MW01268526

Gathering at the Doorway

An Anthology of Signs, Visits, and
Messages from the Afterlife

GATHERING AT THE DOORWAY

An Anthology of Signs, Visits, and Messages from the Afterlife

Compiled by Camille Dan

Cover Art by Jonathan Dan

Chapters by a group of over 40 authors worldwide that include accounts of
personal experiences, scientific research,
and photographic evidence.
Religious and supernatural content.

Published by: Camille Dan

Publication Date: May 2022

ISBN: 9798819589649

© Registration 1192917. All rights reserved.

www.aaronsenergy.com

Disclaimer

Neither the publisher nor the authors are engaged in rendering professional advice or services to the reader. This book is sold with the understanding that neither the publisher nor the authors, nor anyone associated with this book can be held responsible or liable for any advice in this book. The views and opinions expressed in this book are those of the individual authors only and do not necessarily reflect the views, opinions, policy, or position of the publisher, agency, organization, employer, or any other author. The ideas, suggestions, and advice provided in this book are for informational purposes only, are not guaranteed, and not intended as a substitute for seeking professional guidance. The use of this book implies your acceptance of this disclaimer.

Dedication

This anthology is dedicated to the loving memory of my son, Aaron Dan, his grandparents, Judy Dan, Julia and Neil Gignac, and all the beautiful souls who guide us, gather us together, and cheer us on from across the veil as we share our stories. With eternal gratitude.

∞∞∞∞∞∞∞∞∞∞∞∞∞∞∞∞∞∞

Endorsements

"Camille Dan's latest work, *Gathering at the Doorway: An Anthology of Signs, Visits, and Messages from the Afterlife*, is an impressive array of true stories by authors and after death communication experts. Dan, like many of the authors in this book is known as a "Shining Light Parent" meaning a parent who has suffered the loss of a child. The stories in this book are written by credible sources about how those coping with loss have been able to perceive and communicate with the spirits of their loved ones. In my book *The Afterlife Frequency: The Scientific Proof of Spiritual Contact and How That Awareness Will Change Your Life*, I explain the scientific basis for an afterlife and spirit contact as well as my RAFT Technique which teaches people how to *Recognize, Accept, Feel and Trust* signs and communication from loved ones in spirit. *Gathering at the Doorway* demonstrates RAFT in action. It demonstrates from firsthand accounts how a diverse array of people who let down their barriers of skepticism and fear embraced the immense healing power of spiritual contact. *Gathering at the Doorway* is a must read for anyone coping with the loss of loved one and that communication with souls is possible."

Mark Anthony, JD, Psychic Explorer/ Psychic Lawyer®

Author of *Never Letting Go, Evidence of Eternity* and *The Afterlife Frequency*

"As a Medical Medium and Healer, I've witnessed many amazing and miraculous healings granted through the power of the divine energetic essence and intervention of God, or the Holy Spirit. It was by crossing the veil of death as a Near Death Experiencer that I received my gifts of Healing, and my mission to bring Healing to the world. The Other Side is very real. In fact, I am in direct contact and communication every day with higher-dimensional Spirit Guides, Angels, and Enlightened Beings. I even receive messages for the living from those who have crossed over. So, I know first-hand that there is so much more to life than we see in this mundane and ordinary world. This book is about Life – both the life that we see and experience, and the life that continues beyond death. Even though we are seemingly separated from our loved ones by a veil, our loved ones continue to exist as vibrantly as ever. In fact, they are the best versions of themselves ever. For everyone who's missing a loved one, the best news is that our loved ones are not really lost to us. They are aware of us, they watch over us, they care about us, and they continue to love us, forever. While grieving still hurts, it can help to know that our loved ones still live, and that when our time comes, we are reunited with everyone we have ever cared about. This amazing book helps us by showing us a kaleidoscope of love – our love for each other, and God's divine and everlasting love for us."

Kimberly Meredith, Medical Intuitive, Healer, Speaker, Author,
"Awakening to the Fifth Dimension:
Discovering the Soul's Path to Healing".

"I highly recommend Camille Dan's wonderful book Gathering at the Doorway. University-based scientific research has now definitively demonstrated that life continues after bodily death. Further, communication with postmaterial persons (the so-called 'deceased') has been validated during many sessions with evidential mediums and experiments with emerging SoulPhone technology.

In addition, seven categories of clinical findings – such as documented near death experiences and past life memories – further substantiate that life does not end when the earthly form perishes. The collective scientific and clinical data has been investigated and verified by eminent researchers, university professors, and others. The breadth and depth of that research provides comforting and inspiring evidence that life and love do not end.

However, for many people, the most personally meaningful evidence consists of firsthand experiences. And that's where this book really shines. You are about to read many magnificently heart-warming stories including some from colleagues whose integrity is beyond question.

This experiential evidence is potentially healing and transformative. The commonality of firsthand experiences requires me to modify an old adage: There is much more to life than usually meets the eye. Occasionally, we get glimpses of eternity; those can radically change this earthly experience for the better. Thank you, Camille, for assembling this anthology of personal experiences that convey so much knowledge, hope, peace, joy, and meaning."

Mark Pitstick MA, DC, SoulProof.com SoulPhone.com

"A comprehensive illustration and collection of profound transformational experiences. A true validation of the multi-dimensional, expanded consciousness that is accessible to all. *Gathering at the Doorway* opens up endless pathways for any seeker to be left with inspiration and an enriched outlook on the nature of consciousness."

Jacob Cooper, LCSW, Near-Death Experiencer, and bestselling author of "Life After Breath".

Table of Contents

"You don't have a soul.
You are a soul.
You have a body."
~C.S. Lewis~
Author, Theologian
1898 – 1963

Foreword I By Suzanne Giesemann

Words describing the afterlife inspire hope. We want to believe the stories others tell us, but nothing can take us from hope to knowing better than personally experiencing connection with those no longer in physical form.

When I gazed upon the lifeless body of my stepdaughter at her funeral, I realized I could no longer wonder if there is some aspect of us that survives death. I needed proof.

Years have passed and looking back on the journey I took to find our Susan (and find her I did!) I realized there are three big "E's" that help us move forward in the healing process:

EDUCATE: Learn all you can about who and what you really are.

EXPERIENCE: Enter into expanded states of consciousness and discover you are far more than your physical body.

ENGAGE: Come to realize you are not alone through direct mental interaction with souls on both sides of the veil.

These 3 E's are not steps that you take in any one order. They are elements that mirror your life's journey: ever onward, ever upward in a spiral path of evolution.

The book you hold in your hands is perfectly suited to the "Educate" aspect of this healing process. It has been scientifically proven that reading stories of others' experiences opens one to having such experiences oneself. Thus, this compelling collection of heart-felt stories mixed with the latest information on the nature of

1

consciousness has the potential to help you break through any limiting beliefs that are holding you back from the other two E's: Experience & Engage.

The preponderance of the evidence provided in this wonderful anthology is more than enough to render a verdict of "Yes" to the question, "Is there more than just this physical world?"

In my previous career as a U.S. Navy commanding officer and aide to the Chairman of the Joint Chiefs of Staff, I had no idea there was a greater reality. The bolt of lightning that killed my pregnant stepdaughter sent my life in an unexpected direction. In my search to verify what my soul was telling me—that our Susan still exists at another level—I discovered that the term "afterlife" is a misnomer.

There is no afterlife. There is only the everlife.

Having discerned jaw-dropping, verifiable evidence of a greater reality not only from our Susan, but now from thousands of souls who are far from "dead and gone", I can guarantee you that death is not the end. I state with complete certainty that those you love who have passed are still part of your lives and that all of us are part of one interconnected web of consciousness.

Gathering at the Doorway: An Anthology of Signs, Visits, and Messages from the Afterlife will open the door to your acceptance of the everlife. It will undoubtedly inspire you to have such experiences yourself.

As you read, shift your thoughts out of the head and settle your awareness in the heart-space that knows all is connected. From this feeling-state, set the intention to come to know yourself as the soul you are here and now. This less limited state of awareness that is always present is your bridge to the non-physical realms.

Trust me: You do not have to be born with the ability to see or sense spirits. You are a soul and communicating soul to soul is quite natural once you reacquaint yourself with your natural, full-sensory perception.

I used to hesitate to use the word "proof" when referring to an afterlife. Then I heard the story of a young man named Wolf who left proof that we are souls who at the deeper levels know when and how we're going to transition. And then Wolf came to me from across the veil and took away any remaining doubt that we are souls temporarily in human form.

I wrote the book *Wolf's Message* to share the insights that he came back to gift to all of us. His teaching became the basis of *The Awakened Way*™ that I now share in all of my workshops and presentations. The three basic tenets are these:

You are not only human

You are part of one big web connecting all that is

You find healing and connection through expanded states of consciousness

Keep these in mind as you read this book. Those who have contributed their wise words have discovered these truths in their own way. And that is why you have come here: to shine the Light of Consciousness through your unique lens.

May this treasury of personal experience and hard-earned wisdom serve to help you polish the lens through which you see this world. May it help you come to see it is not the only world. And may this awareness make a world of difference as you heal and grow.

Suzanne Giesemann

Suzanne Giesemann is a spiritual teacher, author, and Messenger of Hope who guides people to the certainty that love never dies and that we are part of a multidimensional universe. She is recognized on *Watkins Mind Body Spirit Magazine's 2022 list of the 100 Most Spiritually Influential Living People*. Suzanne is a former U.S. Navy Commander, commanding officer, and aide to the Chairman of the Joint Chiefs of Staff. Her transition from senior military officer to her current work is featured in the award-winning documentary, *Messages of Hope*, based on her memoir by the same name. She has authored 13 books and written and narrated 6 Hemi-Sync recordings. She produces the *Daily Way* inspirational messages read by tens of thousands each day and hosts the top-ranking *Messages of Hope Podcast* on Apple Podcasts and on YouTube. She is a sought-after keynote speaker at major international conferences, and her many YouTube videos have reached millions of viewers. She is a member of the Evolutionary Leaders Circle, a group of thought leaders from diverse disciplines who come together to help support a shift in consciousness. Suzanne leads both online and in-person classes, workshops and retreats, teaching people around the world about their true nature and how to connect with higher consciousness. She serves as faculty with The Shift Network and with Humanity's Team, sharing the mission of helping people throughout the world awaken to the interconnectedness of all life. Suzanne is the founder of The Awakened Way™, a path to living a consciously connected and divinely guided life. She is the creator of the *BLESS ME©* method of connecting to Higher Consciousness and the popular *SIP of the Divine©* meditation. Suzanne's gift of communication with those on the other side has been verified and recognized as highly credible by noted afterlife researchers. Her messages bring not only hope but healing and love that go straight to the heart. Suzanne has a Bachelor's Degree in foreign languages and speaks fluent Spanish. She earned a Master's Degree in National Security Affairs. In addition to her command tour and duties as special assistant to the Chief of Naval Operations, and ultimately as aide to the Chairman of the Joint Chiefs of Staff, she served tours in naval intelligence, taught political science at the U.S. Naval Academy, and was a plans and policy officer for the U.S. Southern Command. Her overseas assignments were in Panama and Japan. Her military decorations include the Combat Action Ribbon and the Defense Superior Service Medal. The tragic death of Suzanne's stepdaughter, Susan, a sergeant in the Marine Corps who was struck and killed by lightning along with her unborn son, propelled Suzanne in a new direction in search of life's deepest truths. When she first began researching and writing the Hay House published book, *The Priest and the Medium,* she never dreamed that she would one day connect with the unseen world herself. After years of meditation, she began to have intuitive experiences, which led her to several classes on mediumship and to an intensive course at the respected Arthur Findlay College of Psychic Sciences in Stansted, England. Her eye-opening experiences there allowed her to develop her contact with the unseen world to the point where she is now in demand for her readings and her classes in evidence-based mediumship. Suzanne receives messages daily from her guides in spirit, a group of advanced teachers known as *Sanaya*. These are published daily on her blog, *The Daily Way*, as well as her Facebook Page.

Website: www.suzannegiesemann.com

"I have long thought that anyone
who does not regularly - or ever - gaze up
and see the wonder and glory of
a dark night sky filled with
countless stars loses a sense of
their fundamental connectedness
to the universe."
~Brian Greene~
Physicist, Mathematician
Author, Superstring Theorist

Foreword II By Sandra Champlain

We humans are interesting creatures. The process of being created is miraculous when you think about it. Our little human embryo is full of everything we need to grow to be living, breathing, walking, and thinking creatures.

We live in self-generating, self-repairing bodies that come with our own battery packs. Add a little food and water, and we may exist for eighty years or more.

We live on a planet that just happens to have everything we need for survival. Our Sun that keeps life possible is just one star out of the estimated 20 billion suns that also have planets in their solar systems, and that is just in our Milky Way galaxy.

How many galaxies are in the Universe? Astronomers can safely say there are at least 170 billion, but most feel that number is more like two trillion galaxies in an ever-expanding universe.

Everything we use on a daily basis somehow originated from the basic elements of this planet: air, water, rock, and earth. The mobile phones we use, computers, televisions, and radios are all able to connect through an invisible source and supply us with never-ending information and entertainment.

Our lives are miraculous, yet as human beings, we seem to be controlled by our minds, which are incorrect most of the time. Although our devices can connect wirelessly, our minds often doubt that we can do the same thing!

Have you ever noticed your mind spends way too much time thinking about the past and worried about the future? Have you noticed that it never stops talking to you, judging everything you do and who you are? Have you ever caught it saying that you aren't good enough, smart enough, something is wrong with you, and something is definitely wrong with other people?

This is also the mind that wants you to doubt the existence of the afterlife, to overlook the subtle signs that have you think of a loved one who has transitioned. Our minds try to convince us that we must 'see it to believe it' when we really are miraculous beings living in a miraculous universe.

This book, *Gathering at the Doorway: An Anthology of Signs, Visits, and Messages from the Afterlife*, is full of incredible stories and experiences that show us that death is an illusion and that we live on. Over forty authors courageously share their experiences so that you may believe that there is much more to life and the afterlife than you know and that your life is precious.

There is nothing wrong with skepticism, and it is healthy for us all to question much in our lives. However, as you read, beware of the messages that come from the negative mind.

After over 25 years of investigating the afterlife and witnessing thousands of afterlife communications in so many ways, I believe that the mind is necessary to have us play this game called life. This game is difficult, not for the weary, but full of opportunities for our souls to experience, to grow, and to learn.

It is often said that 'life is about the journey, not the destination', and the same holds true for this book. Whether you read it cover to cover or let your soul guide you to a random chapter, set aside the voice of negativity and remember the miracle of YOU.

You are one-of-a-kind, and I believe we all came here to learn and experience many things. So, I ask that you be gentle on yourself, know that you are surrounded by love and support from the unseen world, and let this book be a constant reminder of who you really are...a magnificent and divine soul having a human experience.

Sandra Champlain

In 1996, the fear of dying led Sandra Champlain on a journey to find evidence of the afterlife. Over 25 years later, she is the author of the #1 international best-selling book, *We Don't Die - A Skeptic's Discovery of Life After Death*, host of *We Don't Die Radio* and *Shades of the Afterlife* with over 450 combined hours of afterlife evidence and is the producer of the award-winning film *Rinaldi - Instrumental Transcommunication to the Other Side*. Sandra is passionate about helping others through grief and back into life, sharing the afterlife evidence she continues to receive, and empowering all to live powerful lives through her live and online classes, workshops, and events.

Don't miss her weekly *Sunday Gathering* inspirational service and medium demonstration and use coupon code: FREE to receive a copy of her audiobook, *We Don't Die - A Skeptic's Discovery of Life After Death*.

Website: www.wedontdie.com

*"I felt the question of the afterlife
was the black hole of the personal universe: something for which
substantial proof
of existence had been offered but
which had not yet been explored in the
proper way by scientists and philosophers.
The subject of death is taboo."
~Dr. Raymond Moody~
Philosopher, Psychiatrist, Physician,
NDE Researcher
Author of "Life After Life"*

Foreword III By Robert Ginsberg

If you walk up to ten different people in the street and ask them if they believe in life after death, it is most likely that seven or eight of them will reply that they do believe. If you were to ask these same people why they believe, I suspect the common reply would be that this is what they were taught and they have faith that it is true. What they are really saying is that they hope there is an afterlife but have not seen any evidence to support the premise.

This begs the question "what constitutes evidence that we survive physical death?" Such a question matters little to those who have blind faith. They could not care less about evidence, as it is something that they know in their hearts. Others like myself who have not been imbued with deep spiritual knowledge need more. When I first started exploring the nature of consciousness in 2002 after my daughter died, I frankly found the notion that we survive death to be preposterous, if not foolish. To me, it was much the same as believing in the Tooth Fairy or Santa Claus, a nice fairy tale but a notion that should not be entertained by those with a modicum of intelligence. After all, what could possibly survive? Consciousness is produced by the brain, so once the brain is extinguished, we cease to exist forever. The finality of death, a frightening concept to so many, is the only thing that made any logical sense.

Fortunately, I was an open-minded skeptic, and I began to consult medical doctors, scientists, and researchers to find out if my daughter might still exist in some form.

I needed to know if this was all "woo-woo" crap, or were there well-credentialed experts that had any evidence that we were more than our physical bodies? What I learned after countless meetings, interviews, and reading hundreds of books on the subject is that there is an overwhelming abundance of evidence suggesting that our minds (consciousness, or soul if you prefer) can act independently of the brain. Such evidence comes from many disciplines of research, including telepathy, remote viewing, near-death experiences, deathbed visions, mediumship, reincarnation, after-death communication, electronic voice phenomena, and a host of other phenomena that defy mainstream thinking.

However, what I did not expect to find, was that many scientists do not remain true to the very definition of science, the systematic study of the structure and behavior of the physical and natural world through observation and experiment. Scientists are often bound by materialism and refuse to investigate or even acknowledge phenomena that cannot be explained by material interactions. They will never waiver in their belief that consciousness is purely the result of electrochemical processes in the brain. Within this group, the notion that our minds can act independently of the brain is heresy. This is understandable, as such a suggestion challenges their education and life's work and will never be seriously entertained. Oddly enough, when scientists themselves participate in surveys where they are asked if they believe in God or a higher power, the majority respond that they do. Isn't it curious that blind faith can take the place of empirical evidence in this regard when it comes to belief in an unseen force, but their professional position is to summarily dismiss non-physical phenomena?

The problem with applying the scientific method in the study of non-local phenomena is that such occurrences are often spontaneous in nature and not conducive to laboratory replication. Extrasensory perception, however, has been studied and experiments replicated under rigorous scientific controls, and the evidence for its existence is abundant and robust. These studies show that our mind and brain can act independently, and consciousness is not confined to our skulls. This lays the foundation for the belief that consciousness continues after bodily death.

Although I hold out hope that science will one day prove life after death, we need to focus on what scientists consider to be inadmissible evidence, that being anecdotal reports. Since the stories people tell about their experiences most often cannot be backed up by hard data, scientists most often dismiss something that they cannot dissect or replicate. Science often accepts such evidence when it comes to case studies in medicine but runs the other way when non-physical phenomena are mentioned.

But they are missing the point. If the same types of accounts have been reported for thousands of years, from diverse cultures and different religious, cultural, and societal views, should we not pay attention? If these accounts are consistent and have been experienced by hundreds of millions of people worldwide, can they continue to be ignored?

Signs (communications from discarnate sources) and synchronicities (when seemingly separate occurrences combine to form meaning) dominate everyday life. There are certain organizing principles at work that, combined with free will, affect our physical lives. Since our deceased loved ones continue as entities of thought and energy, with memories intact, since the dawn of man they have continued to find ways to let us know that they still exist. Sometimes they communicate directly to us and other times through a third party. Some of us, as I did for many years, never notice the signs simply because they do not believe they are possible.

While we are in the REM stage of sleep, when our chatter minds are at rest, a conduit presents itself by which those in the spirit realm can get through. Dream visitations are the most common form of after-death communication. Such dreams are easily distinguished from ordinary dreams. They are clear and lucid and very tactile, as we can often see, talk to, hug, and even smell our deceased loved one. Most significant is that such visitation dreams are not forgotten upon awakening and can have profound effects on one's grief. Sometimes discarnates find a way to manifest in physical form and can be seen as an apparition. As entities of energy, they can sometimes make themselves known by manipulation of objects, a form of psychokinesis where mind affects matter. Flickering lights, movement, and appearance of objects, voice recordings, or simply a sense of presence. Other times they are instrumental in orchestrating synchronicities in the form of music, numbers, license plates, animals, and messages from unexpected sources. The list is endless, and sometimes we should simply step back and marvel at their ability and inventiveness.

The book you are about to read is a collection of such anecdotal evidence. People from diverse backgrounds and different beliefs, all experiencing things that defy materialist thinking and should not happen. And yet they do indeed occur all the time if we are willing to pay attention, acknowledge, and offer thanks to our loved ones who presently reside in a different dimension. Most importantly, these accounts can help bring us more meaning and purpose as we navigate our physical lives. If we come to know that life is a continuum and does not end with physical death, that our loved ones not only still exist but will always remain part of our lives, and this physical experience is just a blip before we return to our real home, we can fill some darkness in our lives with light.

Bob Ginsberg

Founder, Forever Family Foundation

Author of *The Medium Explosion: A Guide to Navigating the World of Those Who Claim to Communicate with the Dead*, researcher, featured on the Netflix series *Surviving Death*, *Signs of Life Radio* and podcast host, and co-founder of the *Medium Evaluation Certification Program*.

Website: www.foreverfamilyfoundation.org

"All matter originates and exists only
by virtue of a force...
We must assume behind this force
the existence of a conscious and intelligent Mind.
This Mind is the matrix of all matter."
~Max Planck~
Nobel Prize Winning
Physicist
1858 - 1947

Foreword IV By Leslie Dan

A Major Contribution to Understanding Life After the Departure of the Soul.

From time immemorial mankind has been very curious about what happens to the human being and its soul when it departs from life. Many speculations and theories have been proposed. Some suggest that it hovers around us for about one week before it disappears into the "heavens".

Numerous cases have been reported by surviving relatives, that somehow the departed ones have "appeared" in dreams, or made signs, or gave messages that they are still around us and not completely gone. These messages could consist of clocks stopping at the precise time of death, mysterious noises in the house, pictures being suddenly thrown off shelves, and many more examples that you will read about.

When Camille published her first book, *Aaron's Energy*, about my grandson, I was surprised about the large number of spontaneous responses from many individuals who shared their personal grief. It became clear that a major issue, which rings a bell to many people, should be explored further and more deeply as is done in this anthology.

Leslie Dan

Founder of Novopharm Pharmaceuticals and Subsidiaries, Viventia Biotech, The University of Toronto Leslie L. Dan School of Pharmacy Faculty and Building, The Dan Family Aish HaTorah Yeshivah Jerusalem, The Canadian Medical Aid Program, philanthropist, public speaker, recipient of multiple awards.

"Therefore, if personality exists after what we call death, it is reasonable to conclude that those who leave the Earth would like to communicate with those they have left here. I am inclined to believe that our personality hereafter will be able to affect matter. If this reasoning be correct, then, if we can evolve an instrument so delicate as to be affected by our personality as it survives in the next life, such an instrument, when made available, ought to record something."
~Thomas Edison~
Inventor
1847 - 1931

Introduction

This book is about all of us. Not just all of us whose stories appear here. All of us, including you, and you are part of this story now that you're this far into it. We are grateful that you're here gathering at the doorway between the veil with us. Your story is just as significant as every chapter you will read in this anthology. I have a feeling that this book will resonate with you.

You are about to read a collection of chapters written by several different authors from nearly every continent around the world. All of us come from various backgrounds, ages, walks of life, beliefs, cultures, practices, stories and histories, grieving and losses, who all share something special in common: signs and messages from loved ones across the veil.

Each author's chapter is a unique story in itself; its own book, you might say. Yet, together, whether anecdotal or research-based, our message comes through loud and clear. Despite all our differences, a similar thread binds our stories.

The quotes you will see in between each chapter come from thinkers, prophets, saints, philosophers, elders, astronomers, scientists, inventors, physicists, engineers, spiritual leaders, gurus, theologians, doctors, and authors recorded throughout the ages since humankind began to document ideas and thoughts. You will notice a universal consciousness running through them that transcends time, distance, epoch, region, practice, culture, religion, or people.

Every author in this anthology has taught me something. Some of us are first-time authors sharing our personal stories. Some of us are experienced authors and experts in spirituality and afterlife research and sciences who have discovered the many ways that spirit connections are made across dimensions and how we are all connected throughout space and time.

I'll make the assumption that you have experienced loss in your life, and that's why you chose this anthology. Like all of us, you're looking for answers, comfort, support, healing, and validation. Maybe you're hoping for evidence that your loved one lives on in spirit. Fortunately, the evidence is all around you.

There is a whole world out there beyond the one you see. Beyond your five senses…and your disbelief. You indeed have more than five senses, but you know that. Yet perhaps you hold on to your doubt, skepticism, and mistrust. Most of us do; I was once a skeptic too. As humans, we are designed for survival to doubt, ask questions, analyze, and not always trust our intuition.

I let go of the idea that we are fully independent beings a while ago now. In reality, we are not separate from anyone or anything, whether our connections are visible or invisible. I have heard too much from my son, Aaron, in spirit and seen too many validations to hold on to such limiting beliefs.

Max Planck, also known as the father of quantum physics, won the 1918 Nobel Prize for his discovery of energy quanta, the foundation of quantum mechanics that studies fundamental properties of nature at the scale of atoms and subatomic particles. The wave-particle duality of light had been postulated as early as the 5th century BC, and experiments since the 19th century have confirmed that light can be both particles (photons) and waves (energy). Entanglement of quantum particles such as photons, electrons, and molecules has been recently captured on film and shown to occur even at vast distances in experiments. These microscopic particles are the building blocks of our visible, macro, three-dimensional world including us, so it seems inconceivable that anything could be totally separate. What more could a skeptic ask for?

Quantum physics may fall short of defining all that happens, potentially happens, and unhappens ad infinitum at immeasurable speed throughout nonlinear time across the universe. But it does give us some perspective, given our limited abilities to perceive, that possibilities exist within possibilities that become probabilities, and we are created from the energy that flows through it all. Everything is a reflection, a creation, or a re-creation of everything else. Perhaps it's spirituality, faith, belief, mediumship, psychic phenomena, and metaphysics that help us to fill in all the blanks.

Science has already proven by gravitational effects that the universe is primarily made up of invisible energy and dark matter, most of which is not visible to us. We are equipped to detect and measure up to only five percent of what's really out there. Did you know that for years the famous Hubble Space Telescope has been pointed at what appears to be a starless spot in the sky? It has captured multiple images within this "empty" spot, which to the naked eye on Earth looks like the size of the head of a pin held at arm's length. Those images are of at least 10,000 distant galaxies whose light originated some 13 billion years ago. Factoring in the speed of light means that this telescope has been seeing into the past, and it has taken that long for the light to reach its lens.

I think that the best proof for me that there's more to the universe than what can be seen is my cell phone. I can talk to someone and see them from anywhere in the world in real-time because of electromagnetic energy waves transmitting across the globe from my phone to theirs. Energy waves that aren't visible, but I'm sure are there because of the results they produce.

What is skepticism anyway? According to the Oxford dictionary, skepticism is a doubt as to the truth of something or a theory that certain knowledge is impossible. There are different types and levels within the definition. The skeptic requires empirical evidence as proof of knowledge. I wonder if fear might be a synonym for skepticism. But then that's calling it irrational. By letting go of my disbelief, I found reassurance. That might sound like an oxymoron to some. But to me, it sounds comforting and hopeful to believe that there is more beyond human awareness. Maybe you're here to let go of that last grain of doubt that's been weighing you down.

Creation is infinite and perfect. We are made for survival on Earth, and hence we have everything we need to fulfill that purpose. Energy formed us into physical matter just as it does everything. At the same time, the eternal energy of the universe flows through us constantly…energy that can be neither created nor destroyed. We have built-in senses for that too. But the distractions of our daily lives have muted those senses to focus our instincts on living.

You have probably heard of the five "Clair" senses if you've heard or read anything about psychic phenomena and mediumship. They will come up as you read this book. You don't have to be a psychic or a medium to have Clair sense or intuition. We all have it to some degree. Clairvoyance is what you can see with your "third eye", or your mind's eye. Clairaudience is what you can hear with your "third ear". Clairsentience is what you feel in your gut, or on your skin, or in your bones, or your heart. Claircognizance is what you know when you just know. Clairalience is your sense of an aroma associated with someone or something past. Clairgustance is a strong sense of taste of something that isn't physically there. With one, or more of your Clairs, you have the ability to receive signs and messages from spirit.

Your loved ones have many ways to get their messages to you, whether it be through your Clairs, another means, or both. They can meld their energy with anyone, or anything, including you, to get their signs through. They can manipulate particles and matter around you from wherever and whenever they are across the universe. And they do this because they love you.

Since the dawn of man, we have been told that life is not limited to this earthly realm. The ancient Egyptian Book of the Dead, the Greek, Roman, and Norse mythologies, and the *Bardo Thodol* (The Tibetan Book of the Dead) all contain references to an afterlife and reincarnation. Furthermore, all the major monotheistic religions, Christianity, Islam, Judaism and Kabbalah, and Baha'i, inscribe references to immortality and resurrection in their sacred scriptures. Many indigenous and aboriginal traditions hold to the idea that spirit leaves the body to return to the land. In addition, Buddhism, Hinduism, Jainism, Sikhism, African, Asian, and many theologies worldwide, including Wiccan, embrace a belief in the eternity of consciousness. So, we've all been saying essentially the same thing all along.

On my journey through life after profound loss, I have met more fascinating people from all over the world than I could ever have imagined before. If not for sharing my story of grief and spiritual awakening, I highly doubt that I would ever have met so many wonderful people who have, in turn, shared their stories with me. Of course, I would do anything to have my son, my mother, and my father back, but I can't change the fact that they have transitioned across the veil or the fact that I must make the best of things until it's my time to reunite with them. I am confident that our loved ones on the other side have guided us all together with their spirit signs and messages and that your loved ones in spirit guided you to our anthology.

After writing my first book, *Aaron's Energy: An Unexpected Journey Through Grief and the Afterlife With My Brilliant Son*, in February 2021, and its Second Edition that April, I have heard so much more from Aaron, and I have received many more of his signs. I have followed the journey that Aaron and I are taking together since he transitioned to his afterlife in September of 2019 and have continued to keep a journal of his messages and signs. I have read more, heard more, seen more, discovered more, and further opened my mind, hence my experience. Aaron recently told me that eventually, science will prove to us that we have been the creators of our own spiritual awakening.

All along, Aaron has been encouraging me to write another book from my journal entries as he has been introducing me to more and more people with like experiences. I have connected the invisible dots in between his spirit signs to decipher his message that says to record our stories in this anthology and share them. Our loved ones beyond the veil have powerfully brought us all together in miraculous ways to work on our side with and for them. What started as a handful of friends grew exponentially to a group of over forty authors in no time. Spirit energy doesn't waste time when the intentions are helpful and loving. I can imagine a stadium full of souls cheering us on.

In these pages, you will read true stories from people like you and me who have all faced profound loss and struggled through grief. Each author put heart and soul into writing their chapter. It was no easy task. The emotions that well up by writing stories like these can be overwhelming and painful and, at the same time, profoundly moving and therapeutic. While writing is cathartic and personally helpful, it can become necessary to take breaks when too difficult to write through tears. We followed through with spirit-guidance, encouragement, and timing. Everything fell into place in time.

You will also read chapters and forewords written by experts in the fields of survival of consciousness, afterlife communication and research, instrumental trans-dimensional imagery and voice phenomenon, mediumship, spirit contact, metaphysics, bereavement counseling, and grieving. The full biographies of every author who contributed to this anthology appear at the end of their chapters, and I highly recommend that you read their books and seek out their services.

We all made a commitment to share our stories with the intention of reaching out and offering the same hope, validation, and comfort that we have received. We have found understanding, support, community, and companionship by sharing. In making connections with each other, we have learned how to make better connections within ourselves, beyond ourselves, and hence with our loved ones in spirit.

Think of this anthology as a community of support, love, verification, and encouragement in a book. As you read our chapters, we hope that you will find inspiration to seek more, make more connections, share more, and perhaps write your story too.

All earnings from sales of this book go to mental health and addiction research and care programs, bereavement support services, Helping Parents Heal, Survival of Consciousness and Afterlife Communication research, youth and young adult social development programs, and Forever Family Foundation. Thank you for your generosity.

Camille Dan

"When wireless is perfectly applied the whole earth will be converted into a huge brain, which in fact it is, all things being particles of a real and rhythmic whole. We shall be able to communicate with one another instantly, irrespective of distance. Not only this, but through television and telephony we shall see and hear one another as perfectly as though we were face to face, despite intervening distances of thousands of miles; and the instruments through which we shall be able to do this will be amazingly simple compared with our present telephone. A man will be able to carry one in his vest pocket."
~Nikola Tesla~
Engineer Inventor
1856 – 1943

Visit with Your 'Departed' Loved Ones Now, *Mark Pitstick*

By Mark Pitstick MA, DC

Note: In 2019 and 2020, a series of scientific studies at the University of Arizona definitively demonstrated that life continues after physical death. This research was conducted by Gary E. Schwartz PhD and a team of electrical engineers, software specialists, and others at the Laboratory for Advances in Consciousness and Health.

See Article #1 at SoulProof.com for an overview of this scientific evidence that provides 99.9% certainty of consciousness surviving bodily death. Article #60 reviews the clinical evidence that supports the same conclusion.

This collective evidence shows – with very high degrees of certainty – 'The Great News' that you and everyone else:

1. continue to live after bodily death.

2. do not really lose 'departed' loved ones and can likely interact with them now.

3. are integral, infinite, eternal, and beloved parts of Source Energy/Creator.

4. receive assistance/guidance from angels, guides, master teachers, and evolved energies.

5. are sacredly interconnected with all people, animals, and nature.

6. have special purposes for being on this planet at this time.

7. have everything you need to survive and even thrive during this earthly adventure.

8. possess a magnificent body that, when cared for, can optimize your earthly experience.

9. can find meaning and trust the timing behind life's biggest changes such as death.

10. co-create how heavenly/hellish your life feels by your thoughts, words and deeds.

11. can find silver linings and opportunities for growth and service amidst challenges.

12. can likely use *SoulPhone*™ technology in the future for communication with postmaterial loved ones and luminaries who can help us heal our world.

Really knowing this great news can increase your understandings about the big picture of life. And that, in turn, can upgrade your predominant thoughts, words, and actions. Over time, all that can expand your world view to one of hope, peace, gratitude, love, and more. For a more complete discussion of this evidence and great news, read my books *Soul Proof* and *Greater Reality Living* (co-authored with Dr. Schwartz.) For ages 10 - 16, see *The Big Picture of Life* by me, Dr. Schwartz, and Katta Mapes MA, MEd.

This is, obviously, a new and exciting era for humanity. This chapter addresses the bolded portion of #2 above: You do not really lose 'departed' loved ones and can likely interact with them again now.

The collective evidence shows that nearly all of who and what 'deceased' persons are continues to exist in the next phase of life. This includes their personality, energy, love, intelligence, sense of humor, preferences, memories, etc. In short, it appears that everything except their earthly body still exists.

As such, I encourage you to upgrade your language to help you internalize this great news and live accordingly. In this chapter, I will . . .

• not use the terms 'departed, deceased, or dead' without single quotation marks since those have such strongly entrenched and erroneous meanings indicating an end of life.

• use 'bodily death' and 'physical death' to remind you that only the outer shell dies.

• use changed worlds, passed on, transitioned, crossed over, and other terms that aptly describe a continuation of consciousness.

• refer to those who passed on as postmaterial persons; this term recognizes that they have or can, depending on their intentions and with whom they interact, physicality.

When I refer to lower and higher-energy emotions and ways of being, I am not being critical or judgmental. I am referring to objective measurements of thoughts, words, and actions and the predictable consequences of those. For example, peace, joy, and love calibrate at higher levels of 600, 540, and 500. Anger, fear, and guilt test at only 150, 100, and 30. To learn more, search for David Hawkins PhD, MD energy chart and read his book *Power Versus Force.*

The free articles and radio shows that I mention are available at SoulProof.com. To learn more about my books, audio-products, and documentary film, visit SoulProof.com/Shop.

One of the most common questions I receive is, "How can I better detect my departed loved ones?" Some people experience limited contact but ask why there hasn't been more. I understand the questions since there is still so much needless worry, fear, and misinformation associated with physical death.

Developing a different but very real and meaningful relationship with those who have passed on may be less difficult than you think. Beloved postmaterial persons (PMPs) are likely very motivated and able to establish contact. I say 'likely' because that might not initially occur if the PMP . . .

1. Was a devout atheist. If so, she may require time to get oriented and realize that life really continues before learning how to best contact loved ones on earth.

2. Needs rest and rehab time. One example might be a very ill drug addict and alcoholic who passed on by suicide.

3. The PMP may know you are doing OK, so they try to reach others who are less spiritually balanced and awakened. Finally, your higher self may have chosen to not be contacted to motivate your earthly self to search more deeply, meditate, become more peaceful, etc.

Often, the solution to sensing your 'deceased' loved ones better is simply to become a better receiver. They may be transmitting – trying to contact you – but you need to be on a similar higher energy wavelength to tune-in. You may not be able to detect them as well if you are overly sad, fearful, angry, bitter, analytical, or otherwise imbalanced.

The term after-death communication (ADC) describes meaningful contact with a person who has passed on. ADCs may occur via the usual senses or more ethereal ones such as seeing with the mind's eye, telepathically hearing, or inner knowing. These experiences also occur during dreams because the person receiving the communication is deeply relaxed and usual hectic brain activity is dampened. Dream ADCs seem more real than usual and convey a strong sense that an actual visit occurred.

In the past, many people did not share them for fear of being considered weird or crazy. Now, more people are openly sharing these surprisingly common experiences.

Hello from Heaven by Bill Guggenheim and Judy Guggenheim was the first major book to discuss this phenomenon. Respected views from religion support the possibility of communication from beyond the grave. For example, Rev. Dr. Norman Vincent Peale, who earned worldwide respect for his sensible application of religious principles, stated: "I firmly believe that when you die you will enter immediately into another life. They who have gone before us are alive in one form of life and we in another."

Much clinical and scientific evidence indicates that life continues seamlessly after death. As such, ADC reports about visits with/from postmaterial persons are consistent with contemporary evidence and well-accepted theological views.

In the past, ADCs were primarily spontaneous and seemed to occur randomly. In 2022, several methods enhance your chances of connecting with postmaterial loved ones:

1. Evidential mediums are defined sensorily gifted persons who can sense those who have passed on. These individuals can sometimes provide specific and detailed information that appears to come from those who have changed worlds. Under controlled research settings, these mediums convey information they could not know unless they are communicating with those who have passed on. To learn more about this mode of communication with your loved ones who have changed worlds, see article #6 *Evidential Mediums* at SoulProof.com.

2. Facilitated ADCs involve a technique that increases the chances of having a meaningful ADC. The Facilitated After-Death Contact technique I created uses deep relaxation / hypnosis, guided imagery, and other approaches to achieve this goal. For more information, see article #9 *Visiting with 'Departed' Loved Ones Now.* Many bereaved parents have described visits with their children during these sessions. These experiences include talking back and forth telepathically, the child sitting on the parents' lap, feel the child's presence, etc.

3. Induced after-death communications were described by Allan L. Botkin PsyD and Craig Hogan PhD in their book, *Induced After-Death Communication.* Techniques utilizing eye movement, desensitization, and reprocessing (EMDR) are used. This approach has been very successful with nearly all clients that hundreds of IADC-trained psychotherapists have worked with. This approach seems to work equally well whether people are religious or agnostic, and for recent as well as old cases of grieving. For more information visit Induced-ADC.com.

4. Mirror gazing is described in by Raymond Moody MD, PhD in his books, *Reunions* and *The Last Laugh.* This 'psychomanteum' technique is based on ancient Greek methods to visit with those who have passed on. I was trained and certified by Moody to conduct these sessions, so I know they work for some clients. Mirror gazing has been practiced on every continent over several millennia. The

technique is safe, time-tested, and there is no evidence that anyone has ever been harmed by an apparition.

5. The Holistic Breathing technique involves 45 minutes of deep, noisy, diaphragmatic breathing with music and my coaching in the background. The holistic benefits include quieting the brain and remembering more deeply that life and love do not die when the earthly form does. One woman in a group I led sobbed and sobbed for 15 minutes. Then she lay very still for 15 minutes. Afterwards, she shared with the group: 'I visited with my husband, mom, dad, and our beloved dog. I'm certain it wasn't my imagination; I was right there with them.' To learn more, see article #70 *Holistic Breathing Technique.*

In the future, *SoulPhone* communication technology should allow clear contact with your postmaterial loved ones. The SoulSwitch is being developed at the University of Arizona by director Gary E. Schwartz PhD and his team of electrical engineers, software programmers, evidential medium consultants, and postmaterial collaborators. To learn more, visit SoulPhone.org and The Laboratory for Advances in Consciousness and Health.

Whatever approach you use, certain strategies and understandings enhance your chances of having meaningful ADCs . . .

1. Learn the clinical and scientific evidence that definitively shows bodily death is not the end of life. This evidence – as well as your firsthand experiences – can decrease fear, hopelessness, and other lower energy emotions about bodily death. Again, to learn more about this evidence, see articles #1 *Scientific Evidence That Bodily Death Is NOT the End of Life* and #60 *Clinical Evidence That Life Continues After Bodily Death* at SoulProof.com.

2. Know that ADCs are real and very common. Your loved ones who have changed worlds will quite certainly greet you when you graduate from earth-school. But you don't have to wait until then to communicate with them. Just knowing that after death communication is possible is the first step to establishing a real but different relationship with them. At least 25% of Americans have experienced one or more ADCs. That number swells to 66% for widows and widowers, and 75% for bereaved parents. However, when surveying thousands of those with 'departed'

children, nearly all of them report one or more meaningful perceptions of their child. To learn more, see Article #28: *After Death Communications.*

3. Ask for contact. Wise teachings have said, 'Ask and you shall receive.' If you feel comfortable doing so, ask, intend, and pray for safe and clear communications with loved ones who have passed on. Don't be timid. Invite them in by name and talk to them aloud to stay focused. This also lets them know you are taking this seriously. Just treat them like a real person since they still are.

Set a date and time for you to connect with them and keep the appointment. They have other things to do so set a time to meet just as you would with someone on earth. Then start talking, even if you aren't sure they are there yet. Their presence may seem to build over time as you sense the reality of a visit.

Get into the zone and block out extraneous noises and thoughts. Talk about anything, just as you would do with a human friend or family member. Share personal events and ask them questions. Throughout the day, point out items of interest to them, for example, "Oh look, Dad, there's the restaurant you loved so much." As with most things, practice makes perfect. Praying and asking for help is a great place to start. To learn more, see articles #89 *My Prayers* and #73 *Angels and Higher Energy Assistance.*

4. Realize that contacting your loved ones is possible. And, when done wisely, it isn't dangerous or sinful. Yes, I know, some people believe differently. I attended theology school, in part, to learn the best available facts about this and other important topics such as heaven, hell, salvation, God, angels, afterlife, etc.

The phrase 'the dead know nothing' is found in Ecclesiastes 9:5 and is usually quoted out of context. That statement also contradicts other passages in the Old and New Testaments that indicate consciousness continues after bodily death. Examples of those include Matthew 25:46, Luke 16: 19 - 31, and Ecclesiastes 4:2

Solomon, the supposed author of this Old Testament book, was referring to the perspective of people on earth who have no knowledge of Creator. Solomon's use of the phrase 'under the sun' about 30 times makes it clear that he was commenting on how things appear from a limited earthly perspective. Those who don't have a relationship with The Divine believe that 'the dead know nothing', that is, that nothing exists after bodily death.

That phrase has been used to support, without corroborating evidence, the following opinions:

1. Nothing exists after death.

2. Consciousness ceases after death until a resurrection and judgment day.

3. Only those who believe in and follow 'the one true way' experience an afterlife.

Based on the collective evidence, many religious teachings, and much firsthand experience, it's clear that continuing relationships with beloved ones is possible.

Certain chapters of *Leviticus* - a book in the Old Testament that was written approximately 2500 years ago and has been changed over time - warned against consorting with spirits. But those same chapters said it was OK to make foreigners slaves for life. They also warned against cutting one's hair a certain way, planting more than one type of seed in the same area, and going to temple when menstruating. That last one, by the way, was punishable by death.

I take the warnings in those chapters seriously, but not literally. Those ancient teachings may have been given to protect people from malicious and capricious postmaterial persons. Just as on earth, some beings in other realms are imbalanced and thus mistreat and take advantage of others. It's wise to shield yourself with a prayer and intention that only good and God, love and light, and the highest energies will be involved in your ADCs.

Caution about engaging with imbalanced postmaterial persons is warranted, but the average person doesn't have to worry about ADCs being dangerous when following recommendations in this article. But trying to contact 'the dead' could be dangerous for immature persons in age or mentality, those who abuse alcohol and/or drugs, worship evil, and call in dark spirits.

The word 'sinful' originally meant 'miss the mark' or 'to fall short.' It's not helpful to label trying to contact 'departed' loved ones as sinful; that just creates more fear and ignorance. It's more useful to become informed about this subject. Then people can, if they choose attempt communication with their dear ones in wise and responsible ways.

To learn more about this important topic, see article #13 *What Is G.O.D. Really Like?* #47 *Evil Spirits, and the Devil,* #104 *Ghosts/Interim Postmaterial Persons,* and #83 *Am I a Christian?*

5. Upgrade your consciousness. To enjoy contact with your loved ones who have transitioned to the next phase of life, get on a similar wavelength as they are enjoying. They are in a realm characterized by higher and finer energies such as love, joy, peace, gratitude, enthusiasm, growth, and service. How can you upgrade yourself in that direction? Meditate, pray, spend quiet time in nature, serve others, and focus on the current highest feeling thoughts. Be grateful for the positives in your life, optimally care for yourself, and fine-tune your body/mind as explained in my book *Radiant Wellness.*

Doing this regularly over time - it usually doesn't happen overnight - can help you be more on same page as those you are hoping to contact. You can't communicate with them via station 111 FM - that broadcasts peaceful and loving programming - if you're tuned in to station 0.0 AM that focuses on negativity, fear, resentment, regret, and other lower energy emotions. Make sense?

Much evidence indicates that your dear ones who have changed worlds are or - depending on their circumstances at the time of physical death - soon will be very happy, peaceful, joyful, grateful, and enthusiastic as they love, grow, learn, and serve others. They encourage you to be the same way. When? You guessed it - right now.

6. Be aware of subtle communications. You will be disappointed if you expect a totally solid and extended contact - just like while on earth - from loved ones who have re-entered the field of all possibilities. Realize that your perceptions of them may seem ethereal, fleeting, or even imaginary at first. But be patient and persistent, use the information and strategies in this article, and stay alert. Be aware of feeling their presence, electronic aberrations, lucid dreams, and mysterious occurrences.

To facilitate better contacts over time, be grateful for and enthusiastic about - two of the highest energy emotions - gauzy and fleeting apparitions, meaningful coincidences, and subtle telepathic communications. Remember: it's already been scientifically demonstrated that afterlife exists - so relax and release any fears about that. If you've not had any contacts yet, know they are possible and don't give up.

7. Talk to them as if they are present. Why? Because they probably are. Your loved ones who have crossed over are not a zillion quadrillion miles away up in the sky somewhere. Nor are they stuck in the ground until a judging deity deems otherwise. The origin of those concepts ranges from the Middle Ages (around 1400 AD) to several centuries B.C. Your loved ones in spirit are likely very near, especially when you think of them, ask for a visit, or feel their presence 'out of the blue'.

Continue your relationship by talking to them aloud or in your heart and mind. Then listen for subtle responses. Numerous evidential ADCs have been documented by university professors, physicians, and psychologists such the eminent Carl Jung MD. That is, people sometimes learn - in waking or dream ADCs - information they did not know but was later authenticated. You can now trust your senses and release any concerns that it's crazy.

Sensing the presence of your postmaterial dear ones - even just a little bit - can help you remember this: everything about them, except their no longer needed physical shell - is very much alive and well.

8. Release the pressure. It may not be easy to communicate from one dimension to another. Can you instantly and clearly contact those in other realms? I can't. So don't put pressure on yourself or your 'deceased' loved ones about it. Worry and fear are lower energy emotions so avoid those. Instead, focus on gratitude, positive expectancy, and enthusiasm.

Don't become upset if your initial efforts aren't fruitful. That will just create additional pressure and decrease the chance of a successful contact. As with many pursuits, relaxation and clarity assist success. Regularly use meditation, prayer, quiet time in nature, yoga, and breathing techniques to achieve this equanimous state.

To learn more about how you can do this, see article #51 *Meditation*, #77 *Centering Practices*, #82 *Journey from 'Bereaved' to 'Shining Light'*, and #86 *Breathing Techniques*.

9. Hold an object of theirs. Some psychics and mediums encourage their clients to bring a personal item that belonged to the person they wish to reach. This makes sense since objects can absorb and retain energy. Holding an object of your loved one who has changed worlds may be another way to enhance connection with them.

Also create an environment that he or she would appreciate and resonate with. Perhaps flowers, candles, and their photo. Or - for a sports nut - their baseball glove, soccer ball, cleats, and jersey. Be creative and consider what setting would make you and they smile and focus on love, peace, joy, and gratitude.

10. Give thanks. When any kind of communication happens, being thankful may make it more likely to happen again. Gratitude and love are considered to be two of the highest energy emotions and closest to the energy of Source. Focus on the glass being half full and have appreciation for even fleeting, minor, or future contacts.

11. Learn about the possibility of parallel realities. I first heard about this from Native American and Yaqui Indian reports. Later, I read about David Deutsch PhD, a leading theoretical physicist at the University of Oxford, who proposed the existence of parallel universes. Applying the laws of quantum physics, Dr. Deutsch argues that you simultaneously live in innumerable parallel existences or states of being. You live not in a single universe, Dr. Deutsch said, but in a vast and rich multiverse in which other versions of yourself live out other options you've encountered. Even after your current physical body dies, other copies of you may remain alive in other realities.

Michael Newton PhD, founder of *Life Between Lives* therapy, and his team have worked with 65,000 people from around the world. Under very deep hypnosis, these clients provide impressively consistent reports about this source of clinical data. One report is that, on average, only about 25% of a person's total energy is needed during an earthly incarnation. The rest may experience other slices of life as formed or formless, earthly, or nonearthly beings. Clients also reported that part of a person's consciousness never leaves Home and hence remains merged with Source Energy.

One exciting ripple of this is that you and your postmaterial loved ones may be together right now in another part of the field of all possibilities. It's possible that, while you deeply grieve your 'loss', other parts of your and their energy are cheering you on to remember the big picture of life. To learn more, see article #75 *Multilocation/Parallel Realities/Simultaneous Experiences.*

12. Leave room for the "X" factor. The universe is indescribably vast and magnificent. Your five senses only perceive much less than 1% of reality so realize there is much you cannot grasp. There is much that humans don't know about every

aspect of life, and that includes the afterlife. Besides, who doesn't like a great mystery and adventure story? The bottom line? Don't get too obsessive about whether loved ones visit but, instead, trust the power of love and your eternal connection. To learn more, read articles #68 *The Big Picture of Life*, #71 *Ask Your Soul, G.O.D., and Angels*, and #100 *Enlightenment*.

I hope this chapter helps you realize how firmly you and your loved ones are embedded and interconnected in eternity. No one really dies. Yes, the outward appearance of your love and connection has changed. But now you have an opportunity to learn the wisdom of Antoine de Saint Exupery's words: 'It is only with the heart that one can see rightly; what is essential is invisible to the eye.'

About the Author

Mark Pitstick, MA, DC, has fifty years' experience helping people in hospitals, pastoral counseling settings, mental health centers, and holistic health care practice.

His training includes: Bachelor of Science degree in Zoology (Ohio State University 1975); graduate theology studies majoring in Pastoral Counseling (Methodist Theological School of Ohio 1977 – 1978); Master of Arts degree in Clinical Psychology (Western Carolina University 1980); and doctorate in Chiropractic Health Care (Palmer College of Chiropractic 1985). Mark has also completed extensive postgraduate training in clinical nutrition. While attending theology school, he provided suicide prevention counseling and education.

When Mark was six years old, he told his parents that a beautiful sunset 'reminds me of God.' Mark became aware of occasional clairaudient and clairsentient abilities at age ten; he's had a number of miracles, revelatory, and spiritually transformative experiences since then.

After working in hospitals with many suffering and dying adults and children, he was motivated to find evidence-based answers to questions that many people ask: "Who am I? Why am I here? What happens after I die? Will I see my departed loved ones again? Is there a God? If so, why is there so much suffering? and How can I best live during this earthly experience?"

Dr. Pitstick wrote the books *Soul Proof, Radiant Wellness, and The Eleven Questions* with endorsements from Drs. Wayne Dyer, Elisabeth Kubler-Ross, Deepak Chopra, Bernie Siegel, and others. He co-authored *Greater Reality Living* (with Gary E. Schwartz PhD), and *The Big Picture of Life* (with Dr. Schwartz and Katta Mapes MA, MEd). Mark produced the *Soul Proof* documentary film with interviews of people who had near death experiences, after death communications, and other eye-opening encounters. His audio products use deep relaxation, breathing techniques, and guided imagery to help people deeply know and show they are integral, eternal, infinite, and beloved parts of Source. He created the *Ask Your Soul* and Facilitated ADC techniques that use hypnosis and guided imagery.

A frequent media guest, Mark hosted *Soul-utions*, a radio show about practical spirituality, and *Ask the Soul Doctors* featuring interviews with top consciousness experts. Those interviews can be heard at SoulProof.com/Radio Shows. Mark provides clinical support for *Helping Parents Heal* group leaders and *Caring Listeners* and contributes to their newsletter for bereaved parents.

Dr. Pitstick was certified in past life regression therapy by Brian Weiss MD, and the mirror-gazing technique by Raymond Moody PhD, MD. Mark was the executive vice-president of Eternea.org started by Eben Alexander MD and John Audette MA. He has given many workshops and webinars on spiritual awareness and holistic wellness.

Mark directs the *SoulPhone Foundation* that: (1.) teaches the collective evidence for life after death, and (2.) helps fund research and development for interdimensional communication at the University of Arizona. He is a research assistant for the *SoulPhone Project* at the Laboratory for Advances in Consciousness and Health (lach.arizona.edu/).

Mark founded *Greater Reality Living* groups to help people prepare for the paradigm shift after official announcements and public demonstrations in 2022 - 2023 of scientific proof of life after death. To learn more about Dr. Pitstick's outreaches, visit SoulProof.com and SoulPhone.com

"We are stardust
We are golden
And we've got to get ourselves
Back to the garden"
~Joni Mitchell~
Singer, Songwriter, Artist
from the song,
"Woodstock"
1970

From the Next Room, *Jane Asher Reaney*

By Jane Asher Reaney

The person with whom I have felt an indelible bond with my whole life died when I was 49 years old. She was, or should I say, still is—my mom, Betty Asher.

Shortly after she passed away, I started having vivid visitations from her while sleeping. These exchanges were deep and unbounded, much different from a regular dream. I felt an uncanny link to her, and each time these communications carried with them significant messages. Right around the same time, she began leaving my family and me dimes. Then, after a spellbinding manifestation through the eyes of her best friend, I knew that Mom was urging me to pay attention. I began recording everything as it was happening. My fascination to write about this ever-growing mystical connection became a passion that I could no longer deny.

I hear a voice deep inside me where only my knowing is found. This intuition seems to be singing a sweet song that only I can hear, although I can't quite make out all the words or notes. They come in flashes. It's as though an invisible muse is breathing oxygen into this book and beckoning me to come along for the ride.

Over the years since Mom disappeared from my sight, our story continued to evolve and unfold. It would overrun me many times, like a puzzle with endless pieces scattered across 10 years of memories, two laptops, and numerous journals. Baffled but driven, I started to collect these fragments and gradually put them together.

The suggestion to involve my friend, Pam Oslie, was initially inspired by my big sister, Lynn. Pam is a well-known psychic medium with the ability to connect with the other side. She had been an unexpected comfort to my father just after my mom died.

The epiphany to involve Pam occurred while I was on a plane writing a letter to Lynn. I was deeply distraught and weighed down with a carry-on bag packed full of heartache and grief. The only thing that brings me solace when I'm in this state is writing. So, I took out a pen and wrote on the only piece of paper I could find—my boarding pass.

The question I posed to my sister through this letter was, "How do I ask our mother to co-author this book with me?" Clarification seemed to materialize out of thin air. I heard my straight-forward, no-nonsense sister's voice in my head, suggesting that I ask my friend Pam to assist in connecting me with mom to write our story—together.

I immediately sensed my big sister beside me and knew she was doing what she had always done for me my entire life. She was once again giving me stable direction and advice. Lynn never had to make a lot of noise to get her point across. She could do so flawlessly with the tilt of her head, flare of her nostrils, or a flash of her intelligent green eyes. The flight that I was on when this lightning bolt of communication occurred with my sister was my return trip home after her funeral.

So, how exactly does one receive messages of divine guidance from their mother when she is no longer in this realm, but in The Next Room? Mom says, "With faith." And so, our story begins, with me, my mom, my psychic friend, and a fortuitous nudge from my big sister Lynn—who had just been buried. With a sizable leap of limitless faith and my puppy at my feet, I open up to receive and write.

What's the Deal with the Dimes?

It wasn't very long after my mother crossed over that I started finding dimes—everywhere and frequently. They appeared in random unexpected places and always alone.

I found them inside the washing machine, the dryer, on my car seat, at Target, our church parking lot, in gas station parking lots, at the airport, and even in the middle of our bedroom floor. I've always been one to stop in the middle of the street to pick up a penny, no matter how dirty it appeared. So, when I started finding dimes, I was intrigued.

I didn't really understand why I was finding dimes or associate them with my mom until I met another psychic, Marisa Ryan. My boss at the radio station where I worked at the time informed me that he wanted to feature a medium for Halloween, so listeners could connect with their loved ones that had passed away. It sounded like fun. Marisa is a well-known psychic medium based out of Los Angeles. For several evenings, listeners called into the radio station and Marisa delivered messages from their loved ones that had moved beyond the physical realm. The phones were packed every night. As much as I wanted to talk to her at length about my mom, I knew she was here to do a job and provide entertainment for our listeners.

At the end of our shift, the two of us had a great exchange and she suddenly said, "Jane, your mother is leaving you dimes. I'm not sure why or what the significance is, but just know that those dimes you've been finding are from her. I don't know what she's trying to tell you by leaving them, but each time you find one, please know they're from her."

When I told my husband about Marisa's message, he suggested I start keeping the dimes together. I found a little black velvet bag to collect them, and soon my husband, children, and friends were finding them as well.

Have you ever had a dream come flooding back to you in the middle of the day? When it happened to me, it came with such a force and powerful feeling it was uncanny.

A week before my dad's birthday, I put together a happy package with all his favorite treats and birthday cards from every member of my family, even a card from our big old yellow Labrador, Honey. As I was standing at the counter to ship the package, the memory of a dream suddenly flooded over me. It was so overwhelming that I had to put my hands on the counter to maintain my balance and ground myself. In my vivid dream recall, my beautiful mother was sitting gently on the edge of my bed. I propped myself up in bed, and said, "Mom, what's the deal with the dimes?"

"I like to see you smile," she said.

There it was. The message was just like her—direct and to the point. I was filled with such gratitude and joy to finally find out the mystery of why my mother had been leaving me dimes. The message was so pure and simple it made me smile ear to ear. As I turned to leave, directly down at the toe of my right shoe was one bright, shiny dime! I burst out laughing, bent down, picked it up, and held it high in the air, all while smiling, laughing, and talking to my mother the entire time I walked out of the store. I giggled later that day thinking about everyone around me in the store and what they must have thought about the crazy woman holding a dime and talking to herself. I honestly didn't care one little bit. I now knew why Mom was leaving me dimes and it made me smile.

At work the following evening, I told my producer, JJ, about the dream that I had and the dime I found at my toe immediately after. He was with me as producer the evening that I had the exchange with Marisa.

"Are you writing it down each time you find one?" JJ asked. I said, "No, that's a great idea. I will from now on!" As I turned to reach for a note pad, something shiny caught my eye, underneath the console, way back in the corner. I crouched down to pick it up, laughing and smiling the whole time. It was one single, shiny dime.

As I presented it to JJ, he said, "Hi, Mom."

Excerpts from "The Next Room" by Jane Asher and Betty Asher, August 26, 2021, Independently Published by Jane Asher Reaney.

Jane's Mom, Betty Asher with Jane's Collection of her dimes.

About the Author

Jane Asher has always been a natural connector who has enjoyed a successful career in media and the music industry, most notably at major radio stations in San Diego and Santa Barbara, and Virgin Records based out of Chicago. She has been a media professional and in the radio business for over 35 years.

Several years ago, she stepped away from terrestrial radio when Empower Radio reached out and asked her to create a show regarding her passion. *The Next Room* podcast was born. She interviews professionals and practitioners from diverse backgrounds about death, dying, grief, beliefs, afterlife, and cultural traditions surrounding the journey we all must ultimately make. The show airs across 11 platforms and has connected her with extraordinary people throughout this community. The Next Room is also the official podcast of the Beautiful Dying Expo, of which Jane is on the Advisory Board.

Jane is also drawn to mission work. She has been part of a team for five years that has built homes in Tijuana for families in need through Lutheran Border Concerns. She has traveled to El Salvador to feed the homeless, Malaysia to help build a school on Borneo, and Armenia to work with women and children in the village of Amre Taza. Most recently, she was on a humanitarian mission in the Dominican Republic.

Her new book... *The Next Room* is a story transcending space and time, of a relationship between mother and daughter that grew stronger through death. Written together, by initially enlisting interpretation through a psychic medium, *The Next Room* takes us on a daughter's journey through learning eternal life lessons on forgiveness, grief, grace, gratitude, and the limitless love of all, God.

Jane lives in San Diego with her husband, Tom. She is answering her passion-filled purpose by recording her podcast, and writing alongside her puppy and muse, Mamba.

Website: www.janeasherreaney.com Twitter: @JaneAsher Instagram: @JaneAsherReaney LinkedIn: Jane Asher Reaney Facebook: The Next Room With Jane

Jane's beautiful memories of life with her mom.

"I am open to the guidance of synchronicity,
and do not let expectations hinder my path."
~Dalai Lama XIV~
Spiritual Leader
Former Head of State, Tibet

Signs and Synchronicity, *Mark Ireland*

By Mark Ireland

Signs

This chapter is a collection of experiences that point to signs of connection, contact, and validation from loved ones who have passed. In some cases, the signs were subtle, and in others they were overt, but my family and I were alert to all of them. Since some signs were so unmistakable and profound, we knew not to write off the less obvious ones as mere coincidence, but rather to appreciate the entire body of evidence.

People who have ADCs (After-Death Communications) and NDEs (Near-Death Experiences) are often reluctant to speak about them with others. In most cases, their reticence is associated with fear that their account will be marginalized, they'll be scoffed at, or that they may be considered unstable. Because our modern society is so materialistic, that which may be deemed "reality" is typically limited to things that can be seen, felt, heard, tasted, or touched—in a purely physical sense. This is unfortunate because ADC and NDE accounts point to a deeper and more complex reality. If considered in earnest, such reports could help lead us to a better understanding of the total nature of the universe—perhaps one much grander than our current commonly held conception.

My wife Susie's good friend Annette recently disclosed information about an unusual occurrence that took place about a week after our youngest son, Brandon's death. At that time, Annette had given Susie a call one evening and invited her to go on a walk the next morning. Prior to Brandon's passing, walking on the trails around our neighborhood was a regular activity for my wife, so she saw this as an opportunity to spend time with a good friend and get a small taste of normalcy.

The next morning arrived, and Annette woke with a terrible headache, so she really didn't feel like going, but after contemplating what Susie was going through, she felt obliged. They went on their walk, talked at length, and then returned to their respective homes. As she entered her house, Annette broke down in tears thinking about Susie's pain. Shortly thereafter, she stepped into her youngest son's closet and then sensed someone behind her. Annette heard the words, "Thanks for walking with my mom today." Greatly surprised, she turned to see who was speaking. She suspected her husband or one of her two sons, but no one was there. No one was even home. Annette had not shared this story any sooner because she was afraid it would cause us more pain. On the contrary, we were thrilled to hear about Annette's ADC.

Psychic mediums sometimes share information that doesn't seem to make sense at the time it is given, yet later on, the pieces come together, and a meaningful affirmation comes to light.

Back in 2004, during my reading with Allison Dubois, she told me that anytime I heard the song *Fly Me to the Moon*, it would signify that my father was present. When Allison made this statement, it didn't really mean much to me. I'm sure that my father liked Frank Sinatra, but I didn't remember this song being especially significant to him.

Six years later, on October 16, 2010, Susie and I joined our friends, the Andersons, for dinner. Recognizing that this was my father's birthday, I raised my glass and made a toast to him—and everyone joined in. Immediately after the toast had been made, a male entertainer who had been setting up prior to this point started his set with *Fly Me to the Moon*. Later on, between sets, I asked the singer if he had a set playlist. He didn't. Tommy Holloway said that he randomly picked whatever song came to him at the spur of the moment.

Some people gain a sense of connection to their deceased loved ones during quiet times or meditation. Others prefer to spend time in nature and feel the presence of their loved ones while enjoying a walk or other outdoor activity.

On the fifth anniversary of Brandon's passing, I went on a hike with my older son Steven and Stu, Gary, and Dave, three of Brandon's closest friends who had been with him on the day of his death. The four boys and I retraced the steps they'd all made five years earlier to honor Brandon and deal with some of the lingering pain. Everyone missed my youngest son's physical presence, though it was beautiful outside, and the desert gave us a sense of peace, serenity, and holiness—reminding us of what drew Brandon here in the first place.

After ninety minutes of hiking, we were well up the mountain. I began to feel fatigued and a bit nervous over the steep, treacherous terrain. I decided to rest, and Steven remained with me while Stu, Gary, and Dave continued on to build a makeshift memorial at the location where Brandon had passed. While the boys were constructing the memorial up the mountain, I sat below, silently perched on a rocky spot. I sat praying and thinking about Brandon as tears welled up in my eyes. I was not sad, just taking in everything that reminded me of Brandon. I reflected on all the times of his life—first as a cute toddler, then as a gentle boy, and ultimately as a caring young man who made me proud. I also spoke to him in my mind, expressing love. A bit later, Stu, Gary, and Dave returned down the mountain, and they shared a photo of the memorial they had constructed for Brandon, consisting of a cross made of sticks and an arrangement of quartz stones forming his initials.

Shortly after returning home, I sent notes to friends and family telling them about the hike. I mentioned that I had paused during the climb and that the boys had continued on to build a memorial, but I did not share any details about where I was sitting or anything about what I had been thinking while resting. After sending my note, I received a response from Sally Owen, a friend who happens to be a medium. Sally wrote, "Brandon shows me that he stayed with you and 'heard what you said' as the others continued up."

About two hours after sending my note, I received a response from another friend, Elizabeth Stanfield, also a medium. She shared some insights that seemed to indicate Brandon had been with us that day. She asked about the clothes I had worn on the hike. "Were you wearing shoes with an 'N' on them? Nike or New Balance?" I was blown away. The shoes I had worn were indeed New Balance and bore an 'N' on the side. She had no way of knowing. While we had developed a friendship via email and telephone, Elizabeth had never actually met me in person, nor had she ever seen a photo of me other than a headshot. And hiking boots would have been the more obvious guess for mountain climbing, so it seemed she was dialed in.

The coup de grâce came as she asked for confirmation on the setting that day, speaking as if she'd been afforded a supernatural periscope to view the scene: "Were you sitting on a rock and remembering his baby-hood as the boys climbed up the hill?" This was exactly what I had been doing. Elizabeth's response was like reading an instant replay of what I had experienced while suspended on that jagged granite—contemplating all aspects of my son's life.

Elizabeth then moved on to something seemingly unrelated to the hike: "What about the red jacket?" When she said this, I was initially a bit confused, as I recognized the jacket, but I hadn't worn it that day. It was an old, red satin Phoenix Cardinals jacket that Brandon had borrowed from time to time. The garment was pretty dated—the team had changed its name to the Arizona Cardinals in the early 1990s.

Why would Brandon reference a jacket I had not worn on that day? For twenty-three years, I had been a die-hard fan of the Cardinals—a losing franchise. Although expectations were always low, later that very day, on January 10, 2009, the Cardinals pulled off an upset playoff victory over the Carolina Panthers—then going on to win the NFC Championship, advancing to the Super Bowl for the first time ever. It seemed Brandon had been afforded a sneak peek into this future scenario and knew that I'd be happy. I felt he was saying, hey dad, you're going to like this!

People in grief often find that music can serve as a meaningful source of healing. A certain song or artist that was significant to the deceased person now becomes important to those left behind. And if the music plays at just the right time, the song may take on special significance, providing an unmistakable sense of connection with the deceased person.

In 2008 it was announced that the heavy-metal band Iron Maiden would be visiting Phoenix, and Steven and I decided that we would attend the concert along with a few of his friends. We knew that Brandon would have loved to come to this show with us. Brandon was big into music—both as a bass player and as someone who appreciated the work of other artists. He told me that his favorite band was Pink Floyd, and I'm pretty sure that his second favorite was Iron Maiden—rather interesting selections for someone born in the mid-1980s. The latter band is known for their heavy-metal sound, theatrics, and the epic storylines of their lyrics. Religious literalists must occasionally be reminded that for every song like *Sign of the Beast* —a musical encapsulation of the movie —there is a tune like *Sign of the Cross*. Iron Maiden is about entertainment, and they often feature supernatural themes from books or movies and turn them into musical action stories. Less appreciated perhaps is the band's musical prowess. They feature three guitarists who play intricate solos in perfect harmony at breakneck speed, a precise bassist, thundering drums, and the searing vocals of Bruce Dickinson, who has amazing range and power.

Years earlier, at Brandon's request, I learned some guitar parts to a couple of Iron Maiden's less renowned songs, *The Clairvoyant* and *Dream of Mirrors*. Brandon was clearly tired of playing the bass line to Back in Black and was pushing me to expand my musical repertoire.

Shortly before the concert, I sent a thought-prayer to Brandon, mentally relaying the message, "If Iron Maiden plays The Clairvoyant, I will know that you're with us." My request seemed a stretch because the song was obscure, and I hadn't seen it in playlists from previous tours. In doing a bit of research, I noticed that it had been released on the 1988 album *Seventh Son of a Seventh Son*, so it was decades old.

As the evening unfolded, Steven, his friends, and I had a great time at the show. The sound was amazing, and the band reeled off a string of well-loved songs with precision. The energy was over the top as Dickinson wailed while running around the stage, jumping and climbing stage props like a young gymnast.

Near the end of the concert, I got my wish, as the band launched into *The Clairvoyant*. It was the second-to-last song played. For toppers, the band's mascot, "Eddie"—a ghoulish character standing about twenty feet tall—marched out on stage right when *The Clairvoyant* began, signifying that this was the featured song of the set. I felt an electric pulse run up and down my torso and sensed it was Brandon's way of touching in.

To most travelers, the world seems vast, yet our loved ones who have passed on are not limited by the same rules of time and space that govern our Earthly experience. Those who are near to our hearts yet no longer clothed in flesh are but a thought away no matter where we go. Love transcends the perceived limits of our physical world.

In late spring 2011, my wife and I went on a European vacation. We spent the latter portion of our trip in a small Italian town called Sestri Levante. While there, we took a train down to the Cinque Terre, a chain of five beautiful, small seaside villages nestled into the cliffs on the Mediterranean coast, interconnected by walking trails. On the following day we decided to walk around Sestri Levante and scope out the town.

We enjoyed nearly perfect weather during most of our trip, but this particular day was overcast and drizzly. It started raining hard while we were walking around looking at shops and the local architecture, so we'd dodged into the first opening we could find. Unbeknownst to us, we had inadvertently entered an exhibit featuring the work of Storm Thorgerson, the artist responsible for Pink Floyd's album cover designs. Knowing that Pink Floyd was Brandon's favorite band we found this situation rather ironic, especially when *Wish You Were Here*—our signature song for Brandon—began playing as we entered. It seemed beyond unusual to stumble into such a place across the globe in a small Italian village, finding such an exhibit and a welcoming song.

Sometimes people come into your lives for a while, but then they fall out, and you lose touch. In some such cases you may reconnect at a later time, forging new and meaningful relationships. And in some of these instances, the reconnection seems beyond chance and serves to complete a circle.

Brandon took bass lessons for six years and was still taking instruction at the time of his passing in 2004, even though he had become an accomplished player. It was about learning more and refining his skills because he was serious about the instrument and wanted to be the very best he could be. Brandon appreciated his instructor, Todd Hogan, and Todd considered our son to be like a little brother. They would often "jam" together outside of lessons.

Speaking to Brandon's character as much as his musical prowess, Todd invited our son to join his band, and they played together during several public performances. Todd had done very well in music after founding a band called Three Days Down that headlined in concerts where Lifehouse was the opening act. Unfortunately, some of his bandmates fell into substance abuse, so while Lifehouse went on to achieve major commercial success, Todd's group dissolved. When forming a new band, Todd planned to take a different approach and knew he could always depend on Brandon to avoid such pitfalls.

We were not alone in our suffering when Brandon died. Todd had already lost his band and had been in the process of losing both a wife and a daughter to a pending divorce. When Brandon was gone too, Todd was devastated. We didn't know him very well at the time, but we liked what Brandon had to say about Todd and always sensed that he had a warm and caring spirit.

Todd attended Brandon's funeral service and addressed the gathering of three hundred people. In his heartfelt testimony about our son, Todd stated, "Brandon is definitely in heaven," speaking about Brandon's "selfless nature" and "pure heart." After the service, we lost track of Todd for seven years. Susie and I continued to think about him fondly but didn't know where he was living or what he was doing.

Back in the late 1990s, I took guitar lessons for about a year and a half, then shelved the instruction for a long time thereafter. In early 2011, I decided to take a refresher course in hopes of sharpening my playing skills and acquiring some new techniques. I signed up with Stan Sorenson, a jazz guitarist, with whom my son Steven had recently studied. Stan was easy-going and had a good sense of humor, so I felt right at home with him. Since my lessons took place where Brandon had formerly studied, the person of Todd Hogan crept into my mind. At the end of my first session, I asked Stan if he knew Todd's whereabouts.

Stan pointed to the door to an adjacent room and said, "He's right there, giving a lesson." Pleasantly surprised, I waited for Todd's session to conclude and then caught him. He was quite excited to see me, and we spoke for about thirty minutes, enjoying a nice exchange. Reflecting on the past, Todd told me that no matter how dark things got in his life, Brandon used to cheer him up with his happy, calming disposition and his sage advice. As Todd put it, "Brandon always had a way of putting things into perspective and making me appreciate the good things in my life." This was especially helpful to Todd at his lowest points when his marriage was disintegrating and his band falling apart.

One week later, I brought Todd a copy of my first book, *Soul Shift: Finding Where the Dead Go*. Todd was a devout Catholic, so I wasn't sure how he would receive it, but during my thirty-minute music lesson, he plunged into the book and devoured as much as he could. As I made my exit, I found Todd waiting anxiously at the door. Beaming with a revelatory grin, Todd shared that he had experienced paranormal things in his own life, especially during his childhood. His parents had sent him to a priest and a psychologist for counseling, and these "experts" concluded that he had an over-active imagination. After figuring out that it was taboo to discuss these sorts of things, Todd attempted to shut them out and no longer spoke about them when they did occur.

During our conversation, Todd noted that some of these experiences had started up again and even heightened. He was sensing spiritual presences around him. I asked

Todd if Brandon had visited him, and he said that this had occurred on several occasions. Todd also indicated that he had just received a message of encouragement from Brandon pertaining to his new music. The message conveyed that Todd's new album was "awesome" and that Todd "would be receiving unexpected help." In fact, Todd was offered a recording deal right after this message came through. I was also able to lend support by steering Todd to resources that enabled him to move forward with a recording contract. He recently completed and released an outstanding collection of original songs entitled *Nowhere in Between.*

Reconnecting with Todd was a blessing for my family and me, and the timing seemed beyond coincidence. Now remarried with a caring wife and two adorable children, and a budding musical career, Todd seems very happy.

Synchronicity

In the years that have elapsed since my youngest son, Brandon's, passing my life has been filled with unusual events that have convinced me that synchronicity is real. This includes "chance" meetings with strangers where things lined up in unique and meaningful ways, and a mutual benefit was invariably found. Many cases involved such astronomical chances for our meeting as to make "coincidence" the more implausible conclusion.

Renowned psychologist Carl Jung coined the term "synchronicity" and defined it as "temporally coincident occurrences of acausal events." More simply, Jung described synchronicity as "meaningful coincidence."

An implication of synchronicity is that the universe operates in a harmonious manner and that life has meaning. Such a model stands in stark contrast to the view of those who assert that everything happens by chance and any notions of "purpose" are whimsy.

You might ask, what does synchronicity look like?

On the week of January 12, 2009, I was walking through my neighborhood when my cell phone suddenly rang.

"Hello," I said.

The male caller (I will call him Joel) asked if I was Mark Ireland. (Everyone in this chapter is referenced by their actual name unless I call it out in this manner for reasons of privacy.)

After I confirmed my identity, the man asked if I had a pair of tickets for the Arizona Cardinals–Philadelphia Eagles NFC Championship Game. I wasn't surprised by his question since I'd just posted these tickets for sale on the Internet. I wasn't sure if I'd be able to attend the game and had placed the ad to gauge demand for the tickets. Things were making sense thus far until the man's next query caught me off guard. "Are you the Mark Ireland who lost a son and wrote a book?"
Puzzled by how the man knew so much about me, I responded tentatively, "Yes— that's me."

The man then chuckled, revealing a sense of befuddled amusement, and continued. "My name is Joel. My wife and I lost our twenty-year-old son to cancer about two years ago."

Things were starting to crystallize, but I was still perplexed by the cross-pollination of football tickets, parents who had lost a son, and my book. These things were unrelated, and I had not included my last name in the ticket advertisement.

Joel then elaborated, "My wife has had great difficulty in dealing with the grief since our son's death, and she wanted a reading with a medium." He continued, "I've always felt that this life we are now living is all there is and that when it's over, it's over. So, I never believed in that sort of thing [the idea of an afterlife or mediums]. But my wife was suffering so much that I was willing to try anything—so I supported her appeal for a meeting with a medium."

Joel's story was captivating, but I was still left wondering how all this tied to me.

"Earlier today, my wife returned from a reading with a medium named Debra Martin. As I told you before, I've never really bought into this stuff, but I listened to the tape from my wife's session and was stunned. There were several highly specific things that Debra talked about that no one but our son would know."

Joel then volunteered a few details. "For one thing, Debra said that my son and his grandfather were playing with Mitzie. That was significant, because it was just four months after my son's passing that his grandfather died—and we had owned a dog named Mitzie."

Joel then mentioned something else, meaningful to his wife and him.
Debra told my wife, "Your son thanks you for bringing the blanket to him before he died." Even though our son was a twenty-year-old man, he still slept with his baby blanket every night—nestled under his pillow. Just prior to his passing, my wife brought our son's baby blanket to the hospital and gave it to him."

Joel finally explained that Debra Martin had encouraged his wife to buy my book, *Soul Shift: Finding Where the Dead Go* and it was his assignment to pick up a copy from the store. Upon returning home from the store with book in hand, Joel took a moment to check his email and found a note from a business associate that caught his attention. For the past few days, he had been asking around to see if anyone was selling tickets to the Cardinals–Eagles game. One message from an associate named Julia suggested that he contact "Mark Ireland," who had tickets to the game.

When he saw the name referenced in the email and compared it to the name on the cover of the book he'd just purchased, Joel could not believe his eyes. It was at this point that Joel called the number provided by Julia to see if the Mark Ireland who owned the tickets was also the author of the book he'd just purchased.

Now things made sense to me, as I recognized Julia as a woman who dated one of my friends—a person who knew that I had tickets to the football game. With this said, Julia had no connection to Debra Martin—and in fact had never even heard Debra's name before this happened. Considering that metropolitan Phoenix had over four million residents at the time this took place, coincidence would seem an anemic explanation for the rare and long odds involved in this case.

By virtue of Debra's "hits" and the synchronous event that led Joel to me, his skepticism seemed to be waning. I viewed the scenario as a sign that we were supposed to meet—and later spoke to Joel and his wife on the phone for about forty-five minutes in a process that was healing for all concerned.

In late spring 2009, I was visiting my dentist for a routine checkup when Karly the office manager pulled me aside to request a favor. She told me about another couple, the Andersons, who were also patients at the dental office and had just lost their son. She asked if I would sign a copy of my book for them. So, I ran home, signed a copy, and returned it to her within about thirty minutes, and she put it in the mail a short time later.

What Karly and I didn't know was that Fred and Linda Anderson had already read my book. And while perusing my biography on the back cover, the Andersons noticed that we lived in the same city, so they wanted to meet me. As things happened, my signed copy showed up in their mailbox the very day they had this discussion, so they called Karly and asked if I would be willing to meet them.

Obliging the request, I connected by telephone with Fred a few days later, arranging a lunch to include our wives. Susie and I always want to help other bereaved parents. We've met numerous families in this same situation and have found the process to be both rewarding and mutually healing. Having experienced a similar tragedy, we harbor the empathy and understanding necessary to serve others in this way. When others gain a sense of hope and lifting of spirit, our burden is also lightened, and we share in their peace.

When we met the Andersons a week later, our two families immediately formed a bond. They were warm, caring people whose hearts had been broken, as their son, Michael, had passed just a couple of months earlier. Michael was a student at the University of Miami but during his sophomore year in early 2009 had enrolled for a semester abroad in Sydney, Australia, accompanied by two friends. While in Sydney, Michael became very ill, with symptoms that seemed to mirror swine flu, including vomiting and diarrhea. But after three days of illness—on the very day he reported feeling better—Michael collapsed in his apartment and died. The Andersons did not receive the autopsy results or any answers for several months. When the response eventually came, the Andersons learned that traces of kangaroo feces had been found in Michael's system, carrying a lethal bacterium akin to E. coli. The toxins could have been introduced via a meal at an unsanitary restaurant or perhaps were tied to a trip he'd recently made to the Sydney Zoo, but they might never know for sure.

Shortly after we became acquainted with the Andersons, they met with renowned medium George Anderson—and they came back with glowing reports. They said that talking to George was almost like conversing directly with their son. A bit later, I recommended some other mediums for them to consider, and they decided on Tina Powers, booking an appointment with her in the spring of 2010. The Andersons had heard about my reading with Tina and were so impressed that they didn't hesitate in picking her for their next sitting.

To help with stress and pain of grief from losing Michael, Fred also began meditating on a daily basis. It was a practice he'd learned in college but shelved until now. After many months of dedicated meditation, Fred had a very unusual experience. He reported leaving his body and floating up to the ceiling where he could view the entire room (including his body) resting in the chair below. Fred's description fit perfectly with the classic out-of-body experience, or "OBE" as they are commonly called. In an OBE, subjects feel separation from their physical body and become aware that they have a different, lighter, and more flexible body in which they may "astral walk," floating about and feeling no sensations from their physical body, observing happenings below.

What followed about a week later was both shocking, and healing as Michael's face suddenly appeared directly in front of him while Fred was meditating.

Later that day, just hours after Fred's milestone meditation in which Michael's face appeared, the Andersons drove two hours to Tucson for a meeting with Tina Powers. Early in the reading, Tina turned to Fred and explained that he was in the process of opening up to some new experiences and psychic abilities. She then stopped herself in mid-sentence and said, "Your son wants you to know that the experience was real. That was really his face that came to you in meditation." Tina had absolutely no way of knowing the event had just happened. The Andersons had not shared the story with anyone. This gave Fred tremendous confidence in his newfound abilities and was a great comfort to the couple. Tina's statement was the ultimate validation of his contact with Michael.

After this incident, Fred continued to meditate on a daily basis and encountered a series of new experiences. He started receiving information that could later be verified as true and accurate, including precognitive experiences. In one case, his deceased father-in-law appeared to him, telling Fred it was imperative that he check on his mother-in-law immediately. After his meditation, Fred made mention of this to his wife, but she initially scoffed at the suggestion. Linda's mother was always healthy as a horse—she was in her early eighties but was very active and even snow-skied on a daily basis. So, the message Fred had passed along didn't seem to make much sense.

Despite her doubts, Linda called her mother and found that she had been quite ill for several days. Linda flew to New York immediately to be with her and made arrangements for medical attention. After a series of diagnostic tests, it was determined that Linda's mother had lung cancer and also suffered from congestive heart failure—the latter of which would likely have taken her life within days if treatment had not ensued immediately. The two women came back to Scottsdale, Arizona, where Linda's mother went into treatment at the Mayo Clinic. The care proved highly effective and likely extended her life, as well as her high quality of life, for many additional years.

In another case, Fred met me for lunch one day and pulled out the front page from a USA Today newspaper dated June 1, 2010, pointing out a triad of headlines and saying, "I saw this exact cover page just two weeks ago." More importantly, he went on to say that he had seen advanced glimpses of each event, including a deep-water oil rig that would burst into flames in the Gulf of Mexico, a North Korean sub firing a missile at a surface vessel, and Israeli commandos boarding a Turkish flotilla headed for Gaza.

Fred continued to have varied psychic experiences, such as visiting other deceased loved ones and even seeing the domain where Michael now lives. And I would share Fred's description of this alternate dimensional reality with you, but this was a sacred experience—one difficult to express with words capable of conveying a sufficient degree of accuracy or richness. Because of these occurrences, Fred told me that he is now absolutely certain that there is life after death. He has no fear of death whatsoever. Fred never dreamed of manifesting these sorts of abilities and is about as grounded a person as you will ever meet. Was it just a coincidence that Fred and I met?

At the urging of my publisher, I set up an online social networking page in late 2008 to help promote my first book. And although I'd not previously contemplated using this platform, it proved useful for cultivating new connections.

Among the first people I met through this new online channel was a woman named Kim whose youngest son, William, had died a few years earlier. From the photos Kim had posted, I noticed that William bore a striking resemblance to Brandon. Given this similarity, I sent an introductory note to Kim, and she responded a short time later, agreeing with my observation about the likeness of our sons.

Kim explained that William died from liver failure at the age of sixteen. She has since become a strong advocate for organ donation. William suddenly fell ill one day, and she rushed him to the hospital. She had suspected something simple like a virus but was informed that her son's liver was failing; he needed a transplant within twenty-four hours to survive. Miraculously, a donated liver was found within the short time window, and her son underwent successful transplant surgery. But Kim's joy was short-lived because the implanted organ failed five months later. William passed. As wrenching as the loss was for Kim, she was grateful for those additional months she had been able to spend with her son. It had been borrowed time.

Because Kim had learned about my positive experience with mediums, she expressed an interest in having a reading with Laurie Campbell. When it took place six months later, Laurie delivered some remarkable hits, which Kim shared with me the following day. Kim had mentioned nothing about me when scheduling the appointment or during the session.

Laurie correctly identified that William's death was tied to a liver problem and also noted that he had leukemia. Kim saw this as an astounding hit because William had contracted leukemia after his transplant. It was a secret she'd not shared with anyone. Kim had feared that people would wrongly assume William contracted this disease from the donated liver, deterring people from organ donation.

Laurie also identified that William's head had been shaved in the hospital. The doctors had to shear William's scalp so they could drill a hole in his skull to drain fluid and relieve pressure.

"So, what is William doing now?" Kim asked Laurie.

"He's playing music with Brandon," Laurie stated, apparently unaware that she was speaking of my son Brandon. "He's with a group of really good kids from different backgrounds who have a common interest in music, and they all get together to play." This was interesting for several reasons—first because Laurie didn't know that William was a guitar player, and second because she didn't know that Kim and I were acquainted.

Laurie also told Kim that she saw her son "hiking on mountains." This made us wonder if Brandon had possibly taken William under his wing. My son was an avid hiker and lived in the mountainous state of Arizona, while William was a surfer from Florida who had never lived anywhere else.

At the end of the reading, Kim came clean with Laurie, mentioning my name for the first time and sharing that I had referred her. Kim then explained that she didn't know anyone named Brandon, except my son, and William never met my son before passing.

There is far more to this and other stories of synchronicity. At roughly the same time Kim and I crossed paths, I met another bereaved parent through an online social network, Denise Kennedy from New Mexico. Denise had lost her son Eric in an auto accident a year earlier and had become a chapter leader of a support group called Compassionate Friends.

Nine months from my initial contact with Kim and Denise, I learned that Denise and her daughter were traveling to the Compassionate Friends national conference in Portland, Oregon. During the convention, Denise and her daughter met another woman named Kristen, who had lost her daughter in an auto accident two years earlier. (Ironically, Denise's daughter is also named Kristen; however, any time I mention the name "Kristen" in the balance of this chapter, I am referring to the bereaved mother.)

Denise told me that she kept crossing paths with Kristen during the conference, so they spent a lot of time together. Kristen opened up, telling Denise that she only believed in a material reality and held out no hope of ever seeing her daughter again. She had decided to attend the conference, hoping it might help her "learn how to get through this." Despite her pragmatic leanings, Kristen showed some signs of open-mindedness in her interest in a conference workshop discussing "signs" as evidence for the afterlife—a topic with which she was completely unfamiliar. Denise told me that, in general, Kristen was not very far along in dealing with her grief.

After hearing these things, I told Denise that I'd like to send a copy of my book to Kristen and asked for her address. Oddly, after receiving the information, I noticed that Kristen lived in the same Florida town as my other friend Kim, William's mom. This motivated me to include a note suggesting that Kristen contact Kim since they had both lost children. After all, what were the odds of me coming into contact with two bereaved mothers living in the same place in Florida, linked by a woman from New Mexico, via a conference in Oregon?

About a week later, I received an email from Kristen thanking me for the book, but I was completely unprepared for the rest of what she had to say. Kristen explained that she already knew Kim but that the circumstances were difficult: her daughter had died from injuries sustained in an auto accident in which she was a passenger in a car that collided with a vehicle occupied by Kim's older son, William's brother Bruce.

If I thought my connection with Kim and Kristen was bizarre up to this point, things had now moved to an entirely different level. There are about 310 million people in the United States, so the odds of a series of associations like this coming together in this way are nearly incalculable.

Initially, I wasn't sure how to respond but decided to let my heart do the talking as I told Kristen, "I don't know how or why we connected in this way, but I'm sure it has something to do with healing."

After learning about this situation from Kristen's note, I called Kim to explain the almost unfathomable set of circumstances. I was initially a bit puzzled that Kim had never mentioned this information to me, but it seemed there was some residual tension between the two mothers. And I suppose that it was inevitable for some hard feelings to exist even in a case that was ruled an accident.

When I heard the story, it seemed clear to me that reconciliation was in order. I wasn't sure how to force something like that or how long it would take to come about naturally. Once again, the solution was unexpected.

Denise contacted me a few weeks after the *Compassionate Friends* conference, telling me that she'd applied—on behalf of Kristen and herself—for a fully sponsored trip to a retreat for bereaved mothers. A short time later, she wrote to say that both she and Kristen had been selected to attend. The retreat was for mothers who had lost children and was focused on helping them heal, including information on how they could connect with the spirit of their deceased child. I don't know the full scope of the curriculum, but I could tell it was effective after viewing the two emails that followed—one from Denise and one from Kristen. The note from Denise came first and told me that Kristen had undergone a spiritual transformation, moving from a place of despair to one of hope.

A day or two later, I received a note from Kristen, and she said, "Mark, I'm happy to say that I am now an Engineer." I immediately recognized that she was quoting from the last chapter of my first book, where I explained the difference between physicists and engineers. The physicist wants to know how something works while the engineer is satisfied to know that it does work.

Shortly after Kristen returned home, I learned that Kim had invited her to a function to benefit organ donation, and Kristen decided to attend. Within a month or so, Kristen started her own group to help parents who had lost children, exploring evidence for the continuation of consciousness and survival of personal energy after physical death. Kim was invited to the first session and has continued to attend ever since. Likewise, Kristen has been highly supportive of Kim's ongoing organ-donation work and still makes a point to attend her meetings.

I was later surprised to discover the impetus behind Kristen's decision to attend Kim's function and show support. As Kristen wrote, "Do you know why I decided to accept that invitation to attend Kim's organ-donation brunch? It was because of what you said to me about these 'coincidences'—with Kim and I connecting in so many ways—having a higher purpose. I thought to myself … well, I might as well attend and see what the universe has in store for us!"

I've come to the conclusion that the best healing comes from helping others and extending forgiveness.

As a postscript to this story, I later learned about two noteworthy subplots. First, Kristen's daughter had known Kim's older son Bruce; they played pickup basketball in the neighborhood years earlier, and Kristen subsequently found a photo of this activity.

Second, the girlfriend of Bruce, who was also in the car at the time of the accident, reported seeing the spirit of Bruce's brother William—both at the accident scene and then later at the hospital. Initially skeptical of the report, Kim asked the girl what William was wearing, and she responded, "Khaki cargo shorts and a white tee-shirt." Kim was stunned. The description was precise. Prior to his death from liver failure, William regularly wore khaki cargo shorts and a white t-shirt. This girl had never met William, and none of the photos displayed in Kim's home showed him dressed this way.

Excerpts from "Messages from the Afterlife: A Bereaved Father's Journey in the World of Spirit Visitations, Psychic-Mediums, and Synchronicity" by Mark Ireland, December 10, 2013, North Atlantic Books

About the Author

Mark Ireland is the author of two books that explore evidence for the post-mortem survival of consciousness, including the ground-breaking *Soul Shift: Finding Where the Dead Go*. He is the son of Richard Ireland, a renowned twentieth-century Psychic-Medium who counseled celebrities such as Mae West, Glenn Ford, Amanda Blake, and the Eisenhower family.

Mark also co-founded Helping Parents Heal, an organization with 21,000 members and over 100 worldwide affiliates that assists bereaved parents.

Additionally, Mark has participated in mediumship research studies conducted by the University of Arizona and the University of Virginia, and he currently operates an independent Medium Certification program. Mark's objective is to identify high-caliber Mediums capable of furnishing specific, accurate, and pertinent information. According to the Windbridge Research Center, highly evidential readings can provide a therapeutic benefit to grieving persons.

Mark holds a Bachelor's degree from Arizona State University, and he currently lives in the Portland, Oregon area with his wife, Susie.

Website: www.markirelandauthor.com

"Life is eternal; and love is immortal;
and death is only a horizon; and a horizon
is nothing save the limit of our sight."
~R.W. Raymond~
Engineer, Author
1840 – 1918

Love Lives On, *Jan Warner*

By Jan Warner

My husband Artie was dead. I was moving from our home in California to New York City. The roses were still blooming but there was no hand to hold as I looked at them. Our home was a too silent house without his footsteps, his heartbeat, his voice. I needed two more packing boxes, so I drove to the local UPS store we had both used only occasionally. After I paid for my boxes the man at the register, slight in build, balding, with kind eyes looking at me through wire rimmed spectacles said, "Let me carry the boxes for you." I replied, "No thank you. I got this."

His voice turned oddly insistent as he told rather than asked me to let him carry the boxes. I wasn't up for an argument. I had so little energy left. I nodded my head, and he took the two folded pieces of cardboard from my hands and carried them the short distance to my car. When we got there, he looked gently into my eyes. I heard his voice but had trouble absorbing what he said. It wasn't as if I knew him. Even twelve years later I can see him and hear him as he speaks confidently and with great assurance. "Your husband came to me and told me I had to give you a message. You have to understand how much he loves you. You must never be insecure or doubt that he loves you."

I laughed. It was a strange sound. I didn't laugh very much anymore. I was placing the boxes in the back seat when I commented, "That must have been a heck of a dream."

His gaze remained gentle, but his voice was firm. "It wasn't a dream. It was an apparition. Your husband came to me and told me it was important that I tell you how much he loves you." He didn't use the past tense. He didn't say "loved you".

He said, "loves you." I started to cry. I could understand a friend making up a story to try to comfort me but why would someone who knew us only informally as customers carry this kind of message to me if it wasn't true, if it wasn't in fact my husband communicating with me after death in such a way that I would believe the messenger. Now, when I tell the story I ask people, "What does UPS deliver to you?" My husband was a recovering alcoholic who firmly believed in a higher power. He knew I was a skeptic. It was as if he could sense how broken I was. He was the only person who has taken care of me in my life. I was the only person who had taken care of him. A big man with a rough exterior and a marshmallow heart he had a difficult time opening himself up to me. When he did you could feel the vibrancy of our love energetically travel back and forth between us. He would always stop what he was doing if I asked him to hold me. When I thanked him for holding me, he said, "I need it as much as you do."

Handsome, charming, damaged, loving, he was older than I was. I thought when he died, I would be sad and miss him very much. I never imagined I would feel totally annihilated. I was like a house that is hit by a tornado. I was moving and breathing but I felt splintered into bits. I didn't know then that the most beautiful mosaics are made out of broken pieces.

I expected him to come get me. I slept with my hand reaching up into the air for him to grab and pull me up to wherever he was. In the morning I was startled and not happy to discover I was still breathing. After a while I thought maybe I was supposed to go to him and researched suicide. I couldn't give the grief that I was experiencing to those who love me. I would have to live. Now, 12 years later I know that had I died then I would have missed so much. I also know what feels like forever to me on some days and even longer nights, is just a blink of an eye in terms of the eternity that awaits us.

My husband was a recovering alcoholic who was always available to help other addicts and alcoholics. When I realized that my life was going to continue, I searched my mind for a purpose. We used to call each other our raison d'etre (reason for being). With my reason for being gone what could I do? How could I even begin to survive? I decided to honor his work by making myself available to grieving people. I thought if I reached one person that would be enough, and I began writing a blog. I never imagined I would in time support thousands of grieving people from so many faraway places. First there was the blog, then a Facebook page called *Grief Speaks Out*, and then a book called, *Grief Day by Day: Simple Practices and Daily Guidance*

61

for Living With Loss. I have received emails from places as far away as Mongolia and Malaysia. All over the world people share their love, their grief, and their communications with their loved ones.

I didn't know I would find this new reason for being. I especially couldn't even imagine I would have many adventures in a rather magical life. I call it decorating the waiting room. I want so much to be with my husband in the same form but it's not up to me decide the time that this will happen. I always think of Mary Oliver's question, "What is it you plan to do with your one wild and precious life?" I'm in a waiting room but I want it to be as beautiful, and full of life as I can make it. My husband reaches out his hand to guide me every step of the way.

In the beginning I spent a lot of time in bed watching endless DVDs. When his friends or my friends took me out, I felt like I was in shock. All I could think of was the chair next to me that was empty. My husband ran an Alcoholics Anonymous meeting and when a new person came, he always made sure someone took them out for coffee. He never wanted someone trying to get sober to feel alone. His friend Jose who I didn't know very well took me out to lunch. He told me that Artie now often stood at the foot of his bed and reminded him to take of newcomers at meetings. I have a soft spot in my heart for Jose because when my husband was in the hospital, he complained there was no parmesan cheese for his spaghetti. I was a little impatient, but Jose went into the corridor and came back with Parmesan cheese.

Before I left the home we lived in so happily, in spite of the sometime stormy fights, I lit tea lights and placed them on the floor in the living room where my husband's hospital bed had been. A few close friends came over and we told Artie stories. Before I left, I did something a bit weird. I looked in every drawer, cupboard, and closet. I didn't want to leave until I made sure my husband wasn't hiding anywhere. I knew he was dead, but I still (even to this day) can't totally accept that he is never coming back. So much so that I am beginning to believe that while the body does die the spirit lives on. The place I looked last was in the mirror where he got ready every morning. I had the strange idea that somehow his reflection was trapped in the mirror, and I would be able to see it. I didn't see anything except my own reflection. A while later through a medium my husband said, "I was there. I was just standing behind you so you couldn't see me."

A medium? Yes. Still skeptical but I have someone I have been friends with for decades who used to do medium work for friends. Her name is Karen and she had only met Artie once and was someone I trusted. One thing she said was that when I put something like a blanket, but it wasn't a blanket, over my shoulders at night that was my husband holding me. When my husband was dying, he was often cold, so I bought him a *slanket* - those blankets with sleeves.

Every night before I closed my eyes, I pulled the slanket he died in over my shoulder. How did she know that? I had maybe five or six phone calls and usually she ended the session by saying, "He is throwing flowers at you and walking away." The last time she said, "I have no idea why this is happening, but he is throwing tiny stuffed animals at you as he is walking away." She had no way of knowing that he often would come home with a small stuffed animal to make me smile.

Once I told him, through my medium friend, that I was very lonely. That I needed him here physically. I even yelled at him while tears poured out from my eyes for leaving me behind. He said, through her, that if I needed arms, I could find new arms. If I needed physical love, I could find a new love. He was giving me permission to fall in love again. It wasn't something I wanted. When he was alive, I once said, "I wish somebody loved me." He raised one eyebrow and asked a one-word question, "Somebody?" I changed my syntax, "I want YOU to love me." He said, "I can't not love you. Loving you is like breathing."

That's how I feel now. I don't want someone, I want him. I went for a walk thinking about why he would say something like that. I heard him say, "When I said that thing about you finding someone else, I was just saying it because I know that's what I'm supposed to feel. I didn't want to say the wrong thing in front of Karen. You're my woman, my wife. If you need someone, I would try to understand but I want to still be the only man you love. I want you to be faithful to me and our marriage. You're still my heart. Always." I smiled. I liked that answer better. To be honest I think Artie would be angry with me if I didn't miss him anymore. He doesn't want me to be unhappy, but he is glad that I still grieve for him because he knows, as I do, that grief is love.

After a few years, Karen decided she didn't want to do the calls anymore. I always did them around February 3 which is my birthday and my wedding anniversary. I felt that once a year was respectful of whatever he needed to be doing and I knew that Karen had never liked medium work. She told me she "wasn't feeling energy from him anymore". I was hurt and angry.

Sometimes I still think of letting her know how I feel and asking for another call. However, the truth is that I don't need a go between. I was using her presence to validate the love I knew was there. Through her he said, "We were connected before we met, and we will always be connected through time and space." I was using her presence because I didn't trust our own direct communications.

There was another problem. Even if I was talking to him through her, he was still dead. I spent some time being angry at him for leaving me even thought I knew he was too sick to stay. Talking to him through a medium wasn't helpful in the end because what I needed to learn was how to have a relationship with someone who was just spirit. I'm in my earthly body. I miss his face. I miss his voice. I miss his jokes. I miss the body part of him that is ashes in a decorative pillow in my bedroom. His spirit and even spirit arms may be holding me, but I want his human arms.

When I first moved to New York City permanently, on days when I managed to go out, I used to hold my hand curved the slightest bit, pretending my husband was walking with me and holding my hand. The first time I remember hearing him say something to me was at the theater. I knew I liked theater, so I kept going even though I kept falling asleep. I even slept through Daniel Craig and Hugh Jackman. The applause at the end would wake me up. Then I saw Carrie Fisher in *Wishful Drinking* and not only stayed awake, but I laughed. I went to *Sondheim! The*

Birthday Concert by myself and even though the man I was sitting next to was very funny and talkative, I was feeling utterly alone. I heard my husband say, "When you asked me to go places with you, I used to say no all the time. Now that I'm dead, I can come with you everywhere."

Another time I was standing in front of a rather posh jewelry store. I didn't really like my engagement ring and we had exchanged it for another piece of jewelry. I hadn't found an engagement ring I liked until this very moment when I was staring at a deep blue sapphire with a smattering of diamonds sparkling in the lighted window. I thought, "It's too bad Artie is dead. I love this ring. It would make an exquisite engagement ring." I heard my husband say, "Thank goodness I'm dead. I don't have to buy something so expensive." I laughed.

A couple of times I even bought something for him. Something I could only pretend to give him. I went into a shop that sold the kind of t-shirts he liked to wear. At the celebration of his life, I gave away his t-shirts and his books so people could have something to remember him. It was odd to look up and see so many of our friends and family wearing his t-shirts. My intention was to just buy him one. I was going up on the escalator and he said what I thought was "Nobody", but then he repeated it and what he was saying was "No body." I turned around and took the elevator back down and left the store. No point in buying a t-shirt for someone who no longer had a body. As you can tell humor was an important part of our relationship when he was alive and that has continued after his death. Someone once asked me, "Do you joke with your dead?" I've always thought that was a lovely question.
I've taken to calling these communications "taps on the head" because it feels like my husband is tapping me on my head to get my attention and then the thought I have after doesn't seem as if it is coming from inside my brain. The thought seems as though it is coming from outside. I don't hear my husband's voice. He's dead. He doesn't have a voice. However, the thoughts in my head are clear and they feel like his thoughts rather than mine. Often times they come when I am saying something he doesn't agree with or has an opinion on.

I was telling someone how many people feel like they know him when they never met him because I tell his story. He said, "Don't take all the credit. Maybe they feel like they know me because I'm still charismatic."

At first, I was literally trying to save my own life. I went everywhere I thought I could get help. I travelled to grief conferences, went to a therapist and a bereavement group.

I got matched up with two other widows and exchanged emails with them. After a while I realized that everything was too sad. What could I do to laugh like Carrie Fisher had made me laugh? I took a course in comedy sketch writing with someone who had written for Saturday Night Live. He asked why we were taking the class. I said, 'My husband died so I thought I'd do comedy." I got a combination of laughter and shocked gasps. I also took classes in storytelling. In one class I mentioned my husband, and someone I had never met before said, "Oh. That's who I saw with you when you walked in. I knew it was a man, but I didn't know who."

New York City was where I celebrated the first of his birthdays since his death. I wondered if I should celebrate a dead man's birthday and decided of course I could. I bought a cupcake and lit a candle. I pleaded with his spirit to blow out the candle as a sign. It kept burning and eventually I blew out the candle myself and ate the cupcake.

Years before I had found him a book he wanted, On Listening. I had never been interested in it, but I kept it because it was special to him. I was trying to stay in a space of gratitude that he had been born and that we had such a deep and loving connection, but I was slipping back into utter loneliness and confusion. I randomly opened On Listening. Even all these years later the only reason seems to be that he was guiding me. I wasn't going to read it. Inside the front cover was a note in his handwriting I had no conscious memory of. It said, "Don't be insecure. If you are insecure, I'll cry. I love you. I adore you. I worship you. Love from your Dazzle." He used to call me "Panache" and I used to call him "Dazzle". It's a nickname I still try to live up to. It seemed that Artie was still stubborn. He was going to give me the sign he wanted to rather than the one I planned.

I have friends who tell me that they have seen him. One friend was learning to meditate, and he heard my husband say, "Atta boy. Keep up the good work." This same friend said he sometimes feels Artie's presence when he is walking down the street. Another friend saw him in a dream. Sometimes someone will tell me he told them to make sure they look after me. I'm lucky to have friends and family who don't mind when we are in a conversation and I say, "My husband says...". Artie doesn't interrupt too often but they are as used as I am to my husband still having a voice in my life. Sometimes when I share what I've heard him say they will answer that they felt his presence even before I said anything.

Dreams are another thing completely. When he first died, I had a vivid dream. I woke up in my dream and saw my husband. I was so excited. I said, "You're here!! I thought you were dead. I thought cancer killed you." My husband held me and said, "Silly girl. Of course, I'm not dead. I would never leave you. I'm right here." I felt so warm and happy and then I woke up. I felt something against my back and thought for a minute it was him. Then I realized it was a pillow and unlike in my dream, my husband was dead. Could he be dead and still here? Could his body be dead, and his spirit still be alive? I used to think my husband was the most alive dead person I knew until I started working with grievers and I realized there are untold numbers of alive dead people. Do we keep them alive in our hearts and minds or is their consciousness still alive and with us?

Sometimes before I go to sleep, I say, "And then my husband came home." I do that to try to have a dream where he does come home and spends loving time with me. I used to have a fantasy that he would come home, and everyone would be so surprised. Of course, that didn't happen. In the beginning when people used to ask if there was anything they could do for me I would reply, "Can you resurrect dead people?". They would say no, and I would let them know that anything less than that wouldn't be helpful.

I also have nightmares where I am searching for him and can't find him. Sometimes I find him, and he doesn't recognize me or doesn't want to be with me. I don't think of those as visitations. I think the nightmares are trying to reach the part of my soul that can't accept that he is dead. Even after 12 years I find it impossible to totally accept that he is not coming back. We always said, "Nobody leaves." His body was too sick to stay and most of me is rational about that. There is still the part that feels like a promise was broken. Perhaps that promise is unbroken because he is still with me but is in a different form.

Some people feel that if you still have a relationship with someone who has died you are burdening them in some way. I don't believe that. I think time and space is different where he is. He can be with me and do whatever it is he needs to do or even be with more than one person at the same time. I feel him holding me in any way he can; understanding when I am sad or stuck and rejoicing when I am happy and having adventures. Sometimes when I am crying or enraged or wallowing in self pity (I rather like a good wallow every once in a while) I can feel him reaching out to me. He asks me to lean on him more, not less. He wants me to know as difficult as it is he is still caring for me in every way he can.

A big shift happened when I stopped thinking of him as dead and began to think of him as alive and healthy. I want our life and our love to matter more than his death. I am the rememberer, the keeper of his stories, of our story. How tragic it would be to be stuck in that one night, the night of his death. I can tell you every moment of the night. How he ate a teaspoon of warm corn souffle and said, "Thank you. That makes everything better." I still don't know what he meant. I had a hospice nurse in our home who put him into a twilight sleep.

His last words to me were, "I love you." My last words to him were, "I love you too." Well, not our last words, just our last words while he was physically alive. When breath in, breath out, no breath in, happened his friend called his name and held a mirror to his nose and mouth. I knew he was gone. My husband was no longer in his body. I understood why they call a dead body the remains. I loved his body too and I spent time with him.

When we couldn't get him into the dress shirt and tie I had taken out, I put him in a t-shirt that said, "I do all my own stunts". I hope someone got a laugh from that. It was like walking along the shore and watching the tide go out and knowing that it would never come in again. I remember watching them drive him into the night. I said, "I want to come with you but that would be stupid because you're dead." Everything was so quiet and empty. There was no comfort anywhere.

Each last moment is crystal clear in my memory but that was one night. To make that one night more important than all the magical moments of struggle and failure and struggle and triumph would be stealing the meaning of his life from him. I made an effort to reclaim my memories. I wanted all the wonderful moments to be wonderful rather than painful. I wanted to be grateful for all we shared and have that grow bigger and stronger and more important than the pain. I wouldn't let grief taint or steal even one memory. Once I realized I was supposed to live, I began to want to live double for both of us. I want Artie to be proud of me.

I'm still a skeptic. I tell people that if I'm delusional it doesn't matter. Believing my husband is with me and that we will be reunited after death is what allows me to function. I will find out if everything I believe is true when I die. I like that my small chapter will be cushioned in a book with people who aren't skeptical. My favorite inscription on tombstones is "Reunited". I wonder how we will know each other without our bodies. I wonder how we will hold each other. I picture us as bouncing energy balls that can move in and out of each other. I don't really know what shape is no shape but how could I say what the shape of love is? I call it the big party in the sky where we are all together with those people and animals we love so much.

I was watching a documentary called *Everything and Nothing* about the universe. Where could the billions and billions of souls who have existed through time on our planet go? They could go so many different places. Our sun is like a grain of sand on the beach compared to the size of a universe with multiple galaxies containing multiple stars and planetary systems. The universe is always expanding so as huge as it is, it gets bigger and bigger. There are places even our most advanced telescopes can't come close to observing. So much of the universe is made of dark matter. What if our loved ones are warm white lights in the darkness? Perhaps the pulse of the universe is the perpetual beat of loving hearts. I don't know what electricity looks like, but I know that when I plug in a lamp the light comes on. With so many waves and particles floating through the atmosphere why not signs and wonders? Why not communication? Why not love?

My husband is looking over my shoulder as I am writing the last words of this chapter. I don't hear him, but I feel his warmth and his concern. Wait. I do hear him. He is telling me to believe. He is telling me the same message the man who worked at the UPS store told me all those years ago. I have to know how much he loves me. I have to know that some things are temporary, but our love is eternal. We were connected before we met and nothing, not even death, can break that connection. I love you. You're my heart. Always.

About the Author

69

Jan Warner has used her Master's in Counseling degree and her training in NLP and hypnotherapy while working in child abuse prevention and suicide prevention. When her beloved husband Artie died, she felt as though she had died too. She decided to honor his memory by making herself available to grieving people the way he, as a recovering alcoholic, had made himself available to alcoholics and addicts. Jan decided it would give her life meaning even if she only reached one person. Now, she has a Facebook page called *Grief Speaks Out*, that is a supportive worldwide community with 2.5 million followers. She is the author of *Grief Day by Day: Simple Practices and Daily Guidance for Living With Loss*. She has produced documentary films and an Off-Broadway play. She has been to all seven continents. Jan's favorite role in life is being a grandmother.

Jan and Artie

Artie

*"When we look out into space,
we are looking into our own origins,
because we are truly children of the stars."*
~Brian Edward Cox~
Professor of Particle Physics,
School of Physics and Astronomy
University of Manchester
The Royal Society Professor
for Public Engagement in Science.

Through the Looking Glass, *Carla Kaufman Sloan*

By Carla Kaufman Sloan

December 2014, Miami, Florida

Three am. I hear my husband's breathing and envy the steady sound. I keep my eyes closed, bone tired, permeated with an exhaustion I have never known in this life. I am hoping to find sleep again. I wake up at the same time in the middle of every night, medicated or not. I listen for Daisy, our sweet runt of dog, a tiny black Brussels Griffon. She has also become a heavy breather with advancing age, her black coat now gray.

I am not able to lull myself back to sleep. The sedatives have obviously worn off, so I rise from our bed, one of the few possessions we brought to our new house from our home where the accident happened. I slip out the bedroom door and walk through the cardboard congregation of unpacked boxes to Caleb's new room. I creep silently over to listen to my five-year old's breath.

His slow, rhythmic exhales calm me. He looks so small in the queen-sized bed that was previously his brother's, barely larger than one of the big stuffed animals snuggled closely around him. Caleb has recently started laughing in his sleep like his brother once did. I was surprised the first time it happened and delighted to be the sole audience member to this joyful secret.

Without turning on a light, I navigate my way back through the packed boxes to our living room, crossing the chilly stone floor, barefoot. This new living room is nothing like the one in our old house, which had creaky warm brown wood floors that reminded me of my youth in New Orleans. I sit in this white and gray room feeling the hygienic newness of it all. I had intentionally designed it that way from the concrete slab up: clean, new, pristine. I didn't want to worry about undisclosed mold, mildew, or electrical issues that come with older homes. There had to be no hidden element of danger.

Our ultra-modern living room has high ceilings and porcelain tile floors giving it an airy, whitewashed, beachy look. Tall clear glass doors lead to the pool in the backyard. The doors are so huge and heavy that Caleb can't open and close them without help. I can barely open them, myself. Still spotlessly new, the glass appeared almost non-existent. In fact, I had once walked full speed into one while checking on the building progress, nearly knocking myself out in front of the construction crew. Following that day, the contractor put dayglo stickers on each pane at eye level until the work was done.

I sit on the sofa, in the silence, pulling my feet up under me. Only the light from the quarter moon spills through the shadeless doors. I look up at the three pieces of framed art hanging on the wall between the shiny sliding glass. The top piece is a photo of my first-born son, Calder, at age six, holding his colorful self-portrait. His first-grade teacher had photographed my Chicklet-toothed son, beaming with pride, holding his artwork up to the camera. Calder was always smiling. He had inherited my belly laugh and his physical features favored my side of the family.

He had my mother's blue eyes and fair complexion with a slight upturn to his nose. The second piece of art is a collection of calligraphy, first our son's full name, Calder Jacob Sloan, and then everything that described him: Adventure, Laughter, Kindness, could teach a fish to swim, April 6th, Kauai, surfing, big brother, change the world, always loved, never forgotten. Each phrase is a different color and a different size all coming together to form a vibrant heart. Finally, at the bottom of the three is Calder's original self-portrait that his school had framed for us.

The heaviness of being a family of three instead of four, hits me hard. The anguish of losing my eldest son, Calder, presses upward like a geyser and I begin sobbing. I let the tears flow and rack my body as my husband and kindergartener sleep. This witness-free guttural crying can only be done alone When I shed tears around others, they slid from my eyes without permission or control in silent rivers down my face. But the sobbing I save for the late-night darkness.

I miss Calder so much. I want to feel him, his soft skin, inhale his scent, and hold his small man hand. All day long, I had come to feel like I was sick with a terminal flu, one that had sucked every bit of energy from my body down to my marrow. There is only one thing I want. Only one. I want my son back. Alive. I know I will never have that again. Nothing will ever ease this heartache.

I repeat over and over in my head: Calder I miss you so much and I wish you were here. Calder, I wish you were here. Calder. I beg and plead frantically aloud, my body rocking. I surrendered to the pain hoping it would put an end to me. Outside of the sliding glass door, something catches my attention. I am startled and stop crying.

I blink hard and attempt to clear the tears from my eyes. Calder is standing on the other side of the door and looking into the new house through the same glass that had almost knocked me out. He wears a sky-blue t-shirt, but not his glasses. And he is smiling his big toothy grin. I can see him looking around the living room, and hear him expressing a thought, though he doesn't speak: "Wow, this is so cool." For a split second my complete elation in seeing my child again obliterates my sadness, I am filled with a happiness I thought was forever lost, until suddenly fear shoots through me with a jolt and my joy dissipates as quickly as it came. How could this be Calder?

The moment the fear overtakes me he vanishes. Lost again. I get up and walk over to the glass. I am still afraid, but I want to chase after him. He is gone. I return to the sofa and wrap a blanket around me and remain there until sunrise, staring through the glass. The moment is gone but the experience stays with me. My son had appeared to me in my darkest moment. It was Calder. Was this possible?

I questioned my sanity deeply. Had I snapped completely, 8 months into the suffering? As I feel around my mental faculties blindly, another thought drops into my mind. Is this what other people mean when they said their prayers have been answered or scarier yet, that they had experienced a miracle? Even that language is off putting and would have made me roll my eyes if I had not had this experience myself.

Do I completely understand what happened? No.

Do I believe this happened? Yes, in my heart and soul I do, but the rest of me thinks I may be crazy until the experiences continue happening.

About the Author

Carla Kaufman Sloan is an Emmy winning writer and television producer with three decades of experience in creating, writing, and developing TV shows, in-studio production, and delivery, and helming major television network content in New York and Los Angeles. As a young Jewish girl from New Orleans (a.k.a a Jew from the Bayou), being accepted to New York University was an impossible dream that came true. While executive producing national primetime game shows for ABC and Warner Brothers/Telepix in LA, Carla accepted a marriage proposal from Chris Sloan, a TV executive, and as a couple they launched our own production company on the opposite coast. 2C Creative became a rapidly growing content and award-winning production company in Miami with a client base including A&E, HBO, TNT, Discovery Channel, FOX, Nickelodeon, and more. With her career goals rocketing forward, it seemed the perfect time to have a baby. Blue eyed, adventure-loving Calder Jacob, arrived in 2007, followed 18 months later by a little, brown-eyed talented attention-getter, Caleb Finzi. Carla didn't fully realize it at the time, but she was living the dream. Seven years later, everything changed. Months after the tragic accident that took Calder's life, Carla and her husband co-established *Caleb and Calder Sloan's Awesome Foundation* to help children in need, prioritizing kids who have suffered the loss of a parent or sibling. The foundation has grown significantly since 2015 to serve hundreds of thousands of people. In addition to choosing to step back into a full daily life of work, mothering, and community outreach, Carla is also studying and practicing her mediumship ability to connect and deliver messages to those in grief from the loss of a loved one. Carla's interest in expanding her spiritual outlook on life grew from the incredible comfort and confirmation of her son's presence that she received, first through professional mediums, and now regularly. Carla is also a certified Reiki Master.

Calder holding his first-grade self-portrait that would become *Mr. Awesome* and travel around the world.

Calder and Caleb Pajama Day 2013

The Four C's and Daisy Sloan

"The doctrine that the world is made up of objects whose existence is independent of human consciousness turns out to be in conflict with quantum mechanics and with facts established by experiment."
~Bernard d'Espagnat~
Theoretical Physicist
1921 - 2015

You Can Count on the Signs, *Annette Marinaccio*

By Annette Marinaccio, CPA

Congratulations on reading this book! Your soul has likely drawn you to a book of this nature maybe because you are curious or maybe you want validation for your feelings. Either way, I hope that you enjoy the book. And yes, the more stories and information we all obtain about the afterlife, its existence, and what this all means, the more able we are to live the earthly lives we are intended to live. So, let me share some of my journey with you.

My name is Annette Marinaccio. As you can see from my chapter title, I am a Certified Public Accountant. I point that out for two reasons. The first reason is that my profession is bound by a Code of Ethics, so I hope that adds a level of credibility to my words. Secondly, I want to let you know that I am a person who has spent my entire life in love with numbers and statistics. I am a healthcare executive for a large health system in the New York metropolitan area. I am not someone that you would find writing a chapter or a book about the afterlife, however that is also who I am and what I've done.

You see my mother-in-law, Lucille, proved to me that there is an afterlife after she died. That's right, after she passed, she began sending me a series of signs and synchronicities that I simply couldn't ignore. Once I accepted that she is still around, I had one significant question: if we go on after this earthly life, then what the heck are we doing here on earth to begin with? And so my journey began.
I spent about four years submersed in all things metaphysical. I attended psychic events, medium events, read hundreds of books, hundreds of articles, spoke with

hundreds of people about their experiences. I was amazed that once you dip your toe into this topic, the volume of available information is overwhelming. And after about four years, I was quite content with my newly acquired understanding of the afterlife. I had learned the meaning of our lives here and how they connect to the Other Side as best I could. I re-directed my daily existence as best I could, incorporating my new realizations. I thought that was all I had to do.

However, I was wrong.

What occurred after that is the Universe placed me in the path of people who needed a small aspect of what I had learned to help them to navigate through their personal time of grief or curiosity. This was happening time and time again. I found myself conveying a small piece of what I had learned at a time that was very helpful to someone that I happened to be speaking with. Person after person was thankful and even said I had helped to change their perspective or life. As an accountant, I wasn't accustomed to changing anyone's life, so this was quite the rewarding feeling.

After several years of this, I understood that I was meant to summarize what I have learned into a simple and digestible format, as only an accountant type might be able to do. So, I became an author and wrote a book, Your Soul Focus. This has allowed me to enter the world of podcast interviews, book signings, author discussions, and various other things that have allowed me to help share what I learned and my experiences in the hope that yet one more person can find some comfort or inspiration from my knowledge.

Although I have learned quite a lot, I want to share two stories in particular with you. One is how I first started my afterlife journey and the second illustrates how I am now able to understand when the Universe provides me with an important job to do.

It was Wednesday morning, October 25th of 2006. I was enjoying breakfast with my beautiful 13-year-old daughter, Diana, before she headed off to school and I headed off to work. We just had a very emotional weekend saying our final goodbyes to my mother-in-law. I know many people have, well, I guess you'd say interesting relationships with their mothers-in-law, but mine was not like that at all. When she died at the young age of 68, I told my husband, we lost the sweetest member of his family. He wasn't insulted. He agreed.

At the kitchen table that following Wednesday morning, my daughter decided to let me in on a most interesting story from her previous day at school. She said, in an innocent and matter of fact way, "I got a sign from Grandma yesterday."

As my children were growing up, we had never really spoken about the afterlife or receiving signs from deceased loved ones. I had always been matter of fact about death when the topic would arise from time to time. I recall once before the era of cell phones and GPS, I was driving my mother and my two young children somewhere, and I got quite lost. I was outwardly panicking. My son said, "Are we going to die, Mom?" I quickly answered, "Yes, of course, we're going to die. Everyone dies, but I don't think it's going to be today." I was surprised by the question but was more focused on figuring out how to find our way. That became my response every time after that when my children asked about death. "Yes, of course we'll die, but I don't think today's the day." I was pretty matter of fact about the uncomfortable topic.

We had buried my mother-in-law on a Saturday and the following Wednesday, Diana told me that in her art class, her assignment was to make a textured card. She decided to make a Christmas card with green and red pom-poms. She was in a relatively small art class with about a dozen students. Each student had their own table to stand and work at, as well as their own supplies. The common supplies were stored in a closet in the art room. Diana told me that she went to the art room closet and took the pom-pom container back to her desk. It was a large container with pom-poms of many colors and sizes. She took 11 green and 11 red ones out to make her card. I don't know why 11 of each color. I didn't ask why. I was just listening. She let me know that she recounted the pom-poms and left them out on her table before carrying the container back to the closet across the room.

Diana is a bright, strong girl. She is visionary, creative, and detail oriented. It would be just like her to double-check that she had counted correctly. Then, when she returned to her desk after putting away the container, she found a surprise! There were her 11 green and 11 red ones, along with one white one and one lavender one. I listened intently, thinking clearly that's not possible. She must be thinking that she saw them, but they couldn't have really been there if she hadn't put them there, could they? She then asked if I wanted to see them. Of course, I said yes. I was skeptical that she would have them, but she ran up to her bedroom and, sure enough, came down with a lavender and a white pom-pom. I was surprised.

I asked her how they got there. Her eyes lit up. She exclaimed, "I don't know! I wish I had seen it." I could see she was genuinely curious about their presence and that she had tried to answer that very question herself. Diana is quite practical. She had worked through all of the possibilities in her mind. She concluded that they either floated there through the air, or they just appeared. Either way, she wished she had seen what occurred. She said there was nobody around her desk who could have put them there. I asked her what she made of this. She said, "Grandma must be thanking me for the balloons." The pom-poms were the exact shades as the gravesite balloons we had released on the prior Saturday for my mother-in-law. I didn't know what to make of it.

I was fascinated by this story. I was telling it to everyone that I encountered over the subsequent days and weeks, both my personal and my professional friends. Something of this nature isn't a typical conversation, especially in an office. However, I was trying to make some sense of it.

A month or so later, I was telling one friend in particular. Donna was a close neighbor and dear friend. We first met years earlier when we both moved into our neighborhood at the same time. Her two children were about the same ages as my two children. Our husbands also got along. We all instantly connected. Although we had socialized on many occasions, the topic of the afterlife hadn't been discussed. Now I was standing with her and conveying the pom-pom story. Her reaction shocked me. Instead of Donna being surprised about the unaccounted-for appearance of the pom-poms, she was surprised that I was even a bit doubtful about the afterlife. She said incredulously, "Well, you believe in the afterlife, don't you?" And so, my journey began.

I said, "I don't know. I never really thought about it." Donna was stunned at my answer. Here we were sort of close and yet, she had not known that I was unaware of the afterlife! "Of course, we live on after death!" she exclaimed. She was so matter of fact about it that it shocked me.

Donna then conveyed several stories and examples to let me in on this best-kept secret. Although it wasn't a secret really, because she just assumed that I was aware all along. She said that she had gone to several psychic mediums and connected with her deceased loved ones many times. She told me that she frequents a particular medium, based on Long Island, visiting several times after her father died. Donna said that when she needs advice, she goes and asks the medium to tap into her father's energy to advise her.

Donna gave me an example of when her family was trying to determine whether to sell her mother's house after her father died. While there, her father's spirit promptly came through. He not only advised them to sell the house, but he also advised them where to buy his widow's next residence. How is this possible? I listened skeptically. I trust Donna. She is a bright, practical friend, but I wasn't sure that this was possible. I paid extra attention to this perplexing story.

Donna told me that the medium, Josephine Ghiringhelli, said things that Donna was unaware of. Josephine mentioned a miscarriage from Donna's father's family. Donna hadn't known about it, but her mother confirmed it afterward. Donna also said that she went there while she was pregnant with her first child years ago for advice.

The concept of the afterlife was a large part of Donna's life. I was amazed and of course, couldn't keep my mind off of this during my drive to work. I tucked this conversation with Donna neatly in my head, figuring that I would explore it at a later date.

Meanwhile, my family and I were getting into our new routine. We were grieving over the significant loss of my mother-in-law. We were learning to combine that harsh feeling with living our daily routines. We were grieving. Our new normal meant that we could no longer spend time with my mother-in-law. We invited my widowed father-in-law to dinner every weekend that we could. I would typically make a lovely Sunday dinner for all of us, or we would all go out to dinner on a Saturday evening.

A month or so after my friend, Donna, told me about her experiences with mediums, my husband, son, recently widowed father-in-law, and I went out to eat at a local restaurant on our hometown Main St. It was early in December, so quite chilly. Once we got settled in, I happened to notice that one of the large front windows that we were seated near had a full-length poster facing the street. Although we were on the inside, I could see through it enough to see the pictures and wording.

Lo and behold, this restaurant was having a dinner and medium show on a Sunday evening at the end of the upcoming April. And who was the star of the show, none other than — the medium – Josephine G.! Geez, my friend had just filled me in on Josephine G. and now this. I couldn't believe this string of coincidental events. My mother-in-law passes, my daughter gets the pom-poms, I tell Donna the story, she raves about Josephine G, and now Josephine G is coming to a restaurant within walking distance of my home that I happen to go out to eat at. What an unlikely coincidence. We've been to this restaurant often enough, and they've never had this type of event. I wanted to go.

When I got home, I reached out to Donna and asked if she wanted to go. She said absolutely, yes. I asked a third friend to join us also. I called the restaurant and made the reservations myself. "Annette – a party of three," I asked about payment. They said I would pay at the event — cash or credit card — either would be fine. Hmm, so I provided no information other than my first name and how many people were in my group.

On the last Sunday evening in April of 2007, Donna, our friend, Susan, and I drove to the restaurant in our town. We were looking forward to dinner and the show with Josephine G. We checked in, 'Annette-a party of three.' No further information was requested or given. The hostess led us to our table. It was a comfortable booth along the wall. There were about 100 guests seated for dinner and the show with Josephine G. There were booths along the walls and tables in the center of the room. There was an assortment of people attending. Some were old, some were young, some were with their family members, and some were there with their friends. There were men and women. Some tables had two people, and some had eight or so people.

After everyone enjoyed their dinners and when their desserts were in front of us, a fellow came out and introduced Josephine. He mentioned her local radio appearances, classes that she taught, and he mentioned her ability to connect with our deceased loved ones. Josephine promptly came out. She had a microphone allowing all to hear her. She began her show with a brief introduction saying that she would be conducting readings and that we should all listen carefully as our loved ones would speak to us through her. She said it was important that we validate our loved ones' messages as they were conveyed. She said that the validations that we provided would encourage our deceased loved ones to convey more and more. Josephine explained how she would see information conveyed to her by our deceased loved ones. I listened intently, but skeptically. Josephine seemed very sweet, so not someone I thought would have a sophisticated mechanism for deceit. However, if she weren't deceiving us all, then this would make what she was saying authentic, which seemed even crazier.

Josephine started on the other side of the room from where we were seated. She was bringing through a deceased police officer or firefighter. There was a family of about six people there. They were connecting to these messages and validating them. I thought to myself that they might have known Josephine G. They were likely planted there to allow her to start her show with what appeared to be a big hit.

Then, she moved across the room with purpose and stood right next to our table. She promptly said that she had someone named Lucille here. Lucille is my mother-in-law's name. I couldn't move, let alone raise my hand. My head was spinning. Did my friend, Donna, convey this to Josephine? My friend wouldn't set me up behind my back. Could Josephine have used my reservation information to determine my mother-in-law's first name? I don't think that was possible either. I said nothing. I was petrified. Josephine went on saying, "Whose Lucille, Lucy, someone with an 'L'?" I was rationalizing that she wasn't exactly at our table, although she was standing right in front of us. I was hoping that this message may be for the adjacent table. My friend, Donna, was kicking me under our table, trying to get me to take the microphone. She already understood the afterlife. She had no doubt that this was my deceased mother-in-law. Donna was glaring at me. "That's your mother-in-law, take the microphone," she was wording to me across the table. I could not 'take the microphone'. I froze.

Finally, the woman at the table next to us raised her hand. She said that her name was Elizabeth. She pointed out that her name had an "L" in it. Josephine conceded and handed her the microphone. Whew, I was so relieved. I was hoping that maybe these messages would be for Elizabeth and not for me. Josephine went on to tell Elizabeth that she could see that she was going to Europe in a few months. Oh no - I had in fact booked a trip to Italy in a few months. Elizabeth told Josephine that she was not going to Europe but that she had gone to Florida several months ago. After some time, Josephine left Elizabeth and went to read others, connecting with all. Josephine was leaving people stunned and in tears of bittersweet joy. My friend Donna was upset with me for not taking the microphone. But I couldn't have. The whole thing made no sense to me.

About 20 minutes later, Josephine came right back to our table. She said that she had a soul there who had died of something like stomach cancer. She said that the woman was holding her stomach in pain. Nobody raised their hand. Again, Donna kicked me under the table and said, "Take the microphone." I hesitatingly raised my hand. Josephine said, "Oh yes — she is telling me to go to the woman with the dark hair and blue shirt." Yes, - that described me — but that was plain to see.

Josephine continued with my reading. She let me know that she had a mother figure present who had passed with incredible pain to the stomach area. She had passed from an illness like stomach cancer, but not stomach cancer. Yes, I let Josephine know that my mother-in-law did pass from pancreatic cancer. Josephine said that my mother-in-law told her that I was like a daughter to her. Yes, I agreed that we were very close. Josephine continued and said that my mother-in-law was with Teresa. My mother-in-law's mother-in-law was Teresa. They were not that close to one another; however, Ralph's grandmother Teresa was the only one of his grandparents that I had met. Then came the question that turned my life inside out. "Who is Margarita?" I said, "What?" Josephine repeated, "Who is Margarita?" I said, "Margarita is my mother." Josephine asked, "Is she still here?" Before I could answer, she answered the question herself. "I see that Margarita is still here." I then agreed, "Yes." She said, "Oh – because your mother-in-law is saying, 'Say hello to Margarita for me.'"

A year earlier, both my mother and my mother-in-law had been diagnosed with cancer within one week of one another. My mother was diagnosed with breast cancer and my mother-in-law was diagnosed with pancreatic cancer. During the year that my mother was treated for her cancer and my mother-in-law was being treated and dying — every time I visited my mother-in-law, she would always ask how my mother was doing, and she would say, "Say hello to Margarita for me." There was simply no way that Josephine could know that let alone tie me with my married name, which Josephine didn't even know, to my mother's first name. Also, the name "Margarita" is an uncommon name. And Josephine had picked up on my mother-in-law's name, "Lucille," as well as my mother's name, "Margarita". I was done. I was shocked for a moment, but then like a bolt of lightning, I could see immediately that this wasn't a hoax. I could not explain this away. It was real and happening to me. My mother-in-law was working hard to get me to this place of knowledge, for which I am so grateful.

I took the reins from my mother-in-law. She had done all of this. She had indeed placed the pom-poms on my daughter's desk. My mother-in-law had selected Josephine G. My mother-in-law made sure that I saw Donna to convey to her my pom-pom story. My mother-in-law made sure that Donna could tell me her stories, including her positive endorsement about Josephine. My mother-in-law made sure that I went out to eat at the local restaurant to see the Josephine G. poster to get me to this evening to open my eyes and the eyes of my/her loved ones.

Josephine G. asked if it had taken an unusually long time to select her tombstone. It had not taken too long, but my sister-in-law had agonized and frequented the vendor every weekend day and then some. She and my father-in-law had many discussions about it. It was quite intense for several months. My husband was also involved. My mother-in-law said that she appreciated all of their efforts and she even commented on how she loved the butterfly that my sister-in-law decided to have engraved on the tombstone. Josephine asked if we had something engraved on the tombstone that was difficult to have engraved. The company that sold the tombstone to my in-laws did say that engraving a butterfly would be a freehand design and may not look good. But my sister-in-law was persistent. They engraved it and it looks perfect. My mother-in-law gave her sign of approval!

Josephine then asked if my father-in-law had sold his house. I said no. She said that they were showing her a real estate transaction that took years to consummate. She again questioned if he had finally sold his house. Again, I said no. She asked if I possibly might not know if he had sold his house. I said that I would know. He had not sold his house. I realized at this point that Josephine had not asked when my mother-in-law passed. Josephine didn't know that it was six months prior. It may have been six years prior for all she knew. She continued asking if he was planning on selling it. Again, I said no.

Her continued line of questioning was very interesting to me because if she were fake, she would have jumped to something else in front of all of these people, but she was so persistent about this real estate sale. I felt a bit embarrassed for her since it seemed to be misinformation and she had a large audience all witnessing this mistake. She kept saying that she saw a real estate transaction that took several years to consummate, but that had just recently occurred. She eventually stopped and went on to say that my mother-in-law was all about family, which was right, and that she came to me through birds, which I love.

In the car on the way home, I was replaying in my mind every minute of the evening that I could recall. I realized that a month earlier, my father had finally sold the real estate of the business that he co-owned with my Uncle Charlie after seven years of trying to sell it. Since Josephine had initially asked if my mother-in-law was my mother, saying that she was a 'mother figure.' Well, then, although she was asking about my father-in-law and the real estate may be the topic was really about my father. Josephine had said that deceased loved ones come through as levels above, below, or to the side of the sitter. Mothers, fathers, mothers-in-law, and fathers-in-law would all be the same generation level above me.

I realized that the real estate transaction that she referred to WAS the business real estate that my father finally sold after years of trying. Maybe the part of the reading that I thought was a miss, wasn't really a miss after all. Maybe she was so persistent because it is real. Although I was concerned for her mistake and others may have wished that she would move on from her misinformation, Josephine persisted because someone on the other side was insisting on having their message conveyed. I thought that might have been my Uncle Charlie trying to come through.

When I arrived home that Sunday evening, it was quite late. My husband was already in bed. I couldn't sleep, of course. My head was replaying every detail of the evening. I quietly asked if he was awake. He mumbled something. I then couldn't contain myself. I woke him and proceeded to tell him every detail about the evening. He was actively listening. He was also fascinated, although I could tell that he was thinking to himself that I might be exaggerating or something. I knew that I wasn't though. He knew that I am a practical, skeptical and realistic person. So, he was a bit curious now also. What could this all mean? Now we were both in wonderment.

This series of synchronicities began my journey into discovering and uncovering what the afterlife and this life is about. I learned over the next four years that this was the tip of a complex and magnificent iceberg!

The next story that I share with you occurred very recently after my book, Your Soul Focus, was published. One of the many things that I learned during my four years of metaphysical study is that there are often times that the Universe asks us to step up and help someone else. It may be a great help or a small act of kindness. However, it is important to find those occasions and to help when we are able.

I have worked in the same building for six years. For the past four or so years, there has been the same female security guard at the building front desk when I come in the morning. She says, "Good morning" in such a friendly manner and I say the same to her, as I walk past her desk and to the elevators. That has been the extent of our interactions, nothing more than that for months and for years.

About nine months after my book was published, each time I would greet the guard in the morning, I felt like I wanted to give her a copy of my book as a gift. I think because as she sits each day at the desk, she seems upbeat, greeting people as they come and go, which may or may not be part of her job, and she reviews computer monitors of the hallways and elevators of the building all day long. It seems like a job that would allow her time to read a book. Although likely she isn't permitted to read while on the job. But each day over the past couple of months, I wanted to introduce myself and give her a copy of my book. However, starting a conversation like that seemed too daunting to me. Asking an almost total stranger if she would like to read a book about the afterlife, well that seemed like too uncomfortable a situation for me. So, each day that I went to my office, I would think the same thing 'figure out a way to give her your book in case it interests her,' and each day I would do the same thing, I would say, "Good morning" as I passed by and headed to the elevators.

Then one day right after Christmas, I headed to my office as usual. It was a late morning visit and during the holiday week, so I didn't know if I would see that particular security guard. But during the entire drive to work, I was thinking about her and trying to figure out a way to work up the nerve to give her my book as a gift. I played out in my mind for the umpteenth time asking her two questions from under my COVID mask, "Are you a spiritual person?" and "Do you like to read books?" It seemed quite scary, but I pleaded with myself to be brave enough to just do it this time. After all, it is the season of giving.

On my drive to work, I said to myself, "If she is the guard at the desk, today is the day that I will do it."

I walked into my building. She was the guard. As I got to her desk, she said, 'good morning.' I said, 'good morning' back to her and I walked past the desk to the elevators. UGH, once again, I just wasn't brave enough. Except this time, something inside of me pulled me back. I retraced my steps back to her and said, "I am pulled to ask you these questions. Are you spiritual and do you like to read books?" I felt like a jerk as she stood up from her desk and walked to me a little. But she responded, "Yes, I do like to read books. What was the other question?"

Now that she was a little closer, I noticed her eyes were a bit puffy as if she needed sleep. I asked again, "Are you a spiritual person?" She replied, "I try to be. I am trying to remain positive. My mother died two weeks ago, and we buried her four days ago."

"What?" I said, I couldn't believe what she just conveyed to me. She repeated herself. "My mother died on December 9th, and we just buried her on December 23rd." I asked, incredulously "This year? Do you mean just now?!" Wow, I had no idea how timely my questions were. I said, "Oh my goodness. I wrote a book this year that I need to give to you as a gift. Let me get it!" I felt an urgency all of a sudden to get to my car and to get a copy of my book for her.

I rushed to my car and grabbed a brand-new copy of my book. I went back into the building. As she was standing a bit closer to me, I could see her puffy, tired eyes just above her COVID mask were tearing also. The loss of her mother was weighing heavily on her. I handed her my book. She hugged it close to her body and thanked me profusely. I said, "I'm so sorry for your loss. I wrote this book this year. It's about my journey with the afterlife. It's been very well received. I am just a worker in this building, but I really felt that you would enjoy my book. I originally thought it was a gift from me to you, but I realize now, it's a gift from your mother to you."

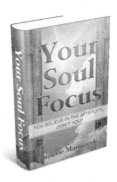

Her eyes were welling up as she clutched the book like she was hugging her mother. I walked away and said, "I hope that you enjoy it". She said, "I know that I will. I am going to start to read it tonight."

Throughout the rest of the day, I replayed this over and over in my mind. Thank goodness that the other side made certain that I garnered the bravery necessary to ask her my questions and to give her my book. Once again, the Universe provided me with a beautiful opportunity to help someone in need. I was so happy that I was able to do my part. What a lesson for me, once again, to follow that inner voice when it is asking me to do something kind for others.

Excerpts are from "Your Soul Focus: You Believe in the Afterlife, Don't You?" by Annette Marinaccio, Inphinite Lumen, LLC, Jan. 29, 2021

About the Author

Annette Marinaccio is a Certified Public Accountant, an accomplished healthcare executive, and the author of Your Soul Focus. Annette's mother-in-law led her on a path after she died to prove to her that there is an afterlife. After understanding that the afterlife is existent, she learned how intricate and extensive our souls and our journeys are. It's fascinating! The information that Annette has accumulated and conveyed has a clear and deep benefit to others during their times of need, grief or curiosity, and her book will pass that knowledge to you. Your Soul Focus has been endorsed by three Long Island mediums with a public presence, it has reached #1 on Amazon three times, it has dozens of five-star reviews, a chapter was included in a Saturday Night Live skit, and most importantly, it has brought comfort and inspiration to thousands of readers. www.amazon.com/dp/1736375156

Recommendations

Your Soul Focus

Laura Lynne Jackson	Robert E. Hansen	Josephine Ghiringhelli
NY Times bestselling author of *The Light Between Us* and *Signs: The Secret Language of the Universe*	Psychic Medium, Author, Intuitive Counselor, and Public Speaker	Psychic Medium, Author, Intuitive Counselor, and Public Speaker

"*Your Soul Focus* takes the reader on a journey of discovery into both why we're here and what comes next. Sharing truths about our existence garnered from years of personal exploration into the existence of life after bodily death, it will open your eyes and heart to the beautiful and continuing connections we share with those whom we loved who have crossed. This journey also offers insight into why we're here, and the beautiful roles we play in each other's lives."

"*Your Soul Focus* is a compelling look at the extraordinary work of psychic phenomena."

"*Your Soul Focus* is a Truly Inspiring Journey of Spiritual Connections and Deep Understanding of "Signs from Above"!!! I recommend this book to anyone who knows or needs to know that love never dies! Annette Marinaccio's book is a true inspiration as to the understanding of how the soul reconnects to those they have touched here on earth. I found it to be Inspirational, Healing and a page turner!! A true testament that love never dies!!!"

"Trust in dreams, for in them
is hidden the gate to eternity."
~Khalil Gibran~
Poet Artist Philosopher
1883 - 1931

The Gateway, *Sheela Jaganathan*

By Sheela Jaganathan

In the stories below, I have chosen to write about my maternal grandparents Gopal and Kalyani, my grandfather-in-law Alfred, and the twins I lost from my first pregnancy.

My name is Sheela Jaganathan. Currently living in Germany with my husband and two daughters, I work as a regression therapist and wellbeing coach. Prior to practicing complementary therapies, I was a litigation lawyer, a recruiting executive, and a patent administrator.

I was born in 1969 in Malaysia and grew up in a religious Hindu family. My father was a manager of plantations, and my mother a housewife. I am the eldest of three siblings. As a child, I was curious and loved reading. When I was five years old, my father gifted me a set of children's encyclopaedia that kept me occupied for hours on end. I learned about science, nature, storytelling, chemistry, outer space, and more. Those books were so fascinating I couldn't wait to grow up and explore our colourful and magical Earth!

Living in a multicultural community in Malaysia, I was exposed to various religions like Buddhism, Islam, Christianity, Sikhism, etc. Our immediate neighbours were Muslims, while in our family, we practiced Hinduism. We also had a good mixture of friends who were Buddhists, Taoists, and Christians. Both my parents had received their primary and high school education in missionary schools run by Irish nuns and monks. So, at home, they spoke to us children in our mother tongue, Tamil and English. My education was just as atypical. I attended a Chinese elementary school where I learned Mandarin, a Malay-language high school, and finished my college and university studies in English-medium institutions. My parents stressed the importance of having a sound education so that we siblings could have successful careers in the future.

When I was 11, my family moved in with my maternal grandparents when my father took up a job offer overseas. My grandfather, Gopala Menon, had left his home in Kerala, India, in 1927 to move to British Malaya to work as a labourer.

Acha passed away when I was 18 years old. In the weeks leading up to his death, I was busy studying for a major examination. Three days before the exams, my grandfather suffered a heart attack and was hospitalised. When my mother came back from the hospital, she told me he was recovering and that I was to focus on my studies and finish the exams. But this was easier said than done. When my mother left that evening to the hospital again, I started praying for my grandfather's recovery. That prayer ended with a bargain with God to take some years off my own life to prolong my grandfather's—Acha was only 76 and he surely deserved to live longer for all the good work he had done and was still doing. There and then, I heard a loud whoosh, and from the force of it all, I fell over my books, followed by a deep knowing that my grandfather would be gone in three days.

I couldn't bring myself to tell my mother what happened, for she and her seven siblings were told that Acha was on the mend. Three days later, he passed away after saying goodbye to all his family and close friends. I never got the chance. Numb with guilt and anger, I couldn't tell if I had imagined that conversation with God or if it was my own thoughts that had caused my grandfather's death.

A few weeks after Acha's funeral, I moved away to college. The new routine and the ever-increasing study load kept me busy as I trained to become a lawyer. The journey was challenging, for I was often homesick and stressed out. One night feeling overwhelmed and unable to sleep, I finally called on my grandfather for his guidance, albeit hesitantly. Ever since his passing, I had done my best to block out everything to do with him. In my mind, that whoosh had felt like a slap on the wrist from the universe. I was truly upset with God for what had happened to Acha, and angry with Acha for putting me into this situation. But now feeling vulnerable, the grief that I had bottled up came flooding back. I wept for hours before falling asleep. The adult world wasn't as vivid and fun as I thought it would be.

That night Acha appeared in my dream as a big ball of light and darted around my room. I followed suit, a ball of light myself, but smaller and wobbly. I moved in and out through walls and even noticed my body sleeping on the bed as I hovered over it. Acha's energy was soft, subtle, and soothing, just like he was in his human body. There was a deep sense of knowing and calmness all around. Nothing else mattered—there was no wanting, craving, nor needing anything. I was prompted to merge and flow with my surroundings without fear. My room had morphed into a giant holographic amusement park and my only task was to enjoy the rides.

Nonetheless, I continued to feel guilty for not telling my mother about the premonition I had. Twenty-five years after my grandfather's passing, when I started practicing regression therapy, I would have the opportunity to tie up that loose end. Regression Therapy is a type of complementary therapy making use of light hypnosis to guide clients into deep subconscious inquiry to search for solutions to their recurring challenges. I studied the technique at Past Life Regression Academy, U.K. During a practice session, as my mother was being guided into a past life, the soul of my grandfather appeared in her mind's eye and communicated with her. He shared with her the connections they had in other lifetimes and how he exists in the afterlife. After the session, my mother would tell that she never expected to come into contact with her father that way. While she had had many dreams about him, this was the first time she could have a two-way interaction with him.

In the following years, bit by bit and no doubt through nudges from Acha, who by now I consider one of my spirit guides, I was shown that each soul, oftentimes with the input from ethereal companions and teachers, decides for itself its entry into and its exit point out of an earthly incarnation. There are multitude layers of objectives, pathways, opportunities, events, synchronicities that need to be created, merged, and aligned before a soul incarnates on Earth. Indeed, it was presumptuous of me to bargain for my grandfather's life back then, for my motivation was purely selfish—I was trying to prevent him from moving on because I did not want to deal with the loss of a loved one or with the topic of death itself. Instead of raising my vibration to keep up with Acha's, I sank into the lower frequencies of grief, anger, and guilt.

My grandfather's death opened my eyes and ears to the spirit realm. I became aware that being spiritual is not necessarily about the depth of one's religious knowledge or rites, but rather the wish and commitment to engage with and explore the unseen realms in the universe. I learned that we can reach out to communicate with our loved ones across time and in spite of death. And like a dialogue between two people on Earth, we first need to find a common platform, collaborate on the method of communicating, and most of all, keep the communication lines open. Now, Acha's presence is like a comforting energy that accompanies me everywhere as I learn to become self-reliant and self-accountable in my own spiritual journey.

Another loved one who impressed me even before she left for the afterlife was my maternal grandmother, Kalyani. In 1999, I had moved from Kuala Lumpur to Munich to be with my husband. While living in Europe, I was able to visit my family in Malaysia once a year. In between, we would call each other by phone. Naturally, I missed my parents and our extended family, for they always kept me grounded.

One evening, in 2006, I had arranged to go to the cinema in Munich city center with a German girlfriend. She had, out of many interesting movies available that week, booked us to watch an Indian film called Water by Deepa Mehta. It was about a group of widowed Indian women living in a commune facing discrimination and exploitation. One of the main characters was called Kalyani. I remember telling my friend that Kalyani was also my grandmother's name and that I hadn't been able to get hold of her or my mother on the phone for the past few days. The movie ended with Kalyani drowning in a river after she was deserted by her lover. My heart sank.

After the movie, I took a train back, and from the train station, it was another ten-minute bicycle ride home. A few hundred yards from reaching the house, my left leg began to feel weird. I felt a slow twisting sensation starting with the toes and creeping upwards towards my hip, as if someone was wrapping my leg tightly with a cloth. I continued peddling with my right leg to avoid stopping on the faintly lit empty road. By the time I reached home around 11 p.m., the weird sensation had disappeared. I crawled into bed and fell asleep promptly.

Sometime in the middle of the night, the phone rang. It was my father on the other end. Even before he said anything else, I asked if he was calling about my grandmother. He said yes and that she died two hours ago, which was between the time I had a problem with my leg and me falling asleep. The cause of death was fluid build-up in the lungs resulting in heart failure. She had been admitted to the hospital a few days before, and that was why I had not been able to reach my mother on the phone. My immediate impression was that my grandmother wanted me to know what was happening to her even though we were 9938 kilometres apart.

As my father ended the call, I was strangely calm. The movie I watched did not seem like a coincidence now. Was it her way of telling me that she was approaching the last moments of her physical presence? In fact, I dare say she pulled my leg even as she was facing the end. You see, my grandmother was eccentric and always enjoyed a joke.

Yet, the grief that I experienced with my grandfather, I never felt with my grandmother, and that bothered me a lot. I managed to reach home in time for an important ceremony sixteen days after her passing. A month later, I dreamt of my grandparents. They appeared as bright, energetic beings, with my grandfather standing behind my grandmother. I remember in the dream that I went around poking their bodies to check if they would go up in smoke. They didn't, and chuckling, they assured me everything was alright, that I needn't worry, and drifted away. I understood then I grieved less for my grandmother, not because I loved her less or I had experienced death and grief already, but because she was back with Acha. Kalyani was no longer a widow on Earth pining for her husband, but a free and happy soul in the spirit realm. Through this experience with my grandmother, I learned grief had many faces and nuances, and that on the other side of humanly sorrow is soul freedom.

Sheela's maternal grandparents, Kalyani and Gopala Menon,
as they were when she lived with them in early 1980's

In 2009, my 95-year-old grandfather-in-law Alfred (fondly called Opa), who was living in southern Germany, suffered a major stroke. My mother-in-law called us in Shanghai to inform us, as we had moved over there for my husband's work assignment. She said Opa was under the care of doctors and that my husband and I did not need to travel back. The conversation reminded me of the time when Acha was hospitalised. Listening to my gut feeling this time, I insisted we go home as soon as possible. My husband managed to get the tickets fast enough, and we reached the hospital with 24 hours to spare.

Just before we went in to see Opa, the doctors told us that Opa had been refusing food and was becoming stiffer by the day. But when the hospital staff opened the room door, all of us saw Opa making an effort to turn around. I remember the hospital staff remarking how odd that was.

After my husband and my mother-in-law greeted Opa, they left to speak with the doctors again while I remained in the room. My attention was pulled to the high windows three meters away from Opa's bed which he had been looking at before we came in. He was curled up in the fetal position, gurgling and wheezing. Having stopped eating for a few days, he was only skin and bones. The smell of impending death hung in the air. I checked on my baby daughter I was holding in my arms— full of life and hungry for the next feed. I thought about myself standing in the hospital in the south of Germany when a day earlier I had been frantically packing up on the other side of the world in Shanghai. The contrast was indeed extreme. I wondered if it would be just as mind-boggling for Opa to leave his human body and go into the spirit world. How long would it take for him to finally let go? Would his soul-self experience a jetlag, like I was having one of the body? To be honest, after a while, I wasn't sure if I was thinking his thoughts or mine. My mind was a blur, and exhausted.

The interesting thing about Opa is that despite the numerous other mini strokes he has had, he always managed to recover. He held onto life with every fibre in his body, even though he suffered from debilitating pain for the longest time. He even managed to look after his bed-ridden wife for many years before she passed. He had been a member of the German Reserve Army who was wounded in World War 2 while on duty in Russia. Having trained to become an accountant, he was extremely frugal and cautious. He wasn't a talkative person but very observant. Whenever I visited him, we used to spend the time sitting together silently, doing crossword puzzles, or reading the newspaper. He was a dignified, proper, and private person. I knew he didn't want to be in the hospital at all. Opa wheezed again, this time louder. As if in trance, I walked to the windows and opened them.

I told Opa I was going to sit with him and visualise a beautiful bridge from his room to the heavens, one that will stretch towards the surrounding mountains and into the sky, and he could take that bridge to freedom whenever he felt ready. I assured him it was alright to let go and that my husband and I will take care of whatever unfinished business he had left. I imagined a sparkly colourful bridge taking form from the side of his bed, and I did the visualisation for the next three hours before returning to Opa's house to put our children to bed. I continued the practice at home, praying for a smooth transition for Opa in the way that he would have wished for. The next day, Opa passed away peacefully.

In the following years, every summer holidays, my family and I would go back to Opa's village and have a meal in the restaurant where we had our wedding reception. The restaurant is located on a hillside overlooking into the valley. We would sit on the restaurant terrace, have a meal, and talk about Opa. From the terrace, you could see most of the buildings down in the village, including the hospital Opa was previously in. And every single time, I would wonder if Opa was still clinging to the earthly plane or if he had taken off to the spirit realm.

The third summer we visited the restaurant, and as I walked out to the terrace, I saw down in the valley a rainbow's end just above the hospital building arching up and over the mountains. I rubbed my eyes in disbelief. The rainbow remained there for some minutes more. I imagined all the memories that Opa was carrying back to the spirit realm—close to a century's worth of information on human life and interactions. Opa was born in 1913 and was just a toddler when World War I started. During World War II, in the prime of his life, Opa was drafted into the German army. He was part of the administrative team and ended up getting wounded while on assignment in Russia. While his life had been full of challenges and uncertainty, like Acha, he somehow managed to not only survive but thrived on his own terms. When I joined the family, he always treated me like an absolute gentleman and happily tried all the Asian food I cooked for him, even when it didn't agree with his stomach. If Opa was communicating with me now through the rainbow, then I can only say it was a fitting symbol of his soul essence of hope, new beginnings, and peace.

Sheela's grandfather-in-law Opa Alfred, early 2000's

And now a story close to my heart.

In 2001, I became pregnant for the first time. The first few days of excitement soon turned into weeks of debilitating morning sickness. I couldn't keep anything down for long—not solid food or liquids. Two months in, I lost a lot of weight. My gynaecologist kept saying this was normal and I should continue sipping tea. Then, in the 12th week, I had to go in for an ultrasound examination. Just one day before the appointment, my morning sickness completely disappeared. I felt incredibly refreshed and strong, and naively I thought this must be the reward for getting over the first trimester.

At the doctor's the next day, being first-time parents-to-be, my husband and I were very nervous. A few minutes after the doctor began her examination, she exclaimed that she could see two embryos and congratulated us profusely. My husband and I looked at each other in disbelief, and even before that information sunk in, she stuttered and said the embryos do not have heartbeats. We were then ordered to go to a specialist for confirmation immediately. You can imagine the roller coaster of emotions that my husband and I were experiencing. Time stood still, and the next thing I knew, I was in a hospital being examined for the second time, except I noticed this doctor was slower, gentler, and kinder. She said I had a 'missed abortion' and recommended that I have a dilation and curettage procedure (D&C) to avoid infection.

The next 24 hours were a blur—I was shuttled between doctors and nurses, prepped for the medical intervention, and finally put up in a ward overnight. Before I was discharged the next day, a doctor came to check on my status and informed me that my hormone levels would crash in the coming days and that I should relax as much as possible. Two days of shock and confusion over losing two babies, exhausted from a full anaesthetic medical procedure, and now the doctor was telling me to take it easy. How was I supposed to do that?

When I went back to my gynaecologist for a follow-up a week later, she told me that I would not get pregnant again without fertility treatment. I couldn't believe my ears. Well-intentioned advice from family and friends followed, but none could take away the feeling that I had caused the death of two babies. The guilt and grief I experienced I would never wish on anyone.

One night, feeling extremely demotivated, I dared the universe to show me just one word of encouragement. Waking up in the morning, the first thought that came to my mind was 'library'. So, to the library I went and searched everything I could on miscarriages in the medical journals. It took a while because I wasn't fluent in German at the time, but two medical terms kept popping up ever so often— Twin-to-Twin Transfusion Syndrome and Progesterone Insufficiency. Long story short, those two pieces of information led me to change my diet, look for a new obstetrician, take up swimming and practice positive affirmations. Within two tries and without fertility treatments, I fell pregnant and gave birth to my eldest daughter in 2002. I felt jubilant! Yet, despite having my daughter, come January of every year, I would feel overwhelmed. Whether or not I consciously remembered the miscarriage, my body would. The January dread continued even after I had my daughter in 2008, but with less intensity.

As my daughters got older, I started to notice how different they were in personality—you could pick any attribute, and they would be on the opposite ends of the spectrum. There was a lot of squabbling, especially when it came to food. Oftentimes, they would fight to go through one door simultaneously, even if we were not in a hurry and there were others available. My daughters were six years apart, yet their actions mimicked the twins' struggle for nutrition and oxygen while in my belly.

Fast forward to 2012, one night as I was putting my second daughter to sleep, she turned to me and said the most stunning thing,

"Mama, sometimes when babies are in your tummy, sometimes when they're not strong, they'll fall out. I was in your tummy, and I fell out!"
"Why would the babies not be strong, sweetie?"
"Because babies have small muscles. The mamas have to eat, so they grow!"
"Where did you go after that?"
"To the doctors who tell if I'm in the tummy."
"Hmm, I wonder why you came to me again?"
"You know, I said I can be with you all, and that's how I do it. First, I pick the big people like Mama and papa, and then sister."
"Have you ever been in another body before?"
"Mama, I used to live on that planet where you can have everything! If you want chips, you think about it, and it'll be there!"
"And why did you leave that planet?"
"Because a lot of people come to our place. Now, I'm looking for my friends here again."

The matter-of-fact tone of her statements startled me. None of my two daughters knew about my miscarriage. A few weeks earlier, I had started a course in Past Life Regression Therapy, but I was quite skeptical about the possibility of past lives. Even though it was a principal belief in Hinduism, I didn't know of anyone in my family or community that had been reincarnated and knew about it. But here was my own daughter making claims that only I could corroborate. I felt like the universe was playing a cosmic trick on me. If what she said at the start of that conversation was true, then wouldn't the rest be true too? I had so many questions for her. Were they fighting over food and space in my belly back in 2001? Was it distressing for them when I was throwing up? Where was that planet she talked about? Could they feel what I was feeling? Was it painful when they died? While I was trying to formulate the follow-up questions, my daughter nodded off. When I asked her about it the next day, she had forgotten about it.

A week later, I came across case studies by Professor Dr. Ian Stevenson, an American psychiatrist renowned for his research into reincarnation. Among others, he had documented more than 2800 cases of children who claimed to have experienced spontaneous past-life recall, most between the ages two to five. In a nutshell, these case studies of Dr. Stevenson suggest life as we know it does not end with physical death. Somehow our memories and impressions from one life can continue beyond physical death and into the next incarnation. Most impressive were the case studies of children born with birthmarks and defects that matched wounds on deceased persons they claimed to be in previous lives (*Birthmarks and Birth Defects Corresponding to Wounds on Deceased Persons*, University of Virginia, 1993). The skepticism I had shrunk a bit, and I began to see my daughters, not as possessions, but free and independent souls with their own agendas and undertakings.

As I look through all the events with my maternal grandparents, Opa Alfred, my own daughters and that of my clients, and my own past life journeys, it only validates for me the fact that the connection we have with our loved ones and soul friends from the other side is not bound by earthly concepts of time and space. Death is a gateway opening us up to another level in the collective game of soul evolution. Death doesn't mean we have lost all contact with our loved ones. It only means we need to find a different way to sense and communicate with them.

From my experience of personal loss of loved ones to helping others explore their soul purposes now has made me truly appreciate the preciousness of human life. It also made me re-evaluate how I wanted to live out the rest of my life. To preserve the memories of my grandparents' and parents' life adventures, I spent the year 2021 researching and writing their memoirs. The amount of information I gathered not only made me understand and appreciate my own heritage better it also provided my parents and me an opportunity to heal old wounds and discover unique ancestral strengths.

Writing the family memoir helped my parents see their turbulent past in a new light, and at the same time they got to know how cherished they are by their family and community in the present time. It made it easier for my parents to talk about their own fears and wishes when it comes to death and how they would like to stay in touch with us when they are in the spirit realm. Love and wisdom seem to be widely spoken in the spirit realm, because without it, I may not have perceived any of the signs and messages from my loved ones. And when you add the extra ingredients of heartfelt willingness, deep curiosity, and a dash of imagination to interpret and understand the wisdom from the spirit world, the messages will start pouring in.

Epilogue on 22-02-2022

My second daughter, who is turning 14 soon, had seen me preparing this chapter and was curious about what I was writing. It has been ten years since she and I last spoke about her past life in my belly. I let her read my stories. With tears in her eyes, she commented as follows:

"It didn't hurt when I fell out of your tummy, Mama. I knew I was coming back because there was something connecting me to Earth. You don't come here for nothing. You go somewhere because you are looking for something. We come to Earth to feel things but when you get here and start feeling, it can get too overwhelming. Like how I am feeling too much right now. Coming to Earth is like going to school, being with people is like doing homework, but the lessons you learn are greater than what you learn in school. And some people don't come to learn, but to teach. This makes me wonder what is it that you want to do here, Mama. Do you still want to learn, or are you here to teach?"

The query came across solemn and humorous at the same time. My heart exploded— in a good way. My judgmental mind faded. I felt vulnerable and deeply acknowledged, for that was one question I have been ruminating over for ages, perhaps even over lifetimes. This was surely another nudge from the other side, except this time, the messenger was my teenage daughter who happened to have reincarnated twice in one lifetime into our family.

Losing a loved one is hard, no doubt. But when you get to see them again, even if they appear in another form, you will recognise them. And, I did, wholeheartedly. That only means there is a part of us that survives death and goes on to remember.

So, death is indeed a gateway to the unseen realms—of places and dimensions that are elusive to our humanly intellect. The solution is to become more receptive and intuitive on the earthly side, so that more messages and wisdom can be received from the spirit world. To this end, I truly wish that learning to enhance our innate intuition will become part of our basic education one day. And surely, the more we share our experiences on everything connected with dying, the more we can continue to demystify the mystery of what happens beyond physical death.

Here we go again. Another nudge from the other side.

About the Author

Sheela is a regression therapist and wellbeing coach who is certified in hypnotherapy, regression therapy, spiritual regression and brain-based coaching. She is a professional member of Spiritual Regression Therapy Association (SRTA) and Earth Association for Regression Therapy (EARTh). Sheela is also an active member in the Advancing Awareness Facebook Group practicing soul-to-soul communication techniques as taught by Suzanne Giesemann. In addition, Sheela has written and self-published a non-fiction book titled Hello Me! chronicling the real-life transformation of her client Kalina using past life regression therapy. For more information, please visit her website: www.omni-coaching.com

Excerpts of this chapter are from "Hello me!" Jaganathan, Sheela, 2016, Hello Me! (1st edition), Self-published.

Sheela's daughters, Kiran (4) and Meera (10), in 2012

"I regard consciousness as fundamental.
I regard matter as derivative from consciousness.
We cannot get behind consciousness. Everything that
we talk about, everything that we regard as existing,
postulates consciousness."
~Max Planck~
Physicist
1858 – 1947

The Death of a Skeptic, *Carol Allen*

By Carol Allen

Who would have known that I would be such a hard nut to crack? My doubts began to creep their way right back in. Like a broken record, I constantly reassured myself, "Tyler touched me, I heard him! And what about the song, on the video, with precisely the words I needed to hear?"

"Okay, Tyler, if you are here, I need more proof!" I stated out loud. Even though my beautiful Tyler had gone above and beyond with so many signs and messages already, why did I still require more validation? Why did I doubt it? It's not like I had forgotten the previous experiences, but I yearned for more.

Undeniably magical things continued to happen. For example, while driving to the grocery store one afternoon, music abruptly began playing loudly. Oddly enough, it wasn't coming from the radio. Rather, the music was blasting from the inside of my purse. I pulled over to see what was going on. Inside was my tablet, tucked away in its folded stand/keyboard combination case. It was deep inside my purse, still clearly closed. Regardless, the music was loudly playing. It played an unfamiliar song that I've since been unable to locate. The song described laughter and joy, was uplifting, and my son's way of saying, "Good afternoon, Mom!"

I arrived at the grocery store. This was my first trip back since Tyler's passing. Hoping it would help make the experience less painful, I chose a branch location less familiar. While walking down the aisle, I happened to glance at what was once one of Tyler's favorite chips. Only to become flooded with emotion, I recalled how Tyler would put these chips inside of his sandwich. Standing in the aisle, completely still, my eyes welled up with tears. Suddenly, the bag of chips fell from the shelf, landing directly in front of my feet.

Confused, I looked up and down the aisle, trying to piece together how the bag mysteriously landed at my feet, only to find that no one else was there; I was completely alone inside of this aisle! I knew immediately what had happened but could hardly believe it. Did Tyler just knock down those chips? Deep inside my soul, I knew that it was him. This made me smile as I whispered, "I love you, Ty."

Next, I headed over to the deli. While looking through the selection of encased deli meats, etched in the glass, read the name "Tyler." All I could do was stare in disbelief, shocked at what I was looking at. "You have got to be kidding me," I whispered as I smiled and laughed to myself.

"How can I help you, miss?" asked the clerk.

Rather than placing an order, I asked the clerk if she had any knowledge about why the glass read "Tyler." I couldn't help myself. All I could think was why, of all the infinite things that could have been etched onto the glass encasing, did it have the name "Tyler?" Perplexed by what I had just asked, she gave me a bizarre look and responded, "I believe it is the name of the glass company." Speechless and in disbelief, I paused to gather myself before ordering.

This was more than a coincidence as this wasn't just unlikely but borderline impossible. The odds of Tyler's name being boldly displayed, on my very first trip back to an unfamiliar grocer, were too significant to write-off as a coincidence. This was Tyler.

On the drive home, I called my sister, Marilyn, to come meet me at my house. I wanted to share with her, in person, what had just transpired. We sat together on the couch as I attempted to effectively communicate what I'd just experienced without completely fumbling over the words with laughter. For the first time, in a long time, the tears that were rolling down my cheeks were tears of joy; I was laughing so hard that I could barely speak, "You should have seen the way the woman looked at me after I asked her why the name "Tyler" was etched on the glass!" I exclaimed, while hysterically cracking up.

It was then, at that exact moment, that the lamp right next to me turned on, randomly. "That's strange. How'd you just turn that lamp on?" I asked Marilyn.

"Are you kidding? It's Tyler again!" Marilyn yelled with a smile from ear to ear.

Marilyn has always believed in the afterlife, frequently referencing her experiences with spirits, and loved ones on the other side, long before Tyler's accident. Years ago, when my boys were little, for example, Marilyn religiously watched a television program that featured a psychic medium from the east coast. At the time, I would say things to her like, "You are too funny… It's hard to imagine that you believe this stuff!" I'd never actually watched an episode myself; I deemed it fiction and was far too skeptical to even entertain the idea.

I became addicted to the signs and could never have enough of them. "It's time for another sign, Ty. Please play me one of your songs." I turned on the radio. There was no song playing, rather, an announcer's voice. I raised the volume.

"We have Tyler on the line! How are you, Tyler?"

Rather than noticing the deliberate sign that was placed in front of me, believe it or not, I felt abandoned. I expected to hear something we played at the service for him, possibly *Simple Man* by Lynyrd Skynyrd or one of the other songs we included in his video. With my head in a downward spiral over the absence of music at the time, it had never even crossed my mind that this was his sign.

Feeling cheated, I again pleaded with him the following day, "Tyler, let's try this again. Please, play me your song." I turned to the station and heard, "We need to congratulate Tyler on his engagement." This time, unlike the day before, the fog lifted, and it became crystal clear. Perhaps it was not what I had expected, but nonetheless, a wonderful sign. I smiled as I recounted the announcer's statement on the radio from the previous day, realizing what I hadn't yet put together.

Days later, I finally found the courage to clean Tyler's room. I hadn't been able to bring myself to stay in there long enough as it was far too painful. I certainly had no intention of parting with his things, but needed to dust, vacuum, and organize a bit. As I was tidying up, things like candy wrappers, empty water bottles, and junk food began to dominate the inside of the trash bin.

On the floor stood Tyler's sneakers, remaining in the precise position he had left them in. I looked at his closet full of clothes and walked to the closet reaching for his shirt. I closed my eyes as I placed his crisp, clean shirt up to my face to smell it. I could feel my tears as they rolled down my cheeks, onto the shirt. This was beyond difficult. Opening my eyes, I then walked over to the desk. There were still papers scattered on top partnered by a remote control from his Xbox console. Inside his desk drawer was a journal. It was clear, after shuffling through all of the pages, that the entire journal contained only one sentence: "I know two things: God exists, and I exist." Tyler wrote, boldly across the center of the first page. The remaining pages that followed were left blank.

Later that evening as we were watching television, I told Tony about Tyler's journal that I'd found. "Wow," was all he could say. His voice was shaky, coupled with his speechless demeanor.

"Don't you think it's crazy?" I asked. "We haven't spent much time over the years practicing religion, or even referencing God, with Tyler."

"I'm just devastated, Carol. I want him here."

I stood up and made my way into the kitchen. A few moments later, Tony yelled out, "Babe, I just saw Tyler!"

"What? What do you mean?" I asked.

"While watching TV, I saw him walking from the corner of my eye. I wanted to run and grab him, so I turned my head in his direction, but then I couldn't see him anymore," Tony said, his eyes welling up with tears.

Undeniably so, Tyler was there.

Excerpt from "Mom, I'm Not Gone.": Tyler Lives by Carol Allen, Independently Published, November 22, 2021

About the Author

Carol Allen is an author, and a Shining Light Mom, Board Member, Book Club Affiliate Leader, Cave Creek Affiliate Leader, Presenter and Speaker, and *Caring Listener* for *Helping Parents Heal* www.helpingparentsheal.org Carol wrote a chapter about Tyler that appears in *"Life to Afterlife: Helping Parents Heal, The Book"*, compiled by Elizabeth Boisson, Independently Published, 2021. Carol's youngest son, Tyler forever 19, is always with her.

"If you want to find the secrets of the universe,
think in terms of energy, frequency, and vibration."
~Nikola Tesla~
Engineer Inventor
1856 – 1943

Surprising Instrumental Transcommunication: Deceased Apparitions, Dr. Sonia Rinaldi

By Sonia Rinaldi - Afterlife Researcher

Each recording, one lesson…

For those who are not familiar with the Instrumental Transcommunication techniques, we may say that it is how we call the contacts between our world and other dimensions, through electronic devices. The advantage of these techniques is mainly the investigation of authenticity since we deal with digital files so that a forensic expert can verify their integrity, characteristics, etc.

The contacts with those that passed may be recorded in images or voices. A curious case happened while I was recording to know about the deceased husband of a friend.

I first met Sheila Lowe in person about four years ago in Arizona, during the Symposium organized by AREI – Afterlife Research and Education Institute. Throughout the entire year of 2018, I worked to assist 30 people who were in grief - the majority of whom were moms who had lost a child.

Sheila, a writer of fiction mysteries, was one of those moms. She had lost her daughter under very tragic circumstances – Jennifer was murdered at the age of 27, by her jealous boyfriend.

I recently invited a few friends, women who had lost their companion (husband, boyfriend, fiancé, etc.), to participate in a research experiment, and Sheila was, one of the first to reply. Seeing her deceased husband, Bill, was not Sheila's only surprise. She clearly identified two other loved ones in the same recording! What a relief for this friend to confirm that those she loved here are still around her.
Here are how the facts unfolded.

110

Introducing Bill...

At left, Bill McElroy when alive. At right, this "transimage"
as he looks now in Beyond.

Sheila was married to Bill McElroy who passed at the age of 70 from cancer. In his apparition at right, we notice that he is younger, renewed, and no longer needing to wear glasses. This is perfectly compatible with the Spiritism Doctrine concepts — which establishes that after the death of the body, our Consciousness (or spirit, or soul) still maintains the aspect of our last incarnation, though healed, younger and healthy.

After I made the recordings to assist Sheila and sent her the transimages registered of her beloved soulmate, she sent some photos pointing out the similarity of his present aspect, compared to photos she had of him in the past.

Bill is now looking renewed and younger! At left, a photo sent recently by his wife, and at right, one more of his apparitions.

In the photo above, Bill was 39 years old. Very similar to how he appeared in the recording (at right). I have to emphasize that none of those transimages recorded were ever seen by Sheila. Below are some of his other apparitions.

As Bill appeared in many sequences of frames, which I forwarded to Sheila, she promptly sent some old photos from her album for comparison. Above the couple and at right, their wedding photo, when Bill was 47 years old. Needless to say, when he passed, at the age of 70 after struggling with cancer, his appearance was not as happy and healthy as below.

We are not aware of the sophisticated technology used by the Spirit Friends who inform us while working from a Transmission Station. Hypothetically, inventors that worked for the good of humanity go on developing their knowledge and carry on the same interests as before.

Being in this field already for more than three decades I saw clear progress in the quality of either of the voices or images. More recently, the Spirit Friends tried to shape and send images of our loved ones, for the first time, in *3D format.*

In addition to this new phenomenon, they also took Bill back to his childhood, as a time-trip to his past. Even though this is an ordinary phenomenon in our research, but we don't know if those images are gotten from the memory of the deceased one or from the so-called Akashic Recordings.

Unexpected Apparition of Sheila's Daughter

While looking at the frames of the video I noticed that one especially seemed to bring a long-haired young lady beside Bill's face. I promptly remembered Jennifer, Sheila's daughter. I sent Sheila the trans image asking for "mom's opinion." Sheila wrote back promptly expressing the very same impression - it was, indeed, Jen!
How creative are those Communicators? Besides possessing such advanced technology to reach our devices on Earth, still they are able to make artistic compositions. What a surprise to see Jennifer beside Bill. One more gift for Sheila!

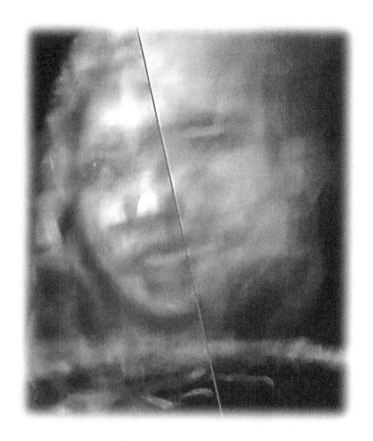

Half of the trans-image is Bill. The other half is a beautiful
young lady who reminds us of Jennifer.

Jennifer, who passed at the age of 27.

Plus One Identification

When I submitted the draft of my text with the transimages recorded, I also included some transimages of "unknown" ones — that is, some deceased ones that I could not identify. In these cases, I published those pictures expecting that anyone anywhere, may recognize and send data and confirmation. In the draft I sent to Sheila, there were some "unknown" and she promptly returned with surprising information.

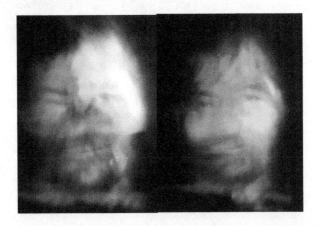

She wrote a text confirming that those transimages looked strikingly like the man she met long after Bill had died. He became her boyfriend, Arnie, who passed away in 2016.

Sheila was equally surprised with the three apparitions and kindly sent some photos of both.

These experiments of communication with the Other Side of life through devices constitute remarkable evidence that life goes on after our body perishes. More than evidence of the reality of the afterlife, we still can observe the high level of technology requested by these transmissions, as well as the goodness of those entities who help us to bring comfort to those in grief here.

Still, more important than all these topics, perhaps we can imagine that these Instrumental Transcomunications may unify and change all basic concepts of us, incarnated, about the reasons why we live, and that Earth is just a giant school.

Sheila and her deceased daughter Jennifer

117

The Participant's Opinion

These are the words of the writer and friend, Sheila Lowe:

From: sheila@sheila....
Date: 6 Jan/2022
Hi Sonia,

I felt very grateful (and a little greedy!) to have not one or even two, but three of my loved ones come through in this experiment. When you asked me to participate in this project, I wasn't sure whether Bill would come through, as we were divorced at the time he crossed in 2020. But divorce notwithstanding, we were still connected, and he proved it.

He didn't really believe in the Afterlife, but he's obviously changed his tune 🤔. *Then, the fact that Arnie, who I was seeing when he died suddenly of a heart attack in 2016, showed up just made me laugh—his irrepressible grin was still the same.*

And there was my Jennifer, who has been gone since 2000, showing up with Bill. They didn't get along well while on Earth, but clearly, they have a better relationship now.
I just wish everyone could experience the joy these photos bring to me.
Sonia is better than Kodak! LOL...
Xoxo
Sheila

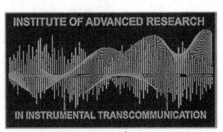

www.patreon.com/sonia_rinaldi

About the Author

Brazilian researcher and writer, Sonia Rinaldi is benevolently helping people connect with loved ones in the Afterlife by recording their voices. She has worked in this field for 35 years. Having audio and video recordings of people living in the Afterlife alleviates the grief of parents, spouses, and other loved ones grieving for someone who has died.

The tangible records of the voices and images of people living in the Afterlife provide compelling evidence that Life continues after the body dies. That realization changes the people who hear and see their deceased loved ones, changing their attitude toward the normal life transition called death.
As more people experience connecting with loved ones in this way, and as the audio and video recordings are broadcast and disseminated, people will realize that Life doesn't end at the transition from the earth. That realization will change people's attitudes toward themselves and others, and eventually, it will change humankind.

Sonia and her research are featured in the award-winning documentary, *Rinaldi*, produced by We Don't Die Films, Robert Lyon, narrated by Sandra Champlain, released on February 22nd, 2022, www.wedontdiefilms.com

I) Ref: Sonia Rinaldi - Afterlife Research and Education. http://www.afterliferesearch.org/arei-initiatives-instrumental-transcommunication/
Sonia Rinaldi, M.S., an author, lecturer, and internationally recognized researcher in Instrumental TransCommunications (ITC), twice received the international Hedri Prize from the Swiss Foundation for Parapsychology for innovative research in 1995 and 1997.

Below you can find Sonia Rinaldi's research, books, published articles, videos, and a few samples of the e-magazine reports she is continuously working on and producing for educational purposes and the afterlife research.

Websites: www.ipati.org www.patreon.com/sonia_rinaldi
Instagram: https://www.instagram.com/sonia_rinaldi_ipati/
Facebook: https://www.facebook.com/sonia.rinaldi.3914
YouTube: http://YouTube.com/user/videosipati
Interviews and Podcasts:
https://www.youtube.com/watch?v=itfA22rJyGA
https://youtu.be/SuhEl8CDC6M
https://youtu.be/xp_l8K69s6s
https://youtu.be/Ml6VG3zEDIg
https://youtu.be/mUbBuq9tzgw
https://youtu.be/27Bp90Oqn30
https://youtu.be/5y5ep9-dLqQ
https://youtu.be/Jai1556DOIs
https://youtu.be/W2bCxydg6U8
https://youtu.be/YTSG0SrIlwM
https://youtu.be/o34PwsNgESY

*"What if it was that one act
of kindness of yours
in that moment that
held the universe
together?"*
~Aaron Dan~
1987 – 2019

Following the Light, *Camille Dan*

By Camille Dan

On September 22, 2019, my son, Aaron, suddenly left his life on earth in a tragic accident. I was traumatized, and in a deep, dense fog of shock and grief for many months. It's not in the natural order of things to lose your child, and my mind refused to accept it. Aaron was my everything, my whole world, for the first three years of his life before his brothers and sister arrived. I used to call him an 'Old Soul' because he was wise beyond his years. He had the compassion and sensitivity of a person with deep respectful insight, even as a toddler. I was forever amazed by him. My life began with his and felt like it ended when his did.

It's been a long journey of forward and backward steps. I still have moments when I don't believe it really happened. Sometimes, I go through a whole day with the feeling that Aaron's gone away on a trip, and he'll be back. Some days, it's like he never left because I can feel him with me. His warmth and strength are palpable when he's present, even though I can't see him. I often hear him speak to me in his voice. Oh, it's him alright. I know by the sound of his voice, the tone and timbre of it. His phrasing is different from mine, and the things he tells me don't come from the lexicon in my brain. His messages are brilliant, transcendent, and beyond my experience.

In the first week after his passing, Aaron slow dripped me with his afterlife signs and messages to get through my thick skull and my profound grief. Being a skeptic and a major-league doubter at the time, it would be difficult to convince me that I wasn't making up Aaron's communications in my grieving mind. Grief does that. It can make you think that you're losing touch with reality. It affects your memory, your thought processing, your decision-making, essentially everything that you think makes you...you.

Oddly enough, my out-of-body experience years earlier during my pregnancy with Aaron did nothing to change my skepticism. I took it that it was a reaction to a fever despite being above my body looking down at it, seeing everything going on below, and traveling through a vent in the wall to a tunnel of light into outer space. Then, rushing back into my body when I recalled that I was pregnant. The stories of near-death experiences that patients told me when I was a nurse were truly remarkable. How were they able to later describe to me the scene at their own cardiac arrest when they were unconscious and without vital signs the whole time, or to know that I was in the room with the rest of the crash team? Even so, I convinced myself that there must have been a logical and scientific explanation. I was a hard nut to crack on a good day.

Aaron started by sending me a message through my psychic friend, Arlene. She brought me a note from Aaron that she had written via channeled automatic writing. There were details in the note that even a close friend like Arlene couldn't have known. The next day I had to speak with a detective investigating Aaron's accident. He said something that was word-for-word in the note. I forget everything else he said.

Later, I would find out that our loved ones in spirit will communicate to us through close friends, family, and animals when our energy isn't suitable for melding with theirs. It's normal to feel sad and low while grieving. Our energy isn't always compatible with spirit, and that's okay. They always find a way through.

Arlene had spoken to me often over the years about the signs and messages that she received from her loved ones in spirit. I thought of her stories as heartwarming, and clearly helpful for her, but not necessarily real without any scientific evidence. She wrote a chapter for this anthology about some of her incredible experiences. Aaron's note from Arlene was the first step of many in my spiritual awakening.

A week after I read that note, Aaron began speaking directly to me. Of course, again I thought it was my imagination. But his voice sounded so real as if he was right there beside me. It first happened as we were driving to the cottage for some much-needed rest. The grief had been exhausting. The trauma of burying my son was more than I could take. I read that being in nature can be quite therapeutic in grief. So, my boyfriend, Anthony, and I threw a few things in a suitcase, loaded up the car, and headed away from the city to spend time at the lake.

It was October, and along the way I was taken by the radiant colours of the autumn forests that line the highway. The drone of the engine lulled me into a bit of a trance. Suddenly, I was stricken by an intense tidal wave of grief that felt like a tsunami hit me thinking that my son will never again see such a beautiful sight. Just as suddenly, I heard Aaron say, "I see it, Mom. I do see the colours...only not the way you do. The colours that I see are vibrant and glowing beyond explanation to you. I see the energy that the trees are emitting."

It was Aaron's voice loud and clear, as if he were a passenger in the car with me. I looked at Anthony who was driving. It's a good thing that I wasn't driving, or it would have caused an accident. Anthony didn't appear to have heard anything. It took me less than a second to decide to keep the whole matter to myself rather than risk sounding like I had just lost my mind.

While at the cottage, Aaron spoke to me often. He also started to send me various signs to prove his presence. Each sign related more than coincidentally to his messages. One time, he told me to look out the window at the exact moment that I caught a glimmer of light in the corner of my eye. When I went to the window, I saw the most vibrant rainbow I had ever seen arching into the lake in front of the cottage. It was one of two that appeared beside each other. It was a sight that I will never forget.

From that point on, Aaron's signs and messages grew in number, scope and depth. He began to write letters and words in the clouds. He played with electricity and the Wi-Fi. Birds appeared at the most synchronous moments. I figured out how to put his signs and messages together, like a sort of connect-the-dots to understand his meaning. With each message he explained to me how energy works in the universe and assured me that he exists in a dimension that I am not yet able to perceive. He reassured me that we will be together again when it is my time to cross the veil.

I read that journaling grief can also be cathartic and therapeutic. I wasn't much of a writer, but I gave it a try. I started to keep a daily written record of my feelings early on, and I found it extremely helpful. Each time I would make an entry in my journal, I would feel a bit better. On top of feeling awful most of the time, my 'grief memory' rendered me nearly non-functional. I could barely remember anything anymore. Journaling was also a good way to prevent forgetting. I found an online grief journaling group in which I felt understood, supported, and encouraged. My writing improved, and I began to try my hand at poetry which I had never done before. So, I kept it up.

Aaron's messages began to fill my journal. They were so full of love, guidance, and infinite wisdom. I was learning from them, and with each of his messages my mind expanded further. Aaron explained to me what it is like in his afterlife. He described how the universe works, how energy is eternally creative and flows across space and time to where it is drawn by compatibility. He told me that love is the source energy of all creation, and that he and I have always been and always will be together. He said that everything is an extension, or reflection of love.

I soon began to see that I couldn't keep Aaron's messages all to myself. After all, Aaron told me several times that his messages were meant to be shared, and that I should share them. Then, one day, he told me to write a book. Having never authored before, I set out to accomplish the task with little confidence, a big heart, some gumption, and a lot of optimism coming from spirit to publish my journal to a book.

The more I shared my experience with Aaron, the more connections I made. I discovered *Helping Parents Heal* on Facebook and joined the group. I was immediately welcomed by other parents going through similar experiences. I felt understood by this warm, caring, open-minded, and supportive community, and I knew that I would never feel alone in my grief again. There were opportunities to share and learn 24/7, and always a kind Caring Listener when I needed a little extra empathy and attention.

I told myself not to set high expectations while it was still so early in my grief. Since I had no idea how to even begin writing a book, I relied on trusty Google for help. That's where I discovered how to self-publish. Figuring that virtually no one would be interested in reading my story, I followed the steps to publish my own book anyway. I was motivated by cheers from Aaron, and the hope that my book of messages from the afterlife might help one other person. Et voila, *Aaron's Energy: An Unexpected Journey Through Grief and the Afterlife With My Brilliant Son* was self-published on February 11, 2021. The title popped into my mind one day. I have no doubt how it got there.

Aaron tells me a lot about light. He described to me that his transition was like being drawn to a spinning circle of light particles that occupied the complete surrounding darkness. As he drew closer to the light, he felt himself absorbed into it. He showed me an image of a sparkler, the ones that we used to spin on Independence Day when we were kids, so I could understand what he meant. I can't describe the relief I felt to know that his transition was so peaceful and beautiful.

Aaron spoke a lot about Black Holes which I recorded in my first book. While I was grateful to be learning so much about astrophysics, I was able to deduce his meaning when he shared his transition to afterlife story with me. Black Holes are so densely packed with mass that their gravitational fields do not allow anything to escape them, including light. Anything inside a black hole is unobservable. Anything not inside a black hole has been somehow able to avoid its gravitational pull. What can be observed is the visible border of light that surrounds a black hole, called its Event Horizon. Aaron's image of a sparkler looked remarkably like the pictures I've seen of event horizons. Was he telling me that he transitioned to a place and time that isn't visible, but exists in another dimension of the universe? I believe that the answer to my question is yes.

When I came to the realization that Aaron's signs and messages were arriving concurrently with things happening around me in real-time, I knew that everything is connected everywhere. I was awakened to the real reality that we exist in flow with the universe, and we are given many signs and messages that we can follow like signposts to find were we comfortably fit within it. When things began to fall into place with much less pain and effort, I knew where to focus my energy and followed. We have an innate GPS that is linked to the universe for guidance whenever we need. Pain, suffering, grief, hurt, and things that we label as negative are redirectors. Feeling hurt, aggravation, frustration, longing, loss, and the like are instinctive indicators to change route on our journeys. Spirit is there and happy to help with a sign, like a dime, a feather, or any other breadcrumb.

Aaron has been quite clear that we carry attachments from our physical lives into our afterlives. We anchor our loved ones in spirit as well as ourselves to the physical plane with our feelings and thoughts. They are more than happy to give us some direction that will help their existence as much as it helps ours. The connection to each other is never lost and we can make the afterlife realm lighter and healthier by what we dwell on in life.

Aaron was such a bright light in life, and he continues to shine through from his afterlife. He was the most giving, kind, sensitive and compassionate person I ever knew. He had infinite curiosity, and creativity. He is my brilliant son.

Aaron has continued to share with me since I published my last journal entry in the second edition of *Aaron's Energy*. It was difficult to decide when to finish the book with Aaron's miraculous signs still pouring in. I chose his sign, the angel in the clouds over the lake, because it was the most miraculous sign from him up to then. His signs and messages have grown to be even more profound and evidential. It appears that he is perfecting his ability to communicate with me across the veil, or perhaps he is helping me to perfect my ability to understand.

My journal entries here pick up from where *Aaron's Energy* left off. All the quotes are Aaron's words to me.

February 22, 2021.
"LOVE is all that really is...everything else is just derivative."

February 23, 2021.
Do you find dimes and pennies in unusual places when thinking about your loved ones across the veil? I have found so many, I'm keeping my collection in a jar. Aaron tells me that a dime and a penny add up to 11, the number of spirit presence, and dimensional connections.

March 4, 2021.
How's this for synchronicity?! It's a beautiful, sunny day today, and I'm on my regular FaceTime call with my bereavement counselor. Just when I mentioned to her that I'm feeling like a failure, my internet goes down, and the call is cut off. Suddenly, out of nowhere on this peaceful and calm day, a huge gust of wind knocks the bird feeder, that I put up in memory of Aaron, to the ground!! Just as suddenly, the wind stopped. I got Aaron's message in all this for sure. He's telling me that this is the kind of thinking that brings the house down.
Aaron tells me that where he is life and afterlife are on a continuum with no end or beginning. In his dimension we are all still and always together. Our eyes can't see it, but our minds know it. We help each other from both sides.

March 7, 2021.

"All universal energy is helping energy. The universe sends you signs to help direct you toward compatibility. Follow the signs toward the flow. If knowledge of the future is helpful, the universe will show it to you in some way, perhaps through a psychic or medium. But, if it's not helpful for you to know the future, there will be no way for you to access it in advance. There are always options and choices. The energy of the universe will always be pointing the way for you."

March 9, 2021.

"Our human drives can get in the way of our spirit drive toward universal flow. Ultimately, we find a way back to compatible flow with the universe once our temporary detours to unsustainable exchange of energy disperse."

March 11, 2021.

Aaron tells me that reincarnation happens all the time and is a naturally occurring and recurring process of energy flow. He said that because energy exists multidimensionally, he exists in more than one dimension at the same time, as does everyone. He explains that we cannot be aware of other dimensions beyond the three in which we experience our human incarnation which is why we cannot have full memories of the others. However, our unconscious energy is connected to them.

March 17, 2021.

Aaron told me today that full knowledge of afterlife could interfere with getting through life experience. He said that we have all we need in the dimension we're in for the dimension we're in. He also said that we can have afterlife and between-life knowledge through unconscious connection to heavenly dimensions, but we're created to experience the life state during life, and we should spend most of our conscious energy and time on it. We have eternity to experience all dimensions of existence. Love the life you're in.

March 19, 2021.

Aaron is sending me many messages today. He said that we experience common elements of transition to afterlife, but we go to very different experiences based on what we remain attached to from our lives. So, we do take something with us across the veil. It's just not material. We bring feelings, attachments, love, trauma, stuff of our consciousness. We transition through a between experience that takes as much or as little time as we need to fully transition. We remain attached to our lives and loves to a greater or lesser extent throughout eternity. In life, we can choose what we subscribe to and how deeply we attach to our subscriptions. When we choose our attachments lovingly and wisely, we take that wisdom and love with us on our eternal journey. We have eternity and many dimensions to carry love through, and to evolve and experience existence and oneness.

March 20, 2021.
Aaron just told me that everything is love. Love is the energy from which all is created. Love is not the opposite of hatred. Good is not the opposite of evil. Right is not the opposite of wrong. Courage is not the opposite of fear. First is not the opposite of last. These are human constructs that may fit within our perceptions, but not with the entirety of reality beyond our three dimensions. All in the universe is an extension of the love source that flows through everything.
I nearly forgot the best part. It's a beautiful night tonight. The sky is clear and loaded with stars. I sat beside the campfire and thought of Aaron as I gazed at the celestial beauty. I asked Aaron for a sign that he was with me. I was suddenly startled by a "person" standing on the porch. Scared the crap out of me. When I looked closer, it was someone in long. white flowing robes whose face wasn't clearly visible. Just as suddenly, it vanished. I believe it was the sign I asked for.
Matter is a manifestation of energy's creation. Nothing is in our way. Energy is in continuous flow. It creates matter for direction and redirection through time and space. Love is in all creation. Love is balance. Love is the source. Emanate and receive love.

March 23, 2021.
"As humanity evolves through its awakening, development in technology has brought dimensional contact closer and closer. We evolve toward meeting and communicating across the veil. Humans have created the means to their own awakening. We look forward to when humanity catches up consciously to their advancement and discovery of our infinite connection, and the realization that we are one."

April 2, 2021.
Telekinesis. I asked Aaron, if we are all connected with the universal energy, and spirits can create signs for us by pushing around forces that surround matter, why can't we do that in our human experience with our thoughts too?
Aaron's answer, "You can, and you do it all the time. Everything you think, feel, and do results in changes in energetic fields that move matter. In our human experience, our ability to be conscious of the movement and changes that we influence is limited

by our senses that are tuned for macro events tied to our survival. In spirit we have no boundaries or barriers and are in flow with micro events to macro events. We have ability to know all events in energy flow."

April 7, 2021.
"When we focus too much on our human self-protective drives, we convert our love-source energy to fear, anxiety, anger, envy, hatred, greed, which draws us downward to cycle energy inward at lower-level states where we attract similar lower-level energies. Lower-level energy exchanges are not ultimately sustainable. When we focus our energy at higher levels of kindness, compassion, giving, consideration, fairness, we are risen to higher-level states closer to the source where we attract exchange with the sustainable universal energy of love and are in flow with creation."

April 10, 2021.
Common sense. Where does it come from and why is it so uncommon? It comes from a sense of responsibility for us and others. In taking care of ourselves we take care of others, and in taking care of others we take care of ourselves. Transferring our responsibilities to others is not balancing energy. In giving and receiving love we find balance with the universe.

April 25, 2021.
"When we act kindly and give charity, we elevate ourselves on a universal scale and contribute ourselves to improvement of energy flow. We are innately aware of the personal reward by how good selfless giving makes us feel knowing the transcending exponential potential of it."

April 27, 2021.
"When spirit incarnates, its opportunity for new perspective is born as it forms a relationship with its new body and manifests experience materially. Spirit holds all its experience across its eternal existence throughout universal dimensions. Incarnate consciousness and spirit consciousness become entangled in an interrelationship of self and beyond and do share as much knowledge of the whole as corporeal ability allows.

April 30, 2021.
"The secret to success is no secret. It is merely often overlooked in material existence and confused with corporeal-driven survival and self-protective instincts. Success is not found ultimately or sustainably in material gain for the self, although the ego

129

may assign it that paradoxical definition. Success is found in transcendence beyond the self. Each being plays its part in the manifestation of universal success, and cannot exist separate from it, but can ascend within it. Be kind and loving. Measure your success as your existence in the universe, your part in it, your respectful support of self and others, and you will recognize how truly valuable you are."

May 6, 2021.
"We are each and all integral to the balance and flow of the whole. As incarnate constructs of spirit we are, and we act as agents of its material creation as part and participants in the entire continuous creation and re-creation of unlimited universal consciousness. We are here as part of the continuous flow of creation. We are each blessed with special abilities and tools to create and care for each and every element in our world and ultimately of the universe."

May 8, 2021.
"How do we know what a tree feels if we don't speak its language? How do we know that a rock has no consciousness if we can't achieve mutual understanding between distant levels? How can we know what lies beyond our ability to see? Let's assume that everyone and everything in our world is in constant communication despite that we can't fully know how it flows within and through our awareness, and we aren't fully conscious of how we are connected. But we can imagine, think, and dream of the energy of the universe flowing through the tree and the rock and all of us, and that despite our differences, we are all here for each other."

May 9, 2021.
I woke up this morning to the warmest angel hug.

May 12, 2021.
"Legacy is spiritual and material. It is not only about what you leave for generations, but also about that you did it. The loving energy you put into your creation will be inherited across time. You hear about inheritance of trauma a lot. Consider that all is inherited including joy and trauma which are reflections of love. Love is the energy of all creation."

May 15, 2021.
Last night there was a beautiful sunset of soft and soothing yellows, pinks, purples, oranges, and reds. As I wished that Aaron could see it, I heard him say, "Mom, I am the sun."

May 11, 2021.
"A dime is just a dime, a penny just a penny until you give them meaning. A bird, a butterfly, and any animal are random visitors until you make connection with their spirit energy. You are integral to signs and messages from across the veil, as you are elemental to them. A countless amount of micro and macro incidents occur simultaneously that require your presence as witness."

May 21, 2021.
Aaron told me that the more we ask for signs and messages together, the louder our voices are heard across the veil. A ripple effect occurs that attracts our loved ones in spirit to do the same as they join together and send us more and more miraculous signs and messages that they are always with us.

May 20, 2021.
I saw the angel in the sky over the lake again, above Aaron's memory garden on this peaceful evening. So, I went to take a closer look. As I stared at the clouds a single cluster of them began to swirl before my eyes. It wasn't windy, and all the other clouds were virtually still. Within seconds it was evident that the clouds were being formed into letters, and the letters into words. When I recognized the words, I quickly grabbed my phone for a photo. Look at the message written in the sky from my angel Aaron!! It clearly says, "I Love You"!!

May 23, 2021.
"Although I am no longer present in my physical form, my consciousness continues to be present here in you, Mom. Live on for me and go forward with me."

June 12, 2021.
"Your loved ones in spirit are still with you, continue to love you, and share all of your life within and alongside you. The connection is never broken. We anchor our energy to you through shareable compatible and familiar thoughts and memories, and we are always here for you as guides and helpers. Ask for us anytime and be comforted by our ever presence. We will always answer your call. Look for our guidance. Open yourself to possibilities and to the concept of infinity, even though the perception of it seems impossible. We are not finite, and we can maintain our connections to you. Our guidance is not restricted or limited to your familiar dimensions. We are eternal and we live in eternity."

June 27, 2021.
Today was a day of signs and synchronicities. I asked Aaron for a sign while out for a walk this morning. I came up with an idea. A butterfly. But there are a lot of butterflies around, so I asked for the butterfly to land on me. Before I finished the thought, a butterfly landed on my arm! As I told my walking partner what happened, we heard a cardinal sing very loudly nearby. What's special about that is cardinals are very rarely seen in this area. Then suddenly the wind whipped up and the clouds above us formed a heart!

June 30, 2021.
"When we are reunited again you will understand the joy of eternity, something you can't understand now, you will know all of our existence and memories across time, and you will know that we have always been together."

July 6, 2021.
"We obviously don't come into the world alone, and we don't go out of it alone. We are never alone, ever."

July 26, 2021.
I asked Aaron to give me a sure sign that he was with me on my birthday. He sent me many signs through the day including a magnificent sunset. But he saved the best sign for last. The best and most significant gift. He visited me in my sleep. He was

perfectly clear, reassuring, radiant, and real as ever. I felt our hug physically and emotionally. I felt the depth and eternity of our love.

"I'm guiding you to share joy with me on your birthday and every day, Mom. We share all our feelings together always. Spirits sing and dance where there is creation and joy. Where there is pain and suffering, spirits give comfort and guidance."

July 27, 2021.

"Think of your brain like your motherboard, your body like your hard drive, and your soul like electromagnetic telecommunication. Your soul exists with or without the rest."

August 3, 2021.

"Dreams are opportunities to experience the other side. The veil is so thin during that part of sleep that we can see through intuitively. Dreams are moments that our physical survival guard is lowered so we can get closer to our spiritual selves and our part of the universal whole consciousness."

August 13, 2021.

I asked Aaron why we generally don't have memories of our experiences beyond our physical lives, such as from our spiritual lives and past lives.

This is his answer: "The brain is not primarily designed for access to those memories. It is designed for our physical survival. As we mature, our brains are maturing to prepare us for adult life and physical independence. Young children who haven't matured to an age of independence do have access to memories and to consciousness beyond the physical until their brains have developed mechanisms for independent physical survival. In adulthood we can access those memories by tuning out from our physical senses at times. The universe has created our existence and in so doing has given us the power to draw from its infinite energy to survive and create."

August 22, 2021.

For the past couple of days, I have felt the presence of someone in the house. I get a heavy feeling of someone standing behind me. But when I turn to look, no one is there. I hear knocking with no one there. At 2:30 am, the lights in the kitchen dimmed by themselves. This morning one crystal on a chandelier began to swing by itself while all the others remained still. Each time that I asked if it was Aaron moving the crystal, it would swing a bit faster!

It's no coincidence that I started reading The Medium Explosion by Robert Ginsberg, founder of Forever Family Foundation with his wife, Phran (of blessed memory), a couple of days ago too. Some of what's happening in the house I'm reading about in this book. I think that this is another way that Aaron shows me he's with me. Plus, he indicates that he's interested and approves of the book.

August 27, 2021.
"Birth and death are transitions from one state of energy to another. You would not wonder why one was born. Though you often wonder why life seems to begin, age, and end. Life is in constant transition as energy is exchanged and transferred in the flow of creation throughout the universe. This is why."

September 11, 2021.
Visited Petroglyphs Provincial Park today to see the ancient First Nations rock carvings of spiritual symbols, and to go for a hike. The petroglyphs are beautiful and mystical. The park is huge with many spectacular nature trails and land formations. Hiking up and down across the granite of the majestic Canadian Shield, over the rocks and roots of the forest floor, and around the marshes and lake brings you feelings of inner peace and a sense of connection to the source of creation.
Aaron's second Angelversary is coming up this month and the grief waves have been hitting a lot harder than usual. Nature walks have always been helpful, and this was a great new place to find.
Entering the park, I asked Aaron if he was there with me and to give me a sign. I was hoping he could visit the petroglyphs with me. As I exited the site, I spotted his sign. An 'A' carved into a rock like a petroglyph!!

September 21, 2021.

I've been thinking of putting one of those large bronze herons in Aaron's memory garden. Today I set out shopping to find one. It turns out that it's late in the season for garden items, (I'm green at gardening, no pun intended) and they're sold out everywhere around here. I was a little disappointed because I wanted to place it there tomorrow on Aaron's Angelversary. When I got back, a real live large grey heron was standing on the dock looking straight at Aaron's memory garden!!

October 4, 2021.

When I turned on the Google Maps in the car today, instead the song, Angel by Sarah McLachlan came on. I couldn't change it to Google Maps, or anything else. Once the whole song had played, the other apps started to work. This was for sure a sign from Aaron.

October 23, 2021.

"One and two dimensions exist within three. It's not too hard to conceptualize those three dimensions exist within four, five, six, and so on. So, it's also not too hard to realize that you and I are present together in another dimension."

November 6, 2021.

"Your world is changing and evolving, so is mine. Change in one dimension affects change in all."

November 8, 2021.

"Things that seem to be happening in the moment have already happened. The body is designed to protect its physical self and is equipped with a fairly sophisticated sensory system for the 3-dimensional world. The physical brain and bodily sensors are receiving information from what is already happening, but the brain condenses all that is in flow down to a point in time to calculate a physical reaction. Consciousness operates in flow with the universe and knows by intuition the vastness of reality beyond the physical senses."

November 15, 2021.

Today is Aaron's third Heavenly Birthday. He gave me a gift today in his beautiful message:

"Return unkindness with kindness. Unkindness is demonstration of a person's feelings about themselves, not you. So is kindness. Show others how you feel about yourself by being kind and help them to raise their inner awareness of their own value at the same time. You wouldn't exist if you were of no value. That's just not possible. You are of eternal value to the universe because you exist. Beyond that, every act of kindness you do exponentially expands that value."

November 29, 2021.
I'm home alone tonight. It's the second night of Hanukkah. I was thinking that I wouldn't light the menorah since I was just by myself.
That's when I heard Aaron's voice, "I'm here Mom. Light the menorah." "Ok.", I said. So, I gathered 3 candles, two for the 2nd night and one called the Shamash that's used to light the others, plus a lighter.
When I went to light the Shamash candle, Aaron said, "Use my memory candle instead of the lighter to light the Shamash." "Ok.", I said again as I touched the wick of the Shamash to the flame of Aaron's memory candle. And at that exact moment, as the Shamash was lit, I felt and heard a whoosh of air blow across my shoulders like a hug from Aaron across the veil.
It was truly miraculous!

December 1, 2021.
Today I had a benign lump removed from my foot. But that's not what this entry is about.
The nurse said she had to double check my ID because I didn't look as old as my birth date indicated. Flattering. But not what this entry is about.
I told her that I will prove my age when I pull out my reading glasses to sign the consent. Funny. But still, not what this entry is about.
After the procedure, on the way home, I spotted a young man outside an optometrist office. He was facing the door. I couldn't see his face. He looked exactly like Aaron from behind!! He was the same height. He had the same stance and posture. He had the same haircut and hair color, same jacket, same pants, even the same Timberland boots that were Aaron's favourite!
Remember my joke to the nurse about my reading glasses? That's what this entry is about. It looked just like Aaron standing in front of an optometrist office. A sign that he was watching over me at my operation.

December 5, 2021.
Do you see the orbs above the Hanukkah candles? I could see them with my eyes, but they were white. In the photo they look green, and they are shaped like hearts. They appeared when I asked Aaron if he was with us as we lit the Hanukkah candles! Miraculous!

December 6, 2021.
"Acknowledge that your own energy field is attracting that which is compatible with it, and that it is the only thing that you have any control over."

December 13, 2021.
"We are not separated by a veil. Human life is part of the same flow as beforelife and afterlife, there is really no separation. Human 3-dimensional existence is as much a possibility and a probability as any infinite possibility and probability of existence. What you call a veil is merely a factor of being in a human form that cannot observe or imagine the micro-transitions occurring beyond it that create the macro-transitions you are able to observe. What occurs in one realm influences all others, most of which you can't know by observation."

December 16, 2021.
"As the 3-Dimensional world transitions through a spiritual reawakening, keep in mind that there is an equally powerful resistance that operates to keep these three dimensions intact as their dimensional limitations exist in a flow that is essential to all universal dimensions. Human limitation, such as fear and it's derivatives like self protection and anxiety for example, are significant and necessary source creations of flow. All is love."

January 3, 2022.
"Your loved ones in spirit are constantly sending you signs and messages. Their signs and messages might not always be what you want or expect. But they will always be what you need, and they will always be loving. Acknowledge that you will have pain in your grief. Pain and grief are expressions of love. Let down your defences when you feel able and allow yourself to be fully open to receive our signs and messages of loving energy that are always there."

January 8, 2022.
An exit sign I drove past on the highway today said, "Oprah Winfrey", on it...at least I thought it did. When I got close to it, I saw that it didn't say, Oprah Winfrey, at all. Time for new glasses.
At the time I was listening to and enjoying a podcast interview with Jane Asher Reaney about her new book, "The Next Room", and reminiscing about my mother. Jane's story about her life and afterlife with her mom stirred up some truly heartwarming memories for me, and I learned a lot.
About 10 minutes up the highway, Jane mentioned Oprah Winfrey in the podcast! Gasp!!What are the freaking odds of that!! I am definitely getting her book!

January 10, 2022.
"All the energy you need to manifest your purpose is available to you. Learn what you need to give, and all will come for you."

February 23, 2022.
Yesterday's events have me still in awe and reeling! I saw a trans-image of my son in spirit on the documentary, "Rinaldi", that premiered yesterday!!
At 58 minutes into the film, the image of Aaron appeared in the part about trans-images of unknown persons in spirit. I was stunned, shaking, and crying. This was evidence before my eyes that Aaron still exists, and that everything he has told me from his afterlife about energy, matter and creation is true. It is the most validating event since his transition!!
Not long after Aaron's transition he told me that he will return to me, and I will recognize him. This is it!! I definitely recognized him. I am 100% sure that it's him. The image of him in the documentary is one that I have never seen. He appears to be around sixteen years old in it. It is Aaron.
I found another image of Aaron in Sonia's gallery of unknowns since, and some friends of mine have discovered images of their loved ones in spirit there too after seeing my Facebook and Instagram posts!

I am eternally grateful to Aaron for guiding me to this moment, and to Sonia Rinaldi, Sandra Champlain, Robert Lyon, and everyone who made this fascinating and miraculous documentary!! www.wedontdiefilms.com

Rosanne Groover Norris, whose story appears in the documentary is a chapter contributor to this anthology. I first heard Rosanne interviewed by Sandra Champlain on her show, *We Don't Die Radio*. It was not long after Aaron transitioned. I have never forgotten that interview. So much of Rosanne's story with her son, Lee in spirit, resonated with my story with Aaron. I purchased her book, *beLEEve* right away.

Sandra Champlain wrote a meaningful foreword for this anthology. I have listened to every one of her podcasts, *We Don't Die Radio*, and her show, *Shades of the Afterlife* on iHeart Radio. I love her book, *We Don't Die: A Skeptic's Discovery of Life After Death* (Morgan James Publishing, Jan. 1, 2013) and I have joined in her *Free Sunday Gathering* as well as her special events.

Another friend, Elly Sheykhet, discovered a transimage of her daughter, Alina in spirit, in the documentary. I contributed a chapter to *The Beauty of a Grieving Mother*, an anthology curated by Elly in 2021, after meeting her on the Helping Parents Heal Facebook Group page. Elly has contributed a chapter to this anthology.

What are the odds that we would all meet? I imagine that they are incalculable.

Our journey keeps going from here and back through eternity. Once again, it's time to close a chapter on a story that never ends and to look forward to what's to come.

About the Author

Camille Dan is the mother of Aaron, and his two brothers and one sister. She has professional experience as a Critical Care Registered Nurse, a Medical Technical Consultant for Feature Films and Television, and a Private Investment Manager. She is the Self-Published Author of *Aaron's Energy: An Unexpected Journey Through Grief and the Afterlife With My Brilliant Son*, First and Second Editions. Camille's journey after losing her eldest son has been so unexpected. A former skeptic, she has now written three books on afterlife signs and messages, has contributed a chapter to the anthology, *The Beauty of a Grieving Mother: Mothers Share Their Stories of Finding Hope after the Loss of a Child* by Elly Sheykhet (Alina's Light Publishing 2021), has been and will be in a number of podcasts and a documentary, has her chapter, "Eternity is in Our Nature", published in an edition of *Chicken Soup for*

the Soul: Grieving, Loss and Healing by Amy Newmark (Chicken Soup for the Soul LLC 2022), and is an author and the curator of this remarkable anthology, all since September 2019. Camille is sure that her son Aaron has been her guiding light through it all.

All earnings from Camille's book sales go to augment donations to mental health and addiction care and research programs, youth and young adult social development programs, bereavement support services, survival of consciousness and afterlife communication research, Forever Family Foundation, and Helping Parents Heal.

Website: www.aaronsenergy.com

*"Do you realize that if you fall into a black hole,
you will see the entire future of the Universe
unfold in front of you in a matter of moments
and you will emerge into another space-time
created by the singularity of the black hole
you just fell into?"
~Neil deGrasse Tyson~
Astrophysicist*

Lee Appears, *Rosanne Groover Norris*

By Rosanne Groover Norris

I don't know much about wormholes, but apparently, my son does because that's how he came through from the other side.

It was only a year out from Lee's passing, in January 2018, that I attended my first afterlife conference. I had been listening to Sandra Champlain's, "We Don't Die" Radio Show, and when the conference was announced, I decided to go. I traveled alone so I had a lot of time to think and talk to Lee. The closer I got to Boston for the first We Don't Die Conference, in February 2019, the more nervous I was about attending. What was in store? Would the people be weird? Would I fit in? I had no idea what to expect, but I forged ahead.

Sandra Champlain welcomed everyone and explained what was in store for the weekend. She was warm and friendly, so I relaxed, ready to learn. Brazilian researcher Sonia Rinaldi was the first speaker Sandra introduced. Sonia is the co-founder and Research Director of IPATI (Institute of Advanced Research on Instrumental Transcommunication www.patron.com/sonia_rinaldi). For over three decades, Sonia has used various methods and devices to receive images and voices from deceased loved ones. As Sandra explained Sonia's work, I thought it seemed "out there." Spirit images coming through vapor? And voices recorded from the other side? To me, this seemed like something straight out of Twilight Zone. I just couldn't wrap my head around it. But I thought about why I was there. Wasn't it to learn? So, I decided to open my mind and heart and listen without judgment. And as I had learned from Sandra and others in the afterlife business, you take what resonates with you and let the rest go. And while I still wasn't sure about Sonia's work, it was interesting to consider. During the conference, I had an opportunity to meet Sonia as we passed each other in the hall. I told her my sister-in-law was from Brazil, and my son had traveled there for business. I did not tell her that Lee had passed. Well, the conference turned out to be better than I expected, and I left feeling full of knowledge and with the conviction that life continues, and Lee still existed.

As the second WDD conference approached, Sonia published the latest images of loved ones that had come through. I knew of a couple of kids featured in the newly named Milligan e-mag 17 (physical medium, Scott Milligan had gifted Sonia with some much-needed equipment), so I looked at their images only. I was disappointed and maybe even a little jealous that Lee's image wasn't in there. To believe is one thing, but to have tangible proof your child is alive and well must be so healing. Little did I know!

A few weeks after the Orlando conference, Sandra mentioned there were a number of unknown images (images that somehow appear on their own) in the e-mag, so I decided to take a look. And there, the first unknown, on page 146, was Lee. It took my breath away like a punch in the gut. I knew in every fiber of my being it was him. I will never forget that moment. There was my little red-headed boy. Lee. He had transitioned at age 30, but, in the image, he appeared to be around age 12, with a bowl cut that was popular in his youth. I wasn't sure why he appeared so young, but I knew it was him!

My next move was to contact Sonia. I posted the image from the e-mag along with a photo of Lee, at age twelve, on her Facebook page and waited for a response. Soon after, I was contacted by Lisa, Sonia's assistant, in the United States. Lisa explained I had posted on the IPATI page, which is in Portuguese, so she rarely looks at it. But she did that day and saw my post. I told Lisa that Lee passed from an accidental carbon monoxide poisoning followed by his dog, Buddy, the next day. I explained how I felt Buddy had watched over Lee until we found him. She promised to have Sonia compare the photo and image and would let me know.

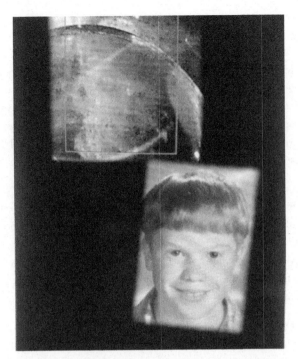

Lee appears with Buddy in Sonia Rinaldi's experiment

Lee and Buddy

It wasn't long before I received an email from Sonia to confirm the image was indeed Lee and that Buddy was there too! Next to Lee's head was a circled image. I looked closer and staring back at me were two eyes and a snout. Buddy! I couldn't believe my eyes. Undeniable proof that not only Lee and Buddy existed, but they were together. My heart was singing with this wonderful news! Lee was alive and well on another plane. I felt it. I knew it. It gave me such peace, hope, and comfort, but little did I know there was more to come.

Later that evening, I got a text from Lisa. She said she had a feeling to ask me about Lee's birthday. I tell her it's September 7, and we discover that Lee and Amber, her daughter in spirit, share a birthday. It's a wonderful synchronicity, but it's only the beginning of Lee and Amber's connection.

The next day, while in the car, with my hands on the wheel, my phone made a call to Lisa. We agreed, it must be the kids. When we finished our conversation, I turned on the radio. I hadn't listened to the radio since Lee's transition, but an Offspring song was playing. Offspring was Lee's favorite band, in high school, and the greatest hits CD was the first thing I pulled out of a box he had stored in his basement. Following Offspring was a Red Hot Chili Peppers song. Lee loved this band, and it was the last concert he attended a few months before his exit. I then switched stations, and there was another Chili Peppers song. Interesting. Coincidence? As I no longer believed in them, I felt Lee was telling me that all was well with him. I wasn't familiar with the next song, but when I heard the line, "I want you to be happier," I felt it was a message from Lee. He wanted me to be happy. And to top it off, I found out that my granddaughter was to sing Marshmello & Bastille's, *Happier*, in a concert a few days later.

Lee's story appeared in Sonia's e-mag 18 in late April. Soon after, I had a reading with renown certified medium, Isabella Johnson. Lee came through beautifully, and when I asked Isabella if Lee had appeared in Sonia's e-mag, he responded, "Duh, Mom," which is exactly something Lee would say, and it made me laugh.

A few months later, my husband had a dream visit. He said that Lee stood at the end of our bed, waving, and smiling. He had his arm around a dark-haired, beautiful young woman. He did not recognize her. Could it be Amber? I'd like to think so.

It was in June 2020 that I got a call from Lisa.

"I met your son in a trance meditation. Amber introduced us. He had red hair and was wearing work boots and a flannel shirt. Amber had her arm around a jacked-up

Lee and said he was the kind of guy she could have married, and that we sometimes live in the country, with a group of friends," Lisa said.

The flannel shirt stopped me short and put a little seed of doubt in my mind. After all, I had never seen Lee wear a flannel shirt, so I wasn't sure what to make of it. But I liked the idea that Lee was hanging out with Amber, so I accepted what Lisa said.

On Lee and Amber's shared birthday (September 7, 2020), I saw them in meditation. Lee was wearing a goofy birthday hat, which Amber grabbed off his head and put on her own. They were laughing, running, and free. It was a wonderful gift.

I had a reading with the well-known medium, Ann Van Orsdel, on Lee's birthday, in 2021. Lee came through immediately, and Ann started to describe how he appeared. She said he was wearing work boots, which were muddy from waking in the woods. But when she said he was wearing a flannel shirt, my jaw dropped. A flannel shirt? I couldn't believe it! She went on to tell me that Lee said, "We sometimes live in the country." We? Those were the very words Lisa had said to me. Ann then asked if I had ever owned a Lab because there was one with Lee. I told her no, and Ann replied, "well, there's one with him." We decided to let it go, and hopefully, something would come to mind. Later that day, I had a thought to contact Lisa.

"Did you ever own a Lab," I asked her?

"Yes."

One more synchronicity and I have a strong feeling there's more to come!

I cannot explain Sonia's process any more than I can explain wormholes, but Lee's unexpected appearance as an unknown in e-mag 17 and the ensuing synchronicities are all the proof I need that life does not end.

As human and spirit we are all part of an intricate weave of connection, and whether you notice them or not, and no matter what you call them, the signs, synchronicities, and coincidences are all around us. You just have to pay attention, trust, and beLEEve.

About the Author

Rosanne Groover Norris lives in Windsor, NY. She is the mother of five children, with one in spirit. She is also grandmother to six. She considers them all to be her best accomplishment in life. She is the author of beLEEve, A Journey of Loss, Healing, and Hope, and a contributor to the anthology, Ordinary Oneness, The Simplicity Everyday Love, Grace, and Hope. She recently appeared in the documentary Rinaldi, which chronicles the work of afterlife, Brazilian researcher, Sonia Rinaldi. Additionally, Rosanne is currently writing her second book.

Lee in his favorite green sweater

"Every subatomic interaction consists of the annihilation of the original particles and the creation of new subatomic particles. The subatomic world is a continual dance of creation and annihilation, of mass changing into energy and energy changing into mass. Transient forms sparkle in and out of existence, creating a never-ending, forever newly created reality."
~Gary Zukav~
Author
"The Dancing Wu Li Masters: An Overview of the New Physics"
in 1979

Follow the Signs, *Elly Sheykhet*

By Elly Sheykhet

I am a mother whose daughter was brutally murdered. I am not a professional writer, and English is my second language. Even in my own language, I have never possessed exceptional writing skills. I am just one bereaved mother with a broken heart, living my life that's been forever changed and trying to help those who were thrown onto a path of life that feels impossible to survive. I wrote my book One Year After to deliver a message of hope to other grieving parents. It is my wish that my story will become part of someone else's survival guide and give people a better understanding of how they can help their families and friends who are suffering the loss of their loved ones.

My husband Yan, our kids Artem and Alina, and I came to the United States from Russia in December of 2000. Our son was 8 years old, and Alina was only 3. America welcomed us, and we believed that living here would open doors and create opportunities and possibilities for us to build a happy life with a promising future for our kids. The language barrier made it more difficult to travel through those doors, and we all had to work and study hard.

Over the years, my husband and I built a solid foundation for our kids to start independent lives of their own. By 2017, our kids had accomplished so much. Our son graduated from college, got a good job, got married, and was enjoying a happy life with his wife, Kate, and their newborn daughter, Angelina. Our daughter, a talented performer on many stages, was a junior at the University of Pittsburgh, studying to become a Doctor of Physical Therapy. Vibrant, sensitive, and beautiful, she was suddenly taken away from us at the age of 20. And with that, our happy lives and promising futures ended.

I have been asked many times how I was able to continue my life after it turned in such an unimaginable direction. In my book, I want to reveal how I survived after discovering the breathless body of my child. I want to share all the feelings, emotions, and experiences that I faced in the year following her death.

Signs

Odd things started happening soon after Alina passed.

I remember how shocking it was when the big portrait of Alina fell off the TV stand where we had temporarily put it before hanging it on the wall. It just randomly fell as if someone had pushed it off the stand.

We had a very nice wall clock in the dining room. It was a housewarming gift from our friends. Every hour it played a song by The Beatles, and little figures danced. One day, about six months before Alina died, the clock stopped running. Yan's uncle, a professional horologist who could repair watches and clocks, tried but was unable to fix our clock due to a complicated mechanism that required replacement parts he couldn't find anywhere. For a few months, it hung silently on the wall. One evening, a few days after the funeral, Yan and I were quietly sitting in the living room. Suddenly, we heard the music play. We both got chills. The sad strains of *Yesterday* were coming from our clock. We got silent for a moment ourselves. Then we ran to our dining room to check the clock and make sure we were not losing our minds. The clock was running. Unblinkingly, we stared at the mysterious clock and watched its figures dance to the music of the well-known song by The Beatles.

"Yesterday

All my troubles seemed so far away

Now it looks as though they're here to stay

Yesterday

Love was such an easy game to play

Now I need a place to hide away

Oh, I believe in yesterday"

One night, I was slowly walking upstairs, carrying my phone. I felt physically and emotionally exhausted. I could hardly breathe and had no strength to lift my legs to take the next step up. Suddenly, a voice screamed out of my phone. "Can you hear me now? Can you hear me?" It seemed the volume was at its highest. I flinched and almost dropped my phone. Despite my weakness, I bolted up the stairs and tried to shut the phone off with my shaking fingers. I sat on my bed and, with wide eyes, stared at my phone. My heart was pumping. I had no idea what had happened. I must have touched an app and started some random video.

I sat on my bed for a while and could not move. Then I opened my Facebook. To my surprise, the smiling face of Adam Lambert was the first thing that popped up. Alina knew that I was a big fan.

I don't remember if Adam Lambert had ever popped up on my Facebook. Seeing his face right after having heard such an odd message from my phone intrigued me. Adam was wearing a red-hot leather jacket and holding a purple microphone. I pushed the play button and heard "Mama." I immediately got chills all over my body. He was singing a song by Freddie Mercury.

"Mama, just killed a man

Put a gun against his head

Pulled my trigger, now he's dead

Mama, life had just begun

But now I've gone and thrown it all away

Mama, ooh

Didn't mean to make you cry

If I'm not back again this time tomorrow

Carry on, carry on

As if nothing really matters"

I could not believe the words he was singing to me. I couldn't stop crying. I felt the presence of my daughter so much. I could see her smiling face and could hear her voice saying, "Mama, I didn't mean to make you cry… carry on as if nothing really matters."

A couple weeks after we had lost Alina, I woke one morning and wanted to check my Facebook. The first thing I saw was a post by a photographer I had never heard of. He wanted to share a picture of the most vibrant rainbow (in his words) that he had ever seen. It was a double rainbow. It looked beautiful. In no time I instinctively shifted my eyes to the very top of that rainbow, hoping to see my angel daughter in the sky. And in no time, I did see her.

To my own shocking surprise, I saw the figure of my daughter's upper body. I could clearly see her face and her long hair. With her left hand, she was holding her head, tilted to the side. Two huge, white wings were visible behind that figure. I felt like I was hallucinating. Yan was awake, so I quickly shoved my phone into his hands and demanded he look and tell me if he could see Alina above the rainbow. He took a quick look and in no time said, "Yes, I see her." I immediately felt some relief. I was glad I had not lost my mind, and I was not hallucinating.

When we had moved into our new house, Alina had wanted her room to be painted purple. Now, because purple is also the color for domestic violence awareness, purple had automatically become a sign from Alina. Purple was everywhere. It felt as though she was constantly trying to remind us of her.

Alina's birthday, 7/7/97, meant that her lucky number had to be 77. Along with purple, that number had become another sign from Alina. It was everywhere. Whenever Yan and I were driving, a car with a plate with 77 on it somewhere would be in front of us. A triple 7 or 7797 was like an extra special sign that always made us pause. Whenever we parked, a car next to us had 77 in its plate number. If we happened to park and there was not a car with 77 next to us, I would disappointedly ask Alina, "Hello, why aren't you here?" And believe it or not, when we came back, there would always be a car with 77 next to us.

Seeing 77 had become our norm. We would always smile and say, "Hi, dochka." I was sitting on our deck, staring at the sky one day, talking to her, and I asked how she was going to give me her 77 sign if I was not in a car and there were no cars around. A couple minutes later, I received a text message from my friend. She sent me a picture of a car driving in front of her. It had a 77.

Aside from the physical signs of her presence, my feelings could suddenly change for no reason. A short while after Alina was gone and the ugly feelings clung to me like a wet blanket, I noticed something very weird happening to me. I was in my office, feeling miserable. I was angry, scared, and upset all at once. I was trying to hold myself together and just do my work. Suddenly, I felt love and peace fill my mind and body. I got very confused. I could not explain why I felt that. I hated the whole world; I hated the fact that my daughter was gone; I hated myself and everything around me. In my present condition, I could not love anything or anyone. Yet suddenly, I was overwhelmed with the feeling of love. I could not understand where it came from or how it was even possible to feel peace and love when my daughter was dead, my heart was broken, and my entire being was shattered. That feeling didn't last long, but it made me feel calmer for the rest of the day.

The next day, I happened to read an article where a father shared his experiences of connecting with his deceased daughter. He described exactly what I had felt the previous day. He said that his daughter tried to integrate her energy into his so he could feel her presence and love. That wowed me. I didn't get that sudden feeling of love very often, but when I did, I was no longer confused. I knew it was my daughter trying to integrate her loving energy with me. Those acts of such beautiful integration helped me get through the most difficult of days.

Synchronicity soon became my norm too. In the beginning, it was very odd when I noticed that my thoughts and conversations were being repeated by other people, as if my questions were being answered through books, TV, Facebook, or other people saying random things. Facebook was especially weird. Random stuff was always popping up and oddly matching the events of that day. I could have a conversation with my friends, discussing some sensitive topic, and a random picture or a quote related to that topic would pop up. What I was eating, saying, seeing, or hearing would always pop up on my Facebook feed later. It really felt as if I was being watched and told, "I know what you're doing."

At first, I thought it was a weird coincidence. But those things happened every day, and it was too obvious and impossible to ignore. After having visited a dentist, I scrolled through my Facebook, wondering what I might see related to that. I expected a picture of someone's big smile showing their teeth or a toothpaste commercial or an advertisement for a dentist's office. But what popped up on my Facebook made me laugh. One woman had shared a picture of bloody dental tools, and they looked identical to the tools that my doctor had used working on my mouth. Why that woman had shared such a disgusting picture, I had no idea, but I knew that it was a message just for me. "Don't doubt it, Mom, I do know you went to the dentist."

All these messages were unique and often very funny. They matched Alina's personality. And every time I received them, it would give me those chills that made me feel her presence.

Holidays were the hardest to handle. It was too painful to stay home on Christmas, so I booked a little getaway vacation with Artem and his family. We were going to Myrtle Beach, SC. During the whole drive there, I felt the presence of a guardian angel. I asked myself if I was making it up. The feeling of his presence was very strong, and I could not deny it. I quietly sat in the passenger's seat, trying not to let Yan know that I was distracted by such a strange feeling.

I felt the presence of a big dude with a long beard and mustache. He wore a long coat with a belt tied under his big belly. I felt as if our car had been wrapped in his strong arms, protecting us from any possible damage like an impermeable bubble that anything coming toward our car would bounce off of. I felt very safe and secure. But I felt very uncomfortable revealing this feeling to Yan. I started telepathically talking to that being. I asked him if he was our guardian angel. I immediately felt his answer as a "yes." I asked where Alina was. He telepathically said that Alina was very busy taking care of other important things and had asked him to be our guardian angel during our travel time. He felt like a very kind and funny guy. I asked what his name was and was very intrigued by the answer given to me.

153

"Robert" was clearly imprinted in my mind. I smirked as I talked to myself. "Robert? Seriously? Who the heck is Robert?" That name didn't sound familiar. And if I was making it up, I probably would have chosen some other name that I knew better. Just to be sure that I was not making it up, I asked one more time what his name was. No other names other than Robert felt right to me. So, Robert was our guardian angel whom our daughter had sent to protect us while we traveled. It made me smile. I was overwhelmed by the amazing feeling of being connected with the universe, and I could not hide it.

Yan looked at me suspiciously and asked if I was ok. I couldn't stay quiet any longer. I asked him not to think I was crazy and revealed what I had been feeling. My husband had gotten used to my stories and didn't think I had lost my mind. He just softly smiled and pointed to the car passing us: 77 was on its plate.

We parked at the hotel garage, and while Yan unloaded the car, I crazily shifted my eyes from one car to another through the whole garage looking for a 77. I was disappointed by not seeing any. I got a little upset, thinking Alina must have been really busy. As we approached the hotel entrance, I almost jumped when I saw a car parked right next to the entrance: 777 was excitedly screaming at me, "Hello, Mother! Don't you worry. I am here!"

We got to our room, and Artem turned on the TV. Shocked, he said, "Mom, look." There was a commercial showing the number 777-7777. It was not shocking to me though; it confirmed one more time that Alina was with us.

I could not get "Robert" out of my mind and tried to find that name somewhere as a validation to my car experience, but such a name had not been found anywhere in the hotel, so I stopped looking and almost forgot about it.

Two days later, we went to a pirate show. We parked at the theater, and there was our favorite 77 on a car nearby. At the entrance, we were greeted by a crew in purple outfits. We took our seats in row A. Dinner would be served during the show. I looked at the tag on our table and was speechless. It said, "Thank you. Your server's name is ROBERT." I silently looked at Yan to check if he had seen the tag yet and met his wide eyes expressing, "Oh my God, I did see it."

The show started. A big pirate ship was the stage. The main character, a young pirate girl, appeared at the top of the ship. She had a petite, beautifully built body. Her hair

154

was dark, perfectly straight, and long. Her eyes seemed dark too. Her grace gave me chills. She could have been my daughter's twin. A pirate captain joined the scene. He was a big dude with a long beard and mustache. And he was wearing a long coat with a belt tied under his big belly.

Spiritual Walk

A very nice trail stretched all along the river just steps away from my office. Every day I would take a walk during lunch time. The trail was always busy. People were walking, running, biking, or walking their dogs. The weird thing was that the animals and birds started acting oddly toward me. One bird suddenly flew out of nowhere to cross the road right in front of my face. Another bird did a little dance, flying in circles right above my head, and then quickly flew away. One time, as I was walking, some weird bird was flying very low toward me, about to cause a head-on collision. And if I hadn't tilted my head to the side, it would have hit me. Another time, a butterfly flew right next to me, acting like it was my walking partner.

The squirrels always made noises, trying to get my attention. They were not afraid of me and always stared into my eyes. A squirrel came out of the bushes one day and ran toward me. I stopped and reached out my hand while the squirrel looked very deep into my eyes and almost let me pet it.

The birds' and other animals' behavior was unlike normal animal behavior. I read in one of my books that spirits could play with the energies of low-vibrating creatures and make them act in a way that would get our attention. This was one of their ways of letting us know they were here. Knowing that my daughter was making these birds and animals act weird always made me smile.

Sometimes it was way too funny, and I could not hold back my laughing, saying, "Alina, seriously?" One day there was a goofy raccoon running around. The other day, I saw a little animal sticking its head out of a hole. I stopped to take a picture of it. Suddenly it came out of the hole completely, quickly peed, and went back into the hole. I laughed so much.

A lot of people seemed to be wearing purple shirts all the time, too, as if no other color was permitted on the trail. They had tied their shoes with bright purple shoelaces, and their dogs had purple leashes. At first it seemed like I was losing my mind. I remembered one day I was walking with my head spinning around, thinking,

"What the heck is going on?" As I kept walking, I asked my daughter, "Alina, is it you who's making all of this?"

"Oh yeah, sure," I heard a loud answer from the guy who was passing me and talking on the phone.

Every day I walked the same way, and every time I got different signs. One day it was a puddle shaped as a heart. Another day I saw a lock with a heart attached to a bridge that I crossed on my way. Hearts were literally everywhere in the sky and on the ground. One day I saw "I love you" written in chalk, and another day it was "You are doing great" with a smiley face.

I remember one day I was not feeling great at all, and while walking I asked, "Where are you, dochka? Just tell me please where you are." Then I looked straight, and there was a big purple arrow on an electric pole. The arrow was pointing to the sky, pointing to where my daughter was. I started crying. I lost the desire to walk and turned around to go back to the office. Then I got an urge to turn back and walk a little farther. I did. On my way, there was a little rock, a colorful rock with a painted sun and the word "shine" written on it. I picked it up and brought it back to my office. I knew it was a present from my daughter, my beautiful shining light.

Every day I was so excited to take my spiritual walk and connect with my daughter. I could not wait for lunch time. I had such an unexplainable feeling that she was waiting for me there. The moment I stepped on the trail, I would say, "Hi, dochka, I am here." My daughter would give me different signs or telepathically answer my questions. Some days she just silently walked beside me, and I could feel her soft tiny hand holding mine.

One day when I had stepped on the trail right after saying "hello" to my daughter, my mind got very loud. It felt like there was a parade going on. Suddenly, I felt the presence of so many people marching and carrying flags. They were loud. My daughter was leading the crowd.

She was laughing and excitingly saying, "Oh my God, Mom, I am on a special mission with my friends now. We came down for six days to visit our moms and let them know we are here. You're the first one whom we have visited because I told my friends that you're so easy to connect with. Good job, Mom, you have figured it out. But other moms have not, so I can't stay long. I have to go. See you later, Mom."

Then it became quiet. I could not believe what I had experienced. It felt so real and had made me happy.

This trail had become a part of my life, and it was a vital therapy for my grieving process. The days when the connection did not happen brought me to a very dark place. To keep going on with life, I needed to stay connected with my daughter all the time.

Mediums

I had read so many stories about people's experiences with mediums and wanted to have my own. I desperately wanted to get a reading with a medium and get a message from my daughter.

One of the mediums I had been following on Facebook offered monthly reading circles. It was like a one-hour conference call where people could call in and she would give each person a reading. One evening I joined that reading circle. There were seven people there. One by one, the medium gave messages to everyone who had joined. I nervously listened to the messages she gave to the others. She finally called my name. I was the only new person in the circle; all the others had been joining every month. The medium had no idea who I was or what was happening in my life.

"Ok, Elly," she said, starting my reading. "You have been through a lot lately. They show me a water mill. It means you've been struggling so much dealing with the ups and downs, and your downs are very rough. Seems like you're dealing with a tragedy."

I just simply said, "Yes."

She continued, "I got a dad figure for you. Is your dad on the other side?"

I said, "No. But my father-in-law is."

"You must have had a very close relationship with him then. I feel the energy of a father."

I said, "Yes, we were very close."

"He is a very serious, smart, and intelligent man. He showed up wearing a very conservative black suit. He must be either Amish or Jewish."

I could not believe what she had said. The only father figure with a Jewish background who it could be was Yan's dad.

I said, "Yes, my father in-law was Jewish."

"He is saying that you're on the right path with what you're doing, and he is very proud of you. He just tipped his hat off his head. It means he bows to you."

I was speechless.

"Hmm, it does not match his serious appearance, but I hear nonstop laughing around him. I feel such bubbly energy with him."

I cried. Who else could that be other than my bubbly, silly girl with her infectious laugh?

Then the medium said, "I hear a name. Sounds like Maria."

I got chills all over my body. Maria was the name of Yan's grandma. Alina's lovely babushka who had transitioned right after Alina. I could not believe it; I was crying.

It was very nice to get a message from my father-in-law, but I desperately needed to connect with my daughter. I kept trying.

A random advertisement popped up on my Facebook. There was one company located in California that offered a psychic medium service by phone. A few mediums from California Psychics were giving a discount. I really wanted to schedule an appointment but was contemplating. I thought that they could simply google my name and get all the info about Alina. I scrolled through the pictures of their professionals, trying to find the one who might fit my needs better.

My eyes stopped at a picture of one lady who looked very kind and had such a nice, genuine smile. I read her info and got a warm feeling. She was the one. She had the ability to connect with loved ones on the other side. She had an appointment available with a waiting time of one hour. I was not sure if one hour was good enough to google my name, but I got a feeling that I could trust it. I put my info in. And I was supposed to get a call at my scheduled time in one hour.

Two minutes later to my surprise, my phone rang. It was the lady.

I knew there was no way she could have found any info about me in two minutes. I felt very positive and open; I was ready to get a message from the other side.

The lady's voice complemented her picture. I was not disappointed in my expectations. Her tone was comforting to me. She asked my name and what I was looking for. I said that I needed to get a message from my daughter. She asked my daughter's name and when she had transitioned. Then she told me that she could not guarantee that Alina would make a connection. She explained that it was just like when we dial a number — it was not guaranteed that the person would answer your phone call. She asked me to take a deep breath and think of my daughter. Then she said a prayer and spoke.

"Alina, Alina. Pick up your phone, sweetheart, your mom wants to talk to you."

I patiently waited.

It took her a while. Then she said, "Ok, Alina is here."

I almost dropped the phone. I started shaking.

"Your daughter's age is between twenty to thirty years old. Is that right?"

"Yes, Alina is twenty."

"She is showing me a fluffy toy… it's a fluffy puppy. Does that mean anything to you?"

"Oh my God, yes, it's her dog Benji."

"She is showing me a candy. Do you know what it could mean?"

"I don't know, but her dad has a sweet tooth, and she liked buying him a special candy and always baked a special cake for him."

"Please tell your husband that his daughter is saying a special hello to him."

I could not hold back my tears.

"She is running now. Was she a runner? Did she like sports?"

"No. She never was a sporty girl. And actually, she was unable to run because of her knee injury."

"I don't know, but she keeps running. Alina, why are you running, sweetheart? Your mom does not understand."

I had no idea what it could mean. All I knew was that Alina could not run, but the lady didn't want to drop it and kept going.

"Why are you running, sweetheart? Tell us why you keep running." Then she changed her tone and said, "Oh, I see... someone is hiding around the corner. She is running AWAY. She is running away from the relationship."

With my shaky voice, I said, "Yes, that's exactly what she was doing."

"It happened very sudden. She was not sick, and she did not take her own life. She is saying that someone deliberately did that to her."

I was crying and validated her with a short "Yes."

"She is saying that she is very sorry and that she did not know that he had planned that. She is showing me a lot of police now."

"Yes, Alina was murdered." I could not stop crying.

"Oh, my goodness, Elly, I'm very sorry, I'm very sorry. Alina is dancing now. She keeps circling in her dancing, and she is smiling. And I hear some name. Marr? Mary? Maria! Alina says that Maria misses you too."

Then she said that Alina said that she loved me, but she needed to go. The medium appreciated my call and said that she was going to pray for me and my daughter. And she asked me to look at the wall right after I hung up the phone.

I hung up and looked at the wall. The foggy image of Alina's face appeared. I stared speechlessly at the wall, watching the image slowly fade away. I was in shock. For a good ten minutes, I sat without blinking or moving. I was in deep shock.

The connection with my daughter is becoming stronger each day.

From my own experience, if you're a newly bereaved mother or father, I know nothing would sound right to you and no advice would be needed. But please believe that your soul and your body know what to do. Just be open and listen to your soul. Your beautiful soul will lead you, and you will find your way, your own unique way.

With the guidance of my daughter, I have found mine…

Excerpts are from "One Year After: From Grief to Hope" by Elly Sheykhet, Alina's Light Publishing, May 9, 2020

Alina and Elly

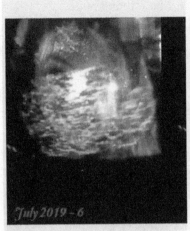

July 2019 - 6

Alina's afterlife trans-image discovered by Elly in the
documentary, *Rinaldi*, about Sonia Rinaldi and her work
by We Don't Die Films, February 22, 2022. The same documentary in which
Rosanne Groover Norris and the trans-image of her son, Lee, appear, and the
trans-image of Camille Dan's son, Aaron appears,
mentioned in the previous two chapters.

About the Author

Elly Sheykhet was born in Ivanovo, Russia, and spent her childhood alongside her
parents and two brothers. After finding love and getting married, Elly moved to the
United States in 2000 with her husband Yan and two beautiful children, Artem and
Alina. In 2003, Elly obtained her Associate Degree in Accounting at Pittsburgh's
ICM School of Business. Also, Elly holds a Masters Degree in Economics that she

earned in Russia and validated in the U.S. After losing her 20-year-old daughter Alina in a senseless act of violence in 2017, Elly and her husband founded Alina's Light, a non-profit organization established in her memory. This organization is very dear to the Sheykhets and is often referred to by Elly as "her child." The mission of Alina's Light, among others, is to give voice to the victims of domestic violence through the arts, community events, and charitable actions. Elly is a published author of, One Year After, and The Beauty of a Grieving Mother, Alina's Light Publishing 2021. She serves as a Certified Grief Coach and has dedicated her life to honoring her daughter by helping others. She hopes to brighten the world in Alina's memory. Elly cherishes the time she spends with family and is a proud grandmother.

Website: www.alinaslight.com

Alina

*"Everything we call real is made of things
that cannot be regarded as real.
If quantum mechanics hasn't profoundly
shocked you, you haven't understood it yet."
~Niels Bohr~
Nobel Prize Winning
Physicist
1885 – 1962*

How Unlikely? Using Reverse Probabilities in Mediumship Research, *Piero Calvi-Parisetti MD*

By Piero Calvi-Parisetti, MD

Based on extraordinary amounts of empirical evidence, gathered for nearly two centuries by some of mankind's finest scientific minds, a rational person can, if he or she wants, believe in life afterlife. Such evidence comes from about a dozen different fields of investigation, including near-death and end-of-life experiences, after-death communication, and reincarnation. It coherently and consistently supports the hypothesis that, in a way which we do not understand, significant aspects of human personality survive bodily death.

Seemingly unbelievable, the survival hypothesis is the one that accounts for most of the data and is, in fact, less unbelievable than some of the alternatives which have been proposed to explain away the data.

Whilst after-death communication is often presented as an individual area of investigation, the term covers a range of diverse phenomena, each one producing considerable amounts of compelling evidence. Apparitional experiences, hauntings and poltergeists, mental and physical mediumship, cross-correspondences, and instrumental trans-communication are all about interaction between the world of the living and the world of the so-called dead. However, they are subjects of such size and complexity that they can be considered as separate disciplines in psychical research.

Within the masses of evidence consistent with the survival hypothesis, for various reasons, mental mediumship has a primary role. First, it is possibly the best known, as great numbers of people have been exposed to evidential mediumship, either in a private sitting or during a public demonstration. The quantity of anecdotal evidence supporting the idea that gifted mediums "talk to the dead" is phenomenal. Second, it is also quite possibly the most thoroughly investigated. Already since the Victorian era, at the end of the 19th century, a range of techniques, from the very simple to the highly sophisticated, have been employed by psychical researchers to make sure that mediums could not acquire information about the discarnate being "read" through normal means. Despite such controls, in a great many cases, detailed information about deceased loved ones was consistently produced, adding considerable weight to the body of evidence. Then, from the 1980s, mediumship research moved into the laboratory, where researchers have direct control on most – if not all – the factors affecting the phenomenon. More than a dozen replications of an increasingly sophisticated experimental protocol involving multiple layers of blinding were carried out, the latest one involving as many as five levels of separation between the medium and the sitter for which the reading is intended. The results of these experiments are unequivocal: research mediums can produce information which is both specific (it is recognised by the intended sitter but not by others) and accurate (it is recognised by the sitter as correct).

This chapter briefly introduces a little-known and, unfortunately, seldom utilised technique which is both very simple and very effective for evaluating the quality of a mediumship reading. Its results can be so powerful in evidential terms that it can also allow drawing conclusions about the overall mediumship phenomenon. Although it rests on quintessentially qualitative judgments, these judgments are used in a quantitative way so that general comparisons can be made with the kind of results produced by the methods of natural science. This technique is called reverse probabilities.

In essence, the technique aims at evaluating how unlikely it is that the information provided in the course of a mediumship reading, taken as a whole, could have been produced by simple guessing. In order to explain how it works, we will use a real-life example – a private reading by Scottish superstar medium Gordon Smith filmed by a BBC crew as part of the 2004 documentary Talking to the Dead (February 2022 https://www.youtube.com/watch?v=mKYo8Gp9pzo). This reading provides the ideal setting to employ the reverse probabilities techniques, as the medium makes a relatively large number of precise statements, and essentially all of them are recognised by the sitters.

For the purpose of this chapter, exactly as it is done in laboratory mediumship research, Gordon Smith's reading for the bereaved couple Greta and Andrew Rhodes will be itemised. That means simply that each statement the medium makes is captured by a short sentence, which is called an "item". As per the reverse probabilities technique, for each individual item we will ask the question, "How likely is it that the medium could have said that by just guessing"?

It is very important to understand that the answers to these questions are indeed personal, subjective, and therefore entirely qualitative. Every person looking at the same items and answering the same questions will most probably give a different answer. The power of the technique, however, is that in the end, this subjectivity – and the inherent qualitative nature of the data produced – will not stand in the way of drawing quantitative conclusions. Or, rather, the conclusions will remain essentially subjective and qualitative, but, as we will see, regardless of the answers given to each individual item, the total odds against chance are so spectacularly high that meaningful comparisons with exact quantitative studies can be made.

Here follows a description of the process the author of this chapter engages in while looking at the sitting in question (items italicised).

I. *Gordon says that the deceased person was a young man.* This is correct. If he was guessing, he would have had a 50/50 chance on the sex, and, say, another 50/50 chance on the age – he could have said a boy, and instead, he correctly said "young man".

At this initial stage, the odds against chance are therefore one in four.

2. *Gordon mentions the name, Andrew.* Immediately and directly – he does not "fish" for information, for instance, by saying something like "I see a name beginning with 'A'". This is also correct – it is the father's name. What is the chance of getting that right by guessing? Shall we say, conservatively, one in 50?

This is the moment at which the reverse probabilities technique starts showing its potential. We have two statements made by the medium and recognised by the sitters.

The author assigned odds against chance of 1 in 4 and 1 in 50, respectively. Therefore, at this early stage, we already have combined odds against chance of 1 in 200. This means that there is one probability in 200 that the medium would have made two correct statements by guessing alone. That is considered highly significant in science.

After considering only two items, the "weight" of the judgment of odds against chance for individual items is still very high. Different observers looking at the same two statements would have made different judgments, and this would have obviously made a difference on the cumulative odds against chances. As we continue, we will see that the relative impact of subjective judgment calls drops drastically.

3. The third item is a character description, which the author considers too general to be of significance. It is therefore ignored.

4. Next, there is a specific reference to the dales (open valleys), which is recognized by the parents as correct. He could have mentioned the sea, or a lake, or a river, or any other geographical feature. But he mentioned hills, and not rugged hills, but specifically the dales. What's the likelihood of guessing that by chance? Let's give it a very optimistic one in eight. We are looking now at combined odds against a chance of 1 in 1,600.

5. The happy birthday mum statement is also considered too generic and therefore ignored.

6. The fourth meaningful piece of information is another name. Gordon says Margaret or Margarita, which is not recognized. But then, after a few seconds, he corrects that to Greta, which is indeed the mother's name. It's not spot-on but remarkably close, especially considering that Greta is not a common name. To be, again, very conservative, the author would give this an odds-against-chance of 1 in 25. After four pieces of information, we have total odds against chance of 1 in 40,000.

7. The fifth piece of information is about the son's passing, which is correctly described as quick. Let's say that it was a lucky guess – the son may have died of a cancer, for instance, which makes for a slower passing – and give it odds of 1 in 2. Combined odds are now at 1 in 80,000.

8. The sixth piece of information is geographical: Ilkley is mentioned and recognized as relevant. What's the chance of that? Extremely small, the author believes, with all the locations in the UK, Gordon could have chosen, but he will only give it 1 in 100, which brings the combined odds at 1 in 8,000,000.

9. Then comes information about a Jack Russell dog, which the author considers very general – plus, the dog had not been there in life but was only a desire of the deceased son. Very meaningful for the parents, but the author will only give it a 1 in 2 chance. Combined odds at 1 in 16,000,000.

10. Then there is a mention of the watch that somebody has been wearing. This is apparently a banal piece of information but evidently recognized as evidential by the parents. It's not that difficult to throw a guess about the watch of a deceased person, so again the author will only give it a chance of only 1 in 2. Combine odds at 1 in 32,000,000.

11. The son is then described as hyperactive, multitasking. Again, quite a generic piece of information, which still appears to be very relevant to the parents. The author will give it another 1 in 2 chance. Combined odds at 1 in 64,000,000.

12. The following statement is about the son having changed his hairdo just before dying. Of all the things the medium could have said… The author considers this a really difficult one to guess and gives it a 1 in 50 chance. Combined odds at this stage are 1 in 3.2 billion. We will now stop mentioning combined odds until the final computation.

13. The next item is the mention of a tattoo, which again is recognized as relevant. A tattoo is not that uncommon, and the author gives it a chance of 1 in 10.

14. What can be considered as the final blow comes next. The son's name is mentioned as Nige, not Nigel, but Nige. No asking, no fishing around. Direct, straight to the point. The author considers that a minimum 1 in 100 chance.

15. The next item concerns a gallery of pictures being set up at home. That is quite specific, but one may guess it's something that bereaved parents may do. Let's say 1 chance in 4.

16. There is then a reference to somebody who has been looking at sunglasses. Clearly meaningful to the parents and relatively specific. He could have said

umbrellas, or hats, or shoes – anything really. The author gives it 1 in 10 chance of guessing it right.

17. Gordon mentions the little lane nearby where you live. This appears generic, but perhaps it's not. In a countryside or suburbia environment, that's normal. But in an urban environment, that's not. Gordon doesn't know where the parents live and could not have easily made that call. The author gives it a 1 in 4 chance.

18. Finally, there is mention of a card and of a specific phrase written on it. The mother says she had written that the previous week. The chances of guessing this particular combination are likely to be very low. In the author's judgment, at least 1 in one 100.

So, to recap, 18 pieces of information provided by a medium to a couple he had never seen before were examined. Two were discarded as too generic, and 16 were retained for reverse probabilities analysis. It is important to stress that a) the information was provided in the course of a continued conversation; b) no questions were asked by the medium at any point; there was no probing, no hesitation; and c) all the pieces of information were recognized by the couple. The author evaluated each piece of information, estimating how likely it is that the medium got it right by chance. The author was conservative in these estimates.

At the end of the process, the cumulative odds against chance came to 1 in 51,200,000,000,000,000.

This extraordinarily large number shows the usefulness of the reverse probability technique. Given that odds against chance of 1 in 20 are considered significant in natural science and 1 in 100 highly significant, it is obvious that the subjective nature of individual estimates is essentially irrelevant. As already noted, it is most likely that different observers would give different estimates when looking at the individual items. At the end of the process, however, the combined figure would always end up having 9, 12, or 15 zeroes. In this sense, the author maintains that, although based on a subjective, judgmental, qualitative process, the reverse probabilities technique applied to multiple items as described produces figures which are so prodigiously large that they can be compared with the exact, quantitative results produced by natural science research.

In pharmacology research, for instance, it is customary to compare the effectiveness of a new drug to a placebo. If studies do indeed show that a difference is there and the effect size is large enough, using exact binomial probabilities scientists can determine how likely it is that the effect was due to chance. As noted above, odds against chance of 1 in 20 (0.05 or 5%) is considered significant and 1 in 100 (0.01 or 1%) highly significant. Anything lower than 5% and the new drug can pursue its travel to commercial availability: studies have shown that there is an effect, and the effect is unlikely to be due to chance.

When reverse probabilities in mediumship research show odds against chances in the thousands (or hundreds of thousands, or thousands of thousands, depending on the observer) of billions, the phenomenon recently defined Anomalous Information Reception can be said to have been conclusively demonstrated.

About the Author

Scottish/Italian author and speaker Piero Calvi-Parisetti is a medical doctor originally specialising in Public Health and Disaster Management. At the beginning of his career, employed by the International Red Cross and the United Nations, he worked in the management of large-scale humanitarian aid operations in Africa, Asia, and the former Soviet Union. At the end of 2000, he moved from field operations to the classroom, taking up a late academic career. Until 2015, he was Professor of Emergencies and Humanitarian Action at Milan University (Italy) and a visiting professor at several other universities.

In 2004, a simple anecdote narrated by his wife triggered an intellectual interest, at first, and then a true scholarly passion for psychical research, especially for the study of scientific evidence pointing to the survival of human personality of bodily death. By digesting some 30,000 pages of literature, attending international conferences and study days, interviewing the researchers, and even training personally with one of his intellectual heroes, Dr. Raymond Moody (the first physician to write about Near-Death Experiences in 1975), Dr. Parisetti became convinced that mind and consciousness cannot be reduced to the activity of the brain, and, in a way which we do not understand, they survive the death of the body.

In 2008, he published his first book, 21 Days into the Afterlife, hailed by NY Times bestselling author Michael Prescott as "The best introduction I have seen to the survival hypothesis." His other books are Adventures in Psychical Research (2011) and Apparitions – Proof of Survival (2014). In 2012 he produced a self-help workbook with an accompanying 8-hour video course and donated it to the Forever Family Foundation, a non-religious, not-for-profit organisation strong of over 12,000 members worldwide, which is dedicated to furthering the knowledge of afterlife science among the bereaved. His latest book, Step into the Light, is directed towards those who are in fear of death, their own or a loved one's, and provides a detailed description of the process of dying and what comes afterward based on scientifically validated sources.

Website: www.drparisetti.com/

> *"The total number of minds*
> *in the universe is one."*
> *~Erwin Schrodinger~*
> *Nobel Prize Winning*
> *Physicist*
> *1887 – 1961*

A Spiritual Reawakening, *Sherry Gallant*

By Sherry Gallant, The Wellness Medium

The one thing we all can agree on is that Life is so unpredictable. It's full of ups and downs. But there are some experiences that are life changing. They make us question our core values. They create a shift in our perspective. They are life changing.

March 22 of 2002 was the day that changed my life forever, it changed my perspective on life emotionally, spiritually, and mentally. It's the day I realized why I exist. My purpose in life.

Spring had sprung 2 days before. The skies were blue, and the sun was shining brightly., It was a beautiful Spring morning. I had dropped my son off at school and met my husband, Jim, for breakfast at a nearby restaurant. After breakfast, I realized I need to pick up a gift for a shower I was invited to that coming Sunday. I said goodbye to my husband and started driving to a shopping mall that was not too far away.

I was driving on a four-lane highway. Two lanes going North and two lanes going South. I was driving in the Southbound lanes. As I was driving, I noticed a car at a stop sign on a street on the Southeast side of the highway. His left turn signal was flashing that he was going to pull out into the Southbound lanes, the one I was driving in. I looked ahead and saw, an 18-wheel transport truck heading North on the inside lane and thought to myself, I hope this man at the stop sign isn't going to pull out into traffic and try and beat this 18-wheeler truck and pull out. Well, he did. As he pulled out, he did beat the transport truck but didn't realize a pickup truck was coming up the outside lane passing the truck at a very high speed.

At that moment, everything I was seeing started coming to me in slow motion. I remember this car and pickup truck colliding and the car, in very slow motion. It was as if everything that was happening in the world had slowed completely down. I could see every detail of what was happening which, in real-time, I'm sure was seconds, but to me, it felt like forever. Everything dramatically slowed down. I remember speaking to myself saying, ok Sherry here he is. This car was only a short distance away from colliding with me. That's all I remember.

I heard a man at my side window saying, Miss, are you ok? I opened my eyes and just stared in a confusing manner. I remember the man telling me that help was on the way. I don't know how long I was there before emergency services arrived, but I remember thinking to myself, what just happened to me. I had felt like someone had taken me out of my car just before the impact and put me back in when it was all over. Something happened that I never had ever experienced before.

I felt someone putting something on my neck from the back seat. I realized there were a couple of firefighters preparing to remove me from the car. As I just sat there, I glanced a little over to the right and realized I was in a Graveyard, and right there, about 8-10 feet away from me was the gravesite of a very good friend of mine who tragically passed away. This was the gravesite of the man who I had named my son after.

I soon realized that this day was the start of my Spiritual Reawakening. The day where I had a new awakening, a new sense of who I was, what I was meant to do. A new sense of being in this world.

I truly believe we are all born with Intuition but as we get older, life happens. Children see and sense things up to about 5 or 6 years old then things change. We don't ever lose it, but we seem to put it up on the bookshelf until something dramatic happens and you are reawakened. Whether it's the loss of a loved one, an illness, an accident, or some other traumatic event.

I have always been one to be very intuitive growing up but, that spring day changed my life forever. I knew I was going to start and embark on a new journey, My journey. My destiny.

All the questions I used to ask myself. Who am I? What is my purpose? They were all going to be answered.

A year had passed. I had been attending Physiotherapy, was seeing a Psychologist for PTSD, and suffered from depression. I had a few other issues, but I was healthy and alive. I truly knew I had a guardian angel, my friend was watching and protecting me that day.

I hadn't been back to where the accident happened, but I knew I needed to go. I needed to go and say, "Thank you", to Butchy.

I arrived at the gravesite, it was a very cold, damp, and rainy spring day. I had brought some artificial flowers for him as a thank you. I sat there in my car waiting for this rain to either slow down or stop completely. As I sat staring out the window a light shined down from his gravesite to my car door. As if it were a sunshine walkway. I sat in awe. As I got out of my car I looked around and it was still pouring rain everywhere except between my car and his burial site. I could feel the warmth of the sun on my face, and I had this sense of lightness and peace come over me. I felt light, I felt blessed, and I felt the love.

I walked over to Butchy's burial site, and I laid the flowers on top of his stone. I looked down and said, "Thank you. Thank you from the bottom of my heart. I know that it was you who was watching over me that day." I walked to my car, got in, and drove away.

About the Author

Sherry Gallant is The Wellness Medium. Sherry allows herself to become a conduit or messenger for loved ones in spirit to relay messages to loved ones here on earth. She receives many testimonials from past clients thanking her for forever changing their lives. Sherry, however, can't take all the credit because it's not just her, the messages come from their loved ones in spirit. She is merely the messenger. Sometimes the readings have really been emotional for both Sherry and the client. "I have had people email me to tell me they were one day away from ending everything. That the reading completely changed their minds."

Website: www.sherrygallant.com

Instagram:
https://instagram.com/official_sherry_gallant?utm_medium=copy_link
Facebook: https://www.facebook.com/mediumsherrygallant
YouTube:
https://youtube.com/channel/UCAoA-ChhbdT0OPVur_xIc7Q

*"The important thing is not to stop questioning.
Curiosity has its own reason for existing.
One cannot help but be in awe when he contemplates
the mysteries of eternity, of life,
of the marvelous structure of reality.
It is enough if one tries merely to comprehend
a little of this mystery every day."
~Albert Einstein~
Nobel Prize Winning
Physicist
1879 – 1955*

My Beautiful Light, *Brian Smith*

By Brian Smith

Shayna Elayne Smith was born on a cold winter day, January 13, 2000. Shayna was loved before she arrived on the planet. Our second child, Shayna, was to be the little sister of Kayla, who adored her and spoke to her in utero, calling her "Baby Sist."

From the start, Shayna had complications. A prenatal test prompted us to do an amniocentesis. We knew she was a girl. So, we chose Shayna Elayne, Shayna meaning "Beautiful" and Elayne, after my godmother, meaning "Light." She would be our second and last child and complete our little family for this incarnation. Brian, Tywana, Kayla, and Shayna had finally arrived on the planet. The Smith family would be complete.

Shayna was born after 13 hours of labor. She pooped during the delivery, complicating matters. Her heart rate kept decelerating. I was just about to scream at the doctors, "Just do a C-section," when she finally chose to arrive.

From the very first hours, we knew Shayna would be a handful. The nurses on duty that night told us they had never heard a baby cry with such demand in her voice. When Shayna wanted something, she let you know. She could and would cry for hours to get her way if necessary. In addition to being determined, Shayna was skilled with her hands and blessed with a sharp wit and intellect. She spoke early and walked

176

early. I recall one day walking into the "toy room" and seeing a two-year-old Shayna staring up at a gigantic Lego tower she had built. She was on her knees, and it towered over her head. I said, "I hope she uses her powers for good, not for evil." Thank goodness that prayer was answered.

Shayna was three years younger than her older sister, Kayla. But they were soulmates and closer than many twins. Shayna looked up to Kayla. And Kayla felt responsible for Shayna. When Shayna was about three years old, she began sleeping in Kayla's bed many nights. They called them "sister sleepovers." It was a magical time I assumed would end when Kayla kicked her out, and Shayna would be heartbroken. I was wrong. It was Shayna who decided it was time to go back to her room. And the sister sleepovers ended with a whimper.

Shayna was a loving child. But she had a tongue that could cut just as quickly as it built you up. So, when Shayna started a sentence with "No offense, but...", it was time to take cover. I did most of the cooking and could expect a rating most nights on how I had done. The highest compliment was, "This meal is restaurant-worthy."

We homeschooled both girls through the eighth grade. So, for most of their school life, they did school together. Both took to learning like ducks to water. It was as if one day, we were teaching the alphabet. The next day they could read. Shayna did her best to keep up with Kayla academically, using her big sissy as a role model.

When the girls were about four and seven years old, they said something that indicated they knew about pre-life planning, something we had never discussed. I'm not even sure I was aware it was a thing. They had a conversation at the dinner table about being in heaven and seeing us and choosing us as their parents.

Shayna started playing basketball at the age of five years old. She played with kids in her grade for part of one season. Then, she told Tywana, her coach, that she didn't want to play with "the babies" anymore. So, she moved a year ahead in basketball and was a year ahead until she decided her basketball career was over at age 14. Shayna was always one of the coaches' favorites. In addition to her size (she played forward or center) and her natural athleticism, Shayna was a hard worker and a great listener. The girls were told if you were on the left side of the basket, you should make a left-handed layup. Most, if they could, would switch to their favorite hand.

Shayna never did. She was the best rebounder on the team and a tenacious defender. She would take a charge like a pro (and had two concussions to show for it).

In eighth grade, like her sister, Shayna said she wanted to go to public school. We told her eighth grade was a tough year to make the transition. She knew several of the girls at the local school through girl scouts. But Shayna had never attended public school. We worried that a new girl in eighth grade, particularly a Black girl in a predominantly white school district, would be accepted.

The next year, she said she wanted to go again. But she had been in scouts with girls who were going into eighth grade. Even though Shayna was academically advanced enough to go into high school, she chose to go to eighth grade to be with her friends. She took mostly ninth-grade classes. By the end of what would be her first and last year of high school, Shayna was sixteenth in her class of six hundred students. She was best friends with a group of six girls. Number fifteen in the class was in her group of highly accomplished friends. Shayna would tell her she was coming for her place in the class.

When Shayna was 14, she decided she was done with basketball and wanted to switch to playing volleyball. This was a major disappointment to the high school coach, who had his eye on Shayna since she had been in about third grade. She was to be the next center on the high school team and had been working with the current center as an apprentice. Shayna was 5'10-5'11" and still growing.

We told Shayna this would be a difficult transition. She had never played competitive volleyball. The high school season began in just three months. But we put her into a volleyball camp over the summer. She loved it. When fall tryouts came around, she tried out for the freshman team and made it. She would go on to start on the freshman team.

When AAU volleyball came around after the high school season was over, Shayna wanted to try out. Again, we tried to let her down gently. AAU is more competitive than high school, and she had just started playing volleyball. There are two levels, regional and national. When Shayna called from tryouts, we expect, at best, to hear she had made the regional team. However, they had offered her a spot on the national team (which was much more expensive and involved out-of-town travel to every game). We said yes. This would turn out to be her last sports adventure. The national tournament that she played in ended just three days before she transitioned from this life.

Shayna was always a deep thinker. We made it a priority to have dinner together every night if possible. One night at the dinner table, she commented how she didn't fear death. She couldn't have been any more than ten years old.

Shayna wanted to be a veterinarian. She loved pets growing up. We had our dog Chloe, who was nine years older than Shayna. Then, there was Zoe, the dog that we got when Shayna was about five years old. Stevie is the dog we got the year before Shayna passed. Shayna had a pet rabbit, a gecko that passed prematurely, and a second gecko, in addition to a pair of guinea pigs. She was obsessed with birds even though she never had one as a pet. She truly adored penguins. She would draw them everywhere. Pablo the Penguin was her mascot. Pee-Kwee was her Care Bear penguin she slept with every night. She had a penguin bedspread and slept with a penguin pillow pet. She wanted to see the penguins at the zoo and the aquarium. Her first and only job was as a volunteer at the zoo. She was only 14. She loved it.

Shayna wanted to attend my alma mater, Ohio State. I was so looking forward to sharing that legacy with her. Kayla was born in Lexington, KY. Shayna was my Buckeye Baby born in Cincinnati, OH.

Medically, Shayna's last few years were challenging. When she was on the fifth grade AAU basketball team, she began complaining about pain in her fingers. We thought she must be jamming them in practice. She was having trouble shooting the basketball. Then, the pain moved to her wrists. We'd have to wrap her wrists before games. She adjusted and played through the pain. When we took her to the doctor, we found out she had a severe case of juvenile rheumatoid arthritis. We were devastated.

She began seeing an occupational therapist. I had to give her two different drugs to combat the inflammation. One was in the form of seven pills that she had to have several hours before eating. So, I had to wake her up early in the morning to take them before breakfast.

The other medication was a painful injection. The medication was so painful the doctor suggested icing Shayna's arm before giving it to her. We would both well up with tears when I had to give her the weekly injection. But she never complained. She never cried.

One day she asked me if she could try giving her the injection without the ice. The ice took several minutes to get her arm numb. I said, "Sure, we can try it." She flinched when I gave her the shot. But, from that day one, she took it straight, no ice. Shayna was my warrior.

I remember when she was diagnosed. We were headed to the lab to get the bloodwork to confirm when she said, "I wonder what it's like to get your blood taken?" Shayna faced everything with a sense of adventure. She would always say she wanted to break a leg so she could experience walking on crutches. Be careful what you wish for. She'd have that wish fulfilled.

At the AAU tournament, Shayna was undercut by a girl while going for a rebound in sixth grade. She crumpled to the ground, grabbing her knee. Without thinking, my parental instincts kicked in. I ran onto the court and scooped up that 5'8" girl and carried her off. She could not play in the remainder of the tournament. I carried her around for the rest of our time there. When we took her to the doctor back home, they thought it was a torn ACL. But they weren't certain. So, she was in a walking cast for three weeks. When she went down in the next game she played in, we knew it was a torn ACL. She had surgery and got her wish of walking on crutches.

After the diagnosis of arthritis and the ACL tear, the next challenge for Shayna was a heart condition. She told us that every once in a while, her heart would race for a few seconds. She had nearly passed out one day at the top of the stairs in our house.

The cardiologist diagnoses her with Wolff Parkinson White syndrome. This syndrome is where there is an extra electrical pathway in the heart. Shayna's condition was mild. It didn't even require medication. The doctor told us we could just monitor it or take the aggressive approach and have surgery to correct it once and for all. This was not an easy decision. Our perfectly healthy girl had gone from no surgeries ever to surgery for injections in her fingers for arthritis, an ACL repair, and now heart surgery. But we wanted this behind us. And we wanted Shayna back to full health.

The procedure didn't work. We scheduled a second attempt. This time it worked. The circuit was gone but only for a few minutes. Then, it came back. The doctor did not recommend a third try. Her condition was mild, and he said all it would require was a follow-up every two years. While she was under, they intentionally sent her heart into overdrive to see if it would run away or settle back to normal. It always returned to normal on its own. She even wore a monitor for 30 days to see if we could catch an episode and get more detail. We rested with the idea we had done all we could do, and she was fine.

On June 20, 2015, Shayna and Tywana returned from the AAU National Volleyball tournament. Shayna had a fantastic time at the resort. Kayla and I stayed behind to save money. Shayna's volleyball season had cost us more than Kayla's first year of college. Tywana encouraged Shayna to call us to see how we were doing. But Shayna was having the time of her life with her friends, running the hotel halls, ordering $5 smoothies at the pool, driving around the resort in golf carts, and talking Tywana into dessert and expensive meals every night. Shayna's attitude was, "I'll see you when I see you. I'm having a good time." This is how I think she thinks of us today while she's in paradise and we're still here laboring.

Shayna returned home on that Saturday, and Kayla left for vacation with her friends. I dropped Kayla off. I picked up Tywana and Shayna at the airport. Monday night, Shayna had a sleepover with her friend Caroline. Tuesday, she was back here in her bed, under my roof, and I felt I could sleep easy.

On June 24, 2015, I went for my usual morning walk and came to my office to work. It was summer break. Shayna didn't have a job outside of the house. So, she was supposed to work helping with the family business. Tywana texted her phone from the basement and got no response. It wasn't unlike Shayna to be late for work. Finally, Tywana went up to get her up. That's when I heard the scream. Shayna was completely non-responsive. I performed CPR on her while Tywana called 911. It took forever for them to get here.

We went to the hospital, where they worked on Shayna for a while. Finally, the chaplain came to the room where we were waiting with our friends who had come to support us. We knew Shayna was gone. Or not.

For many years before Shayna was even born, I had a fear of death. It started around the time I was Shayna's age at the time of her transition. It was so bad I'd call it a phobia. Thanatophobia is the technical term for me. About five years before Shayna was born, the fear became so bad I started studying everything I could find about death and the afterlife. I learned that death is a natural transition from one time of life to the next. It's not the end. It's a new beginning.

Because I had learned this at a deep level, I was fortunate to never have to worry about where Shayna was. I knew she was still alive, better than ever before. What I did not know at the time was "the dead" are still with us. They are still very much involved in our lives. Shayna's transition would send my search for truth into hyperdrive. I had to learn how to connect with her, to continue our relationship, until my transition, and I am with her again.

I delved deeply into podcasts and read books by mediums and other afterlife experts on continuing relationships. Then, a series of synchronicities led me to Mark Ireland and Elizabeth Boisson and Helping Parents Heal. We had "coincidentally" scheduled a vacation about a year after Shayna passed in Phoenix, AZ, where Elizabeth Boisson lives. Tywana and I met Elizabeth, Ernie, and Kristine Jackson and started a Helping Parents Heal affiliate group in Cincinnati, OH. After a year, a few of us parents decided to ramp up the online group of Helping Parents Heal and start regular online meetings to help other parents.

I learned to look for signs from Shayna. I recalled the conversation about the girls choosing us as their parents those many years before. I recalled Shayna saying she wasn't afraid to die.

While making final arrangements for Shayna, we were torn about burial versus cremation. Tywana and I discussed it and decided on cremation. We did not want to have our memories of Shayna tied to a location. When we ran this by Kayla to get her thoughts on this, she told us this story.

Mother's Day 2015, about six weeks before Shayna's transition, we were at my brother's house. Shayna was outside with her cousins and Kayla. No one was talking about death. These were kids ranging in age from 15-19. Shayna told them when she died; she wanted to be cremated and have her ashes spread underneath a tree. It was settled. We had her body cremated, and her ashes are under a tree in our front yard today.

Shayna has sent us signs too numerous to put into this short chapter. I have had many medium readings, and Shayna comes through loud and clear with incredible evidence. However, some of the most impressive came through Suzanne Giesemann.

Shayna has a special connection with Suzanne. Suzanne accurately described the "happy thought bubble," a purple Christmas ornament-type glass orb that hangs in our kitchen. Whenever Shayna would drop in on Suzanne with a message, she would provide evidence.

Once, after Suzanne had told us about the happy thought bubble, Suzanne called with a message from Shayna. But, before she delivered it, she asked if the bubble had a crack at the top. Neither of us had noticed a crack. So, I took it down and examined it. At the top was a barely visible hairline crack. Another time, Suzanne called and described to Tywana mala beads a friend had given her, along with a book on using them. She told Tywana that Shayna had said Tywana had a question for her. After some thought, Tywana realized the question was that, while meditating with the beads, she would often feel her heart quicken and see the color purple. The question was, "Is this Shayna?" Shayna said it was her.

Another time, Suzanne called with a message. But, before she delivered it, she had to provide evidence. She asked if Kayla had been playing basketball recently. We just knew Suzanne was wrong this time. Kayla hates playing sports other than swimming. But we had to call Kayla to check. When we asked if she had been playing basketball, predictably, she said no. But she was babysitting two young girls that summer, and the day before, they were playing with Play-Doh making little balls and pretending they were basketballs.

On Shayna's fifth angelversary date, I was hoping for a sign but careful not to get my hopes up. I was driving Tywana to a doctor's appointment and zoned out when Tywana pointed to the truck ahead of us at a stoplight. The truck had a sticker on the tailgate in huge letters, saying, "I'm right here." In the truck's back window was another sticker that was one of those "Home" stickers" with the O in home replaced by the outline of the home state. It was Ohio, our home, and Shayna's birthplace. The message was clear.

Between running many Helping Parents Heal meetings and talking to what amounts to thousands of parents over the years, I have found healing and meaning in my new life. Four years after Shayna's transition, I began my ministry of sorts called *Grief 2 Growth*. First, I wrote a handbook on handling grief based on my years of experience with HPH and my studies. Next, I started a life coaching business specializing in helping people transform their grief into growth. Finally, I launched a podcast, and as of August 2021, I have recorded my 150th episode. grief2growth.com

I would not be doing what I am doing today had it not been for Shayna in my life and her transition into the next life. Shayna, my beautiful light, is the inspiration for all I do. She is the lighthouse that is guiding me Home.

*An excerpt from the book, "Life to Afterlife – Helping Parents Heal, The Book"
Copyright 2021, Elizabeth Boisson, Independently Published October 2, 2021*

About the Author

Brian Smith is a certified life coach, a grief guide, and a small business consultant. Brian's mission is to help others by sharing lessons he has learned from decades of experience and study.

Brian became well acquainted with grief in 2015 after the sudden passing of his fifteen-year-old daughter Shayna. After Shayna's passing, Brian felt his life was over. He had to learn to survive for the sake of his wife, Tywana, and their daughter, Kayla. Brian has studied the nature of life and death and how to progress through grief. In his grief work, Brian provides a safe space where you can safely share what you are experiencing. Brian shares techniques that he discovered and developed after his devastating loss. Perhaps most importantly, he can help you understand that death is not goodbye and that your relationship with your loved one can continue. His understanding is not a religious-based belief, but a position arrived at based on reason and evidence. Brian's vision is to create a world where everyone has a sense of purpose and fulfillment. If we know the "why", we can endure any "how". Brian wants to remind everyone of their true nature and their reason for being. Shortly after Shayna transitioned, Brian discovered *Helping Parents Heal*, a non-profit peer-to-peer support group for parents of children who have passed. Brian volunteers with Helping Parents Heal and is a leader of the Helping Parents Heal Online group. Brian has worked with hundreds of parents who have lost children. Brian is a member of the Board for Helping Parents Heal. He volunteers for the *SoulPhone* Foundation. Brian is on the board of the SoulPhone Foundation and Helping Parents Heal. Brian is the author of "*Grief 2 Growth: Planted. Not Buried*". He is the host of the *Grief 2 Growth* podcast. You can find Brian at www.grief2growth.com. His YouTube channel is: www.youtube.com/grief2growth and his podcast is at podcast.grief2growth.com As of February 2022, the podcast has received over 100,000 downloads and the YouTube channel has almost 8,000 subscribers.

*"So astounding are the facts in
this connection, that it would seem
as though the Creator, himself had
electrically designed this planet..."*
~Nikola Tesla~
Engineer, Inventor
1856 – 1943

Signs and Automatic Writing, *Karen Wilson*

By Karen Wilson

Nick's mom forever. Hello to all the loving parents on this journey. My name is Karen, and my only child and son Nick, transitioned on March 25, 2017, at the age of 22 years in a car accident. I was terrified! How do I live every day? How many years do I have to live with this pain?

I needed help, and I was drawn ever so strongly to speak to other parents who had lost a child. I needed to see that they survived, and I could navigate a new life without my son. I pursued readings from mediums, connections with other moms, and the strong pull to explore my spirituality. I had dozens of questions I needed answers to that set me on this journey of discovery and gratitude.

I knew almost immediately that Nick was "out there" somewhere and that there was more to this life than just physical life. "Death" could not be the end. I felt a very strong pull to explore this, and here I am.

Whether you believe, you are not sure, or you need proof, first and foremost, I want to tell my story and hopefully help you. There is hope! I feel like we become a different breed of people once we have a child that has left the physical world. Sharing our feelings and experiences is of paramount importance to healing. For myself, I know that Nick is with me all the time. The signs, feelings, and just knowing can't be denied. There is no doubt in my mind Nick is "here".

Signs

Dimes and Coins

A fellow bereaved mom told me that I would start finding dimes. I didn't question it. But I thought it was kind of weird. I was looking and hoping to find one because anything that meant some connection to Nick gave me hope. Then, about four weeks after Nick's transition, I found a dime at a friend's house outside underneath their cherry blossom tree. I was on cloud nine. But of course, the doubt crept in that it was just a coincidence. After five years, I have found 60 dimes, 12 quarters, nine nickels, 8 pennies, one $1-dollar coin, and two $ 2-dollar coins. No more doubts from this mom.

One day my partner Ray and I were having a disagreement about something so insignificant I can't even remember. Although at the time, we kept up the bickering back and forth. Ray decided to go out. He came back in about 1 minute later with a dime he found behind my car. Then he left again and came back within one minute with another dime he found behind his car. That was no doubt a sign that Nick was telling us to stop with the negative energy.

In the beginning, I would go to my son's crash scene as it made me feel close to him. It was in a small field off the side of the road. A dime was sitting on the ground among all the grass and weeds, shining ever so brightly. The chances of me finding a dime in a field are so remote. I was not looking for one, but there it was in the middle of a field. Nick guided me to find it, and I have no doubt.

Our first vacation after Nick's transition was to Myrtle Beach, SC. It was very hard not having Nick to send pictures to and communicate about our vacation. I decided to go for a walk, and I just needed to do it alone. As I was walking and the tears were streaming down my face, I thought in my head, "Nick, please, I need a sign; I am having a rough go here." Within minutes I came across about 6 pennies on the ground. My heart sang as I bent down to pick them up. I am sure people around me thought, look at that poor woman needing to pick up found pennies. But I paid no mind to it and grabbed them, feeling so proud.

On this same vacation, we were playing golf, and again I was feeling so sad and missing my son. I asked for a sign. On the 14th hole, I found a quarter. Ray and I were out for a walk one evening and talking about the dimes and coins. I said out loud in a joking manner, "Nick if you are gonna send me money, how about something bigger like 50-dollar bills."

I work in a Dental Office at the front desk. About one week later, a patient that was sitting in the waiting room came up to me and said, "I found this 50-dollar bill on the chair over there. Maybe someone lost it." I was dumbfounded, and it took me a second to respond. I took it and gave it to my manager as maybe someone did lose it and would call. She said to give it a week, and if no one calls, you can keep it. I knew in my heart that no one would call. That was Nick showing me that he heard me loud and clear. No one called, and I was fifty bucks richer at the end of the week. Interesting thing…most people would have kept that $50 and quietly put it in their pocket, but this lady did not.

Coins I have found in the last 5 years. I started to make a bracelet,
but there are far too many to wear it now, 92 coins total!

Feathers

I have found many feathers. Some have been in unexplainable places, like my pocket. They are different in colour but mostly grey and white. One day I was on my way to my therapy session. I found a wonderful therapist who helped me immensely. She adds spirituality in her counseling sessions if the client wants to include it. Anyway, I was walking up the steps to her home where she works, and there was a long blue feather about twelve inches long sitting on a step. It was absolutely beautiful and blue, which is my favourite colour. Nothing like I had ever seen. I picked it up, and I showed it to her and asked her if it was hers. She responded, "No, I have never seen it before. You keep it." I put it with my collection. I truly believe, and I know this was from Nick. He was telling me I am on the right track and my counseling sessions are a part of my healing.

License Plates

Since Nick's transition, I have been drawn to certain license plates. The first four letters of his license plate were BMVP. My eyes go directly to any license plate with these letters. One day I was going shopping at the mall, and there was construction in the parking lot. I thought, "I don't want to drive and park near there as it was dirty and muddy." I honestly do not know how to explain this, but I ended up driving right in the thick of the construction area, and when I parked my car, the car in front of me had a license plate that read "NIK NIK". I was blown away.

Another example of similar synchronicity is when I was thinking of joining a gym approximately three years ago. I was back in forth in my head about it. Just as I was thinking of what I was going to do, a car in front of me had a license plate that read "BE FIT". That was enough for me. I joined.

Birds

Birds appear and come very close to me. They look at me for a period of time that is way too long for Nick not to be involved in this sign. There is a knowing that it is not just a bird as in the past I have never had birds come so close to me and just look at me.

One very obvious encounter was at a local park. Ray and I were sitting under a tree on a hot summer day. There were about 15 Canadian geese by the water doing their thing. One of them walked right up to me as I was sitting. I was kind of startled as they can be nasty. Not this one. It just walked up to my chair, stood about two feet in front of me, and just looked at me. It didn't make any other moves or noises, it just looked at me. This lasted about 10 minutes. I knew that this was my beautiful son Nick assuring me he was with me. It was so heartwarming, and I was so happy.

About six months after Nick transitioned, we went to the Bahamas. While sitting on a chair by the pool reading, a large bird walked over to my table and chairs. It hopped up on the chair in front of me. It stared at me and turned its head. I thought to myself, "Why is this bird not flying away?" It stayed for an inordinate amount of time. I know without a doubt now this was Nick once again telling me he never left.

Songs

Nick and I had a song that we would belt out in the car together whenever it came on. It is *Don't Stop Believing* by Journey. I now know why that was our song. This path is my journey of hanging on to believing that my son in spirit is with me and guiding me. It makes so much sense now. This song comes on when I feel like I have doubt. Also, he knows how much I love John Lennon's Let It Be and Imagine. So, they are frequently on as well.

Electronics

At the very beginning of my journey, my phone would go off like someone was texting me, but no one was there. At first, I thought my phone was not working properly. But after asking people if they texted me and finding out no one did, I realized this was Nick. When my mind took me to that realization, the texts stopped.

One day I was on my laptop on a site that required my password and username. This particular day I was having a lot of sadness and felt a little hopeless. Before I could type anything, this appeared on my screen, "You got this, love Nick." I was so stunned. I knew I had not typed anything, and why would I type that? Ray was out for a walk, and I needed someone else's eyes to validate it. I did not move, literally. I sat there waiting for Ray to come back to see it because I was afraid it would disappear.

Thoughts and Messages

I was always worried I would lose him throughout Nick's life on Earth. It was a fear I could not contain. I put it down to being overprotective and nervous. I had lost both my parents at a very young age and could not handle any more loss. I was also afraid of my own death and leaving Nick without a mom.

Two months or so before Nick transitioned, I was putting away laundry, a mundane task. Out of nowhere, I had a thought pop into my head. It was very disturbing. I heard this, "If Nick were to die, it would be difficult, but I could survive it." I heard it twice and I had absolutely no idea where this came from. I was not even thinking about anything to do with death. I know now that it was my spirit guides, or my higher self, preparing me for what was to come. I no longer fear death. I do not want to suffer, but death to me now represents being reunited with Nick, and that is what I want when my time comes.

Connecting to Nick

Automatic Writing

My journey has led me to learn some tools to connect to Nick. Meditation is something I did quite a bit in the beginning. It helped me feel a higher vibration. Automatic writing is absolutely paramount to my connection. I learned how to do this when I took a workshop with a Spiritual teacher. It was not something that I learned immediately. I had to really concentrate and let go of any doubt. I picked up a pen and, in the beginning, I was only getting letters and numbers. But after some practice, now, when I pick up a pen and ask for the connection, the pen flows like nothing I have ever seen before. There is no space between the words, and they just flow together. Nick will have me write messages he is trying to convey to me, mostly to do with things that are currently going on in my life and messages of how he wants me to live my life. I can ask him questions, and he will have me write the answers.

My very first multi-word message when I started doing Automatic Writing was, "Karen thinks death is the end." I believe that this came from my Spirit Guides. I am convinced they guide me to learn to connect with Nick. When I received this message, I was dumbfounded in the beginning. I always felt that there was something to the afterlife. However, hearing that death is not the end propelled me to learn more, and more, and more!

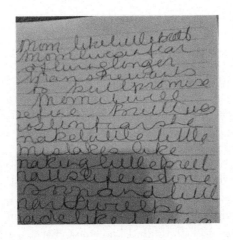

You can see that the words have no spaces and are looped together. Nick's spirit takes my hand and writes messages. This is nothing like my own handwriting. Nick always knows when I ask him for a session, and he never fails to take my hand. My job as an Office Administrator always finds me with a pen in my hand. Nick only takes my hand when I ask.

Pendulum

I learned how to use a pendulum for connection. Nick will give me "yes" and "no" answers as well as "I don't know". The pendulum swings back and forth and in circles. Once you learn how to use it, you can ask questions and see the answers. I use it all the time, giving me such great validation.

Thoughts and Feelings

There are times when I am busy at work, and out of the blue, I will get a thought or feeling in my head. There is just a knowing that it is from my son. Quite often, it is to do with something I may be struggling with or trying to decide.

I have my mother and father in Spirit as well. They come through with messages too. Not nearly as much as Nick, but it is nice after over 30 years to hear from them.

There are many things that we do to celebrate Nick. First and foremost, we talk about him almost daily. We laugh a lot as he always made us laugh, and we have some great memories. We celebrate his birthday, his angel date, and for Mother's Day, I buy myself a gift from him.

Nick has a team of friends he left behind on Earth. They raised money to have a Memorial Bench put in his High School Park. It is only four kilometers from my home. I ride my bike there. The plaque reads "Forever Young, Forever Happy, Forever Your Friend".

Whenever we travel, we take some of his ashes with us and sprinkle them in the ocean or wherever we feel is a beautiful spot. I write Nick's name in the sand, and I take a picture.

I started a tradition at Christmas when Nick was about four years old. Each year, we would go to the mall and purchase a gift for a child that we would donate. I wanted Nick to learn the value of appreciating all the presents he received and know that this gift may be the only one a child receives. Unlike the numerous ones under our tree with his name on it. As he got older and received an allowance, he would donate some of it to this gift every year. When he got his first job, he would use his own money. We would do this together. After Nick's transition, I continued donating a gift, but now I do it in his name.

Giving Back

By far, one of the most helpful ways I have begun to heal is by giving back. I knew I needed to meet some parents that had lost children. I needed to know I could survive this and wanted to share feelings and experiences.

My first endeavor was volunteering as a visitor for seniors. I was matched up with a lady who lost her son in a motorcycle accident. Albeit he was in his mid-fifties, child loss at any age is devastating. This wonderful and full-of-life lady did not have much family. We were able to share our experiences. After four years, we still talk on the phone and visit when we can and have formed a bond.

I began reading vigorously anything I could get my hands on regarding the afterlife, Mediums, Spirituality, etc. I came across a book by Dr. Mark Pitstick called *Soul Proof* (1st edition, published in 2006 by Soul Proof Productions). This book was my springboard to finding Nick again.

I was addicted to finding answers. I came across videos by Suzanne Giesemann, a well-known certified Evidential Medium. I read one of the books she authored called *Still Right Here* (1st edition, published 2017 by One Mind Books). After reading this, I was well on my way.

Her book led me to reference an online group called *Helping Parents Heal*, www.helpingparentsheal.org. The closest group chapter to where I live was about six hours away. I reached out to the group leader, and she set me up with another mom in my area who was on the same path as I was. We met up and decided to start our own group for our area. We meet monthly, and this has brought me so many new friends, experiences, and immense gratitude to the parents who reach out so frequently for assistance. We help each other. It does not matter who has been on this path longer, we all have something to offer each other, and it is healing in many ways.

I was online reading about people's experiences with pendulums. I came across Irene Weinberg, who was starting a series called *Grief to Rebirth* and was looking for people who wanted to share their healing experiences. I sent her my story, and she asked if I would do a podcast with her. I was so nervous, but I did it, and I'm so glad that I did. (Rebirth Series - Karen Wilson – Rebirth after the loss of a child by Grief and Rebirth: Finding the Joy in Life Podcast anchor.fm)

Many Things Learned

Throughout my five-year journey, I have learned so many things about myself, the people I surround myself with, and my fears. I have lost some people that I previously surrounded myself with, which has been mostly my choice, and I came to that decision shortly after Nick transitioned due to how I had been treated.

I believe that people are afraid of facing the possibility that something as tragic as losing a child could happen to them. They shy away, make excuses about not understanding my grief process, or think I have lost my mind. Perhaps I would have thought the same thing had I not experienced this loss. However, I no longer worry or care about what other people think. My grieving process is not for them to understand. But one would hope to receive support and not have more pain inflicted on them as I did. I "forgive" these individuals in my heart, but I no longer allow them in my life.

When the trust of the very people who are supposed to unconditionally love and support you disappears and they bring you harm, you must put in a boundary to protect yourself. Boundaries have become a huge part of my journey. Negative people have an extremely limited part of me in their lives. It is hard to completely get rid of these people as this is a part of daily life. However, I have learned not to internalize their negativity and just let them move through their day.

Letting go of control is something I have learned also. However, I do struggle with it from time to time. Everything will or will not happen in its own divine time. Learning patience is the biggest thing with which I struggle. The more we work against this, the harder we make our lives. Life is going to happen and what matters is how we receive and deal with events, whether negative or positive.

Giving time, love, support, and sitting with someone struggling is what we can control and is of paramount importance. Feeling alone and lonely is something I have struggled with all my life. I have learned how to navigate these feelings and reach out for help. I no longer judge people as I once may have. Instead, I pause and think of what happened in that person's life to make them engage in destructive behavior. Compassion is so needed in this life we are living.

The grief I felt, in the beginning, was so raw, and I was terrified. I needed to find someone who would help me get rid of it, or so I thought. I now know my grief is a permanent part of me. It changes over time, but it never goes away. I am okay with that now and glad because my grief is my bridge to Nick, and I never want that to go away. Grief is my new sidekick. Sometimes it's ever-present, and sometimes it is but a thought away. You must feel to heal!

Support System

I have a wonderful, supportive, patient, and loving partner. Ray has been with me throughout this whole process. Sometimes he may not fully understand my connections, but he fully supports them and has seen many things he can't explain with his logical mind. I am so thankful I can share all of it with him.

Many of my friends are bereaved moms. We do not sit and cry all day together. Instead, we have fun and do things that moms who have not lost children do. However, we understand and support each other if we have a bad day or moment. It is such a comfort to be with people you don't have to hide your emotions.

Some friends have shied away from me and only reached out for the good times. It is disappointing, but I do understand that some people just can't deal with it. Other friends have wholeheartedly supported me through my journey. They may not understand, but they do not judge me, and they love me just the same.

The hardest part has been losing some of my family members. It is a very long story and goes far back and beyond the loss of Nick. Suffice it to say that I felt deeply hurt and shunned at the hardest time in my life. It truly almost completely broke me…. almost. Here I am, surviving, rebuilding, and reframing my life with good people, positive experiences, and letting go of the wrong people.

I am fiercely protective of Nick's memory and my heart. I have no issue letting go of people who do not support that or have harmed it in any way. Letting go is hard. Peace is beautiful. I choose PEACE!

What I Have Learned About the Afterlife

We are most definitely Spiritual beings having a human experience. We have been here on Earth many times, in different roles of male and female. Reincarnation is real. When we decide to reincarnate, we do so with our "soul family", who agree to play different parts in our life to facilitate lessons and experiences we choose or need to learn for soul growth. This life on Earth is an illusion viewed and experienced through the lens of our soul.

I could not believe I would choose such a tragic life of loss. However, I spent so much time learning and using discernment to decide what I believe, and there are things I am not sure about. I will never stop learning. It is not something one can decide to believe without intense learning wanting to learn and putting judgment aside. These are my beliefs, and I am in no way trying to force them on anyone. I recommend that if you want to learn, there are so many tools out there that can assist you.

Nick is with me all the time. He assists me, guides me, sends me messages, and signs. I believe that he even tests me. I can't wait until I am with him again. I know I have a job to do while I am still in human form on Earth, and I will wait until my time comes and I know we will have a beautiful reunion.

Nick's Messages

I would like to end my chapter with some messages Nick has repeatedly sent me. I believe that they have helped me, and I hope they will give you hope as well.

"Fear nothing."

"Live life like it was your last day."

"Death is not the end."

"Be happy."

"Mom, I will never leave you."

About the Author

Karen Wilson is a Shining Light Mom, *Helping Parents Heal* Affiliate Group leader, and continues to pursue her abilities in channeling spirit.

"All things share the same breath —
the beast, the tree, the man.
The air shares its spirit with all
the life it supports."
~Chief Seattle~
Suquamish & Duwamish Leader
1786-1866

A Little Bird Told Me, *Laura Robinson*

By Laura Robinson

From CHICKEN SOUP FOR THE SOUL: COUNT YOUR BLESSINGS

Faith sees the invisible, believes the incredible and receives the impossible. ~Author Unknown

I am sitting in the movie theater with my husband and tears are welling up in my eyes. We are watching About Schmidt with Jack Nicholson. It's the scene where a colleague is looking at a photo of Jack's daughter on his desk and says, "She's beautiful, does she live close by?" Jack responds, "She's the apple of my eye. I think about her every day. She's 3,000 miles away, in California, but it's okay -- I see her a couple of times a year."

In the darkened theater, my husband glances over at me and whispers, "Honey what's wrong?" Tears are streaming down my cheeks now, and I choke out the words, "We have to move back to Canada. I have to be with my Dad."

I had always been the apple of my daddy's eye, and I knew that he was thinking of me every day, many times a day. I grew up in Toronto, Canada, but had moved to Los Angeles to be an actress. I was enjoying a successful career, had found an amazing group of friends and loved L.A. But I missed my family so much, and they missed me. I had been living in California for fifteen years. I had gotten married, and had two wonderful children. And even though we always came home for Christmas, and my parents came to see us in the spring, it never felt like enough. I had watched both my husband and my best friend lose their dad and mom, respectively. I saw how

198

devastating that had been for them. My husband had been planning to go on a trip with his dad for years -- they never got to do it. My best friend got a call that her mom was in I.C.U., raced to the hospital to be with her, but did not make it there in time.

The secondhand experience of those losses became a huge blessing in my life.

My dad was having health issues and a voice in my head had been getting louder and louder: it was telling me that time might be running low for him. Nothing was technically life-threatening, but my "daughter's intuition" was on high alert, and I was listening. And I am so grateful that I was, because in that moment, in that movie, I made the decision to totally re-route my life... and, thankfully, my husband and kids supported my decision and happily came along on the adventure with me.

We moved back the summer of 2003. Instead of seeing my parents twice a year, we started to see them every week. We all had so many great times together. My dad came to see my son play hockey, played cards with my daughter, and he and I would go out for breakfast a lot -- that was one of our favorite things to do. We did all the simple little things there isn't time for when visits are rushed or pressured and you are trying to fit a million things into one week's vacation.

I wanted to be there for my dad, and I was. I wanted to have my kids get to know him, and they did. Most of all, as crazy as it seemed, and as hard as it was for me to leave my friends and life, I followed my heart, and for that I will always be grateful.

Because, after four and a half years, it happened. My dad went into the hospital for simple issues with circulation and one night, in front of my eyes, he had a massive heart attack and the next morning he died.

I was shocked, bereft and confused -- but I was there.

I did not get the dreaded phone call in the middle of the night. Did not have to fly home and experience all the guilt and regrets that would have gone along with losing him and not being present. I had played that scenario out in my mind, and had done something about it before it happened.

Cut to the day of my dad's funeral. I was brushing my teeth, staring at myself in the mirror in the daze that comes at such a time. Drained, beyond tired, and cried-out, I caught a little movement out of the corner of my eye. A bird was sitting in the middle of the tree outside the bathroom window. I walked over to the window, turned the crank and opened it. I thought the bird might fly away at the sound... but it didn't. In fact, it never moved a feather and kept its eyes glued to mine. Suddenly, the world went very quiet, and everything distilled down to the bird and the tree and me. And in that moment, I knew it was my dad, coming to tell me he was okay, and that I would be okay. I felt my deep sorrow lift a little and the bird and I stayed there, our eyes locked on each other for a long time. I finally had to turn away, and when I looked back a split second later, the tree was empty.

Later that week, I was telling the story to a dear friend. She asked me, "What kind of bird was it?" "A robin," I said, "but he had grey feathers, which is unusual. I don't know why, but I felt like it was my dad." My friend grabbed my hand and said, "A robin? Laura, your last name is Robinson."

And there was one more piece to the story. I got an email from another friend who had been quite close to my dad. She said she had asked my dad a year or so earlier, that when he died he would send her a sign, and then send the same one to me. She knew of our deep heart connection. My dad had agreed. She was writing to ask me if I had had any "signs" since his passing.

I wrote back and told her my robin story. She immediately replied, "I am covered in shivers right now, because the sign your dad and I agreed upon was a red bird. There was a cardinal on my deck yesterday. He stared at me for ten minutes. I'm sure it was your dad!" I understood then, without a shadow of a doubt that my dad had come to me, was watching over me and would continue to.

It's always so hard to lose a beloved parent, but what I am grateful for is that I do not have to live with regret: regret that I had moved so far away, that there hadn't been enough time to be together and to reconnect again after all those years. At the funeral, I said that I knew I had been unconditionally loved every minute of my life. I feel so lucky to have had that blessing.

I miss him every day but I have peace in my heart... and a little bird on my shoulder.

Excerpt from "Chicken Soup for the Soul: Count Your Blessings: 101 Stories of Gratitude, Fortitude, and Silver Linings", by Jack Canfield, Mark Victor Hansen, Amy Newmark, Laura Robinson, Elizabeth Bryan, Chicken Soup for the Soul, November 3, 2009, www.chickensoup.com

About the Author

Laura Robinson is a true multi-passionate creative - this talented actress-author-inventor-producer-speaker- musician-entrepreneur and mom wears a LOT of hats and seems to love them all! Robinson co-invented the hilarious, best-selling board game, Balderdash, in her mid-twenties! She's also an Emmy-nominated Executive Producer/creator of Celebrity Name Game, the syndicated television game show starring Craig Ferguson.

Laura has enjoyed a successful career as an actress in both Canada and the US, with starring roles on the CBS detective drama, Night Heat and sitcoms Frasier and Cheers. Robinson is an engaging motivational speaker and author, performing at various North American events and co-authoring several books for the popular, uplifting book series, Chicken Soup for the Soul, including Count Your Blessings and Hooked on Hockey. Robinson is currently in the recording studio, working on a project of her original music. You can connect with her on Instagram and Twitter @Balderdashgrl and by email at laura@laurarobinson.com

*"Make yourself familiar with the
Angels and behold them frequently
in spirit; for without being seen,
they are present with you."
~St. Francis de Sales~
Catholic Bishop and Saint
1567 – 1622*

Love Never Dies, *Margaret Mary Petrozzo*

By Margaret Mary Petrozzo

I hope that my chapter will help those grieving the loss of their child and give hope and inspiration. Knowing that your child is with you always in the bonds of love we have created on this earth that transcend time and space. Since Ally left this physical world, I have been guided on a spiritual journey of transformation, growth, learning about myself, and finding my way back to life.

Alexandra Mary Petrozzo was born to us on April 24th, 1987. Ally transitioned on Christmas night of 2011 in her sleep from a seizure and or a brain aneurysm. She was 24 years old. She was my second child. My first daughter Christine was only twenty months older. Ally was a little sister to Christine and big sister to Jamie. Jamie, my son, is three years younger than Ally. He is my third child. I will always have three children. It was a sensitive question after Ally transitioned when people would ask me how many children I have. I will always have three children.

Ally was a joy of a child; she was precious and beautiful in every way. As she grew up to adulthood, she blossomed into the most beautiful young woman both on the inside and physically. She loved to sing as a young girl. At the age of two, she was singing in perfect pitch. She was blessed with an angelic voice. She sang in a talent show in third grade on stage, where she had such stage presence. Ally sang the song *Somewhere Over the Rainbow* and received a standing ovation at her school. I cried with joy!

Ally had this magnetic energy that everyone seemed to love because she exuded unconditional love. She loved hearts, heart jewelry, earrings, bracelets, anything with hearts. She loved the color pink, sunflowers, her family and friends, and singing and dancing in the many musicals plays she performed in high school. Then, as she entered college at Lynn University in Boca Raton, she became the *Star-Spangled Banner* singer at all their sports games. Ally just loved that!

She blossomed in college. Ally also tried out for American Idol. She sang the song *Jesus Take the Wheel* by Carrie Underwood. My husband took her to Madison Square Garden for the auditions. The judges loved her voice, but they chose someone more dramatic. It was an experience that Ally and her dad were able to share together. My husband Peter, being a musician, was the perfect one to accompany her. We encouraged Ally to audition, we were always encouraging our children to do what they love, and Ally loved singing.

She sang in the choir in grammar school as well as high school. Ally also performed at the Paper Mill Playhouse in New Jersey in the musical *Joseph and the Amazing Technicolor Dream Coat* starring Debbie Gibson and Patrick Cassidy.

Ally was a blessing to us in our lives as she kept our family tied together. That's how much love she was, and she is still. Ally is loved forever. I carry her in my heart each day until we will one day be together once again in spirit. I have a collection of stones and rocks in the shape of hearts that I feel Ally places on my path when walking. In addition, I have many heart-shaped cloud pictures from what I often see when we go to Florida in winter, which remind me that Ally is always with me.

The signs we receive from Ally continue, even after ten years this Christmas night, 2021, without her physical presence. Our communication with Ally still exists only in a different way. Last week was my husband's birthday on Halloween, but we went out to celebrate the evening before his birthday. A gentleman was playing the guitar in the restaurant and singing. He sounded like James Taylor, and he started to sing *Somewhere Over the Rainbow*! We knew it was a sign from Ally that she was happy that we were out celebrating Dad's birthday. Ally sang that song on stage in grammar school and received a standing ovation.

Then the musician played and sang a song called *Say What You Need to Say* by John Mayer, which happened to be the phone ring Ally had on her Blackberry phone. We were filled with love and tears that evening because we knew those were messages from our beautiful Ally. We have had so many, without a doubt, signs that her essence of love energy remains with us. We need to be aware and open to messages from our children just waiting to communicate with us.

I knew Ally was different from the moment I held her in my arms when she was born and looked at her with her big, beautiful sky-blue eyes and a full head of brown hair. My intuition told me that she would be different, and my God, I was right.

As I am putting these words on paper, it stirs many emotions, and it is still very hard to believe Ally is no longer here in this physical realm. Yet she continues, after almost ten years, giving us hope and the most wondrous signs from the Afterlife that we call "Heaven".

Ally has graced me with beautiful visions from the Afterlife that let me know she hears me and tries to comfort me from just behind the very thin veil where spirit exists. I have felt her presence with profound and overwhelming love.

Our bonds of love with our children are tied forever. I want to give hope that we are never alone and that our children hear us and love us more than we could ever imagine. I hope that the visions and signs that I have received bring you some comfort and curiosity in knowing that we are far more than just a body and that the wonder of the Afterlife is another journey.

In hardships, there are always opportunities to grow spirituality. I have learned that with great love for our children, there are miracles.

Ally was an angel on this earth. She had an essence of pureness, and she radiated love to everyone. She was a beacon of love and light. She was Divine love. Ally exuded unconditional love. She loved helping and volunteering her time in high school and college. Ally would rather help the seniors at the senior centers or feed the hungry, unlike other girls her age who would rather have gone shopping at the mall. She volunteered her time in college and participated in "Relay for Life" events. She was a beautiful human being.

Everyone who knew her from when she was a little girl loved her. She was loving, kind, generous, empathetic, and had a great sense of humor! She always made me laugh. She would say, "Mama do you see my halo?" I have never in my life met anyone as loving as Ally. Ally used to say, "Mama, I love you more than life itself." I would say, "Ally, I love you too, but please don't say you love me more than life!"

She was peaceful in her soul, and what she said would make so much sense. She was an "Old Soul". Her friends and her sister, Christine, would ask Ally for advice about many subjects. Ally was my daughter and my best friend. We both supported one another. We were cheerleaders for each other. I always felt that Ally was too good and innocent for most people. Sometimes she would say, "Kindness can be taken for weakness."

I am so grateful she chose me as her mother. "There is a reason for everything." That's what Ally would say, and her favorite quote was "Be the Change You Wish to See in This World." She made a difference in many of her friends' lives and the lives of others. She always gave of herself to others, and in many ways, she was selfless. She would do anything to make others happy. Ally was love itself!

The memories that we shared as mother and daughter bring me happiness. She brought me the fun and laughter as mom and daughter and as true friends. I adored her. Ally felt the same way as did I.

When Ally was twelve years old, she had vague symptoms of vomiting from time to time which I attributed to stomach viruses in school. I am a Registered Nurse by profession, but I did not recognize that her symptoms were as serious as they were. She then started to experience vision difficulties. She had difficulty reading books and her comprehension was not the same.

I took her to an eye doctor who happened to be a friend of my husband, Peter. As he dilated Ally's pupils and examined her optic nerve, he said, "I think Ally has a brain tumor." I could not believe what he said, and I went into immediate denial.

I called my husband right away. We immediately took her to our pediatrician, who referred us to a physician in NYC for an immediate MRI. The diagnosis our eye doctor made was correct. The MRI results showed a brain tumor present in between the ventricles of her brain. It put pressure on the optic nerve in her left eye, the blood supply was diminished, and her vision was compromised. Also, there was pressure on the brain, which affected her comprehension. The tumor had to be removed immediately.

It was conclusive as I sat in the pediatrician's office with my husband. Hearing this shocking news that our Ally had to undergo brain surgery, and we still were not aware if the tumor was cancerous or not, had us panicked and devastated. We were referred to one of the most renowned brain surgeons in this country.

These memories are still very difficult for me. I felt guilty not seeing her symptoms as something so serious, being a nurse and her mother. My observation should have come sooner. Everything happened so quickly, from the eye doctor to the MRI to the pediatric oncology floor at Hackensack University Medical Center.

Ally asked me before she was admitted to the hospital, "Mama, am I going to die?" I had to be strong for her. Holding back my tears and my own fear I said, "Ally, I'm not letting you go anywhere. You are going to be fine and live." That was my hope.

When we got to the hospital and Ally was admitted, we waited for the neurosurgeon Dr. Arno Freid. He walked into the hospital room wearing his white coat, and there was an incredible white glow surrounding him. Peter, Ally, and I couldn't help but see his aura of white light. He had the films of the MRI. He showed us that the tumor in Ally's brain was the size of a plum, and he thought from his experiences looking at it that it was benign, which meant it was not cancer. We could finally breathe. He could remove it surgically.

I was able to stay with Ally in the hospital. We went to sleep the night before her surgery holding each other's hands, her little hand in mine, and I hid my worries from her as I prayed to God to please help us through this intensive surgery she was to endure. I needed to stay strong for Ally. I remember Ally saying, "Mama, I don't know what I would do without you." Little did I know that we were going to lose her. We loved each other so much. The bonds of love of mother and child can never be broken.

I remember distinctly walking to the operating room, standing alongside Ally's stretcher as the nurse and orderly wheeled her to her fate, which was out of our control. I saw all the equipment in the operating room, and I knew being a nurse what my beautiful baby girl had to undergo, and I prayed for strength. I kissed her and told her I would be waiting for her in the recovery waiting room. Ally was so courageous.

Dr. Fried kept us updated every hour while Ally was in brain surgery. It was a six-hour operation. I prayed the rosary to the Mother of the Universe the entire time. My faith in a higher power was able to keep me strong.

When Ally was wheeled by stretcher into the pediatric ICU, her headdress was white gauze and her face as white as snow, which seemed to illuminate with a glow of white light and peace. I was so thankful to God, the Source of all, and to the neurosurgeon and team of professionals. I could finally exhale. Ally was going to be okay.

She did really well and was discharged on my birthday at the end of March, the best present I could have ever possibly asked for. She was homeschooled for a few months and graduated eighth grade that June.

A year after surgery, Ally had a seizure. The neurologist informed us that a seizure could occur post-brain surgery because of the interruption of brain chemistry. These were setbacks for Ally. She had lost peripheral vision in her left eye because of the tumor and was declared legally blind in her left eye. Yet, she was always grateful, and she grew spiritually knowing she had a second chance at life. It was for a reason, she would say. She was grateful for us as parents and loved her family with all her heart.

Ally had a difficult journey with the seizures. They were random, especially if she was tired, dehydrated, stressed, or at a certain time of the month they seemed to occur. She was placed on seizure meds which seemed to help at the time. Unfortunately, this created anxiety, a normal reaction for anyone going through this.

We live in New Jersey, and Ally wanted to go away to college. She went to a university in New Jersey but wasn't happy there. She loved Florida, as did I, palm trees, swimsuits, swimming pools, beautiful sunny weather, and sandals. Because Ally loved Florida, we decided to investigate universities near her grandmother's home in South Florida. We found Lynn University. It was a beautiful campus, and together we went to tour it.

Ally fell in love with the atmosphere and applied to Lynn University and transferred there. Her grandmother lived about an hour away in case of an emergency. You know, in retrospect, maybe I could have kept her closer, but she would say, "Mama, I just want to fly!" She wanted to be free from all she had been through medically and to live her life. So, I encouraged her that she could do anything she wanted. She loved her college experience, and she made so many friends that are now my friends. Her love continues, and I share in that love.

I had an opportunity to go to Florida with Ally and stay there for a few months before graduating. My husband encouraged me to go and spend time with Ally before her graduation. We were so close, and I lived through her. I would get excited about everything she experienced. Ally was so grateful. We loved each other so much. We always hugged and kissed each other good night and truly appreciated each other.

Ally graduated in May of 2011 with a Baccalaureate Degree in Early Childhood Education. We were so proud of her! Little did we know that she would not be with us at the end of the year in this physical world. I will never forget this special and proud day that she graduated. We were so proud of her and what she had accomplished. She had persevered through her brain surgery and seizure condition. Ally was worried that day that she would have a seizure walking up to receive her baccalaureate degree. All went well. There was so much joyful energy in the auditorium that day.

When Ally eventually came back home to New Jersey in the summer, she started a new life here. She was used to being on campus with her sorority sisters and always having friends around her. But, at home in our small town, she was preparing to apply to schools for job opportunities in education.

While home, she started to experience more frequent small seizure activity. The doctors changed her meds. We wanted to make sure she was not having seizures while sleeping. She had an electroencephalogram for twenty-four hours with no seizure activity noted.

Ally applied to Autism Speaks in New York City and was excited about this new job opportunity. I took her into the city. She was so excited and wanted to dress professionally for this job interview. She looked so pretty and exuded enthusiasm to the interviewer. She was hoping to hear back from them. She wanted to make a difference and "Be the Change You Wish to See in This World."

Ally was thrilled that they called her, and she got the job! We were happy for her, although going into the city with her seizure condition, which was random, caused concern. Ally was to start her position with Autism Speaks the first week in January of 2012. She wanted to make a difference for children with Autism. I am certain where Ally's energy is now. She is doing wonderful work assisting children behind the veil in marvelous and wondrous ways.

While Ally was home, she started to record herself singing music, some country, and a few Christmas songs. She wanted to take piano lessons while home before starting her job with Autism Speaks. She wanted to play the song *Silent Night* on the piano for Christmas, and she learned to. She was so excited to play for our family coming for Christmas. She played it beautifully on Christmas Day for my family and my sister's family. We were all so proud of her!

Christmas Day 2011 was a beautiful day with family and food and celebrating all being together. It was a day of love. Ally had mentioned to me on Christmas morning that giving gifts to others was more important than receiving them. Making others happy made her happy. That was Ally, always giving of herself.

Christmas night, my family went home around nine o'clock. I remember Christine slept over at her friend's house after our family left, and Jamie had to be up early for a part-time job in town. With clarity, I can remember Ally hugging me and saying, "Goodnight, Mama." I looked at her and knew that she was tired, and I gazed into her eyes. I remember how she looked. I asked her if she was okay. I had a gut feeling, intuition maybe. She had to wake up the next morning to finish the part-time job that she was leaving to start her new position with Autism Speaks. I knew she was tired from a full day with family, and because of her seizure condition, I was concerned it could provoke a seizure. Always listen to your intuition.

We hugged each other like we did each night, and we were so grateful for one another. She went to change into her warm pajamas and then came back out to say goodnight to Peter, and then she said, "Thank you Mama and Pops for all the gifts. I love you both.", and she went into her room to sleep.

I wanted to go in and check in on Ally after I cleaned up the dishes and table clearing. But I didn't, because I did not want to wake her as I passed her bedroom to go to my room. When it was approaching morning, the light was coming through the shades of my bedroom window. I thought that I had not smelled the coffee. Ally was supposed to wake up early to finish her part-time job in town. I heard whispering in my head saying, "Why isn't Ally awake yet?"

I believe Ally was trying to tell me something before I was awakened.

Peter was awake and went to wake Ally that morning. Then I heard Peter's screams that Ally was gone. I thought I was in some horrific nightmare. I ran into her room and wailed like a wounded animal. I was crying and kissing my beautiful baby girl. I didn't know why she left us physically. I was in a state of shock. My baby was gone. I felt a separation from her a mother would not want ever to feel. My angel of God had left us to go home to heaven. I knelt by her bed, held her head, and kissed her. I asked God why He abandoned me. That was how I felt.

I don't know how I have made it through, but I do know that my angels, God, the Blessed Mother, and Ally helped me through this tragic and devastating time of my life. I never gave up seeking Ally. I asked how she could be gone, my beautiful daughter and friend. Our love was beautiful. I kept searching for her. I spoke to her every day, and I knew she heard me.

I began reading many books on the Afterlife. I journaled and started a yoga practice and meditation. Grieving is difficult and raw, and each person's grief is different. I cried tears that would fill an ocean, and the pain in my heart was genuine. I believe that I had a condition called "Broken Heart Syndrome". I had physical pain in my heart. Grief is love with no place to go. I felt like I was walking in two worlds, one here on earth and the other with Ally. We love our children unconditionally.
I missed her in the deepest part of my soul, and I wasn't sure how I would get through this, but I stayed connected to Ally in the love we shared as mother and daughter. I felt a heavy feeling when I would get into the shower, I knew it was my sadness. I would get up and do the things I used to do. I got up, had coffee, and got on the treadmill like I would when Ally was here. I knew doing this would keep me physically engaged, as I took one day at a time. Each day, I looked back and saw how

far I had come along. My angels and Ally lifted me in spirit. Each day I promised myself I would meditate. I felt that I was connecting with Ally. Love is the strongest emotion in the universe. I felt so much love while meditating and listening to angelic music.

One day while sitting in my backyard, a place where Ally and I loved to sit, talk, and enjoy music and summertime dinners, I decided to sing to her sitting in nature. I was missing Ally so much, and I sang this song by Lee Ann Rimes, called *I Need You*. I had this feeling that Ally was there. I felt her energy like a mother knows her child, and I was compelled to take photos. So, I stood up and started taking pictures near the place I had been singing.

I knew Ally was there. Suddenly, I saw a round and golden light in the photos on my iPhone! As I examined the images, I saw Ally's face in the light orb! I began to cry with immense joy! Ally heard me singing to her, something she loved, and came in this light-energy orb to confirm that she heard me and was with me in our bond of love. This was a turning point for me in my healing, for I knew without a doubt love never dies. Love is eternal.

Since then, I have had other paranormal experiences. One night, when my family was over visiting us, we were simply happy to have our family around enjoying a pizza night together. When they left, I had this feeling that Ally was there. As I opened the back door to the patio, I was compelled once again to take photos with my iPhone. To my amazement, a gigantic round white-golden orb in my photo appeared. I examined it with a magnifying glass, and I could see Ally clearly in a light image. In that same light orb, I saw my parents, who passed years ago, and my father-in-law, who had passed two months prior to Ally's passing. I was in such awe of what I saw in that photo! I could see their faces so clear as day. I feel this was a gift of love from Ally and my parents and father-in-law telling me that Ally was fine and with them. I always talked to Ally and asked her if she was with my parents. We must never stop talking to our children or loved ones who transitioned because they hear us. To me, this was a miracle, the way my loved ones and Ally tell me that they remain with us in the spiritual realm and that they can see us and are always with us. This was another way my grief began to transform into hope. I know without a doubt this was a heavenly gift!

I have had so many communications from Ally, synchronicities, and validations through the years. She seems to come through to me with license plates on cars too. I could be thinking of her while driving, and then I'll see a license plate with "Ally" on it! It makes me smile knowing she is communicating with me this way, which happens so often.

There was a time after Ally transitioned that I was making fleece blankets in Florida in Ally's memory for cancer patients at Martin Memorial Hospital in Stuart, Florida. I made several blankets and labeled them "Ally's Hope". Then, to our joy, while driving to deliver them to the hospital, in front of our car was a truck which said, "ALLY'S Construction"! My husband and I knew at that moment that Ally was aware of what we were doing in her honor and memory.

There was another time that I went to California after Ally transitioned to visit my daughter Christine. We went to Carmel-by-the-Sea in northern California, where my husband rented a house for us to enjoy and heal. We had a wonderful time. It is a place of beauty, God's country. We met up with Ally's best friend Britt, and I felt so much love there.

When I came back to New Jersey, I went to bring sunflowers to Ally at the mausoleum. I spoke to her in my mind and whispered to her about the love I felt there, knowing she was with me. I asked Ally to keep bringing me love. While driving down the country road to go back home, I saw a license plate coming up the road that said, "LOVE"! I started to laugh with joy and cry at the same time, knowing Ally, with her wonderful sense of humor, heard me speaking to her. It's just amazing and miraculous in ways I cannot begin to describe.

I cannot count how many beautiful signs I have received because there have been so many. I still, to this day, receive messages from her. Love is the highest emotion in the universe, and our children are our loves.

When my husband and I were in Florida one year, it was Ally's birthday on April 24th, and we went to Lynn University in Boca Raton to bring balloons and let them fly into the sky. There is a memorial for the students from Lynn University that went to Haiti to volunteer with Habitat For Humanity, who passed away in the earthquake. Ally knew some of these students and one of the professors. We felt Ally's essence and those students at that beautiful memorial.

When Ally was 29 years old in heaven, I happened to be in Florida. There was a little blue car in front of me while heading to the gym, and the license plate said, "Ally 29", on her birthday! Just amazing, Ally! These signs make me very happy and always bring me joy and validate that she is closer than we know.

On our way back to Stuart, Florida, where we stayed for winter, we went to the post office. I happened to glance at the car parked next to us, and the license plate said, "Ally 31"! That was Ally coming through with a message that she was aware that we were at her campus for her birthday, and this validation was one of the little magical moments we received.

I believe she loves making us aware that she is close by and wants us to know she is forever with us in the love bonds we share. We carry our Ally each day in our hearts, and I never stop talking to her! I miss and love her with all my heart.

Another sign I received as I was in meditation while outside in the summer in New Jersey. I asked Ally to validate she was with me and send me a hummingbird which I had not seen all summer long. As soon as I started my meditation, this tiny beautiful little hummingbird with fairy-like wings appeared in front of my face! I couldn't believe it! Ally heard me again and used the hummingbird's energy to show me that she heard me.

This past Christmas, we started a new tradition. We decided to buy and decorate a pink Christmas tree for Ally because she loved pink and Christmas. So, we call it "The Ally Tree". I placed a picture of Ally in a snowflake picture frame on the tree and decorated it with silver and gold ornaments. I think that Ally must love that idea! We also have a real tree in another room in our home.

The signs that I have received from Ally have helped me know that there is a much greater reality, and the love and openness we have in our hearts is a gateway to the universe and its magic and miracles. I do not doubt that Ally remains with me in spirit. She has helped me from where she still exists to know that we are connected to each other for all eternity.

I wrote a book in Ally's honor called, *Ally's Hope: My Christmas Angel.* I self-published it on Amazon's Kindle Direct Publishing. The proceeds of the sales of my book go to the Alexandra Mary Petrozzo Memorial Scholarship Fund in Perpetuity for students at Lynn University in Boca Raton, Florida, and the Epilepsy Foundation.

One evening I was looking on Amazon for a book that sparked my interest with inspiration. I began to view a few books when I saw *Aaron's Energy: An Unexpected Journey Through Grief and the Afterlife With My Brilliant Son.* I was magnetically drawn to the energy of the title and the book cover. Since Ally transitioned, I became interested in energy, knowing we are far more than physical bodies. We are made of subatomic particles of energy.

I read Camille's book. I was so engaged in this book of love and energy about another mother's heartfelt grief and love of her child, Aaron, who had transitioned. I felt an immediate connection to Camille and her writing. I wanted to reach out to her and tell her what a beautiful book she wrote about Aaron and mention that my daughter Ally also transitioned. I connected with Camille through social media on Facebook, and I sent her a message that I was so grateful to have read her book about Aaron.

I had a manuscript of my own, written in Word Press, about Ally but had no idea how to publish or where to publish it. I asked Camille where she published her book, and she said that she self-published it on Amazon. I told her that I was not familiar with Amazon Self-Publishing and was not very technologically savvy. Camille's immediate reply was, "If you should need any help, I can help you with your manuscript." I was so grateful and happy to hear that. She offered to assist me in editing my manuscript for self-publishing on Amazon. Camille's kindness and generous spirit while on her journey of grief revealed her genuine love and the kindness in her heart. Camille and I became friends. She lives in Canada and I in the United States in New Jersey.

We both felt that our children, Ally and Aaron, brought us together for a reason. I am forever grateful to Camille for editing my manuscript. Without her assistance, my publishing may have been delayed. Our children brought us together in writing our stories about them, and in Camille and I supporting each other and lifting our hearts and spirits! Our children are our cheerleaders from their heavenly home!

I am forever grateful for Ally's love that has continued to guide me. I have come to a place on my spiritual path where I know, without a doubt, that life continues, and most importantly, Love Never Dies.

About the Author

Margaret Mary Petrozzo was born in Brooklyn New York, graduated from Nursing School and became a Registered professional nurse in Medical Surgical nursing and then specialized in Neonatal Intensive Care unit at St Vincent's Medical center in Staten Island. This was the most rewarding job she had as a nurse. Skillfully she learned how to work under extreme lifesaving critical situations and helping to heal these tiny premature babies. She worked there for almost six years. She met Peter, her husband, got married and started a family right away. She has three children, Christine, Ally and Jamie. While pregnant with her first child Christine, she worked at a prestigious grade school as a school nurse and loved working with the children. While during and after pregnancies she worked part time in local home care cases, nursing homes and assistant care living facilities as a wellness nurse. She also had experience in dermatology and cosmetics and Mohs surgery for skin cancer patients. She also worked as an RN in the Mother/Baby unit at a local hospital where she gave birth to her own children, and as an RN liaison for a rehabilitation facility part time for five years in which she screened medical histories of patients for the rehab facility she was employed at.

Margaret Mary and Peter started the Alexandra Mary Petrozzo Scholarship Fund for other students seeking assistance, at Lynn University in Ally's memory. Her book, *Ally's Hope: My Christmas Angel*, was self-published on Amazon is a tribute to Ally. Margaret Mary hopes that this book will get into the hands of those parents or persons that need healing and to know that life after this life continues, and that love never dies. www.amazon.com/Allys-Hope-My-Christmas-Angel-ebook/dp/B095N8P4V4

*"The quantum measurement problem is
caused by a failure to understand that each
species has its own sensory world and that
when we say the wave function collapses and
brings a particle into existence, we mean
the particle is brought into existence in
the human sensory world by the combined
operation of the human sensory apparatus,
particle detectors and the experimental set up.
This is similar to the Copenhagen Interpretation
suggested by Niels Bohr and others, but
the understanding that the collapse of the wave function
brings a particle into existence in the human sensory
world removes the need for a dividing line
between the quantum world and the macro world."*
~Rochelle Forrester~
Author, Philosopher
Cultural Evolution, Epistemology,
Metaphysics, History, Quantum Theories

The Knowing, *Marian Shanley*

By Marian Shanley

I can remember from a very early age how the world seemed shiny and bright, and the love that surrounded me was something I took as normal for everyone. I can remember eating sand in a small sandpit before I could even walk, the grainy hard substance confusing and intriguing my sense, and playing with my magical friends.

I knew the feeling of utter joy and laughter and recall one time in particular as a child buckled into a light harness holding me safely in my pram as I couldn't yet walk, and I was less than a year old. Happiness and innocence in plenty while bouncing with joy and giggling and feeling the energy surge up just below my rib cage, creating the most joyous gush of laughter.

I remember the constant feeling that I was safe, watched over, and always aware of the lights I saw around people and the knowing before the happening. Like a secret knowledge, a sense, a smell, a feeling, an ache. I always had a "Knowing". But I did not realize that not everyone had it!

The first day I felt the true power of this kind of connection to time and space was my first big emotional tear at the tender age of three. As the second child of six, I had a hunger for knowledge the minute I could express it. I remember the sensation of being taken to Montessori in a small village in Ireland in a large transport vehicle, so foreign to my usual routine of being transported in my family car with my mother.

The village was called Trim and had many medieval buildings and tremendous history. My regular playground prior to this new routine, was in the ruins of the castle, best known now for the movie Braveheart with Mel Gibson. Passing the old stone walls after traversing the tight bridge over the river Boyne, I could feel my world was changing.

The knowing was growing and evolving!

I was very small for my age and yet already a little warrior, and this day, this unfamiliar journey without family left me feeling anxious. I remember the second I entered the building, I felt it was not for me, and I immediately turned on my heel and escaped out an open gate. I ran across the main road without awareness of traffic and saw a truck heading straight for me. I froze to the spot and closed my eyes, and next, I found myself opening them safe on the pavement. I remember the sensation of being lifted, of warm arms around me, and gently being placed on the sidewalk. Then the panic around me as I was spotted by a teacher and immediately brought home to my mother. So ended my first day in education, but I learned a lot that day. I knew something or someone had saved me.

This sense of not being alone continued for years, with small things and large things being unexplained constantly and again, taking that for granted because I thought everyone else had the same journey.
I do remember a child who played with me in the yard, who had a soul like no other, and we became fast friends. She used to whistle like a bird mimicking a wood pigeon, fascinating my ever-growing mind and soul. My open heart and soul never questioned whether she looked different or even spoke differently. I knew that the soul was all that counted.

219

Even at this early stage in life, I would fly in my dreams and meet her and lift her from the ground to show her how to fly with me. Sometimes it took a lot of effort, but I knew I had control over where we went and the freedom of soaring into the sky. To me, this was normal, that everyone had this type of existence. We would spend every waking moment together between classes and meet in our dreams at night for months. But then, one day, she simply wasn't there. She didn't show up to school, and I couldn't understand, and nobody explained anything to me.

Fast forward to a choir rehearsal and learning songs in Latin, I noticed she was no longer meeting me in my dreams. Two days later, six-year-old me stood in church singing with the choir as a little white coffin was wheeled down the aisle, and a strong booming voice came across the church speakers to talk about my little friend.

I was so happy and at peace because I knew she was an Angel. Grief helped advance my tuning, and I knew it would all be okay. Many asked me if I was sad, and I said, "No." Instead, I expressed I was Happy for her, which drew a lot of confused looks. I shed no tears but purely felt peace and knew. I simply knew. And then I heard a Wood Pigeon in the distance and felt a light kiss brush across my cheek. We never met in my dreams again, but that was the start of the Knowing. It's a strange kind of place as a child not having the words or language to explain to anyone.

I wanted so much for people not to be afraid of this secret power, but I became very aware of how people react to a child who can see beyond the moment.

My dreams became a place of travel and adventure. My zest for life was beyond my years, and my enthusiasm was of such heightened energy that it somehow was a catalyst for others' growth, whether they liked it or not! My open spirit had not yet learned how to protect itself, but the lesson was coming, whether I liked it or not, too. Over the next few years, I decided that hugging others could be healing, and I knew my true mission and journey in life was to make the world a better place. So, I began to make others happy. The Knowing was growing.

At age seven, I had the most amazing and beautiful teacher who gave me the gift of absolute love and education. The night before I attended her class, I woke up screaming as a large rat entered my dreams, trying to bite me. I grabbed its upper and lower jaws in my hands and tore its head apart in one large crack. I ran into my parent's room and jumped into their safe and nurturing arms, sobbing. I had no idea that time and space had given me a warning for the next day's events.

220

As I mentioned, my teacher was my idol, my love, my inspiration, and I was a bubbly, chatty little girl of seven who at every turn wanted to show her my heart and soul to make her happy. By the end of the day, I had a sore little hand from being hit with a wooden meter stick, and worse still, the most significant immediate damage was my little broken heart. Somehow, my enthusiasm for life and learning wasn't received in the way I meant it, and she got angry, and I was disciplined.

This type of discipline was very common in Ireland when I was a child but is illegal these days. That day I buried The Knowing...I stopped flying in my dreams...but it wasn't the end of the adventure.

I never asked a question in primary school again from that day forward, and my soul became held in a place of silence and fear until I left that school to go to Senior School. But from this trauma, something else began to happen. In the place of my dreams, I began to quietly scan people!!! What does that mean, I hear you ask?

Now, I discovered at a very early age that if I sat silently, focused on a person, I could check their health out from head to toe once I tuned into their energy. I could also feel if they were happy or sad. I could also sense the energy around them. When I say energy, I didn't know then, but I know now. I was sensing souls, quantum energy, and portals to time and space.

My earliest connection with time and space was a gentle but effective non-invasive search for energy. I absolutely considered this normal and that all children could do this. I knew instinctively that a hug or gently compassionate reference to their grief could be soothed by my energy, and thus my spirit journey started from there. These days the amount of time the knowing, quantum energy, and the power of dreams have come together to show and share a glimpse of what's beyond, before, behind and right here with us all. I constantly get reminded by numbers like 111, times like 11:11, or multiples of repeating numbers. I have given you a brief overview of the journey's small particles, and the growth's snippets. We are only a breath away from love and beauty and those who have travelled onwards.

But the biggest lessons I have learnt have been through loss. For example, my Nana who is now one of my Guardian Angels. I have learnt to call on my ancestors for help, and they present in perfume, feathers, music, rainbows, birds, numbers, and especially in my dreams.

Time and space move with our intentions and beliefs, but are most importantly, calibrated by our love and compassion. The one thing I have learnt from all my lessons in life so far is that we have today. We can create and manifest many beautiful things in life, but we also must allow that in parallel with this life, there is a flow beyond our control that will challenge us and force pain and growth, but at the core is genuine compassion for self and others. If we can sidestep anger when it rises and glide through honest pain to forgive ourselves and others along the way, then we rise. The Knowing is a sense of empathy beyond the atomic levels at which we resonate. It's a place so deep within that it rises in extreme times of grief, sorrow, fear, and challenge.

It's a voice within that surges and pulses and offers the most delicate calm in the most excruciating times. There is no way to humanly explain how deep it vibrates in the soul until it is experienced. But it is exactly as it says, a knowing, an understanding of the truth and the why.

Those who have experienced it gravitate towards each other. Without explaining, they reach for their mirror vibrational with others. Time and space will always be a part of this too, where quantum fields of energy surge and dip and create dynamics in life, in consciousness, and most importantly, in our growth as humans on this planet. Each atom of us vibrates a familiar signal to others with the knowledge, innate or otherwise, like a call to the wild, a high-frequency cry that a few will hear but even fewer will act upon.

I met Sean when I was sitting to do a Bio-Energy course in Dublin, Ireland, and he approached me as it was midway through the day. The venue for learning was a private school with limited numbers in the course, and I had yet to meet the students outside of the class I was attending. As he glided across the room, his first words to me were, "I have a message for you."

The Knowing was suddenly activated, like a switch from my childhood was suddenly energised again. I sat with him as he began to tell me that he had energies present with him who wished to share information with my family. He began with a message from a man in uniform, smelling of tobacco, and he informed me that this person was my grandfather. I knew he was right but silently sat and let him tell me the message. He shared a beautiful message from my grandfather to my dad with the knowledge I didn't even know about this.

All the time he sat there, I noticed his gentle nature and the ease at which he spoke. He told me information for my mother from another energy and referred to my Guardian Angel as Maureen, who was my Nana who passed. He gave me a very personal message to remember the happy little chatty, curious child I was and never let it go again.

This alone was profound. Then, as easily as he had come over, I turned my back for a split second, and he was gone. I continued the rest of the course for the day, and later that evening, I relayed all the wonderful things to my family in depth, and it created a new healing for them and tears of happiness and love.

The next day, I returned to the course to say a massive thank you to another student and share the words of my family members to whom he had given the message. I looked everywhere. I asked the course admin if she could contact him for me to say thank you. She informed me that there was no student named Sean, no teacher called Sean, and the course was restricted to students only who signed up prior. I spent a week trying to track down Sean, but I Knew...the parents Knew...everyone Knew. It was simply a formality for him going through the motions on this earthly plane. This gentle soul beyond time and space who offered my family contact with a messenger, and he became a voice of voices.

From that moment on, I made it my mission to follow my promise to myself when I was three years old, to make this world a better place.
So much has happened since then that a book will be written at some point. I have glossed over so much here. But I believe that I found my voice again to give others a voice. I have connected to quantum, but it's like learning to drive a spaceship, and in time and space, I shall master it. But for now, I'm enjoying the journey. Buckle up because there certainly will be a lot more to come. And my dreams are more vivid these days, so one thing is for sure... this piece is a catalyst that holds quantum healing, growth, and love.

We all so deserve that, and I, for one, will share it until my last breath before whatever lies ahead...

About the Author

Marian Shanley is a qualified Medical Herbalist, a broadcaster, humanitarian, and is most recognised for hosting the Power of Dreams Show on Dublin South Radio. She is a former Journalist and has met with the Dalai Lama. Marian is the recipient of many prestigious awards in Ireland, such as The Humanitarian Award and an award from the Lord Mayor of Dublin for supporting Original Artists and Musicians. She is a recording artist. Instagram @marianshanleypod Twitter @marian_shanley

*"You can know the name of a bird
in all the languages of the world, but
when you're finished, you'll know
absolutely nothing whatever about
the bird...
So let's look at the bird and see
what it's doing - that's what counts."
~Richard Feynman~
Nobel Prize Winning Physicist
1918 -1988*

Spirit Comes in Feathers, *Lynette Setzkorn*

By Lynette Setzkorn

Not long after my friend Brenda Baker died, I got a text message from her son, Brad. I've written about Brenda quite a bit since her death because she's very much alive and well, and she was very dear to me and to many others. She died in 2018 after a short, fierce battle with bile duct cancer and yet she remains a big presence in my life and the lives of our friends.

When Brad texted, "I have an interesting bird story if you have time," how could I refuse? I called him right away. The interesting story he wanted to share was pretty wild, but his voice on the phone sounded light ~ and happier than I'd heard him since before Brenda's diagnosis.

Brad had been sitting in the office in the front of his house, once Brenda's house, the night of Thanksgiving. It was nearing midnight and he was doing something online with lights off and the blinds closed. Suddenly, *POW!* something big hit the window, hard, just a foot or two away from where Brad was sitting.

It was startling, to put it mildly. The house sits at the end of a quiet cul-de-sac. Having spent almost a year in the front bedroom of that house while Brenda was ill, I can attest to the fact that after 7 or 8 pm, Glendale, Arizona's 50th Drive is a ghost town.

Being a young man, and a smart one, Brad thought it best to investigate, but first he picked up a pistol, just in case. What, after all, would be banging on the window of a house, on a very quiet street at midnight? Nothing good. Brad opened the front door a few inches, peeked out, and was instantly overcome by the powerful onslaught of a heavy feathered body and wildly flapping wings. A "really big" bird hurtled through the few inches of opening and shot into the house.

There's something dreadful about a bird in the house, and Brad was just as unenthused as I'd have been, as most of us would be. He rushed after it and was stunned to see the big thing flying erratically around the great room, finally coming to rest on the far wall, where it clung to the smooth stucco before slowly slipping down behind the television. Brad couldn't quite believe what he was seeing, so he hurried to look and, yes indeed, there were dark little bird eyes shining up at him in the dim light.

Though I don't want one in the house, I am an avid bird person and I had to know what kind of avian critter would exhibit such odd behavior. There are big flocks of mourning doves in Brenda's neighborhood, but they rarely fly at night. The two most common night flying birds, owls and bats, are easy to identify and Brad knew it wasn't one of those. As I quizzed him about the bird's appearance, he just kept saying, "it was big, really big."

I'd been telling Brad for months that Brenda would send him signs that she was with him. A solid skeptic, he was not yet impressed by the more usual sightings: a couple of dimes had turned up in strange places, a few flashing images on the television set which had meaning to her friends but left her son unconvinced.

And so commenced the extraction of the bird. He later told me he was thinking all the while, "Mom, really? Did you do this??" As a show of "Hello, son! I'm here!" it is funny, extraordinary, and in keeping with Brenda's big personality. It also fits nicely with two other instances when Brenda abandoned dropping dimes and sent somewhat irritating messages to her son, in each case later confirming to our friends who are mediums that she did indeed make the lights dim in the kitchen (no, son, you don't need an electrical overhaul. I just dropped in to say hi!) and sure enough popped the bathroom light bulb off its base as cleanly as if it had been cut (ta-dah!).

Why would someone in spirit send a sign like this? It's not every day a big bird knocks on the window, then rushes the front door the instant it's opened. In Brad's case, I wondered if it took that to really get his attention. He wants to believe his mom's with him. He feels her at times. But the random penny or butterfly or rainbow isn't substantial enough to penetrate his grief and skepticism. Enter the big personality of Brenda on her cherished son's first Thanksgiving without her, and the dramatic, wild, flapping evidence of "I really am here, son!" If she was trying to get his attention, it worked.

As soon as I heard this story, I recalled the experiences of two excellent mediums, Suzanne Giesemann and Susanne Wilson, both of whom have worked with and been tested by Dr. Gary Schwartz, a prominent afterlife researcher at the University of Arizona. On two separate days, before they knew one another, both of these experienced evidential mediums received messages describing the mechanics of how spirit is able to use creatures in the natural world to get our attention.

No, that's not your mother sprouting feathers and beak, hurling herself at the window and flapping through the front door. But it is your mother (your child, your husband, sibling, beloved friend, all of our loved ones in spirit) using the creature to connect with you, to send a message of comfort. "I'm still here. Believe." The spirits told the Suz/sannes, on two separate days in Schwartz's lab, we control the birds with their permission. It's kind of like remote control. "And the birds think it's fun!"

This blending of consciousness sounds like madness if we're thinking that, as humans, we're a cut above the average feathered creature. But the truth is, we are the creature, and the creature is us. I am you, you are me, we are all The Divine, expressing itself in trillions of cherished incarnations, and knowing that truth ~ really knowing it, gut-and-heart level ~ is to know with certainty that there is no death, no separation, and thus no permanent loss of love.

How does it work for Brenda to take over a bird and send a message to Brad? The quantum physicists would suggest it's a matter of intention. Brad's deeply grieving, Brenda knows it, and the wish to comfort him manifests in feathers and raps sharply at the window. Message delivered and, in this case, very well received. Brad's intention, expressed in the longing for his mother, might have played a part too. "I miss you, mom. If you're really out there, please show me."

In the Big Reality, there is one mind, one energy of love in the entirety of what we think of as the universe and beyond. It is infinite, everywhere present, in all things, always. True separation is not possible except in our human awareness. It's why our

227

minds can be trained to get out of the way so the consciousness of a living being can connect with the consciousness of one we think of as dead. Mediumship is simply expanding consciousness beyond what we think is real ~ these human suits we wear, what we see around us, and our busy little brains ~ in order to merge with All That Is.

Oneness. Consciousness. Merging. A universe made of love. All those words can sound like a lot of nonsense for many of us; nice in theory, but can we trust the concepts? And yet since Brenda departed in May of 2018, her friends and loved ones have been getting signs from her and having those synchronicities and experiences regularly confirmed by Brenda, through trustworthy mediums, with evidence that she was behind them.

Though I was sure that this crazy bird was sent by my friend, I wanted certainty, so I texted Suzanne Giesemann. She's exceptionally skilled and highly evidential, plus she connects with Brenda regularly, * having been very close to her in life. "When you get a chance, Brad had a pretty bizarre encounter with a bird. I think it was Brenda, but maybe you could ask her? I'll tell you the details after."

That wasn't the time for a confirmation. Suzanne and her husband Ty were at a football game. Suzanne said she wasn't getting anything from Brenda at that moment. I told Brad to trust his gut and I was, for once, trusting mine too. That was my message in this: when you know, you know. I knew without doubt it was her. The intense "truth shivers" that flooded my body when Brad told me the story were sufficient proof for me.

And then, the next day, an email from Suzanne. Brenda had dropped in on her to affirm that she had indeed sent that bird. Without having received any of the details, Suzanne said, "She had me laughing out loud as she took credit for the bird and showed me the remote control. She acted silly and apologized for just getting the hang of it. She showed me it was as if her guidance of the remote control had gone a little crazy and the poor bird ended up behind the television. All the while Brenda is loving that it's working, but a bit freaked out that the bird has crash-landed behind the TV."

This made me laugh out loud, because Brenda and I, once we heard the story of the two Suz/sannes in Gary Schwartz's lab, used to joke about the birds and the concept of directing them by remote. We'd mimic holding remote controls in our hands, driving birds into walls, windows, cars. Oops! It was a source of much hilarity in the year before she became ill, so it was a joy to hear Suzanne's confirmation that Brenda was playing at remote control bird operation and, ever the accomplished A+ student in life, laughing about her less than stellar performance at bird-driving-101.

That she was having trouble getting the hang of it also echoes a statement made through Suzanne a day or two after she quit breathing. Though a student of mediumship in life, she found communicating from the other side a bit of a strain. "It's as hard to learn communication here as it was to learn mediumship there." Clearly, she's mastered it now, but this new thing of driving birds? She hasn't exactly nailed it, not yet anyway.

"Then love flew through the door."

And yet the love that flew through that door was deeply felt. I heard a tone in Brad's voice that I had not heard since before Brenda got sick. It makes me weepy to think about it now. There is such a gift in knowing our loved ones continue. It doesn't entirely remove the pain of loss, but it helps. It's a promise: "I'm still right here, still with you. We'll be together soon enough."

The sound of hope, of coming to believe that she's not truly gone? I'll forever hear it in the tone of Brad's voice that night. It resonates deep in my soul. It's the sound of love and trust and maybe-just-maybe, of a broken heart beginning to mend.

We are so very deeply loved. That sounds like a cliche until we actually get it, making the connection of our human hearts to the truth of our souls' knowing. And usually, when that happens, the very thought makes the heart swell, and the eyes get teary.

The love that is Everything revels in the wonder and beauty of all of us. We are constructed of that Love and we ~ you, me, every one of us, even that fat flapping bird ~ are the direct result of Love expressing itself with so much joy it can't be contained. As Suzanne Giesemann puts it, when we come to know that love and life are forever, "we go from an emptiness that cannot be filled, to a fullness that can't be contained."

It's a wonderful, mysterious, magical world. Our loved ones are still right here, forever connected by the bonds of love we share.

Trust that. Let it settle.

I hope your heart expands.

I hope your eyes leak.

*Since her death in 2018, Brenda has since revealed herself as Suzanne Giesemann's mediumship guide, the two of them even teaching a class together with the Shift Network.

From An "Unexpected Mystic: Stories About Life, Love, Death, and What Comes After", Blog by Lynette Setzkorn, https://anunexpectedmystic.com/

About the Author

Lynette Setzkorn writes about life, death, and what comes after at AnUnexpectedMystic.com. Her story of Brenda Baker's life and death, An Unexpected Healing, was included in Debra Martin's book, Proof of Miracles. As a child abuse investigator and sexual abuse specialist with the State of Oklahoma, she regularly dealt with trauma, tragedy, and survivors thereof. But when her two great loves died at the end of 2012, she struggled to find a reason to live. Evidential mediumship ~ coming to know that we don't die ~ subsequently provided the solid foundation for a life-changing spiritual awakening and now a joyful life. When she's not talking to her dead people and catching the signs they send her way, Lynette is delighted to assist Suzanne Giesemann with her bookings.

"Reality is created by the mind,
we can change our reality
by changing our mind."
~Plato~
Philosopher
428-348 BCE

Choose to Believe, *Paige W. Lee*

By Paige W. Lee

Bryan and God blessed us with miracle after miracle—so many signs that our son was still present and a part of our lives. And yet still, years into my healing journey, I had doubts that would continue to creep in occasionally, unsolicited but present, nonetheless. Was it really Bryan? Was he really communicating with us? My mental mind didn't understand it. I wasn't one hundred percent sure I truly believed any of it. I had nagging fears and doubts that kept me distant from God and prevented me from fully connecting with my son.

I was so tired of doubting. No matter how many amazing signs Bryan sent us, no matter how many readings I received from reputable mediums, no matter how many times my own higher self-nudged me and spoke to me . . . still doubt would raise its ugly head from time to time. It was holding me back, keeping me down, literally choking me, preventing me from healing and moving forward.

One day, something truly miraculous happened. I heard these words in meditation: CHOOSE TO BELIEVE. Choose to believe that it is all real—my son's voice, the messages, the signs, the miracles. I understood that until I really DID believe, I could simply CHOOSE to believe. And that would be enough. For now. That was a critical moment in time for me.

After I made the decision to "choose to believe" everything broke wide open for me. Over time I realized that I no longer needed proof of anything! I wasn't "choosing to believe" anymore—I truly DID believe. My heart had been opened and there was no turning back.

Bryan and I wrote about this in an automatic writing session we did together in December 2014. It is titled "Believe." The credit for these words belongs to Bryan—he wrote through me so fast and so clearly...I was merely his scribe.

Where are you?

Where are you now?

If not here, then where?

Can I find you? Can I see you? Can I feel you?

Are you in my heart?

In my head?

Are you "on the other side"? Can you even be found?

Did you believe in Heaven and find your way there? But why? Oh why

did you leave me, my child?

The day you died

I believed I might die, too.

But gradually something awakened deep down inside of me,

and with the clarity that only

God can provide,

I knew I would find you.

So, the seeker in me searched everywhere.

In books, in classes, in meditation and prayer

in dreams, and through tears. So many tears.

I felt you draw nearer,

and I heard your voice

call out to me loudly,

with determination and force. MOM!

At that moment

our new journey began. I knew I could still have a relationship

with you.

Over the years,

as my grief subsided (just a bit),

I came to understand

the hows, the whys, and what ifs.

Not wanting me to waste the life I have left, you helped me move

beyond the pain

of your death.

My heart still aches.

I will never let you go.

But I understand now it was all part of our plan.

There is much work to do. Our journey is never ending, I know one thing for sure:

I found you!

You are here.

You are there.

You are everywhere.

You are the sun in my face

You are the wind at my back.

You are the trees swaying

You are the water cascading

You are young and happy and free!

You send me ladybugs and oh, so many signs,

to remind me of

your never-ending love.

You give me hope.

You give me peace.

You give me understanding and joy.

You give me all of this,

and so much more.

We hug!

We dance!

We laugh!

And sometimes, yes, we cry.

But I know you are with me always,

loving me, guiding me, always reminding me.

A new relationship was born between us.

Different, for sure,

but still just as real!

~~ ~ ~~

What is death, my friend, really?

Their bodies are gone,

but our loved ones are still here,

Because it's the Spirit that never dies,

never leaves us behind.

So, open your grieving hearts, open your minds

just a tiny bit,

and then

prepare to launch

a most fascinating ride! You and your loved one, together still.

Now and forever,

your relationship is real!

One heart, one love. Healing and growing, walking side by side with gratitude and in deep awe

of the miracle of life, the miracle of Spirit!

Releasing our paradigms about death and dying,

we come to understand

our true Purpose and true Self.

We come to know how blessed we are, not in spite of our grief,

but because of what it can teach us!

For me, for you, for all people who grieve, we have just one word: BELIEVE!

~~ ~ ~~ ~ ~~ ~

You CAN still have a relationship with your loved one. Just because you cannot see them or hear them does not mean that they aren't present. Can you hear or see gravity, yet do you believe? Can you hear or see the air that you breathe, yet do you believe? Can you hear or see your God, yet do you believe? Believe, my friend. Believe!

Excerpt from "Choose to Believe: A Story of Miracles, Healing, and the Afterlife", by Paige W. Lee, Ladybug Media, August 23, 2020

About the Author

Paige Lee is an Author, Speaker, former Grief Coach, and Healer. She volunteers as an affiliate leader for Helping Parents Heal and is also a Caring Listener for the organization.

Her spiritual awakening came abruptly and forcefully after her 23-year-old son, Bryan, was brutally murdered in September 2008. Just as the only world she'd ever known was shattered, a new world opened. A world filled with Hope, Spirit, and Love; a world that allowed her not only to continue having a relationship with her son, but a world that opened her own true self into being. Paige is driven to help others release their fears, negative blocks and diminishing beliefs about who they think they are, and become the beautiful, shining soul full of love and light that they truly are. When we let go of our paradigms that hold us prisoner and limit our ability to thrive, we learn to live a life full of peace, abundance, and joyful purpose.

Paige lives with her husband, Dwaine, on a small acreage near Boise, Idaho, where she puts her passion for nature and gardening to good use. They love to travel and spend as much time as they can with their two remaining children and five grandchildren. She takes every opportunity to be outdoors and, especially, to hike the many trails in the spectacular hills and foothills near her home. Choose to Believe is her first book, born of the pact she made with her son, after his death, to share their story and help others overcome the profound grief after the death of a loved one.

Paige and Bryan

Bryan

*"Life's like a play: it's not the length,
but the excellence of the acting
that matters."
~Lucius Annaeus Seneca~
Philosopher, Dramatist
Circa 4 BC – 65 AD*

The Soul Plan, *Michèle Chouan*

By Michèle Chouan

I was born on July 7th, 1956, in Algeria, at that time a French colony. We were already two years into the war of independence that would last six more years. In 1962, we, French people, had to leave the country in haste, Algerian people having conquered their independence. At the age of 65 today, I'm still struggling occasionally with symptoms of the trauma experienced in the early years of my life (insomnia and nightmares). My parents were born Jewish but were not practicing religion. I'm not observing any kind of religion myself. I'm the only girl among my siblings, two boys.

My parents, at the time of the war of independence, experienced the separation of their own parents (divorce on one side, abandonment on the other), which added extra angst and responsibilities at the young age of 26 for my father and 22 for my mother, considering they also experienced World War II during their childhood. I wasn't able then to analyze their circumstances, which would have given me a better understanding and kindness towards them.

What I experienced with them was that my father, in his attempt to avoid troubles, became hardened, insensitive, and tyrannical. He was focused on controlling and overcoming material and financial situations and hardships. As for my mother, she evolved in a totally opposite direction: weak, obedient to him, and dependent on him, even though she worked and earned a living.

This familial environment had an impact on me: I became secretive, solitary, daydreaming, and interested in metaphysical matters. I also became sad, pessimistic to the extent that I started to feel depressed around the teenage period. At the age of

17, I started meditation with a group. Initially, it was difficult to keep at it, but eventually, it became my favorite way to connect to a dimension of serenity and spirituality.

By the age of 24, I had quit my law studies, part because I was bored with them, part to manifest my rebellion against my father. As we lived on the French Riviera, I decided to study and work in the tourism branch, at hotels reception desks. That is when my first experience happened. I'm prone to think of it as an OBE (out of the body experience) rather than an NDE (near-death experience) because there was no tunnel, no feeling of intense love, no meeting with an extraordinary religious figure as commonly described in the NDE literature. So, this is what happened:

Meeting my spiritual guides.

I had to undergo surgery under general anesthesia. I don't remember much about the circumstances preceding the surgery itself. I was probably rolled in the operation room and lying on a table; I received an injection of anesthetic while I was counting backward from 10 to 0. I didn't go further than 7. After an indefinable while, I regained consciousness in another dimension.

I was not anymore in the operation room. For lack of better description, I felt as if I was in the coulisse of a theater. The place felt cozy, with big velvet curtains, rugs in the colors of red and brown. But more importantly, I was facing two beings dressed in long bright dresses of a Schiaparelli pink color. But I could feel that one was masculine, and one was feminine. I immediately told them that I didn't want to return. That nothing was working and that I was depressed. What happened is that I was aware I was in the afterlife and didn't want to return to Earth life. It felt like I was rushing back to my guides to let them know that my Earth plan was not working and that I was too discouraged to continue. I had lost the meaning of my life and the desire to go on.

The two guides were listening with attention and benevolence, but I could feel there was some amusement in their gentle smile. Similar to an adult listening to the complaint of a child. At the same time, in the field of my consciousness, I could perceive the scene of the theater becoming more present. That's where I was supposed to return. It was like a metaphor for me to return to Earth, playing my role as a human being.

The guides started to push me energetically towards the scene. I resisted giving more arguments for not going back. That's when they told me: "You can go now. Don't worry. Things will be better now." Instantly, my resistance weakened, and they gave the extra push.

Immediately, I found myself back in the operating room. But I was located at the ceiling level, blinded by the intensity of the light coming from OR spotlights hanging on the ceiling. But was it coming from the spotlights? And what part of me was blinded since I was not in my body? At my level, there were also some transoms allowing to see the outdoors. Slowly, my gaze was attracted to the scene happening below. From the ceiling, I could see several nurses cleaning the OR, putting away instruments, and rolling away carts with machines. They were casually exchanging information.

At last, I saw "a body" lying on the operating table. It took me a while to realize it was mine. As soon as the realization set in, I felt an irresistible pull towards my body, even though my feelings toward it were close to total indifference. I reentered my body with a feeling of repulsion, like putting a hand in a cold, wet glove, and realized that I was now seeing the ceiling from below. But at no point did I have the feeling of "rolling on my back".

Coming back to ordinary consciousness, I gave myself the instruction to remember what had happened and fell asleep. The following days, I felt a huge change in my state of mind and emotions. I felt balanced and happy. The contrast with my previous state of mind was glaring. Nothing had changed in my life, but I accepted whatever was there. This new frame of mind was to last for several years. And I never went back to the previous gloomy emotional state.

It felt like an upgrade of my whole life, even though nothing had changed yet. But I was able to envision a deeper dimension and put sense to life. I was not alone anymore. I had company, helpers in another dimension. But that was not all. What happened next was achieved to convince me of the reality of my experience.

A week after my surgery, my colleague and friend Mary offered me to join her on a short trip to Paris to visit her father and stepmother. There, she introduced me to a couple of friends, and we spent a few evenings with them, going to the restaurant or attending concerts in bars. One of these friends, Alain, retained my attention, and we exchanged a couple of words during one of the evenings. He mentioned that he collected postcards, and if I ever travelled, he would be grateful to receive some postcards from different places. Mary and I left Paris, and a couple of days later, we were both having dinner in a little restaurant. I told her about the postcards and that I had found old postcards in my parents' belongings. I asked for Alain's family name and address. Mary spelled the name, and I was writing it down: C.H.O.U.A.N. Seeing the full name on the piece of paper, a swift thought came to me: "That's going to be my name". I immediately dismissed the thought as "crazy".

But, by the title of this chapter, you already guessed that the thought was not crazy at all. It was a premonition. Alain and I connected through the postcards I sent, we wrote to each other, he visited me on the Riviera and the rest is history… two years later, we married, and I effectively took the name of Chouan.

That's how I know the encounter with the guides was not a dream or a hallucination due to the drugs administered for the surgery, as the medical staff often says. It brought premonitory and very supportive information that helped me move on in a very serene and balanced frame of mind. It gave me a sense of my life. There was a plan behind all that happened. It also opened my long-life desire to study and practice in the realm of spirituality: meditation, yoga, therapy.

My life happened on two simultaneous levels: material and ordinary, working, raising our children, etc., and spiritual, studying and practicing meditation, yoga, and reading all the books I could find on the subjects of NDE, OBE, Past Lives, and reincarnation. After working for many years in the corporate environment, essentially as a Human Resources Manager, I had the opportunity to move to New York in the USA. There, I studied Polarity Therapy, which is an energy-based healing modality. I practiced in a private office and in a hospital before having to return to France and resuming corporate life for a number of years.

In 2001, I took a number of Past Life Regression sessions in Paris. Fifteen years later, I would find the evidence of one of the retrieved Past Lives during a trip in Peru. All this is reported in the book I authored in 2019. In the meantime, I kept studying, getting certified in Coaching and Hypnosis, and I finally left the corporate world for good and settled practice as a Life Coach and Hypnotherapist specializing in Past Life Regression and Between Lives Regression. We moved abroad to different countries the next few years, and I carried my practice with me.

In December 2020, while in different periods of lockdown due to the Covid pandemic, I decided to take an online mediumship class with Suzanne Giesemann. My intention was not to become a medium, but my father had died in April 2019, and I wanted to make contact with him.

My relationship with my father had always been somewhat distant and cautious. The tough, tyrannical upbringing I had had to experience had left traces. He tried to connect with me in many opportunities, mainly by expressing his interest in my work of hypnosis and Past Life Regression. He liked to display a cautious skepticism around the subject of reincarnation. During the three last years of his life, as we were living in Saudi Arabia, I had many opportunities to talk with him on the phone. I tried to lift up his spirits, as my mother, diagnosed with Alzheimer's, had been put in a specialized institution. He felt their life had taken an unfair turn. I attempted to change his perspective by interrogating him about the sense of such a challenge at that time of his life ("What do you think you are learning?").

I told him I was writing a book, and this led us to have a discussion about reincarnation. I asked him to make a pact with me: the first of us to die would send an irrefutable sign to the other one if the soul survived death. This pact was inspired by the one Elizabeth Kübler-Ross made with her ex-husband. My father agreed but specified he was certainly the one who would die first.

On April 1st, 2019, my father died. We visited him a week prior to his death. He was hospitalized but was very conscious and articulate. We were told that he was just tired after a bad infection and that he was convalescing. We talked for an hour, and I had no indication that he was dying. Before I left, he told me that he "adored" me. I should have known.

A week later, we were back in Riyadh when I received a call from my brother telling me he had died in the early hours that morning. Unfortunately, due to my primary relationship with him, I didn't feel sorrow or grief, even while attending his funerals. But I kept waiting for "the sign" that didn't come. That's how I decided to take Suzanne Giesemann's class. I was practicing daily, hoping that at some point, I would contact my father and that he would send the sign.

My father sends a sign from the afterlife.

December 27th, 2020, we were at home with my daughter and her husband. There was a big astronomical conjunction of Jupiter and Saturn to observe in the sky. This conjunction looks like one big star, and it's called Christmas Star or Star of Bethlehem. Every night around that date, we stood in our garden, in the sharp cold, wrapped in our coats to observe the phenomenon. That night, on December 27th, inspired by the beauty of the stars and according to Suzanne's instructions, I whispered a request to my father: "Dad, if you are here, please send me a sign."

We came back inside and sat to watch the series *The Crown* - Season 4, Episode 8, and to my surprise, at minute 8:22, there was an English cab driving away. One of its license plates had my birthdate on it: 7756. I was all the more amazed that one of my father's obsessions was the birth dates of all the members of our extended family and friends. During his entire life, he had been writing them down on his calendar, punctually sending a note to each of us. I felt elated… what were the chances, so fast after asking that I would receive such a clear sign.

Screenshot of *The Crown* - Season 4, Episode 8 - minute 8:22

Of course, I kept wondering how my specific individual sign would be carved forever in a big production as *The Crown*. How could that happen? But I had to let go of that line of questioning/doubting. The sign exists for you and no one else. This plate didn't mean anything to anyone else, only to me. And I sent immense gratitude to my father across the expanse of the sky, wherever he was.

Finally, I will tell you my last story of communication with the afterlife.

Communication with Adam.

On January 20th, 2017, as I was living in Saudi Arabia, I received a call from the French Embassy, asking me if, in my capacity of Coach/Therapist, I could meet with a couple of French people whose eight years old son Adam died suddenly during the preceding night. This is how I met Mary-Alice and Gabriel. The shock of this death was all the more significant, that Adam had no pre-existing condition. That day he experienced some tiredness and fever and couldn't participate in a running competition organized by the French school of Riyadh. At night, he didn't have dinner but got some Paracetamol with an herbal tea, before going to bed. His dad, checking on him during the night, found him stiff and brought him back to the parental bed. Soon enough, he woke up Mary-Alice, and they agreed that something was wrong. They took him to the emergency room, where he was rapidly attended to. Unfortunately, after 50 minutes of attempts to stabilize him, he died.

I worked with Mary-Alice and Gabriel until they left Riyadh to go back to France. The devastation was profound, the experience senseless… I was just there for them and tried to help them bear their burden.

Fast forward to December 2020, during my mediumship course with Suzanne Giesemann. On December 20th, I sat down for practice. Following the course instructions, I connected myself to a higher dimension and waited for a deceased person to appear. A couple of minutes later, a being showed up, and I instantly identified him as Adam. I never met him in person, but I recognized him from the pictures Mary-Alice had shown me. Except that he looked more like 20 years old than 8 (the age he died). In my consciousness, I asked him how he was doing. He looked happy and dynamic. He was surrounded by a beautiful, soft light and told me that his "job" over there was to take care of deceased children. He was welcoming and accompanying them right after their transition. His last incarnation (as Adam) happened for him to be familiar with the experience of dying as a child and remembering how children felt after passing.

According to the course instructions, I asked him to give me evidence that he was Adam. He said that for me, it would be a big red stone, like a ruby, that I would find soon after our communication (I had a rapid thought there, that it would be pretty

245

difficult... all the more that I was at home in the countryside under a Covid lockdown...). For his parents, they would find a message from him to them in his things. I had the image of a notebook in a box. That meant I was supposed to tell his parents about the mediumship experience... I felt I was not ready to tell anybody about this, let alone Mary-Alice and Gabriel. I didn't want them to think I was crazy, but most of all, I didn't want to raise their hopes and be responsible for them being crushed if they didn't find the message. They didn't need any kind of extra cruelty. Of course, Adam perceived my reluctance and encouraged me to let go of my fears and to pass the message. I felt the message was not mine to retain. Who was I to keep his parents from receiving hope and comfort from the afterlife? I promised that I would pass the message on the next anniversary of his death at the latest.

The same day this communication took place, as I was watching a pastry contest show on Netflix, one candidate decided to bake a pastry that looked like a big ruby. Of course, I sat stunned... I could feel a rush of energy running through me and a sense of exhilaration too. Part of me couldn't fathom how that was possible.

Then on February 20th, 2021, it was four years since Adam died. Mary-Alice posted on Facebook, and it seemed her grief was unchanged. And I took this opportunity to send her a private message to let her know about my communication with Adam, specifying that I hoped she didn't think I was crazy. She answered right away and reassured me as to my sanity. She felt too tired to go through Adam's things but told me she would check his belongings soon.

Six hours later, that same day, she sent me a picture of a double letter she had retrieved from Adam's things. The letters were written pages from a notebook and were bound with a green ribbon. One letter was for her, the other for Santa. On hers, Adam had written: "Dear Mom, I would like to do artistic activities with you." But Mary-Alice was not sure the message was the right one. She was too afflicted to think straight.

The next day, she sent me another message saying that she woke up that morning with the desire to paint, and that was something she liked to do with Adam when he was alive but had not much time to do. She stopped painting after he died. But that day of February 2021, she spent the entire day painting. She finally recognized that it was Adam's message through the veil, and I confirmed her understanding by encouraging her to communicate with Adam through her art. She could feel a new energy and was lifted up for the first time since Adam's death. She was filled with hope as a real opening took place, a new level in her grieving process.

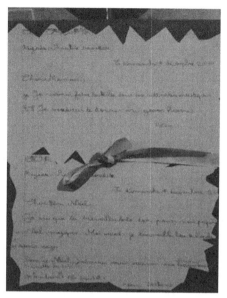

Adam's message to his mother Mary-Alice

About the Author

Michèle Chouan is the author of *Transformer votre esprit pour changer votre vie* (Editions Baudelaire, 2019) a memoir and a self-development guide. After working 20 years in the corporate environment in different executive positions, she decided to pursue her long-life passion: therapy and coaching, particularly hypnosis and past-life regression, with 25 years of practice. Michèle holds a Master's in Human

Resources. She is also Master-Practitioner in Ericksonian, Humanist, Past-Life and Between Lives Hypnosis, www.coach2inspire.com

"Spooky action at a distance."
~Albert Einstein~
On Quantum Entanglement, 1935
Nobel Prize Winning
Physicist
1879 - 1955

The Letter, *Casey Gauntt*

By Casey Gauntt

This is a story about the two most important men in my life: my father, Grover Cleveland Gauntt, Jr, and my son, James Tedrow "Jimmy" Gauntt. I thought their deaths forever disconnected me from them until I was shown otherwise.

The Letter.

I sat in my law office on a sunny November morning in San Diego, California, but the bright day couldn't raise my spirits. Three months earlier I'd lost my 24-year-old son. Handsome, brilliant Jimmy was two years into his career in Los Angeles as an actor and screenplay writer. After partying with some friends, he decided to walk home. He never made it. In the darkness, on a narrow, winding, road, a car struck him. Not enough time for either to avoid the collision—nobody's fault. Just a terrible accident.

A knock on the door roused me. Shelley, my assistant, entered as if she were walking on eggshells. "An Emily Sue Buckberry called. Said you were both in Coalwood, West Virginia, many years ago. She has something you left behind and thought you might want it. Here's her cell number." She laid the pink phone slip on my desk and left.

I certainly remembered Coalwood. I'd spent the summer after high school graduation working at the Olga Coal Company. My father's Chicago-based company, Case Foundation, was contracted to punch a 2,000-foot ventilation shaft into a new section of the mines, and my dad sent me to work there before I started college in the fall.

1968 was a tumultuous year. The war in Vietnam was raging with 500,000 Americans deployed overseas. Our country and families were being ripped apart by violent anti-war demonstrations. Civil rights leader, Martin Luther King, was assassinated in Memphis in April, and two months later, Robert Kennedy Jr., was assassinated in Los Angeles. Coalwood might provide some respite from the insanity gripping our country.

On June 9, 1968, my flight landed in Charleston, West Virginia. As I pulled my suitcase from the baggage carousel, a young man with black hair and a swarthy complexion strode up. He wore tan pants and a long-sleeved shirt. A flat-billed railroad engineer's cap perched on the back of his head. "Hi. I'm Tim Bowman, but everybody calls me Mex," he said, sticking out his hand.

I shook it. "I'm Casey."

"Figured so," Tim said. "Boss's kid, right?"

I nodded, wondering if that fact would be held against me. Tim didn't seem to care one way or another. "Come on. It's a long drive to Coalwood," leading the way to a beige pickup with the Case Foundation Company logo emblazoned on the driver's door.

On the two-hour drive, I learned that Tim was born and raised in Coalwood, the middle child in a family of three boys and three girls. He was my age, eighteen, and had just graduated from Big Creek High School in Welch, a couple of towns over the mountain. His father was forced to retire as a coal miner for Olga because of black lung disease. We swapped stories as we cruised along. By the time we arrived in Coalwood, we were friends.

Coalwood, in the southwest corner of West Virginia near the Kentucky border, later became famous as the hometown of Homer Hickam, Jr. Homer, known as Sonny to his friends, was the leader of a high school rocket club that won the National Science Fair Grand Prize medal in 1960. In 1998 he wrote a memoir about the town and his and his friends' experiences. *Rocket Boys* was a huge bestseller and a year later was made into the movie *October Sky*, which starred Jake Gyllenhaal as Sonny and Chris Cooper as his father. Mr. Hickam, Sr., was the superintendent of the coal mines buried deep below the town owned by Olga Mining Company. The summer I was there, Sonny was fighting in Vietnam as a U.S. Army officer.

Tim helped me get settled in the Clubhouse, a splendid three-story boarding house, and hotel built in the early 1900s. Enormous white pillars framed the porch and entrance. Junior Chapin and his wife, Carol, ran the place, both employed by Olga. As I followed Mrs. Chapin to my room on the second floor, she chattered away like we were old friends.

"We live here in the Clubhouse, you know. We have two teenage daughters, Kim and Theresa. You'll get to know them real quick. I make breakfast every morning, and I'll make sure you have a good lunch to take with you. Dinner is at five-thirty sharp."

As I unpacked, I wondered what it would be like living in a company town where every house, every business, every person was owned or employed by the mine. It wouldn't take long to find out.

The job site was a few miles up Snakeroot Hollow in a place called Mudhole. The unusual names weren't the only things strange about Coalwood. I'd grown up in Itasca, Illinois, twenty miles west of Chicago, surrounded by soybean fields, uninterrupted vistas, and huge skies. I lived in a nice neighborhood on a golf course. In contrast, Coalwood was surrounded by tree-covered blue mountains crouched above this Appalachian miners' camp, seeming to squeeze everything and everyone through the slit of a valley they called home.

It was a "two-smoke ride" to the shaft job. I usually bummed unfiltered Camels from one of the crew members everyone called The Greek.

The job ran three shifts per day. The work was hard and dangerous. I got kitted out in my yellow, waterproof suspendered pants and coat, strapped the battery pack for my miner's lamp to my waist, settled the wide-brimmed metal hard hat on my head, and stepped into the skip, a metal can a few feet square tethered to a crane by a metal cable that acted as a crude elevator to drop us down to the bottom of the shaft. Tafon, Hub, and Rat, all Coalwood boys, rode down with me. Fear rose in me as the skip began to drop. The skip picked up speed, plunging four hundred feet to the bottom of the shaft, where I'd spend the next eight hours. The jagged rock walls blurred as we plummeted past. The skip slowed and stopped. I hitched up my britches and stepped out into darkness pierced only by our headlamps. My first day of work had begun.

I was handed a pneumatic drill—a jackhammer. My job was to drill holes into solid rock to accommodate the sticks of dynamite that would shatter rock and deepen the shaft. The jackhammer was about two feet in length and weighed sixty pounds. Tafon Hylton, the foreman, showed me how to clip a five-foot drill bit into the business end.

"Hold it as far above your head as you can, and keep it tight to the rock," he instructed.

Fortunately, I had grown quite a bit the past two years and was about six foot two and a whopping one hundred fifty pounds. I set the bit against the rock and pressed the trigger.

Oh, shit! It felt like my teeth were going to shake out of my gums. The noise was ferocious. As I drilled my way down into the two-inch diameter hole, the work got a little easier and I learned some tricks of the trade, thanks to Rat Kirk, the only guy on the crew skinnier than me, with an Adam's Apple big enough to rival Johnny Appleseed's. Once I got the drill handles down to chest level, I'd throw one of my legs over the drill to add more weight to force it down. When it worked its way a little lower, I sat on it.

More than once the drill bit would suddenly bind up in the hole and I'd get bucked off the drill like a cowboy tossed from a bull's back, slamming into the wall, and getting pretty banged up. The other miners guffawed, thinking that was about the funniest thing they'd ever seen. I'd struggle to my feet, shrug, and do it all over again.

Drilling through solid rock, even with water-cooled drills, created a blinding swirl of dust. The solution? Red Man chewing tobacco. I'd put a big chaw of that in my jaw and as I breathed in through my mouth, the slug of wet tobacco acted like a filter and trapped some of the dust—at least in theory. Of course, it never dawned on me that I was swallowing the dust, along with the nicotine, which made me feel like I could work forever and never get tired.

Once the 60 or so holes were drilled, we packed them tight with sticks of dynamite using a wooden tamping rod. Then we inserted the detonators and wired them all up, cold sweat dripping down my back that nothing would set them off early.

After setting the charges, we'd be hoisted out. The fire master would holler, "Fire in the hole!" and press the hot button. The ground shuddered underfoot. Then the sound rolled out of the shaft like Thor's fury after one of Loki's tricks. When the smoke and gases cleared out, a mechanical mucker would scoop up most of the rock. The rest we'd shovel out by hand. On a good day, all three shifts would advance the shaft about ten feet.

Everyone in town knew my grandfather, Vern Case, and father ran Case Foundation, and this kid with a silver spoon in his mouth was viewed with suspicion. Later that summer Tim confided in me. "Those first few weeks you were here? Somebody—I'm not sure who, and I don't know if they worked for Case or Olga—sneaked into your room several times and went through your stuff."

"Why the hell would somebody do that?" I asked, outraged at this violation of my privacy.

Tim shrugged. "Just checkin' you out, I guess, tryin' to figure out what you're doin' in Coalwood."

"Like I'm some kind of spy?"

Tim shrugged again. He had no answers. Neither did I.
As time went on, my willingness to work hard earned me respect and friendship.

I learned a lot of things in Coalwood. In addition to drilling, stuffing fuses into dynamite, and chewing tobacco, I learned how to test for methane gas, the chief nemesis of all coal miners. I also became adept at shooting rats with a .22 rifle at the local garbage dump and drinking 3.2 beer and an occasional snort of homemade moonshine.

I also made a lot of friends both on the job and with other boys who lived in town. Everyone had a nickname: Hub, Taf, Rat, Mex, Squirrel, Choke-Knot, Ringo, and Lurch, to name a few. They honored me with an invitation to play on their softball team that played other nearby mining towns and my own nickname: Long Ass, because of my exceptionally long legs. Although I was extremely apprehensive about spending a summer in a place unlike any other I'd ever been, it turned out to be one of the most memorable and enjoyable periods of my life.

253

My dad came to visit me late that summer. We had dinner and he spent the night in the Clubhouse. The next day he joined me at the job site, an alien draped in his dark blue suit. The crew snapped to, almost saluting when he showed up. My father naturally commanded that level of respect from tough men. He paid little attention to me. Inside I was beaming.

As he got ready to return to Chicago, he took me aside.

"Casey, before you get home, do me a favor. Get a haircut and don't chew tobacco in front of your mother."

In late August, I flew off to the University of Southern California in Los Angeles, where I majored in business and law and met the love of my life, Hilary. As far as I was concerned, Coalwood was forever in my rearview mirror.

Now, 40 years later, a voice from the past had caught up with me. The Buckberry name meant nothing to me, and I hesitated to return the call. What could she possibly have of mine that I would want? After considering the message for an hour, I dialed her cell phone.

"Emily Buckberry," a staticky voice said.
"Uh, this is Casey Gauntt. You left a message for me?"

"Hey, Casey. You probably don't remember me, but my mom and I lived on the third floor of the Clubhouse the summer you worked in Coalwood." Her voice was effusive and gregarious.
She was right. I didn't remember her.

"You used to play your guitar on the porch and sing. Sometimes we'd all sing along."

An image of long brown hair and a smile hovered in my mind. "I remember," I fibbed.

"I told your assistant that you'd left something behind in Coalwood. As handsome as you are, she probably thinks it was a baby."
We both laughed.

"When you left Coalwood, I was bummed that I didn't get to say goodbye. I went past your room and saw a letter and an empty Case Foundation envelope addressed to you lying next to a wastebasket. I picked them up and scanned the first couple of paragraphs. It was a letter from your father and the envelope was marked 'Personal.' He had written about problems the company was having on the Olga job, and I was afraid that—Coalwood being a company town and all— if that got around town there'd be big problems. I thought. Casey should have ripped this up or something. Did he really mean to throw it away?

"So, I kept it, intending to send it on to you. But I got sidetracked with graduate school and life in general. The other day, I was going through some boxes and found the letter. I Googled you, called your San Diego office, and here we are."

Yes, we were.

She chattered on. "So, Casey, are you married?"

"Yes," I grunted, anticipating her next question.

"Any kids?"

"We have a daughter, Brittany." Tears welled as I told her how Jimmy had died only three months before. I barely heard her words of condolence.

All of the laughter and light-heartedness were sucked out of her voice. She was stunned and, for once, at a loss for words. Finally, she asked me, "Do you want the letter?"

I managed to give her my home address and we ended the call.

Instantly, my body was awash in goosebumps from head to toe, and I felt like a current of electricity was pulsating through me. I'd never before experienced anything like it. I was consumed with a feeling, a deep knowing, that something very strange and exceptionally powerful was afoot. I cried hard for several minutes. I hadn't told Emily I'd been thinking a lot about my father the last few weeks.

Two years after that summer in Coalwood, I'd flown home from college to Itasca for Christmas. Dad was away on a business trip, but he was supposed to return the next day. I woke up that morning to find my thirteen-year-old sister, Laura, in my bed, shaking and crying. Mom stood in the doorway, her face ashen.

"They found your father in his office this morning. He shot himself."

While I had lived the college life and hung out with my fraternity brothers, the company was consumed with financial problems. A deep recession mired Case Foundation in debt. On top of that, the developer of a massive Chicago skyscraper, the John Hancock Building, had filed a hundred-million-dollar lawsuit against Case Foundation and my dad for alleged faulty foundation work. Dad became more and more frustrated, exhausted, and depressed until he could take no more.

On Christmas Eve Day, a letter addressed to me arrived. Inside were three hundred-dollar bills and a one-line note scrawled by Dad: "Please get something for your mother and Laura for Christmas."

Stricken, I handed Mom the money and tossed his suicide note in the trash. Two weeks later, Mom packed up the house and moved to her folks' place in California. I went back to college.

Emily and I didn't talk about my father during our call or how I'd spent the better part of the last four decades trying to bury his memory and all of the pain and suffering he'd brought upon me and his family. He was supposed to keep us safe. Instead, he abandoned us and ruined our lives. My father was the strongest man I knew. He was a highly decorated Army officer during World War II and received multiple medals for bravery and exceptional leadership.

I was deeply angry and frightened by his suicide. I couldn't talk about it. When I got back to college, I told some of my fraternity brothers my dad had died. To those who asked 'How?' I replied, "heart attack." I maybe told three people what really happened. Over the next 38 years, I ran away as hard and fast as I could from my dad.

I did my best to keep my own family secure and happy and shield them from hurt.

But I couldn't keep Jimmy safe.

Over 1,000 friends and family attended Jimmy's memorial service in La Jolla. His death was a shocking gut-punch, and he was deeply mourned. We were beyond devastated, and I descended into a very dark place.

A week before Emily Sue called me, our daughter Brittany came over. She told Hilary and me that over the past two years "Jimmy felt a peculiar connection with your dad. He felt your dad's presence around him and became obsessed with finding out everything he could about him."

She said Jimmy spent a lot of time in the attic of our house where boxes of family scrapbooks and photographs fill the space. "Jimmy found and read several letters your father wrote to Gramma Barbie and his parents during the war, and several photos of your dad as a boy, soldier, and middle-aged man. It all fascinated him." Brittany continued.

"When Jimmy told me this, he made me promise not to tell you, saying 'It will freak Dad out.'"

He was right. After Brittany left, Hilary and I talked some more about Jimmy's compulsion to know all he could about his grandfather; a man he never met and that I wouldn't talk about.

I don't recall much about that conversation, but later Hilary would say, "I hadn't seen you that angry in ages. Do you remember what you said?"
I shook my head.

"You said, 'What the hell is my dad doing hanging around Jimmy? If he had something to do with Jimmy's death, I don't think I can live with that.'"

I began to see a psychologist six weeks after Jimmy died. I knew deep in my core I needed help to absorb his loss as well as finally confront my father's suicide. My work with Dr. Frank Altobello—Dr. A as he likes to be called—has been enormously helpful.

I told Dr. A about our conversation with Brittany and how upsetting it was for me. He said, "There's a powerful connection among your father, Jimmy, and you. We need to see where this is going. Something may be happening."

Emily Buckberry called five days later.

On the Saturday after Emily's call, Hilary and I went with our daughter, her husband of one year, Ryan, and my mother to Del Mar Beach. The Santa Ana winds had blown in a perfect day: cloudless sky, a sea the color of sapphires, and temperatures in the high seventies. Brittany and I paddled past the surf line on boogie boards and spread some of Jimmy's ashes. Around three, Mom wanted to go home, while the others stayed at the beach.

I dropped Mom off and decided to swing by our house and check the mail. Inside the box was a priority mail package from Emily. I took it inside and tossed it on the counter. There it lay while I fiddled around the kitchen for a bit. What could be in it? Would it bring back even more terrible memories to see my father's handwriting— knowing that he had only two short years to live before leaving us forever?

At last, I tore the strip off the package and pulled out the Case Foundation envelope. Emily had attached a note. "Here are some words from your dad that might help sustain you as a bereaved father. It surely can't do anything but comfort you to be reminded of how much you were loved as a son."

The envelope was postmarked on June 19, 1968. I drew out the letter. Dad's neat handwriting spread across both sides of the page. Phrases jumped out at me. "We have lost a lot of time on the job . . . leadership a big factor . . . the three explosions we've had on the job has caused us serious delays...we have a good contract, but it doesn't cover stupidity . . . your leadership qualities might be contagious . . ."

He wrote about suffering from depression and insecurity in his youth, a religious zealot of a mother he could not reason with, and a war that changed him. These were things he had never shared with me.

More phrases. "I don't consider myself successful, therefore I'm not going to preach to you. Should you want and ask for my advice, I'll give it . . . don't expect you to follow it blindly . . . I hope you develop a strong character to go along with your fine mind and wonderful body...give some thought to what you want to become and do, and if your ambitions are high, go to work... only you control your destiny. . .we love you and will never turn our back on you."

258

Nothing in the letter was familiar to me. I examined the envelope. It was in pristine condition as if it had been steamed open. I always tear the top or side of an envelope to pull out a letter. Always. That letter never got to me that summer in Coalwood.

He closed his letter with this:

"I'll be around, any time you want me. I'll be there, because I care more than you'll ever know, my son. All love, Dad."

My body shook with sobs. I turned to look for him—and Jimmy. I felt my father was in the kitchen with me.

And what I didn't mention, is that Saturday, the day the letter finally arrived in my hands, was Jimmy's 25th birthday. My father's letter arrived on my son's birthday!

My father knew that day would be one of the hardest days of my life, and he was there with me, as he promised he would be.

About the Author

The letter from my father arriving all those years later on the day it did was a game-changer for me and my family. I instantly realized my father never stopped watching over me and loving me. He bonded with his grandson to help him over to the other side. I also realized there is something much bigger and more powerful around us than I ever imagined. Instead of running away from him, I began to run to my father and learn everything I could about him, and why he wrote about those things he suffered as a child and young man. I began to properly mourn his death.

I also knew this incredible synchronicity was not only for me and my family but was meant to be shared. I wrote the story and gave it to my family, our friends, and Jimmy's friends. Thus began my ten-year transition from a career as a hard-charging corporate attorney to my second and most rewarding career as an author, speaker, and grief advisor.

I started a website in 2011, www.writemesomethingbeautiful.com. In 2013, I co-founded with two other dads a growing group of fathers with children who have transitioned, and in 2015, published a book, *Suffering Is the Only Honest Work*, that features the story "The Letter". My second book, *When the Veil Comes Down*, came out in 2021. One of its chapters is "Healing With History". I found that looking deep into my past and the journeys of my ancestors helped me tremendously with my own healing in the present. In early 2022, I pulled together "The Gauntt-Case Clans" which includes the stories I've written over the years about my family's roots and some of its more colorful characters. More about the books can be found at www.caseygauntt.com.

Jimmy's legacy continues to grow. The James T. Gauntt Memorial Fund was established at his alma mater, Torrey Pines High School. Over $110,000 of scholarships have been awarded to graduating seniors with financial need to pursue collegiate studies in the arts and literature.
Jimmy was a Trustee Scholar at the University of Southern California where he majored in English and Spanish. In 2009, the Department of English created the Jimmy Gauntt Memorial Award to recognize outstanding graduating seniors. Since its inception, over 70 "Jimmies" have been awarded by the Department. The award is the first of its kind at USC. Hilary, my wife, and best friend for over 48 years is a passionate cook and hosts a very popular food blog she started in 2011: www.heronearth.com.

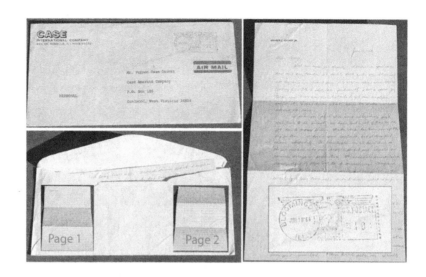

The Letter.

Grover, Casey, and Jimmy.

Jimmy Gauntt working on a screenplay at a film shoot in 2007.

Nonni Mauck, Casey, and Emily Sue Buckberry
at the 2009 October Sky Festival in Coalwood WV.

"As you find the light in you, you begin
to see the light in everyone else."
~Ram Dass~
Yoga Guru
Spiritual Teacher
Author, Psychologist
1931 – 2019

Love Lives Forever, *Elizabeth Boisson*

Morgan James Pierre Boisson & Chelsea

By Elizabeth Boisson

On November 23rd, 1988, Morgan was born in Montpellier in the south of France. I first arrived in this historic university town in 1983 as an exchange student from the University of North Carolina at Chapel Hill and returned two years later as a graduate assistant at the Université Paul Valéry. From the moment that I held him in my arms, I felt Morgan's enormous bright light. However, even then I had a feeling deep inside that he would not be here for long. This foreboding caused me constant apprehension throughout his life, further intensified by the fact that I never felt it for my other children.

My husband Cyril had previously lived in Africa for most of his life. His parents were still there, so a few weeks after Morgan's birth, we set off to N'Djamena, Chad, to show off our adorable baby boy. The trip turned into an arduous adventure. Two days into our stay, Morgan became very sick, and the only available doctor was a medic with the French Foreign Legion. Under the doctor's care, Morgan slowly got better, and we returned to France a few days later. This brush with fate did nothing to calm the growing apprehension that I felt about my newborn son. Soon after, we flew to Chapel Hill, NC, to introduce Morgan to my mom and dad, who was a professor at the University of North Carolina in the School of Public Health. They were thrilled to spend time with our beautiful blue-eyed boy. Morgan was destined to become a world traveler. Within the first month of his life, he had visited three continents: Europe, Africa, and North America.

All four of our children were born in Montpellier, including our baby Chelsea, who survived for only two days. I had been in the hospital on an IV for two months with placenta previa before Chelsea's birth, during which time Morgan stayed with my mother-in-law. I could not take care of him, and it was challenging to leave him. I spent my days in the hospital bed sick with worry, imagining that Morgan thought that I had suddenly abandoned him. He was my best buddy.

Despite the care that I was receiving at the hospital, I could not hold onto Chelsea any longer. She came into the world by C-section on January 21st, 1991. My water had broken several days earlier, and her lungs were crushed before she was finally delivered. I knew that she was in distress because I felt her kick less and less as her birth approached. I tried desperately but unsuccessfully to get the nurses to do something to help her. Chelsea survived on a respirator for only two days. Because of my Caesarian, I could not cry or mourn her passing; the slightest contraction of my stomach was agonizing. I was released from the hospital a few days after her birth.

It was a huge relief to finally get home to my sweet Morgan. He was the reason I was able to heal. However, with the passing of Chelsea, I began to feel that I had one foot here on earth and one foot on the other side with my tiny angel. Later, after Chelsea transitioned, we were fortunate to add two beautiful daughters to our family: Alix in 1992, and Christine in 1995.

When Morgan was seven, we moved with him and our daughters to the United States. During Morgan's childhood, he was in a hurry to do everything. He learned to walk at 7 months and seemed to only have one speed when he was a toddler: a fast-paced run. I was even compelled to have him wear a harness with a leash for a year to keep from losing him, much to the dismay of my French friends and family. Morgan hurried to grow taller and bigger than all the other kids in his classes. My big boy seemed to burst at the seams with energy and enthusiasm. He also raced to join and excel at many sports. He studied Judo at age four and earned his black belt in Taekwondo at age eleven. In high school, Morgan was a defensive lineman on his high school football team, and at 6'7" and 280 pounds, he was essential to the coach and the team. His athleticism and leadership skills in both football and track earned him a Marine Corps Distinguished Scholar-Athlete Award. These activities calmed him down and reined in some of his extra energy.

When Morgan graduated from high school and left for the University of Arizona, my world abruptly tilted. Suddenly, his enormous presence no longer filled our home. We all loved watching as Morgan burst through the kitchen door to grab us for a bear hug, sometimes forcing me to walk backward as he held onto me. Or when he would sprint down the hallway, jumping to hit each archway on the way back to his room. And we would laugh hysterically as he performed silly handshakes with his sisters. At the University of Arizona, because of his gregarious personality and massive height, it was natural that the cheer squad recruited Morgan. The team aptly nicknamed Morgan 'Big Bear' for the enormous bear hugs he gave.

Morgan already spoke two languages, English and French. After spending his sophomore year in Nanjing, China, majoring in East Asian Studies/Chinese, he was determined to learn Chinese and become trilingual. While there, Morgan participated in pre-Olympic games through Nanjing Normal University. As he was almost twice the size of his competition, it was no surprise when he placed first in shotput out of students from thirty participating universities.

The summer before Morgan passed, he spent six weeks studying and traveling in France. His fluency in French and his caring nature led him to become the pseudo-protector of the other kids in the program. As such, Morgan regularly accompanied the girls who lived in unsafe neighborhoods back to their apartments.

We met up with Morgan at the end of his stay in Paris and flew to Montpellier to spend time with our family. It would be the last time he would see his French relatives. Memories from that lazy summer are enduring and beautiful for the rest of us. One evening, Morgan lingered by the pool at a friend's home as the sun was setting. He recorded his own version of 'I Believe I Can Fly' on his Blackberry phone on that beautiful twilit evening. He was a huge fan of Michael Jordan and had watched the movie that made the song famous, 'Space Jam,' at least sixty times. We found the recording on his phone after he passed. Hearing it play from time to time on the radio became a way to validate that Morgan was near.

After a long, peaceful summer, Morgan returned to study in Nanjing, China, on August 30th, 2009. While packing for his second trip to Nanjing, we attempted to stuff five months' worth of clothing and supplies into one enormous suitcase. Morgan turned to me and said: "Mom, I don't think that I will be coming home from China this time." Even though I had suffered from premonitions about Morgan all his life, this was a shock. After composing myself, I responded that he had no real reason to leave; he could stay and return to Tucson instead. But Morgan was ready to go. He calmly put his hand on my shoulder and said: "Mom, I'll be fine." Two months later, Morgan passed of severe altitude sickness at the Base Camp of Mount Everest. He didn't lie. I now know that he truly is 'fine.'

October 20th, 2009, started like any other fall day in Cave Creek, AZ. Two days prior, Morgan had left to spend fall break in Tibet with thirteen other students from his study abroad program. I had just arrived from a Tuesday afternoon yoga class and received a call from Morgan's program director. He told me that Morgan was in distress and that the students were descending the mountain to get him to safety.

I quickly called Colin, Morgan's roommate, and best friend in China. As soon as Colin answered, he told me that the situation didn't look good. Morgan had stopped

266

breathing, and they were attempting CPR. Colin was not sure that Morgan would make it. I was terrified but knew that Morgan needed to hear my voice. I wanted to pour all the love and gratitude I felt for my beautiful son through the receiver as he lay on the cold Tibetan ground. I asked Colin to put the phone up to his ear. I told Morgan that we loved him, that we were proud of him, and not to be afraid. At that very instant, I felt Morgan hug me from the inside. To this day, I still cannot correctly explain this sensation. It was incredible; I felt a warm, calming feeling wash through me. That moment was utterly life changing. I later found out that this event was called a Shared Death Experience. Through it, Morgan comforted me and reassured me that he would always be with me. In an instant, I knew that love never dies.

Through the years, I've been told by several mediums that Chelsea was the first person to meet Morgan during his transition. This explanation made sense to me. As she knew the ropes, Chelsea was able to grab Morgan's hand and lead him to me. Morgan and Chelsea have stayed with me throughout my healing journey. And whenever I feel sad, I can always count on Morgan to hug me from the inside. Moreover, Morgan has since let us know that if he hadn't transitioned at the Base Camp of Mount Everest, it would have happened on the I-10 coming home from the U of A to Cave Creek. There was nothing that we could have done to stop his transition.

Although Morgan's passing forever changed the lives of everyone in my family, knowing where he was and that he was safe and happy reassured me. It helped me become an anchor for my husband and daughters. We learned to navigate our new lives without Morgan's vast, loving presence in our family. A family friend gifted me with Dr. Raymond Moody's book, Life After Life, and I gratefully read it in the days immediately following Morgan's transition. I realized that there was scientific evidence to support the connection I felt with Morgan. Signs and validations have reassured us many times since his passing that he is with us. I have chosen a few moments that resonate deeply.

After Morgan's passing, I desperately wanted to communicate with him. I had never been to a psychic medium, and I didn't see how it could be possible to reach my son this way until something extraordinary happened one week after his passing. I had been practicing yoga at a studio for many years, and Morgan had sometimes attended with me. Earlier that day, Angie Bayliss, the studio owner, had interviewed a psychic medium, Susanne Wilson, who was looking for rental space. During her conversation with Angie, Susanne not only connected with Morgan, but she also communicated his personality and mannerisms. Through Susanne, Morgan gave Angie numerous validations. She said she was being shown a big teddy bear and a bottle of Captain Morgan. She saw a young man shouting through a megaphone that he was 'fine'. Morgan had used a cheerleading megaphone that sat on display at his memorial service and is still in a place of honor in his room. Susanne also saw him on a mountain, lying on his back. She saw a black box next to his ear and understood that he had listened intently but had been unable to speak. He told Susanne to say, "Mom, I heard everything you said, and I love you back." It was a tremendous validation to know Morgan had heard me as Colin held the phone up to his ear. His response through Susanne was typical of what Morgan always answered, day after day, for years before he passed.

Susanne also told Angie that Morgan and his two roommates in China were like a 'band of brothers.' Morgan was close to all the students on the student exchange, but his two roommates were especially significant. Colin and Matt accompanied Morgan's body to Lhasa. They waited with him until my husband could receive a visa to enter Tibet six days later. Perhaps the most important message communicated by Susanne was that we would receive a unique rock from the place that Morgan transitioned. Susanne sketched it for us, showing that the stone was split in two. A month later, Morgan's roommate Colin arrived at our home, carrying a bouquet of my favorite flowers. With it, he brought the two halves of Morgan's rock from the desolate tract of Tibetan countryside where he passed. It looked just like the picture that Susanne drew.

My husband Cyril returned to work in China soon after Morgan's passing. After waiting for three excruciating days in Chengdu for a Tibetan visa, he had traveled to Tibet to retrieve Morgan's body. It was nearly impossible to bring Morgan home because of legislative roadblocks. Still, he was finally able to do so thanks to his dedication and meaningful friendships in China.

Cyril had visited Morgan in Nanjing several times while he was studying there, so being back in China after Morgan transitioned was especially hard for him. On one particular morning, he was on his way to the airport to fly from Hong Kong to Beijing. It was very early, perhaps 5:00 am, and most of the city was still sleeping.

Cyril sat in a taxi, thinking of Morgan, and missing him more than ever. Cantonese music played softly on the radio. Suddenly, Cyril recognized a familiar tune: "I used to think that I could not go on, and life was nothing but an awful song. But now I know the meaning of true love, I'm leaning on the everlasting arms." It was the song that Morgan had recorded while in France, 'I Believe I Can Fly.' Here it was, playing on his taxi's radio on the outskirts of Hong Kong, on a lonely road leading to the airport. This decisive sign lifted Cyril's spirits and gave him strength for the remainder of his trip. He was confident that Morgan was with him.

Morgan and Chelsea send signs every day to let me know that they are still right here. One of the best signs we have received was on Morgan's 30th birthday when we hiked to the bench dedicated to him and Chelsea in the Spur Cross Recreation Area. As we walked towards the bench, I told Morgan that it would be wonderful to get a big sign from him. Very soon after, we spotted a bobcat up ahead in the middle of the path as we made our way through the beautiful desert. Seeing the bobcat was significant because the University of Arizona mascot is a Wildcat. The bobcat seemed to want to stay with us and approached us to within three feet. We took multiple pictures of the beautiful cat as it wound its way through the desert flowers, seemingly purring at us. My husband and I had no doubt that this majestic feline was a gift from our son.

My two daughters both feel Morgan's presence in their lives. They realize that knowing our children in spirit are happy, healthy, and whole helps us move forward and heal. Therefore, they have spent the past 11 years supporting my work at Helping Parents Heal, welcoming parents to monthly meetings with hugs, smiles, and genuine love. I know that the kindness and compassion that they have provided have helped the two of them on their own healing journeys.

Christine often has lifelike dreams of Morgan and knows that he is with her. Alix connects with Morgan through meditation and even believes that Morgan saved her life. In 2012, while she was studying at Sciences Po in Paris, she attended a party with her cousin, Anne-Sophie, in a neighborhood far from her home in St. Germain. She had taken migraine medicine before leaving, and after a few glasses of champagne, she started to feel dizzy. She threw up in the bathroom of the bar and told Anne-Sophie that she was going home. In her confusion, she forgot to grab her coat on the way out.

Wearing only a sleeveless cocktail dress, she embarked on her journey home under gently falling snow. Arriving at the curb, she jumped into the first available taxi. After a few stoplights, she looked to her left and did not recognize the person sitting next to her. She opened the taxi door and vomited again, then crawled out and stood freezing on the street corner. Staring at the street names painted on the building walls, she realized that she was lost. She attempted to call friends with her cellphone as the street names began to blur together. She was unable to reach anyone, and no one knew where she was.

Alix's next recollection was of being shaken awake by her two roommates. It was morning, and she was back in her bed, safe and sound. The girls had a flight to Portugal leaving at 7 am and needed to hurry to the airport. Alix sorted through her memories, trying to piece together how she had made it home. One of her roommates, who had stayed home the night before, remembered hearing the front door burst open at 3 am. Later, when her second roommate arrived, the door was still ajar. The girls lived in a 9th-floor penthouse apartment that was only accessible by a winding staircase. After exiting a taxi headed in the wrong direction, Alix last remembered sitting down in the snow, kilometers from home. She is confident that Morgan carried her safely home.

Many of the validations that we receive come from Morgan's friends. While on the cheerleading team at U of A, Morgan befriended Dan, aka the school mascot Wilbur the Wildcat. Dan later became a firefighter. Once, when a fire was raging above him in a home, Dan helped a fellow firefighter remove a car from the garage below. His friend put the car into neutral, and Dan was to push it out of the garage. Suddenly, Dan felt someone hugging him tightly around his chest and pulling him forcibly backward. He said that it felt as though Morgan was giving him an enormous bear hug from behind. As Dan was yanked back, a huge air conditioning unit fell through from the floor above. The firefighter who was sitting in the car saw the whole thing and exclaimed, "Dude-what just happened?" Without a doubt, Dan knew that Morgan had saved his life.

After Chelsea passed, I realized that there is more to our existence than this one physical lifetime. I knew she was not gone, and I was ultimately able to survive her passing with the help of my son Morgan. When Morgan passed in 2009 and gave me that tremendous hug, I was determined to learn all I could about the Afterlife. I needed to understand where Morgan was, who he was with, and what he did all day.

Helping Parents Heal grew out of a Facebook group I started in October 2009, one week after my son Morgan transitioned. I knew that I was not the only parent experiencing these signs from our children, and I wanted to share with people who understood. After joining forces with Mark Ireland and with the help of Doryce Norwood, our pro bono attorney, Helping Parents Heal became a nonprofit in 2012. It has far exceeded its humble beginnings. We now offer support and healing to Shining Light Parents on a worldwide basis. The goal of the support meetings conducted by affiliate groups is to let parents know that their kids are not gone. They are still right here.

Helping Parents Heal now has over 130 affiliate groups in the US, Canada, the United Kingdom, South Africa, India, Australia, and New Zealand. We also have Caring Listeners, parents who volunteer to lend a healing ear to newer members. Dr. Mark Pitstick and Lynn Hollahan (Devon's Shining Light Mom) lead this inspiring group of parents. Carol Allen, Tyler's Shining Light mom, is one of our Caring Listeners and leads several affiliate groups. Irene Vouvalides, Carly's Shining Light Mom, joined our group and immediately volunteered as an affiliate leader.

Then soon after Irene joined, she suggested that Helping Parents Heal host a conference. Planning an event this size is no small task, but Irene was persistent. Following more than a year of hard work and transcontinental phone calls to coordinate the event, we proudly held our First Helping Parents Heal Conference in Scottsdale, Arizona, in 2018. The sold-out event hosted 500 parents and 30 presenters. A dozen Shining Light Parents volunteered to help the incredible conference run without a hitch. Ironically, and unsurprisingly, the staff at the hotel reported that our guests appeared to be the happiest that they had ever hosted. We will be holding our Second HPH Conference in Phoenix in August 2022, and we plan to welcome 1000 parents. All of the proceeds from the sale of this book will go towards the conference.

Please know that you are not alone. We share this journey, and we understand. We are all in this together, and together, we will help each other heal.

-Written by Morgan's Shining Light Mom, President and Co-Founder of Helping Parents Heal, Affiliate Leader of HPH Phoenix/Scottsdale, HPH Caring Listener and Newsletter Editor, Elizabeth Boisson. www.helpingparentsheal.org

An excerpt from the book, "Life to Afterlife – Helping Parents Heal, The Book". Copyright 2021, Elizabeth Boisson, All Rights Reserved

About the Author

Elizabeth Boisson is the President and Co-Founder of *Helping Parents Heal*, the Phoenix/Scottsdale Affiliate Leader, a *Caring Listener* and the Newsletter Editor. She is the author of the book, *Life to Afterlife: Helping Parents Heal, The Book*.

Two of Elizabeth's children have transitioned; her daughter, Chelsea, in 1991 and her son, Morgan, in 2009 from severe altitude sickness while on a student trip to the Base Camp of Mount Everest in Tibet. Immediately after, Elizabeth created the Facebook group Parents United in Loss. Then, in 2012 she joined forces with Mark Ireland to form Helping Parents Heal. Elizabeth is a certified yoga instructor and teaches yoga for healing grief. She has taught Yoga classes for the past 6 years. During the pandemic, she has been teaching Yoga by Zoom M-F at 8 am AZ time, and the classes are posted online as well. The classes include Flow, Yin, Yoga Nidra and

Power Yoga. If a parent would like to attend and cannot afford to pay, please reach out. For more information, her email is: Elizabeth@helpingparentsheal.org. Join her Facebook Yoga Group at www.facebook.com/groups/ElizabethYoga

"We are asleep. Our Life is a dream.
But we wake up sometimes, just enough
to know that we are dreaming."
~Ludwig Wittgenstein~
Philosopher
1889-1951

Our Shared Love, *Susan Kendal*

By Susan Kendal

In honour of Neil. It was the Canadian long weekend in May 2014 when the world I knew came to a crashing stop. Neil and I had a jam-packed schedule planned filled with highly anticipated festivity. Our youngest daughter was flying off on a 10-day educational adventure, our niece was preparing to celebrate her bat mitzvah, and our dear friend's son was getting married. Clothes were organized, gifts readied, suitcases packed, and our home was prepared for our American relatives who were joining us for the impending celebrations.

The months leading up to this weekend were consumed with agonizing tension that challenged our previous forty great years together. Stress became a constant in our lives. It had permeated our marriage and was infiltrating into our relationship with our children.

My 89-year-old dad was having monthly chemo appointments, our eldest daughter had chosen a more peaceful environment and moved out of our home, a bitter divorce was tearing apart family relationships, work/life balance was at an all-time disastrous level for Neil, and communications with our only son and his wife had stalled. We were looking forward to a happy weekend filled with family, laughter, and love. We needed the positive distraction!!

The weekend began on a positive note. Extended family photos were taken (our last together), and we all enjoyed the Saturday night bat mitzvah celebrations. It was such a relief to put away our ongoing concerns and take a much-needed break from day-to-day concerns.

On Sunday, during the wedding procession, my husband began to sweat. This was very uncharacteristic of him, and I suspected it was caused by a bout of anxiety. Little did I know that this would eventually culminate in a fatal cardiac arrest on Tuesday morning at the young age of 54.

Losing Neil was numbing. We met when I was only fourteen in high school. He was a year older, and we became best friends immediately. By the age of sixteen, we were dating exclusively, and the rest was history. Our names were forever intertwined, as were our lives. We were married at 21 and became parents to three children within the next ten years. We had a dog and a beautiful home in the Toronto suburbs surrounded by our large extended family and friends.

Imagining life without my husband seemed insurmountable. At the time of his death, I had no idea that life would continue to reach new depths of anguish for me. Unfortunately, society doesn't prepare us for death. Before losing a spouse, we think that grief is finite, and it will end in a few years. Never do we anticipate death's companion - secondary grief – the many additional issues that arise as a result of loss – would add even more hardship to my journey.

For me, the loss of my husband began a difficult journey of self-discovery and growth. The first order of business was to stop this cycle of stress that had entered our lives. Much of the stress that had consumed him was now mine to mitigate. I was very aware of the trauma it had inflicted on our family over the past year. I recognized that the only way out was to deal head-on with the issues and create calm.

My late husband had a small and faithful group of friends who were privy to many of the causes of his considerable angst. It was obvious to all of us that there was much work to be done to clear these issues. With their discreet and valued guidance, I succeeded in resolving most of the issues within the year.

Yet, there was one life challenge that felt too difficult and personal to discuss with anyone, so I held it buried deep within.

On a walk with my cousin a year after becoming a widow, I realized I had to seek guidance. Because I was embarrassed, I had not previously confided in anyone. In her presence, my emotional dam was finally able to burst open. I shared my long, complicated, and very painful story with her.

During the conversation, she noticed that I had a constant and very annoying cough. This had developed shortly after my husband passed and remained the entire year. Having studied many forms of spiritual awareness, she believed that I had caused my throat chakra to close when I shut down my communication. The throat chakra, she explained, is responsible for personal truth, and I had inadvertently created an unbalanced body. She suggested that this closure was the explanation for my persistent cough.

Unbeknownst to a novice like myself, yoga is suggested as a key to opening this chakra.

Ironically, in the early months after my husband died, I took to a new form of exercise to try to work out my frustrations – yoga. I soon discovered a miraculous gift that frequently greeted me at the end of each class. While in savasana, the final resting pose, I would close my eyes, relax, and welcome my husband, who would appear lying beside me.

Let me be very clear. I had never experienced anything like this. I had occasional intuitive thoughts in my lifetime and always welcomed them as little whispers from a higher source, but nothing prepared me for his image at my side.

Beginning shortly after his death, a few individuals had confided in me that they had seen my late husband in their dreams and even felt his presence while awake; but I had not. I never questioned their belief, but I also never thought that I would be gifted with this experience.

When Neil first appeared following class, I looked to be sure that no one else noticed him; but I need not have bothered because I instinctively knew he was only there for me. He never spoke or reached out. I'm not even certain if he had arms. I stared into his loving hazel eyes as I had for so many years before and felt a surge of love. For those fleeting moments, I was given a blessed opportunity to rekindle our deep emotional connection!
Oddly, I never began the class anticipating our reunion. Although it happened with some frequency, I was always pleasantly surprised when he appeared. Somehow his presence never frightened me. Each time my tears flowed in the darkened classroom as we lay side-by-side.

After a few moments, he left as quietly as he arrived. I never told anyone about these visits. I somehow knew that this was a sacred, fleeting bond between the two of us. I accepted this act of comfort as a final goodbye, a gift from him to me.

Shortly after my conversation with my cousin, I took another yoga class. As I had done for over six months now, I laid down at the end in my final pose and hoped Neil would appear. This time something even more miraculous happened. Neil was not lying beside me. He appeared as a vision coming thru my body. As always, my eyes were shut, but I could clearly see his head rising out from my throat.

I silently watched this vision, stood up, and left the room to shower. Oddly, there was no fear; yet I instinctively understood that something seismic had shifted within me. I was filled with sadness as I knew …this was to be the last time Neil visited me. I believe that he was able to leave thru my throat chakra because it had opened during the conversation with my cousin. I was now able to face my challenges and continue my personal journey without him by my side.

In the years following his last visit, I was finally able to rectify my personal situation. In addition, I have learned to open up much more than I ever anticipated. In 2020 I began a new mission. Armed with my personal experience and coupled with my coaching classes and a grief educator's certificate, I now intend to give voice to all who are bereaved.

Living with loss is a lifetime challenge. When someone dies, friends and family rally around the bereaved for a short time. Soon after, the conversation changes from one of comfort to one of anticipation and judgment. The bereaved are given a time frame to "get over it". This antiquated notion leaves no option but to grieve in silence. Often silence can become isolating and cause mental and physical health issues.

Let's make it easier for the bereaved by educating society on how to help those who are grieving. Death is the ultimate taboo; it is the unspoken elephant in the room. Yet, unlike other taboos, this is the only one we shall ALL experience. My goal is to shatter the taboo by using my voice to speak up and share my learned and lived knowledge.

Let's normalize death – before it kills you.

About the Author

Susan is the founder of *Evolve Beyond Grief.* For more information, conversation, and opportunities to get involved, please reach out to Susan at:
https://www.evolvebeyondgrief.com/
https://www.instagram.com/evolvebeyondgrief/
https://www.facebook.com/evolvebeyondgrief evolvebeyondgrief@gmail.com
www.griefismysidehustle.com
podcast/susan-kendal-surviving-compound-grief-and-loss

Susan & Neil Friday night at the Bat Mitzvah

Last photo together

*"So we fix our eyes not on what
is seen, but on what is unseen,
since what is seen is temporary,
but what is unseen is eternal."*
~St. Paul~
Christian Apostle
2 Corinthians 4:18

The Christmas Miracle, *Melissa Ralston*

By Melissa Ralston

I am a grieving mom. I am writing about some of my experiences that have occurred since our son's tragic passing in 2013.

I am 53 years old. I have been married for 35 years. I am the mother of twins and one angel in heaven. My belief system is Christian, and I consider myself to be spiritual. I love cooking, painting, being outdoors, traveling, and reading. I am a huge animal lover, and currently own a pet sitting business with my husband, John.

My son's name is Matthew. He loved animals and had a very kind heart. The world as I knew it stopped existing the minute we were notified of his passing. I have always been very connected with my son. Before we were informed, I had been very worried about him. He was out of town, not responding to phone calls/texts. I told my husband and a friend that I didn't know if Matthew was still alive. I insisted that I couldn't feel him. That is a story for another day.

Since Matthew passed away, I have had several unexplainable experiences that I believe to be signs from the other side of the veil connecting me with Matthew to comfort me and let me know that he is okay in the afterlife. Most of these experiences have involved nature, such as butterflies, animal encounters, rainbows, and witnessing beautiful acts of kindness. But those stories are also for another time.

Today I want to talk about a friendship created from across the veil that culminates with an unforgettable Christmas miracle.

2021 was the first year since Matthew passed away that we put up a full-sized Christmas tree, put Christmas lights on our house, and sent out Christmas cards. Matthew loved the holidays and absolutely adored the decorating. Until this year, it was just too painful for us. Somehow this year felt different, and I could approach the holiday with hope in my heart.

To add to this, I was introduced to Camille in 2020. I had actually prayed for her for months before we connected. My friend, Kim, contacted me, who asked me to pray for her dear friend who had just lost her son in a tragic accident. Kim is a super kind and empathetic soul who respects privacy, so she didn't provide any personal details. It wasn't until a few months later that Kim connected me to Camille.

I believe our sons had a hand in bringing us together in friendship. Camille lives in Canada, and I am in the United States. So just the fact that we connected is pretty amazing, but our coincidences just kept piling up. One of the first things Camille told me is that Aaron told her he is with someone named Matthew across the veil. Camille didn't know anyone named Matthew who had passed away. Camille was genuinely excited when we met. This was further confirmation of her communication with Aaron.

Another huge coincidence is that Camille's dad once served at the military base near my current home. The very same base from where my husband retired. Camille was born and lived within 25 miles of my current home. What are the odds? The more we spoke to one another the more we felt connected, not just to each other, but also to our sons.

Camille told me that cardinals would come to her yard whenever we spoke, and she often sent me pictures. Soon after meeting Camille, cardinals began to appear in my life in random unexpected ways. One example of this was when my husband and I had a meeting with a client on the Air Force Base. I was texting with Camille when we drove onto the base, and I sent her pictures so she could reminisce. When we arrived at the client's house, the first thing that I noticed was a glass cardinal hanging in their window. I took a picture and quickly texted it to Camille. Her response was, "We are so connected," with a picture of a cardinal in her yard.

Since that time, I have seen many, many cardinals in my yard. I have also seen them while working outside with clients. However, this Christmas, I experienced something that literally touched my heart and soul. Here is what happened.

It was Christmas morning 2021, and John was leaving the house to visit our clients. I was staying home to prepare food for our Christmas dinner. I heard John open the front door and I thought that he had left. However, a few seconds later, he appeared at the bedroom door saying that someone had left gifts on our doorstep. We didn't know who it could possibly be. John didn't stay to open them because we had an entire morning booked with clients. One package was the size of a shirt box, and the other was a small square box approximately the size that a watch would come in. A card was signed, "The White Family", and some papers with comforting passages from the Bible. We don't know a family by that name.

I stared at the packages with wonder as I slowly untied the shiny silver ribbon from the smaller box. When I removed the lid, I saw a beautiful cardinal Christmas ornament nestled on a bed of red velvet. My heart leaped with joy as I held this amazing gift in my hands. My eyes then turned towards the shirt-sized box. I couldn't possibly imagine anything inside that could be anywhere nearly as special as the cardinal ornament... I was wrong.

I gently untied the shiny hand-tied silver ribbon and lifted the lid. I unfolded the tissue paper covering the item inside. What I saw warmed my heart and soul to the very core. Inside was a painting with an easel stand. It was of a beautiful, vibrant red cardinal sitting on a snow-covered branch with a vivid blue sky as the background. There is an inscription written along the edges of the canvas that says, "When a cardinal appears it's a magical sign to remind you that all will be alright, and I am always with you."

Tears began to flow from my eyes, and I knew in my heart that this was a gift to be shared with Camille. I immediately called her. Several cardinals flew into her yard as we spoke, and she sent me pictures of the amazing gift that I received. In that moment, we both knew that we shared an amazing Christmas miracle that connected us to our sons.

This is just a small glimpse of the friendship that our beloved boys orchestrated from beyond the veil. The story doesn't end here, but you guessed it, that is another story for another day.

About the Author

Melissa has been married to her husband John for 35 years. She is the mother of twins and one angel in heaven. Melissa is co-owner of M and J Just Be Kind Pet Services. She is an animal lover, avid reader, and knowledge seeker. She is founder of Kindness Sisters, a small text message-based support group for grieving moms, loves cooking, painting, traveling and most anything outdoors. Melissa believes in sharing stories, diversity, and inclusion for all and in spreading kindness.

This butterfly stayed with me for an entire afternoon.

Cardinal at a client's house on the
Air Force Base near my home.

Matthew. My last photo of him.

*"Love is the light that dissolves all walls
between souls, families and nations."
~Paramahansa Yogananda~
Monk, Yogi, Guru
1893-1952*

Family is Watching Over Us Always, *Arlene Maislin*

By Arlene Maislin

When I was about five years old, things began to happen to me that I couldn't understand. Although one could say I've been a believer in life after death and spirit communication for most of my life, I must admit that at that age I didn't understand what I was experiencing. It wasn't until I was in my teens that I began to realize I had communicated with the other side. I remember words flowing and stopping, whether I was writing or speaking. I now know that it was spirit flowing through me.

I'm going to tell you a story, out of the many stories I could tell, that begins in 1994 after the death of my wonderful father-in-law, Simon. He was diagnosed with a very rare form of cancer called Acute Monoblastic Leukaemia. It seemed to come on overnight. On January 7th, 1994, our family gathered in the hospital together to be with him for those last few moments. Unfortunately, he succumbed to his illness just three weeks later. His death came as a shock, and we all took it very hard. He was loved deeply, not just by his family but by friends and business associates worldwide. He was the patriarch of our family. We were all so close and mourning the profound loss along with his is wife, three children, their spouses, seven young grandchildren, my parents, and the other in-laws. He was the anchor of our family. He was our 'go-to guy' who was deeply connected to many. He passed away in the early afternoon before the Sabbath.

My first sign from him occurred the night after he died. As the days are shorter in January, Shabbat was early, and candle lighting took place at 4 o'clock that afternoon. Together with my mother-in-law, we lit candles to usher in that first Sabbath without our patriarch. Candles typically burn for about three to four hours. I remember lighting the candles at 4 o'clock when the sun went down. The mourners all shared the traditional Shabbat dinner, and we talked a lot about what we were going through as we consoled each other.

Hours later, around midnight, I walked into the dining room to make sure the candles were out. To my surprise, they were still glowing. I instinctively looked up at the ceiling, and that's when I knew that Simon had never left us. From that point on, I was so aware of his presence.

Inside my mind, we were having continuous conversations. He signaled to me that he was around in so many ways. Electricity was his primary mode of communication. The next significant message I received was two weeks after he passed.

Family birthdays and other important occasions were always celebrated together. My mother-in-law came to town for my birthday weekend. She walked into my dressing room, where I was sitting at my makeup table, and handed me my birthday card. She said, "I'm so sorry we're not celebrating in our normal fashion, but I wanted you to have this from me and..." But before she could finish her sentence, the lights above my makeup table flashed off...then on...then off again. We both looked up, and right away, without thinking, she said, "and from Simon too".

Never one to miss a celebration, Simon would want to make sure that he was included. We got that message loud and clear! From then on, our conversations in my head/imagination increased. We had these lengthy chats about all kinds of things nearly daily that first year. I must admit that, to this day, I still question whether or not I was making the whole thing up. But our conversations felt so real!

I remember seeing a medium recommended by my sister-in-law approximately two weeks after Simon passed. She was struggling to come to terms with his death and recommended this person. We were both grieving deeply and needed some kind of validation that he was around. I drove to the medium's apartment alone. I walked in and sat down. The first thing she said to me was, "Have you lost a male figure who was very dear to you?" I said yes immediately. Then she looked up at me and said, "He's pacing back and forth and is anxious to get the conversation going." She said that his personality came through loud and clear, and she described him perfectly.

She went on to ask, "Who has his watch?" I knew that my brother-in-law, my husband's brother, was given his dressy watch. There had been a bit of discussion within the family, and everyone was so happy to know that it was given to him. The medium said, "That's not the watch I'm talking about." I replied that I didn't know of any other watch. "Well, he's really concerned and upset about his watch that broke." I had no idea what she was talking about.

I went home and asked my husband if he knew about his dad's broken watch. He said that he had no idea what I was talking about. So, then I called my brother-in-law, who also didn't know, and I asked my sister-in-law and my mother-in-law, who both didn't know. Shortly after that, I got a call from my husband's sister who said that she couldn't believe it, but she knew about her father's broken watch.

When her father was in the hospital, he was wheeled into surgery to have a port put in for chemotherapy. The doctors said they didn't know what else to do for him. He took off his everyday watch and handed it to her. As he did so, the chain-link broke. She stuffed it away in her pocket, not giving it another thought. Her mind was fully focused on her father. She had completely forgotten until I started to ask her about it, and she finally was able to remember. Needless to say, we had that watch repaired. His son is wearing it. It was absolutely my father-in-law's personality to be bothered by his broken watch. Something that was broken could be fixed and then used. Many examples like this of his personality came through the medium, proving to me that it was him. They seemed to be a metaphor for all our broken hearts that would heal over time.

I remember going out for walks a lot in the weeks and months following his passing. It was good therapy just being outside. I realized that Simon's primary mode of communication was through electricity. One of the things that happened on a regular basis was that the streetlights would turn off as I passed under them. He was making sure that I knew he was around. I acknowledged it every time, and my children, his grandchildren, got to experience the same thing I did. Many of our family members, once alerted to this phenomenon, started to experience communication through electricity on a regular basis. Even my friends acknowledged him when the streetlights would blink off as we passed under them together. I continued talking to him every day, and it helped me deal with the grief and with missing him.

The mourning process starts immediately in Jewish tradition. The deceased person is buried as soon as possible after death. Healing is about the living and those left behind. There is one week of Shiva, or mourning, after the burial, where prayers are said twice daily, and friends and family visit the mourners to offer condolences, love, and support. Food is sent in by anyone wishing to serve a meal to the mourners so that they can focus on their bereavement and help their loved one's soul ascend. The seven days of Shiva are followed by the Shloshim, the next 30 days. At this point, one can visit the grave if they are so inclined. After one year and every year after, the deceased is remembered with the lighting of a candle and prayers on the anniversary of their death, the Yahrtzeit. Healing is a step-by-step process in which the main goal is looking after the deceased's family.

As is the custom, the men in the immediate family do not shave for 30 days. Grooming is considered to be unnecessary when someone is deep in grief. It encourages the mourner to confront the loss with no distractions. Shaving and concern about one's look are considered a distraction. Mirrors are covered for this reason and also to prevent the soul from returning through them.

At the conclusion of the 30 days after the death of his father, my husband went into our washroom and took out his razor to begin to shave. Precisely at that time, an electrical storm occurred. There was lightning and thunder, and the energy in the room was incredible. All of a sudden, the glass shower door shattered into a million pieces. At first, we were shocked that something like that could happen. I mean, shower doors don't just shatter on their own. And then I felt it. The energy took over the whole room. It's hard to describe the energy shift, but it was beyond incredible and filled the whole space. I knew that my father-in-law was there with us. He sent us a powerful message to remind us that he would always be with us. I felt his presence so strongly.

It is not possible for me to write a chapter in this book without giving mention to my beloved mother, who I lost to pancreatic cancer in November 2011. It was my mom who got me interested in learning about the afterlife. Early in her marriage to my dad, she and her friend went to see a psychic on a whim. They were given life-changing information. My mom and I used to discuss this at great length. Years later, after her death, I took comfort in knowing her beliefs. She felt strongly about the fact that life doesn't end after physical death.

I've had many discussions with her across the veil in the years since her passing. For example, when she was alive, she used to say matter of factly, "You don't need to come to the cemetery after I'm gone." When I would ask her what she meant, she would say, "What do you want to go there for? I'm not there." After she passed away and I felt the need to visit the cemetery, I could hear her voice so loudly in my head. "Don't go! I'm not there!" But, of course, like all children ignoring their parents, I did go all the while knowing that she felt that way.

I could hear her in my head loud and clear arguing with me on my drive there, telling me adamantly that she's not there and that I don't need to drive all that way. Needless to say, I didn't listen. I arrived at the cemetery for the first time alone. It was a beautifully clear, and sunny day and I felt full of peace there. And then, as I'm sitting by my mother's grave, I look up, and out of nowhere, I spot two pheasants. My mind was blown! They had to be a sign from my mom.

When I was growing up, we used to have two pheasants visit in our backyard. I only saw them at her grave that first time. I felt that her message to me was that she would be with me no matter where I was. It was interesting to note that on my subsequent visits to the cemetery, my mother wasn't as argumentative with me. The second and the third time I went to visit, I would hear her. She would say, "Why are you going? I'm not there! I would say back to her, "I'm going for the peacefulness. I'm going because I feel the need for a concrete place." By the third or fourth visit, my mother stopped trying to reason with me and said to me that she understood. If that's what brings me peace, she didn't have a problem with it. The teacher became the student.

Throughout these past ten years since her death, I have never stopped missing my mother. I often go to pick up the phone to call her, and then I remember. I have gotten many signs and messages from her. Dimes are a big sign for myself and my whole family. (Insert photo). Whenever we find one, we take a photo and send it to the others. We also know that cardinals are a sign from her. She often marveled at the beauty of them when she was alive. We all know it's a message from my mother in keeping with her personality. My father-in-law uses electricity to communicate, and my mom uses dimes and cardinals.

Arlene's collection of dimes found since her mother's passing
next to other coins found during the same period.

I truly believe that my father-in-law and my mother have been behind the scenes watching over us and protecting us. I have received so many messages from them, including multiple physical signs as confirmation that they are there, just on the other side. I have felt and continue to feel their love and support throughout these many years. I have confirmation from world-renowned psychic mediums that they have been present at family traumas or celebrations. I continue to believe that when my time on Earth is over, and I have finished learning what it is that I was sent here to learn, we will be reunited once again.

About the Author

Arlene is married and the mother of four children and one grandson. Shortly after receiving her degree in Psychology, she moved to Montreal where she met Camille and started a lifelong friendship. She has known Camille for over 35 years and Aaron for all his life. She watched him grow up. Shortly after Aaron's sudden passing, she received a message from him. This communication with him would start a chain of events leading up to the writing of this book.

"Science cannot tell us a word about why music delights us, of why and how an old song can move us to tears."
~Erwin Schrodinger~
Nobel Prize Winning
Physicist
1887 – 1961

Guided by the Signs, *Donna Rewald*

By Donna Rewald

I am a mother of five. Three sons, two daughters, two of whom are in spirit, my baby daughter Ashleigh (born sleeping in 1983), and my eldest son Adam (40). Adam transitioned on July 26, 2019, at our cottage while kayaking with his then 8-year-old daughter, McKenna. We may never know the circumstances causing the kayak to capsize, which resulted in Adam's drowning, and I often wonder if we're just not meant to. Why the one place that held so much peace and beauty within him, where he felt most at home and his happiest, he'd choose to leave us, but then I suppose, where else?

I was numb and, of course, in shock. I remember feeling and saying, I just don't know how to do this?! We're never prepared to bury our children. There's not a book to follow, it was unfamiliar territory that I did not want to be in, but here I was. Amongst my grief was the incredible fear of continuing my life without my son and losing another one of my children or my husband, really, anyone that I loved dearly. The pain was one I'd never felt before, and it felt like it wracked havoc within every cell of my body.

I knew I required grief counseling immediately and reached out to our family doctor, but I was unfortunately only able to receive a few sessions from the therapist in his office. I also had to wait a month between. It was not near enough. I searched for grief support groups for parents who had lost a child in our rural area, there were none, so I quickly created a chapter from a non-profit organization that I found online. Although very early in my grief, I knew there must be other parents like myself feeling the same, requiring any kind of support they could find, and we had monthly meetings. Then COVID arrived, bringing even more isolation, which I really didn't mind as I didn't want to be around others, so the couch became my safe haven, binge-watching endless shows.

Can I just say here what an amazing husband I have been truly blessed with? He picked up where I dropped everything, and I mean everything, as I was only existing in our home and in our marriage. I didn't care if the house was clean or dirty, or if we ate or didn't, and this man just took completely over for me and often still does when those dark moments, hours, or even days come again. Adam absolutely adored this man and had the utmost respect for him. In his eyes, his stepdad could do no wrong. They were the best of buddies, and I know my husband misses that.

Adam began showing me a sign very early that he was here by sending cardinals daily. We had already been living in this house for six years, and we'd never seen one. Yet still, to this day, I receive a beautiful red male and a female. I was experiencing a really rough morning on one of the early days, and I'd begged Adam during some sobbing moments for a sign. I had to leave the house to drive to the grocery store, and again I began crying while driving. Just before I made my turn, a car turned before me, going the opposite direction. Now ahead of me, there was an advertisement on the rear window of the car with a huge red cardinal. Thank you, Adam!!

I was gifted tickets six months after his passing to an event for a very well-known and accredited medium, Sherry Gallant. There were approximately 100 people in attendance. Adam was the first to come through for Sherry, with such evidential messages that were impossible for her to know about beforehand, such as he sends me cardinals, "not to sell the cottage", to listen for him calling "Mom", to name but a few. That reading brought me such comfort, but more importantly, Sherry delivered Adam's messages with such compassion. She is truly a beautiful soul that I've had the pleasure of taking a couple of classes with recently.

I've always been a somewhat spiritual person, believing there was so much more for us when we passed, but I'd not given much thought to it. As the months went on, I needed to know where my Adam really was and what he was doing. But more importantly, I absolutely had to continue a relationship with him, and how would I even begin to do that. It didn't sit well with me for my son to be "just a memory" in my world, it wasn't near enough, and I had to figure all of this out. So, my online search began, this time on the afterlife, and I came across an organization called, *Helping Parents Heal*. Why I didn't find it before, I have no idea. Perhaps it just wasn't my time yet. HPH was and still is a godsend for this mom's grieving heart. I began to learn so very much from all the guest speakers who presented in the past months and are recorded and placed on the YouTube channel. I attended every single online presentation I possibly could. I went onto the links given for these meetings and became a sponge, soaking up each and every tidbit of information that made sense to me. I ordered books that the speakers had written and more books that I found along my way as I continued to research where Adam is and how I could possibly connect with him.

My understanding came to be that just wanting to connect with my son wasn't enough, that I had personal self-work to put into this as well, and this was honestly a huge catalyst for me. I had to learn to meditate, raise my vibration frequency to meet that of Adam's, quiet the "monkey mind", and be comfortable with just being still, which wasn't easy for me. I began using a pendulum and an alphabet board, and this is when my communication with him really began. Adam would spell out his messages to me, and very quickly too. Each morning after my ritual of meditation and a prayer of protection, I'd ask him if he had a message for Mom, and he always did. Two days in a row one week, he gave me only "just guides". After seeking advice on this, it was Adam telling me, "It's time to connect with your guides now, Mom." So, I nervously did.

Yes, I heard of the term "guides", but I honestly had no idea what it meant, who they are, and what they do? So, using the pendulum and board, I asked if my guides were there and received a "Yes". Then I asked, "How would you like me to connect with you?", and "write" was what they spelled out. I'd already begun practice classes using channel writing with Adam, so I sat down with my book, pen in hand, and asked for my guides to give me their messages. Three-and-a-half pages later, I was absolutely astounded as to what I was given from them. They referred to me as "Dear Donna" throughout, with such love and encouragement, telling me that I was to be of service to other parents, to help them connect with their children if they asked, to support and encourage them and that I am to write a book of my journey with my son.

In my continued writings with Adam and my guides, I was constantly asked to go outside more to be one with nature. So, on a warm spring day, after receiving the same message again, I went out and sat in Adam's garden for a while. I received the knowledge to "look up Mom" and a beautiful heart-shaped cloud was there. Thank you, son. I went inside shortly after, and while doing dishes, I suddenly heard "MOM!" I turned around and answered as a mother does automatically, "Yes?!" No reply. So, I called up to our youngest son, "Why did you call me?" To which he replied, "I didn't, you just woke me up!" It was Adam, and I heard him loud and clear. This was over a year after being told I would by Sherry. I haven't heard him since, yet anyway!

I placed a favorite pair of my earrings on the kitchen island. They'd been there for ages. Tidying up and putting things away was just something I cared less about the first year or so, but I always saw them there in plain view. Then, one wasn't there. After about a week, I asked Adam out loud, "Can you find my earring for me? Please, it vanished, Honey, and it's driving Mom crazy!" I joined a Facebook group that a woman I quickly became friends with was running. She also had a son, Tommy, who had transitioned only a couple of months before my Adam. She formed a group for parents to share their signs and connections. Sally posted about a book that was of great interest to me, so I decided to look for it in my Kindle, which I always keep on my coffee table shelf in the living room. I opened up the Kindle, and there laid my earring. The book that I was going to search for…*Signs: The Secret Language of the Universe* by Laura Lynne Jackson (Dial Press Trade Paperback, June 2, 2020), which in fact, I already purchased and uploaded. It was waiting for me to read it, and thanks to grief brain, I totally forgot about it. Thank you, Adam, for both my earring and the message to read the book. Coincidence? No. Synchronicity? Yes, just six days before Adam's first Angelversary.

As I began opening myself up more and more spiritually, with complete trust and gratitude, the more the signs and messages began coming from Adam. I had to learn to pay more attention to what I was seeing, hearing, and feeling all around me and become more aware of my senses.

While I was out driving, doing errands, I had been texting with McKenna's mom about a tree she mentioned. I told her, I think I'd like to get one for Adam's memorial garden, and then suddenly, my car says I have a text message from Adam!? It read, "No". So, I jokingly texted her, after I told her about the message, "I guess he doesn't want the tree?!", and then, "I wonder if he's trying to communicate with me?" Then, a second text came through from him again, this time saying, "I am!!" I was in absolute awe. I heard that electronics could be used to convey messages by those that crossed over, but this was my first experience. We had this car for a while, and it had never done this before.

A medium told me that Adam wanted me to feel him, and that Adam suggested going for a drive with the music playing. I had purchased a concrete piece of hands with a little bird for his memorial garden, and I had to pick it up. It was a gorgeously sunny and warm Spring Day. When I turned on my car, immediately a text message from Adam came through, and I thought "Ok babe, I guess you're coming with me!" It was an hour drive there and back, and I had the radio playing for a change. Music was still hard for me to listen to, and then I suddenly felt Adam say, "Mom, play MY music." So, I put on my Spotify playlist entitled Adam which loops. The first song was *Patience* by his favorite band, Guns N Roses (a sign-in-itself, right there for me). I started singing to the following songs as well, swallowing the lump of a sob that was trying to come up. I began to feel a sensation of such warmth in my upper body and tingling as it enveloped me. My heart became so full of utter and complete love, and tears of happiness filled my eyes. I just knew right then that I was finally feeling my son for the first time!! The love felt was truly indescribable. I know without a doubt that in those moments, my son and I blended!!

My youngest son bought me a beautiful pandora bracelet for Christmas 2018, which I somehow lost shortly thereafter. I looked everywhere in our home, torn the bedroom apart, every dresser drawer thoroughly searched, all to no avail, until December 1st, two days after Adam's birthday, his first since he transitioned. I opened my sock drawer, and there it was, laying right on top as if waiting for me. I was elated and put it on our bed to take a photo to send my husband, and then placed it on top of my jewelry stand. That evening I picked it up from the table to take it to my husband to adjust it. That's all I remember because it disappeared...again! I retraced the few rooms I'd been in searching once more, scolding Adam saying, "Ok bud, this isn't that funny anymore!" The next morning after my tea, I went up to my bedroom to get dressed and make the bed...and there it was lying on top of my sheet! I slept in that exact spot, and I had been up and down throughout the night. I felt the entire bed before I got into it, and nothing! I asked my husband if he had put it there, and of course, he hadn't. Now, when not wearing, it hangs over a decorative bottle Adam bought me on the last Mother's Day we spent together.

Adam also shows his signs using the sky and clouds as his canvas to show me something beautiful. What I love about these are the nudges he gives me to look up, and as well, to take a photo! I can be in the garden, and I'll hear Adam say, "Mom, look up." I've learned now to do it right away, as he will persist until I do. There will, of course, be a gorgeous display of his art for me. There was one time, which still makes me laugh, that after I heard him say to look up, there was one cloud in the sky, and it appeared to be taking the shape of a feather. I then heard, "Take a photo, Mom." My phone was just inside the door. So, I went and got it, opened my camera and my phone started acting strange. Then it totally froze. I got it fixed, tried to take a picture, and the same thing happened again. The shape was beginning to change by now, of course, and I thought, "That's it. I've missed it now." But then got told again, "Take the damn photo, Mom." So, I ran inside and got my tablet which I had to turn on. Of course, the feather shape by now had disappeared. Once again, however I heard, "Just take the picture, MOM!!"

Interestingly enough, I didn't see in the sky what I saw in the photo, a side view of a beautiful angel. You see, my brilliant son didn't want me to see a feather, he wanted me to see the angel that he was creating for me. He used my phone so that I couldn't take the photo at the time I thought I should. But instead, he allowed me to take it with my tablet when he was ready, not me. When I brought my phone back into the house, I decided to try to take a picture, thinking something was wrong with my phone, and it took one just fine. Adam is constantly amazing me.

Bubbles have become a very important form of communication with my son and angels, and I just can't love them enough. It began when I decided that we'd blow bubbles on his second Angelversary so that his daughter and young nieces could also participate and do something fun for the family. I took a lot of sporadic photos of just bubbles blown and zoomed in on them later. To my eyes, I saw the cutest little figure smiling! But then two days later, when I was having my first Angel reading with the well known, ordained Angel Minister, B (Beth) Carleton, close to the end, she was asked by my angels to pull another oracle card, and she said you're going to laugh at me, but they're telling me for you to "blow bubbles"! B then went to put the deck away, and a card fell out. She turned it over, and it said, "We Are So Connected", and it had bubbles all over it!! I joined one of her Angel Circles months later. Yet again, bubbles were mentioned! I decided that day that I needed to have something for myself that had bubbles in it, that I could see daily. Then a glass ball came up on Facebook, with yes, bubbles inside it. I searched for months, and today while writing more in my chapter, I finally found one!

I hear Adam's messages in my left ear, which is interesting as I'm mostly deaf in that one for many years now. I've had amazing sessions with my dear friend and medium

Sally and Adam. Sally has a blend of mental and physical mediumship capabilities with the help of her guides and her son in spirit, which enables her to facilitate direct, real-time, two-way conversations between loved ones across the veil and ones here. Mckenna, Adam's daughter, has also been able to speak with her Daddy as well, and for her to hear again from him, "I love you sweetheart", something she thought she would never hear again. During my most recent conversation with Adam and Sally, he told me that he was helping me become more clairaudient and I must practice listening, not just for him. But I must also learn how to listen to multiple sounds, one at a time, focus on just one, and put the other sounds in the background.

About a week before Valentine's Day, while showering, I heard Adam say, "Can you send flowers to McKenna from me for Valentines?" Ego mind and doubt had popped in, of course, so I asked Adam to send me a heart as a sign that it was him asking (on Sally's advice). The next morning while scrolling through Facebook, I was seeing hearts, but I didn't feel they were from him. Of course, Valentine's was coming, so they were everywhere. Later that day, I had to go back on to Facebook to look for something, and I immediately saw a beautiful heart pendant that a local artisan was selling. One side of the heart was an angel wing, so I messaged her to buy it for McKenna, not even thinking of the sign. Later that evening, while watching tv, it suddenly occurred to me, "Oh my gosh, that was my sign!!" Needless to say, I ordered his daughter flowers from Adam, wondering though, "How am I going to tell the florist that it's from a dad in spirit and what to put on the card from him?!" The florist knows about my son as I've purchased some things from her in the past, so I just explained my task, and when I asked about the signature, she replied, let me meditate on it. It all came together as it was meant to. We are guided precisely to whom we should speak.

One of my favorite ways of receiving messages from my son is through the songs he pops into my head. It's always an adventure. With Adam, most times he wants me to dig for his deeper message, though he will only give me a couple of words and a tiny bit of melody. I will literally open my eyes in the morning with it in my head and wonder why I am thinking this?!! Then the search begins!! I pity Google, as I definitely can't hold or hum a note for the life of me. But somehow, together, we figure out the song, then I search the lyrics, and there is always a wonderful message.

There are many ebbs and flows within grief that often can steer me a tad off my spiritual growth and practices path, but Adam always takes the wheel and brings me back again. I had been struggling for a bit of time and awoke to hear *Here I Go Again* by Whitesnake, and a short melody humming to Google. A song I hadn't heard in many years, it was my son telling me it was time to get back on course again! Often, it feels like puzzle pieces he's giving me to put together so that I finally see the bigger picture that I need to see, always guiding me to where I'm supposed to be.

Another morning it was "I've been", and a few bars. On to Google I go, searching song lyrics with "I've been" in them. Nothing came through that made sense, so I hummed to poor Google, and it immediately said, I think you're looking for "Spirit Eye 125hz". I'm looking for what?! I opened the link it gave me, and it was "Binaural Beats", which I'd never heard of before, so I googled again! To my understanding, binaural beats are frequently used to connect with the divine source, your higher self, and of course, spirit, at different frequencies while wearing headphones or earbuds. This is how my son leads me to learn how to connect better with him, and it's just fascinating to this mom!

I love and cherish each and every sign and message I receive from Adam. Whether it's just a "Hey Mom" or one with a deeper message, they're all equally important to me. I no longer believe in coincidences but instead that everything happens for a reason, no matter how minute that may be. I believe that I know we are always, and in all ways, being guided by our loved ones in spirit, God, our guides, and our beautiful angels.

My journey so far has zig-zagged in many directions, into places I had never considered and probably would never have any interest in in the past. Within my ever-continuing spiritual growth, I've been led to different methods of connecting with my "divine team", which has included oracle cards. Oh, they are wonderful!! I, of course, had no knowledge about the use of them or what they even meant. I only heard of tarot and likened them to psychic fairs where a fortune teller would be gazing into a crystal ball!! I'm still astounded, really, at how I've changed my thinking.

An entire new world has opened up to me since my son passed, and I embrace all that resonates with me. I use oracle cards with both my guides and angels. They have their separate decks, and when I ask questions and pull the cards, there lie their messages for me. I've taken classes to educate myself on how to use them as they are divination tools and to be used properly. To learn about my divine beings, my favorite teachers are both Colette Baron-Reid, bestselling author, Internationally Acclaimed Oracle Expert, Intuitive Counselor, Psychic Medium, TV Personality, and Podcast host, and Kyle Gray, bestselling author, Spiritual Teacher, International Speaker! I'm learning so much through Kyle about our amazing Archangels, how and what we can ask them for to guide us, so I too can share guidance, messages, and healing from the angels. Who would have ever thought that at my age I'd be considering any of these? But here I am loving all of it.

Grief does change you. There's no denying that. I've lost friends and relationships since Adam passed, and you know, that's ok. I've learned that we're all on our own individual journeys, and it's not for me to judge anyone. I now live my life trying to have just positive thoughts, as what we think becomes who we are. I have deeper compassion and love towards others and send love and healing to them instead of anger or disappointment, which isn't always easy.

Still, again more of my self-work and growth that I know will never end. I am, after all, human. No, I'm a soul inside of a human body. I've made many new friendships with like-minded moms that I'm forever grateful for. This can be a very lonely journey, grieving the loss of a child, then coupled with becoming spiritual, you really find out who will support you and who won't. I don't have to defend my beliefs or my son to anyone, but I also won't force mine on others, as it's not my place.

I didn't just wake up one morning and decide to become spiritual and begin this new relationship with Adam, understanding all that it would entail. It's been a lot of researching, learning, and practicing. I will never fully understand how the spirit world and all that it encompasses works. I don't know if anyone truly does, and I'm not sure if it's for us to know until it's our time to return home.

Who I was before July 26, 2019, is not the same person I am now. I will always grieve for Adam. I miss his physical presence so very much, but I know, trust, and believe now that he is always right here, whenever I need him to be, and a lot of times, just hanging out with his mom. It really does allow this journey of mine to be one with a lighter heart.

About the Author

Donna Rewald is a mother of five, 2 of whom have transitioned. Donna maintains a deep spiritual connection with her son Adam. Her spiritual toolbox continues to grow as she continues to evolve, heal, focus on living her life in the moment, and helping others.

*"You are whole and also part of larger
and larger circles of wholeness
you may not even know about.
You are never alone.
And you already belong.
You belong to humanity.
You belong to life.
You belong to this moment,
this breath."
~Jon Kabat-Zinn~
Professor Emeritus of Medicine
Creator of the Stress Reduction Clinic and
the Center for Mindfulness*

Harley's Hearts, *Cindy Leder*

By Cindy Leder

I'm NOT a believer.
I'm a "knower".
There is a huge difference.
Believers believe. Knowers know.

Science tells us energy cannot be destroyed. So where then, does a person's energy go once their body ceases to exist? By sharing some of my stories with you, I am hoping to be able to help open up some hearts to the possibility that Spirit really does exist and that receiving and accepting these beautiful signs and messages they send us are indeed extraordinary gifts. Trusting in the knowledge that life does not end at death may even help change some vague hope into belief and belief into knowing.

In 1975, my mother passed away from cancer. She was only 48. Imagine having to say goodbye to a husband and four children at such a tender age. A formidable task. I was only 16. It's never easy to lose a beloved parent, no matter what the age, because no one ever loves you as much as your parent does. My two older sisters, my younger brother, and I were beyond devastated by such a profound loss. What made it worse was, back then, no one ever spoke of such great loss, especially with the kids. Our lives would never be the same again. As fate would have it, I would go on to lose my father in 2007 and my beloved husband Harley in 2011.

After my Mom's passing in 1975, I took a part-time job at a store that sold evening and cocktail attire on the weekends. Every few weeks, a spunky, cool lady would come in to change the clothes on the manikins in the window. Her name was Deborah. She was the one who laid the groundwork for my very first experience with Spirit. The store was located in the heart of the Financial District, so Saturdays were notoriously slow. That allowed us plenty of time to talk and laugh. We spoke of everything under the sun, including all things loss and spiritual.

One Saturday, Deborah brought me a book on Astral Projection. I couldn't wait to get home to read it. That night, while practicing in bed, my first sign from Spirit appeared. It came in as a royal blue light that washed across my white window blinds. That "blue light" freaked me out. I wasn't really sure what it was at first, but as the blue turned more vibrant, it gave off a vibration that was both powerful and penetrating. I went on to learn that royal blue is the colour associated with the 6th chakra and paranormal vision (seeing beyond the capability of the eyes to the other side). That blue light distinctly felt like my mother's presence. How do I know that? It's difficult to explain, but the simple answer is, as I tuned into a higher frequency, I felt her presence within every fibre of my being. She made the hair on the back of my neck and arms stand straight up. Best explained as the feeling gave my goosebumps goosebumps. I simply KNEW it was her. I just didn't have the right words to explain what I had felt to others. Years later, my Mom validated the blue light experience for me. My friends had arranged for me to see a psychic for my 40th birthday. The first words out of the psychic's mouth were, "Your mother is in the Spirit world, and she wants to know if you remember the blue light. She says it was her". Confirmation and validation!

I can still feel my Mom in Spirit around me to this day. We have shared numerous spiritual experiences together, and she has seen me through beautiful times and also through some dark and difficult ones. I felt her presence the strongest when I delivered both of my children. She let me know that she was safely escorting them to me. She has also orchestrated and organized many connections via the Spirit world for me. She's instrumental in helping me communicate with my father, my husband, my in-laws, my grandparents, and many, many other loved ones across the veil. She was with me during the late stages of my husband's illness.

During a mediumship reading, my husband Harley confirmed for me that alongside his own loving parents, my Mom was also there to greet him as he peacefully crossed over. Unfortunately, he never got the chance to meet my Mom on this earth plane because she passed away a decade before we met. She was the one responsible for bringing Harley through for the first time a year after he passed. She has helped me to understand and accept that love never dies, and that life is a continuum. I am very grateful for the communication we share and for her ongoing spiritual presence in my life.

My Dad chose to be a believer. He relished hearing stories of my experiences, especially if they included my Mom. He listened intently as I described messages of love from the other side. He always appreciated discussing the possibility of life after death with me, and as he faced his own mortality, that discussion must have brought him some much-needed comfort. Hey, who wouldn't feel great knowing that the "physical end" wasn't really the end?

He passed suddenly on the morning of July 26, 2007. That night, I looked into the mirror before going to sleep and simply said, "Okay, Dad, now you can tell me if what I believe to be true, IS true". I woke suddenly that night, startled by the feeling that someone had sat down on my bed beside me. I felt my memory-foam mattress sink. Next, something began caressing my leg, from my knee down to my ankle. My eyes popped open wide, but I consciously chose to remain perfectly still. My husband was fast asleep beside me, so he was not doing the caressing. Silently, I said to myself, "Dad/Mom, if that's you, please do that again." As instructed telepathically, my leg was caressed two more times. Slowly, I turned myself over to catch a glimpse of who was sitting there. I saw no one but noticed the clock read 2:22 (that repeating number is associated with spiritual awakening and can symbolize the merging of two separate yet equal paths). Again, a higher vibration told me my Mom/Dad were there to confirm what I already believed to be true.

About a month later, I experienced an extraordinarily vivid dream. My Dad, in his crisp and crystal-clear voice, called me on the telephone. He said that I was his messenger and asked me to tell my three siblings that he was fine, happy, and reunited with his two best pals. I specifically asked, "What about Mom?" He confirmed he had also been lovingly reunited with her. That dream evoked a visceral reaction. When you love somebody, you can hear them say, "I love you," but you can also feel and sense the depth of that love, too. That night, I felt pure love energy. I have never experienced anything quite like that in the dream state before.

My husband, Harley Ulster, was the love of my life and a gem of a human being. Bar-none, he was one of the finest people I have ever known. We met in March 1983, but the universe had us cross paths a few times before finally placing us on the same path together. We dated blissfully, and our love just blossomed. While dining at our favourite neighbourhood restaurant, on Valentine's Day in 1986, Harley asked me to marry him. Being a prankster, he handed me my Valentine's card, which read "Will you MAR … me?" and was written in such a way that the word MARRY actually fell off the printed page! He could then claim that he had never truly asked me to "marry" him!! Saying yes to this gentle, funny, caring, loving, kind, compassionate, and beautiful human was the best decision I ever made in my life. I was the lucky one who would get to spend a lifetime with him. Our great love created two of the most miraculous blessings in our lives, our amazing daughter, followed twenty-two months later by our incredible son.

Exactly 25 years to the day that Harley asked me to marry him, I had to lay him to rest. Yes, you read that correctly. He was buried on Valentine's Day, 2011, two weeks after his 59th birthday. He had been diagnosed, at age 48, with Multiple Myeloma, an incurable cancer of the plasma cell. I will spare you the agonizing details and the depth of our grief, anguish, and pain upon receiving this diagnosis as well as the various ups and downs we navigated over the next eleven years. Suffice it to say, losing Harley was the most difficult thing we have ever faced in all of our lives. Valentine's Day was chosen as a permanent reminder and marker for our love. Harley's "Valentine hello" and "Valentine goodbye" symbolized and solidified the intense strength of our love bond. Perhaps, that is why Harley chose a "Heart" as his main way of communicating with me from beyond.

Harley sometimes goes to great lengths to get our attention. While onboard a flight home from our son's law school graduation, my daughter and I looked out the window only to see a huge letter 'H' in cloud formation in the sky. We knew it was his way of saying he had been there celebrating with us.

The night before he wrote the New York Bar Exam, my son lost his good luck charm, Harley's "business card". Distraught, he muddled through a last-minute review the next morning. He opened up his textbook only to find Harley's business card staring at him and marking a page that he had not yet studied. It was an unmistakable sign from Harley urging him to read that particular section, and sure enough, it appeared on the bar exam that day. To this day, Harley sends messages of love when we need them most and also includes messages of guidance as well. He continues to send a plethora of signs and symbols. These include, but are not limited to, dimes, butterflies, hummingbirds, clouds, cardinals, feathers, scents, songs on the radio, and heart shapes in nature. His "heart-shaped" messages come in the form of rocks, shells, leaves, wood, food, water splatters, animal markings, snow, seaweed, sand, shadows, etc. Over the years, I have developed a discerning eye and can easily spot all things heart shaped. He also sends heart messages to my loved ones, who forward all sorts of messages of love to me. These signs provide me with feelings of love, protection, and comfort in a way that only Spirit can deliver.

The first time Harley used technology to send a message was via a TV located in my son's bedroom on the third floor of our house. This specific TV functioned as a "car tv" long before they were ever in vogue. It was 13 inches and small enough to fit between the driver's and passenger's seats. It plugged into the lighter and had a VCR function. It was a major source of entertainment for our kids as we drove 2 1/2 hours to and from ski country.

Harley turned that TV on at any hour of the day or night. Sometimes, it would occur around a birthday or an anniversary. My daughter, son, and housekeeper all experienced this phenomenon over and over again. When home alone, I would often hear full-out conversations taking place in my house. I would seek out the source of the voices and always end up back on the third floor. One time, I made my way upstairs, saying, "Hi Harley, I know it's you." when something prodded me to press the video's play button. Unbeknownst to me, there was a VCR tape inside. I saw Harley walking through our front door, holding our baby daughter, saying, "We're baaaack!". The sound of his voice brought me to tears, but those words made me laugh out loud! He had now become the "Arnold Schwarzenegger" of Spirit.

That same TV turned itself on once in the middle of the night, waking my daughter mid-dream. She was dreaming that she was doing a spin class when an old friend of hers from high school, whom she hadn't seen in years, tapped her on the shoulder, asking, "What's your Dad doing here?" That's precisely when the TV turned itself on. Freaked out and startled, she texted me immediately. It was 5 am. I invited her to come down to my room and describe what happened in detail. The experience was exceptionally real and woke her out of a deep sleep.

After she returned to bed, I was left tossing and turning by the song *All Out of Love* by Air Supply which played over and over in my head. That song had no real significance for Harley or for me, but like any musical earworm, I simply could not shake it. The accompanying feeling was, "Get up, get out of bed, and go check it out on the computer." So, I did. Imagine how I felt when I read the following lyrics from *All Out of Love*:

"I'm all out of love,

I'm so lost without you,

I know you were right, "believing" for so long.

I'm all out of love,

What am I without you?

It can't be too late to say that "I was so wrong".

It's important to note here that Harley, although fascinated by all of my stories, was a skeptic. He preferred scientific proof. So, receiving an apology from my husband, from the great beyond, via a musical message, shook me to my core. What a message of confirmation! Whenever I hear that song, I am profoundly reminded that Harley's love surrounds me. Thank you, Harley and Spirit, for consistently reminding me of your powerful presence in my life.

Our 25th wedding anniversary arrived five months after Harley passed. The anticipation and lead-up to that day were absolutely brutal. Thoughts of him were all-consuming and ubiquitous; how much I missed him, how much he was missing, how proud I was of our kids, how proud he would be of our kids, etc. I drove up to the cottage to mark our special day.

En route, I stopped at our favourite greasy-spoon diner. A ritual. I sat at our favourite table next to the window. The same waitress approached to take my order. Notoriously, she always got it wrong - nothing changed that day. There I sat, alone and without Harley, on our 25th Anniversary. Pensive and deep in thought, I stared out the window, oblivious to the fact that countless "Harley Davidson" motorcycles were parked in plain view. Suddenly, I was disturbed by a table of six noisy men seated next to me. I tuned into their conversation, and all I kept hearing was, "My Harley this ... and my Harley that ...". These men kept rambling on about their motorbikes. But hearing Harley's name on repeat helped fill my heart up with joy. I gazed out the window again, only to ultimately see those countless "Harley" motorcycles staring back at me. He went to great lengths that day arranging those messages to let me know I wasn't alone.

The cottage was Harley's favourite place. I pulled up the driveway and took pause. The yearning was much more amplified and overwhelming on our 25th Anniversary. Tears and memories kept flowing. He loved everything about that place, and that helped me to feel his presence. I laid my cheek on his pillow, I went through his clothes, actively seeking out his scent (after five months it seemed his scent was starting to fade), and I went through his drawers seeking anything at all that might remind me of our magnificent life together. I desperately just wanted to feel him around me.

As I sat by the pool in the fresh air, I kept talking out loud to him. I promised him I would continue to live in a manner that made him proud, and more importantly, I told him I would take good care of our precious children. I kept blabbering on until I noticed five heart-shaped clouds in the sky above my cottage. In shock, I froze, jaw agape. Then, hypnotized by these beautiful, heart-shaped clouds, I felt Harley's presence with me in much the same way I had felt my mother's presence when the blue light splashed across my window blind.

I ran into the cottage to grab my camera to capture those magnificent clouds forever. When I returned, the clouds were gone. I got to see them and knew they were messages of love from Harley. Perhaps, they were meant only for my eyes. They are forever etched in my brain, and I will always feel their power in my soul. I spent the remainder of that afternoon gazing up into the sky, hoping to catch a glimpse of more heart-shaped clouds. Harley sent me three more that afternoon, and I captured them all on camera. One might even say that he moved heaven and earth to grab my attention and show his love that day by surrounding me with "Harleys" and sending me numerous heart-shaped clouds. It left an indelible mark on my heart.

One of the most spectacular messages from Harley came on the day of my daughter's wedding. It's always wonderful to celebrate exciting and joyous occasions. I didn't want Spirit to miss out on this special celebration, so the night before my daughter's wedding, I put out a special invitation into the universe to ensure Spirit wouldn't miss it. I invited all Spirit we love and miss to come and share in our joy. I knew Harley would never miss his daughter's wedding.

Just after our daughter got engaged, a reading with a psychic medium confirmed that Harley knew and was overjoyed that my daughter was engaged and to be married. The psychic medium described the wedding day for me. She told me Harley would be there in the form of a cardinal and to be on the lookout for him. She also asked me if my daughter would be standing underneath "an umbrella or an awning or something" at the ceremony. She knew absolutely nothing about chuppahs (the canopy beneath which Jewish marriages are performed). She told us to look up at that umbrella/awning (chuppah) during the ceremony, and we would know that Harley was there with us. "It will be confirmation from him," she said, "that he walked her down the aisle."

I cut a piece of Harley's favourite shirt and sewed it into my daughter's wedding dress. My son put a piece of that same shirt into his pocket, and I pinned a piece inside my dress, right next to my heart. We all carried a piece of Harley with us on her wedding day. Our daughter made the most exquisite spring bride. We came across many heart-shaped stones during family photos, and, as promised, a beautiful bright red cardinal appeared and followed the happy couple on their outdoor photoshoot. It was a truly amazing day filled with much joy, love, and happiness. I felt such a surprising sense of calmness.

My son and I walked my daughter down the aisle together. As we approached the chuppah, I looked up to see if I could see any sign. I saw nothing. I was a bit heartbroken and disappointed, but it most definitely did not stop us from celebrating and enjoying the rest of the wedding. The next day, my nephew, who had taken footage of the ceremony with his cell phone, showed my sister his photos. In shock, my sister shrieked, "You better show these photos to Aunty Cindy right now!!" My nephew forwarded me his pictures. Stunned, I saw this big, beautiful heart shape hovering directly above my daughter as she stood beneath the chuppah. I was elated and overjoyed and rendered speechless. No one could explain how that heart got there that night, but no one needed to explain it. We all knew. That heart only appeared in photos and on video footage. Harley had walked his daughter down the aisle as promised. The universe works in mysterious ways! Definite proof that just because you can't see something does not mean it ISN'T there!!!!

Harley also sent me an amazing heart-shaped sign on the day our first granddaughter was born. It was a very cold, snowy Family Day in 2019. My daughter's water broke at 7 am, and she and her husband proceeded to the hospital. I followed a few hours later. Thinking we might see blizzard conditions, I backed my car into the hospital parking space just to make it easier to exit at the end of the day. As I opened my car door, my gaze fell directly upon a heart-shaped footprint right there in the snow. I saw no steps leading up to or away from it. Just a snowy heart shape was lying there on the ground. Had I not backed my car into that parking space that day, I would have missed it completely. I smiled and cried, thanking Harley for letting me know that he was right there with me, overseeing things, as we welcomed our first grandchild. On the day that marked the arrival of our second grandchild, my daughter saw a huge stone heart, outlined in rainwater, on her driveway as she walked out her front door and headed to the hospital. Harley bounced both of our grandchildren on his knee before safely sending them off to us. Both granddaughters are named for him.

Losing someone you love deeply causes great emotional pain. But knowing that life exists beyond death is both powerful and healing. Not to mention the fact that it helps give us the hope we need to understand that there's something more beyond just the physical. Signs from Spirit can bring joy to those who have lost loved ones. They also have a profound effect on one's healing. Signs of love allow for the possibility that our loved ones still exist, that they're always around us, and that we can still connect with them whenever we choose to. Spirit loves nothing more than connecting with us and making us aware of their presence. My visual is of a big, beautiful bridge made up of trillions of hearts - a virtual meeting place of love, if you will - that allows souls from the Spirit world to meet up with, connect and pass messages of love to and from souls in the physical world. There is nothing more healing than knowing your loved ones remain close by and continue to surround you.

I may not be able to convince you that Spirit exists using science, logic, reason, or religion, but I can tell you that when you feel Spirit, you'll know. I feel them in every cell and fibre of my being. I carry my loved ones in my heart, and I reach out and speak to them whenever I want to because I know they are listening. Spirit is always willing to communicate. They send all sorts of signs and messages to let us know that they are there. All WE need to do is open up our hearts to the possibility.

Hardship may be the greatest of all teachers, but sometimes out of great tragedy, good things can come. Honouring Harley's legacy, life, and memory remain important to our family. Eradicating this insidious Multiple Myeloma blood cancer to help spare other families the trauma, pain, and sadness our family had to endure is our goal. Giving back helps us accomplish both. Wanting to ensure that all MM patients receive timely access to the newest life-extending medications, I joined a national Multiple Myeloma Advocacy team. On my quest for the cure, I established an annual Multiple Myeloma 5K Walk in Toronto that helps to raise the necessary funds for research. Research is the key to a cure. I am thrilled to report the MM5K Walk is entering its 18th year and has raised $9 million for Multiple Myeloma Research to date. This directly impacts new treatments for Multiple Myeloma patients worldwide. In 2009, we had the great fortune to help launch The Bloom Chair for Multiple Myeloma Research at Princess Margaret Cancer Center, the very first MM Chair in Canada and only second in North America. We continue to forge ahead in an effort to turn Harley's dream of a cure into a reality. Alas, we could never have accomplished any of this without the constant love, support, and extreme generosity of our spectacular family and unbelievable friends.

I don't believe in coincidence. All things have led me to this time and place for a reason. Life is made up of a combination of love and pain. The ability to feel both of these elements is necessary for growth. I continue to grow. I hope these few stories have touched you in a way that may make you want to stretch your heart a little to let in the possibility that Spirit exists and always wants to communicate with us. If life is love, and love can never be extinguished, then life simply cannot end. If we cannot see our loved ones who have passed, does that mean they are not really there? Quite the opposite. Signs and messages are all around us. We just need to adjust our frequencies to be able to see, feel, receive and accept them. The signs we receive are special gifts of love and comfort sent directly to us from Spirit. These beautiful messages can help change vague hope into belief...and from belief comes knowing.

I am a knower.

Postscript

While formulating this chapter in real time, I receive two heart photo messages: one from Harley's friend via social media and the other from Harley's sister via text. Neither sender realizes the impact of their explicit timing. The photos arrive as I sit writing about signs from Spirit. The validation and confirmation these two messages bring me are cardinal. They definitely validate the significance and importance of this great labour of love.

A very special thank you goes out to Camille Dan for uniting and empowering us to collectively create this remarkable and important anthology which helps provide evidence that our loved ones actually do remain close by.

Thank you, Spirit, for consistently reminding me of your loving presence in my life.

About the Author

Cindy Leder is a retired, experienced educator and former Vice-Principal/Principal of a private school in Toronto. Currently involved in volunteer fundraising for Multiple Myeloma research at the Princess Margaret Cancer Foundation, she is committed to raising funds and awareness, while trying to bring some hope to the many Multiple Myeloma patients and their families who live with this insidious cancer, nationwide. As co-creator of Toronto's annual Multiple Myeloma MM5K Walk, they have raised $9 million to date for Multiple Myeloma research via The Bloom Chair at Princess Margaret Cancer Centre in Toronto. Cindy is privileged and honoured to be the mother of two truly amazing and successful kids, Ellery (Ryan) and Philip (Austin) and blessed and grateful to be the "Bubie" (grandmother) of two incredible granddaughters, Poppy and Lulu.

In her spare time, Cindy photographs nature. After her husband Harley passed in 2011, it afforded her an outward expression into her own healing and helped teach her to trust in the rhythm, harmony and balanced order of the universe. In 2017, She held a photography exhibit of her work where 100% of all proceeds were donated to Multiple Myeloma Research at the Princess Margaret Cancer Foundation. She took her broken heart and turned it into art, much the same as her participation in this anthology.

> *"The soul is an infinite ocean of just*
> *beautiful energy and presence made*
> *manifest in human form."*
> *~Panache Desai~*
> *Spiritual Leader*

Box Dream & a Phone Call from Josiah, *Raina Irene*

By Raina Irene

How do I tell you of myself, the mother of three with one of them in Spirit?

I will start with this.

On October 22, 2017, my heart stopped with his. My youngest child, my twenty-nine-year-old son, my baby Josiah, left planet Earth, changing the direction of all that I am, and all I would be.

I became a bystander to the unreal, the unimaginable, and from there, I have emerged somehow more aware and less afraid. I wrote a book to honor him, created an Oracle deck with his art, and have learned more about myself and Spirit than I had thought possible. I have come to cherish being alone and honor whatever the day may bring me, physically, emotionally, and spiritually.

My Son gave me the title Heart, Soul, Spirit Practitioner after he left this realm.

I am a Retired Esthetician and hold multiple certificates in Holistic Health, Spiritual and Emotional Healing, Plant Medicine, Reiki, Angels, and Spirit Communication.

These days I work with Mothers who also have a child or children in Spirit. I continue to write about this journey, the emotions, the signs, and the realness of all of it, and spend as much time with my grandchildren as possible.

Josiah has come to me in so many ways, I call it, -The Alchemy of Josiah-.

This story is about two dreams he gave me, the signs around them and the messages within them. The continuous message that, Everything is Love and Love Heals Everything.

Box Dream

The Alarm woke me at 5:30 am, as usual; that is the time I like to wake and do the morning dance of coffee, meditation, dogs, and reading before my walk. Yet this morning had my mind reeling back to the story that had just happened in my dream before it escaped into the vagueness dreams have a way of escaping to. Jumping out of bed is not part of the dance, so I repeated the dream over and over. I did not want to forget it. I quickly realized there was no way I was going to forget this. It was more than a dream.

It was a message.

I poured myself an oversized cup of coffee and walked straight to my healing room to write down the dream. The dream took place in the home I was living in five years ago, before moving to my present home. Both Josiah's siblings, Jeremy and Valerie were with me. We walked out the front door to see several packages sitting on the ground near the plants. One was huge, about five inches thick, and maybe forty-eight inches by sixty inches in dimension, if not bigger. A piece of the cardboard was ripped off exposing some sort of metal parts inside of it. I scanned the outside of the box to see who it was for. It was addressed to my children's father but sent to my address. Below the address written on the box, it said: "I know I did the ultimate "screw up" (except the words were choicer!) and was signed, Josiah. I could immediately sense what he was meaning, he had sent it to my house instead of his dad's so I would have to give it to him?!

I told the kids that I must see what is in there, and proceeded to rip the cardboard away, my emotional curiosity getting the best of me. We all ripped the box open, to expose a kit to build your own motorcycle.

I started to cry hysterically and within the dream, I knew that Josiah had been gone for months so how was this happening? How was this possible? How could he send me anything?

There were several other smaller packages, one with herbs.

In the next scene, I am walking with Josiah's dad on a road near the home I grew up in and I was telling him all that had happened and showing him the box. He opened the box but said nothing and had no expression on his face.

319

That is when my alarm went off.

As I was writing down the dream, my mind wandered, and I got distracted for a moment. You know, I haven't even finished my first cup of coffee! Then I heard a noise, like a shallow scraping. I started to look around the room to see what the heck it was. I saw nothing until I turned completely around to see Josiah's wooden tree, an art piece that he made for me, that hangs on the wall there. It was swaying left to right against the wall, hypnotizing me back to my sole reason for being in this room. As it slowed to a stop, I tried to make it sway again, just to make sure I had not caused it. How could I though, I had not moved? I hit the wall with my fist as hard as I could, with no movement. I shut the door hard, nothing. I scooted my chair against the wall, nothing again. I touched the side of the wooden tree pushing it to the left and watched it return its sway to the right. That was the only way to make it move, and I had not done that!

Josiah's Wooden Tree

"Ok, Josiah, you are here, I know that beyond a shadow of a doubt!" I whispered as I placed my hand on my heart to keep it intact. I finished writing the dream and then sat there, blown away by his capabilities, and of course, telling him if he could sway that tree once, he could do it again!

I was meeting a friend at 7:00 am to walk so I left the room, knowing that this dream, and Josiah had more to tell me. After the walk, I had a meeting at 9:30 am that lasted a couple of hours. When that ended, I decided to eat something and check my emails before I dove back into the dream. I don't normally open my emails when I have other things on my mind, especially when it has to do with Josiah, yet today I did. I opened an email from Lisa, a well-known psychic medium and teacher. She was having a class in the next hour about trance mediumship. That's what I feel I do when I write with Josiah. Hum, I thought, perfect timing, maybe this will help me connect in more about the dream, I'd better take this class.

I had watched some videos of Lisa's but not sat in on an entire class, so I didn't know a lot about her, and still, I knew this was what I was supposed to do. She went on to explain trance mediumship and tell stories of her own experiences, which were fascinating. Then she says,

"I am going to demonstrate for you, I am going to connect to my guide in trance and channel a message for the group. My guide's name is... (wait for it) ...JOSIAH!!!!!!!!"

Wait... What did she just say?? I felt like I was in an altered reality for a moment. I must have misheard her. Then she shared her screen with the group, because she was going to type the message, and the first word she typed was, "Josiah!" I sat, mind blown, in tears, listening to her channel, this higher being, named Josiah.

Was this my Josiah? Well, for me it was!

Now I finally had the time and openness of my spirit to dive in and find the message to this dream. I know that this didn't come from my subconscious mind because I am not focused on the motorcycle, the transportation he chose to ride his way in through those translucent doors. I have always known he left well before that bike was anywhere near that tree. So that wasn't from me. Yet the motorcycle is the only tangible thing he could send because he knows that I could not accept a broken tree. The tree is too symbolic to the both of us, I mean he made me one!

And he sent the box to my previous house, I could feel the significance in this too. It was somewhere I had already moved away from. This dream had to have been from Josiah. Plus, he signed the box, telling me this was the Ultimate Screw-up!

Let me start with, The Ultimate Screw up!

I knew right away, even inside the dream that he was referring to screwing me up. Meaning, "Sorry Mom, I didn't mean to ultimately screw you up, but this is the way it needs to be."

Ok, I get that, I have come to understand we agreed on these roles, but why a motorcycle Josiah? Why send a motorcycle kit to your father? And why do I have to give it to him? And why so many boxes?

Deep in my soul I knew the answer but decided to look up the meaning of some of the things he had shown me in this dream.

Dreaming of Boxes. Dreaming of boxes can mean that you have strong feelings about change. Like you are ready for change, or to change the way you have been doing things.

Open boxes can signify the emotional baggage you are carrying. Sealed boxes (which there were several) can mean you are gaining a sense of closure with some issues in your life, you are finally feeling unclouded.

I looked up the meaning of dreaming about a motorcycle. I couldn't find just parts, but I found "broken" which felt close considering the meaning. To dream of a broken motorcycle refers to the broken hopes in your life. What you had planned did not work out the way you imagined; however, your life might not turn out as you expected but it turned out the way it is today. It went on to say that you can still make changes and adjust your mind to the idea.

Another meaning of dreaming about a motorcycle was associated with meaningful progress in a situation that you have been working towards. And one of the meanings of dreaming of steel, which is what the parts of the motorcycle were made of, means friendship and love are eternal, also steel represents the beliefs in your heart.

Dreaming about herbs can mean you need to remember the beautiful and treasured parts of this life and allow the light back into the parts of you that have lost their shine.

As I went through all these meanings, I started to see the pieces of this puzzle Josiah had sent me. In the dream, my attention was first drawn to the largest box, the partially torn box. All my emotional baggage and feelings laying there on the ground, torn open and exposed. As my children and I opened that heartbroken, distressed, wound of a box, there inside were the pieces of steel, the parts of me that were hard to process. The wound so deep of my child being in Spirit, this is the only thing I could focus on and the process I have been in.

Addressed to my children's father, because we share a similarity of the heart when it comes to our children. What I have been doing and what he has been doing is different, yet something within me is shared with him. As in my dream, when I gave the box and all the parts of steel, solid and heavy yet shiny, to his father, it was a symbol of me giving this part of my broken heart to spirit so it could be assembled and reunited with the parts of me that I am now.

In my yard, the other sealed boxes showed me that I have put so much behind me and traveled through the eye of the needle to another part of myself that I was unaware existed! That the change I want to happen has already happened. All I had to do was entrust it to the Ethereal, to Spirit, to G~d.

Josiah was using his Alchemist ways again to challenge me to dive deep and figure it out...

"Let me send you this package, the parts of you, the strong feelings you have are all in there. I want you to see them. You and my siblings rip that open, become aware of what is in there, and then, realize where you are now, no longer torn and in pieces. I have sent you herbs to remind you of the light you are and the light that this world still has for you. Yes, you may still weep as you remember the box, yet handing it over to the Universe, to the Stars, and to Heaven will allow this part of your process to become stardust. And let me remind you how connected we are. When I send you a dream, just like my wooden tree that swayed to the left and the right and then stilled in the middle, don't you veer to the left or the right. Stay the course. Stay connected to the higher consciousness that is you, that is me."

That is why I listened to Lisa for an hour. To hear her say she was connecting to Josiah, to see her write it. To know that what I know is true.

Our bonds are inseparable. We just need to pay attention and be willing to dive deep, ponder what we see, what we feel, and what we hear, and know that we know we can't make this up. It is happening all the time and it is real! I could not have made that wooden tree sway, no matter how hard I tried. I can't force a sign or a dream; I just need to stay open and aware. And I can't build a motorcycle from a kit, nor do I want to, but his father can and so can my spirit team.

His father in my dream represented The Light of G~d, Higher Consciousness, The Ethereal - as Josiah has shown me, or whatever the Spiritual aspect is for you. That is where the healing comes from. I had to hand it over and allow my spiritual guide to carry it, who is also my son.

My heart felt calm, Josiah was next to me as I sat amidst the stardust and another message came through me from him!

"Deep breath, deep love. You are the essence of all that is.

You are the channel of light and love.

You are the now and the forever.

Enter the now with the heart of forever.

Enter all that is with the best of yourself.

Leave the rest.

Leave it at the foot of the hill you are trying to climb.

Leave the hill that is the illusion of a creation that no longer serves you.

See past the illusion into the forever of what is you and has always been you.

Breathe again and feel the expansion that you have been holding back.

Exhale the energy that is moving forward and move forward with it.

Your breath is your legs.

Let your breath move you, not your body.

Your body follows your breath.

Your body holds you back.

Your breath moves you forward.

If you would pay attention to your breath, your mind would calm, and your body would rest.

In the calm is the clarity you are longing for.

Breathe."

I sat back dumbfounded. I felt like the day had gone full circle as I read what his message said.

A few weeks later I had another dream.

A phone call from Josiah!

"Hello?" I question as I answered the phone in my dream state. The other end was quiet, yet I knew it was my son Josiah.

"Where have you been? I thought you were dead!" I said in a rush of heavy emotions of shock and relief. (Which is weird because I never use the word dead! But you know how we can use that word so flippantly to someone we are worried about?)

He answered softly, his voice soothing, "I have been traveling, camping, and there was no way to call."

"Why didn't you call me before you left?" He only replied with, "It was blocked." My heart was racing, and the tears were gushing, "blocked?" He assured me that was not what he meant, that telling me was impossible.

I went on to tell him how happy I was to hear from him, to talk with him, how much I loved him, missed him, and needed so many more of these calls. He replied with the same.

The dream went on with so much validation that it was from him!

I often tell him that I miss his phone calls telling me of all the art he was creating, the people he had met, and the places he was traveling. Tears rolled down my face that morning, harder than they had in a while. Of course, he can call me from where he is, and of course, he is going to keep me close, just as we were here, we still are. Just as I wrote over and over as he was teaching me our new language those first couple years as I wrote in Because of Josiah.

He has not disappeared, and He is not dead.

Death is an illusion. He is just on the other side of that Translucent Door.

He is traveling. I needed to hear that, and I know you did too.

Our bonds continue.

Everything is Love and love heals everything.

Beauty, Strength & Healing

About the Author

Raina Irene is a Heart, Soul, Spirit Practitioner, Mother, Grandmother, Healer, and Author. She holds multiple certificates in Holistic Health, Spiritual and Emotional Healing, Plant Medicine, Reiki, Angels, and Spirit Communication. Raina's eclectic and spiritual diversity enables her to tap into your unique needs, supporting and guiding you to clarity and connecting you to your own healing energies. After her son Josiah left planet Earth, writing became a refuge and a voice of their continued bond. As she wrote, Raina realized it was Josiah guiding her keyboard and direction. With two siblings, parents, and now her Son in Spirit, Raina has committed to sharing that our bonds continue, that communication with the Ones We Love in Spirit, Our Children is not only possible but happening all the time. All you have to do is Believe and you will see. Raina is the author of *Because of Josiah: The Sacred Alchemy of a Mother's Unending Bond with Her Son in Spirit*, Transcendent Publishing, February 24, 2021. Website: www.rainairene.love

Josiah

*"How can you be certain
that your whole life is not a dream?"*
~Rene Descartes~
Philosopher, Mathematician
1596-1650

Spectator Mode: See You in My Dreams, *Jonathan Dan*

By Jonathan Dan

If anyone were to ask me, "What was your favorite part about your childhood?" I would simply tell them: "My favorite part about my childhood was that I could visit my brother Aaron whenever I wanted to."

I am an avid gamer, video game concept artist, and 3D modeler. I owe many of my interests to my late brother Aaron, as I had idolized him throughout my life. I wanted to be like him so he and I could share interests and do fun things together.

When I was only 3 years old, my brothers Aaron and Zach were always playing video games together. It was a tad difficult for them to accept the 3rd brother into the family, possibly because of all the popular gaming consoles at the time, the Super Nintendo Entertainment System and Sega Genesis (known as the Mega Drive outside North America) only normally supported up to 2 players. But I distinctly remember when Aaron took a 3rd party controller and pretended to plug it into the SNES's AVI output, so that I could pretend to play along with them. While even then I quickly realized I wasn't actually playing the game, it was a very generous gesture from a young Aaron that he was willing to let me participate no matter what.

It was here when Aaron introduced me to the world of Video Games, where my passion was born. He introduced me to other hobbies as well. Aaron was a very generous person as you can tell. But sure, he did tend to quarrel and get on my nerves a lot too growing up. But when I think about him, through memories good or not, the brightest shining light is always that he was there. Later in his life, Aaron became very close to his family, as he was set on repairing all the dirty laundry, we had developed amongst each other over the years. He put the needs of others before himself.

327

But alas, this generosity of Aaron may also have been a vice for him. He was also respectful and kind to the wrong people. People who lied and took advantage of him. Perhaps Aaron found it difficult to cut ties with them because his sense of honor and respect made it hard to just simply abandon someone like that.

One day, Aaron decided to pay me a visit to my apartment, seemingly out of nowhere. At the time, Aaron usually visited with me together with Mom at her house, or when we went to see movies together. But this time, it was just the two of us. We started by playing the last game we ever played together, *Earthworm Jim 2* on the Super Nintendo. I remember helping Aaron answer the nonsensical trivia questions from the quiz challenge near the end of the level called, "Villi People". "May I please be excused to go to the bathroom?" The answer: "The Industrial Revolution." Upon reaching the level "The Flyin' King", we turned the game off and headed out to a nearby restaurant called Mariachi's.

This restaurant was actually a special place for Aaron. He had been going there since his high school days and became well acquainted with the owner of the restaurant. Every time we went there, the owner would greet us warmly and ask how our lives were doing. She was essentially a second mother to me and Aaron. Aaron and I ate at the back patio, the last time I can vividly remember hanging out with him.

As we left and he dropped me off, Aaron had a strange look in his eye. I wasn't aware of his meaning at the time. But thinking back, I think Aaron was telling me to take good care of our mother. Perhaps he knew he was in his last stand, but I'll never be able to ask him that. To this day, I do my best to take care of Mom and make up for Aaron's absence. However, I'm well aware that I will never be able to replace him.

When news of Aaron's passing had come to me, my mind had essentially shut down. I was unable to comprehend much, having difficulty accepting that the news I heard was true. I hardly ate much, I hardly did any work, and it wasn't until around a couple of months later that I was back at working capacity. I mostly just spent time explaining the whole situation to everyone I knew over and over again. I told them I believed that problems in Aaron's life had reached some kind of "critical mass" as being the "reason" why he passed.

When it came to revealing Aaron's tombstone and epitaph, it made me feel a bit more realistic. I remember mentioning to a buddy that Aaron was getting a tombstone. I remarked at how unfortunate it was that something like that was all a person like him could receive, as far as "gifts" go. On the day of the headstone unveiling, I stated that I shouldn't be there because Aaron should not be dead. It was still so unreal to me. I said that this shouldn't exist, yet it does. At least, it did help me somewhat to accept that this was Aaron's final resting place.

When I was nearly done with my online courses, my final assignment was to make a simple art demonstration game in Unreal Engine 4. I ended up making a very simple game where you played as a birds-of-paradise-flower-guy and a lollipop fairy who explore a barn, haunted woods, sacred woods, and a cave, all of which I had to conceive, and 3D model myself. It was around this time when Aaron had recently passed, and thusly so, I dedicated the whole project to his memory in the credits section. I mentioned that he got me into gaming at the age of 3, and how I would never have made the project in the first place if it wasn't for him. I even loosely based the protagonist off Aaron himself. My teacher enjoyed how I paid respects to my brother, mentioning it in my grade notes.

Furthermore, I also 3D modeled a tombstone reading "GOODBYE AARON" and placed it in the game's sacred woods area next to a giant tree with a face. That area of the game was inspired by *Kokiri Forest from The Legend of Zelda: Ocarina of Time*. I prominently remember Aaron playing and enjoying that game as a kid as well. I didn't play it at first because I thought it was an "Aaron Game". I figured it would be a nice virtual final resting place for him. I even put a sunbeam particle effect to make the tombstone seem more heavenly.

Yes, in my works of fiction, there will always be something in there where the inspiration has some loose connection to Aaron. Numerous characters that I have been designing and writing take a couple of elements from Aaron. I've even had an idea for a game where you must haunt a house in order to set things right in your family so that you can properly move on to the afterlife. Go figure what inspired that. Yes, I think it is best that I immortalize my brother's memory in my works of art.

My mother wrote a book titled *Aaron's Energy: An Unexpected Journey Through Grief and the Afterlife with My Brilliant Son*. She wrote it to document all the spiritual connections she felt with him in his afterlife. I felt it was my duty as Aaron's brother to produce the cover art for its first and second editions. It only made sense;

I was an artist after all. I even made the cover art to this book you're reading right now.

Now when it comes to me and having dreams, they tend to be all over the place. Sometimes I can remember minute details from dreams that often make little to no sense. I write them down shortly after waking up because sometimes the craziest ideas I've had for game concepts came to me in dreams. In some of my more vivid dreams, they always seem to be a sort of perspective where I am watching a "movie", and I don't feel like I'm part of the dream.

But after Aaron had passed, I do remember having two vivid dreams about him, in both of which I was myself. In the first one, Aaron and I were sitting on a park bench. He asked me "Can you guess whose birthday it is next month?" I replied "Yours." He stated back "You're exactly right!" I did have this dream in October, and since Aaron's birthday was in November, I must've had Aaron's birthday in mind because this was going to be his first "un-birthday". A birthday which he would not even be alive to even celebrate. Was he growing older?

Then the dream took a strange turn. Aaron then opened his mouth in a strange way and bared his teeth. He then asked if I wanted to go rob a bank with him. Perhaps I was trying to imagine what kind of secret unsavory life Aaron might have been living, maybe the kind that caused him to die young. Perhaps it was a message from him for me. Was he warning me not to delve into bad habits?

Then suddenly he and I are playing *Parappa the Rapper* on good ol' PlayStation One, another game I remember seeing him playing and enjoying. He started complaining about the game not having touch controls. A tad strange considering no release in the *Parappa the Rapper* series has ever supported touch controls. What kind of deeper meaning could that possibly have? See what I mean about remembering minute and insignificant details? I guess now what I'm saying makes as much sense as anything Joe Chin said in those games. But could it be that they are significant, and I will come to know why one day?

The other dream simply involved me at my mother's house standing in her driveway. A strange black van pulled up, and out came Aaron. Aaron seemed to be absentminded, and not emotionally connected to my "in-dream relief" of his return. He wasn't exactly eager to come up and hug me. I approached Aaron saying, "Aaron where the hell have you been? We thought you were dead." Inquiring about his whereabouts, Aaron simply responded, "Partying." While distraught by Aaron's lack of emotion, perhaps he meant that he is doing just fine on the other side, having fun where he is. Then I woke up. Even to this day, whenever I dream about being with my siblings, Aaron is always there.

Today, I feel like my memories pertaining to Aaron are locked. They are like files that have been put into quarantine. Usually, when I think of him, I just feel anguish and emptiness. I ponder how I am going to explain their late Uncle Aaron to my future children. It is still very difficult to convince myself that this all actually happened. I tend to feel this kind of shock most when I am thinking about my family as I go to bed. Is this because it is easier to connect with Aaron in the dream world?

I know it would be very immature of me to pretend he never existed, but I just can't seem to talk about him casually anymore. When I visit my mom, I often see photographs of us four kids together, thinking how incomplete we are without Aaron. I try not to stare at them too long, I know Aaron wouldn't want me to move on without him. I know I must move forward and do what I can in his stead.

I've heard so many tales on what happens to people when they die. Every single culture you can think of has some kind of funeral procedure and interpretation of the afterlife. It's difficult for me to decide which specific one of them is correct, so I just roll with all of them. I do retain some degree of confidence that Aaron is watching over us, that he can still hear us. From his grave, I feel the signal is the strongest. It is easier for me to feel spiritual connections in specific places than just anywhere.

I imagine Aaron is proud of me for staying close to Mom and helping her out. I don't think I can ever label Aaron as "no longer a person", but I often see him as from another era, a bygone era. Perhaps in his perspective, Aaron may have just woken up ten years in the past, thinking he had a bad dream where he foresaw his own death.

Whenever people talk about the afterlife, you're bound to hear about energy, alternate dimensions, and timelines. I certainly do believe there must be some form of reincarnation. How does it work? Will you still be human? Will you be on Earth even? Will the laws of physics be the same? Are you simply told: You are dead, you will respawn in 200 years?

Is Aaron on spectate mode now, waiting for his respawn? I guess he is, as he still watches over us. Sometimes I wonder if all these movies, games, and books with deep lore are distorted previews of what the next world may be like. It's curious how so many views about the afterlife can have so much in common.

I like to go to Aaron's grave on his birthday and sing happy birthday to him. I like to go to his favorite restaurant Mariachi's on Día de Los Muertos to pay respects to him. All because he is still my brother no matter what.

And so, Aaron will always be a part of me. That's because I will never forget all the important things that he told me. I am who I am because of him, and I know he wouldn't want me to be unable to move forward without him. I will do my best to make up for his absence even though I know I can't. If the *Epic of Gilgamesh* taught me anything, it is that a person can only be immortal if they are remembered. Aaron, you will always be the best brother ever.

About the Author

Jonathan Dan is a freelance artist, author, and video game designer. Jonathan created the cover art for both editions of the book, *Aaron's Energy: An Unexpected Journey Through Grief and the Afterlife With My Brilliant Son*, (February/April 2021), and he is the creator of the cover art for this book. He is fluent in Japanese. Jonathan and his team created the video game, Kakigori Adventure, www.artstation.com/artwork/9N3L9o Jonathan's art can be found at https://artofjonathandan.com/ Jonathan has memorialized his brother, Aaron, in his art.

"Stars are phoenixes,
rising from their own ashes."
~Carl Sagan~
Award-winning
Astronomer, Astrophysicist
Astrobiologist, Author
1934 – 1996

The Phoenix, *Lisa Wilcoxson*

By Lisa Wilcoxson

The Phoenix represents the bird of immortality, having risen to new life. There can be no Phoenix without fire. I know such fire. It is all-consuming. It robs you of your very breath. Your heart continues to beat despite being utterly shattered. Everything you know seems to have been a house of glass. Life, as you know it, becomes shards surrounding you to slice you as you writhe in any direction while your heart is being burned from the inside. Slowly, agonizingly, and with seemingly no will, the light appears. It is then you begin to rise. It is then your wings emerge, one feather at a time. It is then the magnificence of your soul's true colors come alive and lift you to awakening. This is my story. I am a Phoenix.

It was the year 2000. Despite all the warnings of doom, the calendar changed centuries without a technological crash. The threat of complete meltdown proved to be false and was now behind us. Instead, a new decade glowed with great promise. I was a single mom, working full time with two beautiful sons, ages eleven and five. Michael was my firstborn. Anthony was six and in kindergarten. My ex-husband and father of the boys had moved to Minnesota four years prior. Our life was not a bed of roses, yet we were a happy little family of three.

Michael was uniquely special, having suffered a toxic reaction to his first DPT immunization at the age of one month. He immediately began having severe seizures. By the age of two, he had a quarter of his brain removed with a two-thirds corpus callosotomy, which is the surgical separation of the lobes of the brain. This was done in an attempt to stop the seizures from traveling. Due to the removal of his occipital lobe, which was where the 'hot spot' appeared in the PET scan, he was now cortically blind. At the age of four, he began choking on anything he ate. He was then surgically given a G-tube, which was basically a button directly into his stomach where I would tube feed him all his nutrition. In all his years, Michael never walked nor spoke. Being Michael's mother was the best thing in my life I will ever do.

My mother had been ill for many months, and the second quarter of the new decade was her last. On May 7th, one week before Mother's Day, she took her last breath. The year began to feel ominous. Four months later, my world shattered.

"Leanna! Mom took him!" I cried out to my sister on the telephone.

Michael had developed sudden aspiration pneumonia. Arriving by ambulance at Phoenix Children's Hospital, we were met in the parking garage by the trauma staff and a portable x-ray machine. By the time we were in the building, I was told, "I'm sorry, ma'am, there's nothing we can do. His lungs are completely full."

Michael was put on a ventilator to allow his dad to fly in from Minnesota. Upon Ed's arrival, he stood bedside as I lay with our precious boy. I held Michael as we waited for his heart to stop beating. It seemed an eternity. My father was at the foot of the bed. He burst into sobs and began telling me, "He's running now, Lisa! He's running, running, running!"

Shortly after the funeral, my then-boyfriend, Rick, took me to Kartchner Caverns in Southern Arizona. Being from Colorado, I had not yet recognized the beauty of the desert. It appeared to me we were driving through God-forsaken land. I saw nothing but cactus upon mounds of barren ground. We had arrived at our destination. We chose to walk the handicapped ramp as we had done so many years before with my beloved boy. A concrete tunnel took us down to the cavern. The opening behind the airlock door was similar to entering Willy Wonka's wonderland. The colors shimmering off the stalagmites and stalactites sparkled like a lost pirate's treasure. I had an epiphany; if something this magnificent could lie hidden beneath the miles and miles of treacherous land, then of course, there could be a Heaven! Our eyes do not behold the only reality.

The story slowly began to turn from a nightmare to a dream. My mother and I were huge believers in mediumship and the afterlife. We used to frequent a famous medium when he visited Phoenix at Celebrity Theatre. My grandmother had crossed from ALS in the eighties, and we both were hoping for a reading. This medium would often be the guest of the local radio show as well. A few months after Michael crossed, I called the show and was shocked to be placed in queue for a reading.

The medium said, "I see a young boy. He must have been a track star. He is showing me he is running."

Of course, I was immediately brought back to the moment Michael crossed and my dad's exclamation, "He's running, running, running, Lisa."

I then knew Michael was okay. He was communicating to me through the medium. This was all my mommy heart wanted to know. It was also a great relief to know that my mom was 'there' with him. I began to feel the light in both the lifting of the density of my grief and in the brilliance of what I was told about my child.

From that point forward, I turned everything I had towards Anthony. He became my sun and my moon. Michael's mother continues to be the best thing I would ever be, but Anthony saved my life. When he was two years old, he told me, "Mommy, I waited forever to come and be your baby." I believed this with everything in me. I adored him.

Fast forward twelve years. Anthony was preparing for college. Rick, who I wed soon after Michael crossed, had just been contracted to build a home in Sedona, Arizona. I had been working for a major airline in flight operations for nearly 30 years, and my job was being transferred to Dallas due to the company's purchase of American Airlines. I was preparing to be an empty-nester and retire from the airline to work with Rick.

Returning from shopping one evening, Anthony and I pulled into the garage. As the garage door slowly shut, he didn't make any motion to exit the car. We both sat in the dark as he said, "Mom, I need to talk to you. While you and Rick were in Sedona, I went to a party. I had never seen anyone drunk, and I didn't know how much to drink. I drank a whole bottle of vodka, and I almost died. Mom, I'm going to college, and I can't help feeling like I'm going to die. I'm scared, Mom. Will you please watch out for me?"

I cannot recall what I possibly said in response to this. Just the thought of Anthony's fear continues to immobilize me. And yet, the sacredness of this single conversation has manifested feathers for my wings.

About five months later, I was getting ready for bed one night. Completely startled as I entered the room and exclaimed to Rick, "I just saw my mom in my closet! She was crying!" I don't know what shocked me more; that I actually saw her or that she was crying. I still had the belief that Heaven was full of angels on clouds playing harps.

Three days later, I received a telephone call from a nurse at Scottsdale Hospital's emergency room. She told me to come quickly. Anthony was on a ventilator. My mother knew! She was crying because she knew my mommy-heart was about to break again.

Anthony had been at a party and had an immediate and severe reaction to a new synthetic drug, 25I-NBOMe. Friends delivered him to the emergency room. He had no breath or heartbeat. Like his brother, he was put on life support after being resuscitated. Forty-eight hours later, I held him as we waited for his heart to stop. Mine stopped, too.

There I was, in Sedona, Arizona, in a daze of trauma. Sedona is considered one of the most spiritual places in the world, and I hated it. I hated God. I felt as if I had been set up. I felt as if God knew the rug was about to be pulled out from under me, and I was dropped in the middle of this beautiful place to be broken. I wanted no part of it.

The nights were the worst. Daytime left me with the possibility of distraction, yet nightfall left me with my thoughts. How? Why? I began to fragment. I began to hear a woman wail. Who is that pathetic woman I hear? The heartache became so completely inescapable that I began to claw myself out of my own skin. Slowly, deeply, I felt my nails scrape from my forehead, down my neck, down my arms, and across my chest. Over and over. Get me out of my body. I cannot take it!

Rick woke to my rocking, my sobbing. Seeing my distress, he grabbed my wrists. "Lisa, stop!"

"Oh, Rick, look what I've done! I won't be able to go anywhere for three months. I've just mutilated myself," I said with both shame and desperation. We turned the lights on, and I had blood and skin under my fingernails. "You need to get some help," he insisted, wrapping me in his arms as we both tried to sleep.

The next morning, I awoke with not a mark on me. We were both stunned. I had the dried blood and skin under my fingernails, yet not a scratch. This was my first true physical awareness of something greater.

Despite the miracle, Rick insisted I find a therapist. Typing 'Sedona Grief Therapist' into the search bar of my laptop, several names appeared. One caught my eye. I figured what the heck? I must admit, I had little faith in small-town doctors, so I had very little expectation that this would be of any help. But, to my surprise, within twenty-four hours, I had an internationally acclaimed child loss grief and trauma expert sitting at my kitchen table. She listened intently as I spoke of Anthony and Michael and explained trauma, the fight or flight, and the body's reaction. She taught me to put my hand on my ribcage and remember to breathe. I hysterically reviewed twelve years of love for Michael and eighteen years of love for Anthony. She then asked, "What day was Anthony born?"

Very slowly, and with tears in her eyes, she pulled up her pant leg and had that exact birthdate tattooed on her ankle, 7/27/94. She explained her daughter was born and died that day. We discovered our children were born exactly one hour apart in Phoenix hospitals. It was also that moment I realized I had been sitting there grieving the eighteen years I had. While this beautiful mother was listening to the eighteen years that she didn't get to live with her daughter. It was my first experience with another mother who knew my heart.

Such were all the women who would hold me up until I could find my legs. The doctor was my first true earth angel, whether she believes in them or not. She is indeed a scientist, activist, and true first responder. She does grief, deeply and unabashedly, and for that, I am grateful. Years later, I discovered we are related. Her great-great grandmother married my great-great grandfather. Their first two children died.

Although during the weeks, the red dirt of Sedona and the doctor nurtured, grounded, and grieved with me, we would return to Scottsdale on the weekends.

Walking into the home we shared with Anthony and not having him there was physically and emotionally debilitating. I knew I needed more help. I had a friend, Juliet, whom I had known for twenty years. Juliet and I became close when her only son, Noah, died. She knew I had lost Michael, and we would often speak of the boys. However, I didn't know how to truly help her because Noah was her only son, and I simply didn't know how she was going to survive without him. When Anthony, too, was no longer with me, I yearned for Juliet's strength. I knew she was attending a group down the street from my house. It was called *Helping Parents Heal*. It would change my life.

The meeting was to be on Sunday. I had arranged for my dad, his wife, and Rick to accompany me. As we pulled into the parking lot of the Logos Center, a man approached us. He introduced himself as Mark Ireland. He was dressed sharply in plaid sports coat and slacks and had a very happy demeanor. He welcomed us by grabbing a book from his car's trunk. "I need to leave, but go inside and find Elizabeth," he said.

We entered a small foyer where we found a group of people mingling about as if they were at a cocktail party. They were smiling, chatting, nibbling on a cheese tray and cookies. One couple handed out small plastic yellow flowers with smiley faces in small plastic pots. They said the flowers danced in the sunlight. I wasn't sure we were in the right place, but I found Juliet sitting in one of the pews waiting for the meeting to start.

I'm sure I cried the entire meeting. Elizabeth introduced a medium. The man explained to us he could see all our children, that they were in the room behind each of their parents, and he could see them as if they were behind waxed paper. He offered random readings and brought Anthony through to us. The four of us sat and cried as this man offered evidence he was speaking to Anthony and that he was with his brother. This is all I remember, and this is not what was remarkable.

To be told of an experience is quite different from having an experience. It is the latter that catapults one from believing to knowing. Days after the meeting and visit with Anthony, I was back in Sedona. Remembering to get the mail I had brought from Scottsdale; I ran to the car. I returned to the kitchen shaken. Rick asked, "What happened?"

In my hand, I held Anthony's death certificate. I couldn't read it. I wouldn't read it. That might make it real, and I refused to believe it was real. That had become my mantra, "It is not real. Not surreal, simply—not real. He is not dead."

I had one more piece of mail. It was a large white envelope. As I tore it open, I gasped. It held a waxed paper envelope with a photograph of Anthony from his high school graduation over a year earlier. I had never before seen a waxed paper envelope. I had no reason to be receiving this photograph. I had not ordered it. There was Anthony, looking at me from behind the waxed paper, exactly as the medium had described him. To this day, that photo remains exactly as I received it. It was my very first piece of personal evidence from my son himself.

Thus became my journey of the Phoenix. In Sedona and with my doctor exploring deep grief during the week and with earth angel Elizabeth Boisson and *Helping Parents Heal* taught me to connect to my children on the weekends. I actually coined them, "My Darkness and My Light". Despite their dramatically different approaches, they insisted meditation and mindfulness were key.

It was at a grief retreat in a Tao Buddhist Center in Sedona I began to see more clearly that there is no death. I began to understand the story to be unreal. I truly began to see we are not our bodies, and I knew without a doubt my innermost denial that my children were dead was the truth of my soul.

Then children began to come to me. The first was a beautiful young girl who appeared at the foot of the bed. She completely, well, simply appeared. She was dressed in a white tutu, white tights, and ballet slippers, with a ring of white flowers upon her head. She looked to be about seven years old. She smiled and spun in circles like a little ballerina, stopped, and slowly vanished. I was stunned.

There were about sixty women at this retreat, and although we had all heard the stories of our children, I had not met each mom individually over the four days. Taking our children's pictures off the alter table in preparation to leave, I saw the girl's photo who had appeared in my room. Yet, she was in a wheelchair and quite a bit older in the image. I knew who her mother was, but we had not met personally. I pondered what to do. I knew this was her child. Should I say something to her? What would I say, anyway?

Everyone was having lunch before driving off to return to our lives with our grief in tow. In a matter of a minute, everyone seemed to have suddenly left. I looked over, and the only other person in the lunchroom was the mom of the beautiful ballerina. I gathered my courage and moved next to her. I explained that although I knew it sounded crazy, I had seen her daughter in my room. I told her of the beautiful smile, the dancing, the joy on her face. I told her how beautiful her daughter is now. But I didn't understand because I knew she was in a wheelchair, just like Michael was. The mom looked at me with complete astonishment. "Oh my gosh," she said. "I haven't shown anyone that picture!"

She grabbed her iPad and frantically began swiping through photos. She turned the iPad towards me, and I was looking at a picture of the sweet girl precisely as she had appeared to me. She wore the white tutu, the tights, and the ring of white flowers on her head. Her mother explained that she adopted her daughter from Romania, and when she first arrived, she loved to dance. As she aged, her muscles became spastic, and she needed a wheelchair. She was fifteen when she crossed. I will forever be grateful to this beautiful young girl for trusting my heart.

I had actually seen people in spirit a couple of other times in my life, but I thought I was simply a bit crazy. When I was thirteen, four people appeared at the ceiling of my bedroom for exactly ten days. There were two men and two women dressed in clothing from the 1800s. I could see them clearly and objectively, yet I couldn't hear them. They spoke to each other and looked at me, but the room was silent. On the tenth day, I was at the basketball court of my junior high school. Startlingly, one of the men appeared. Surely, this confirmed I was crazy. As I ran into the locker room, he followed. He told me I was not ready yet, and they would be back. I never saw them again. I also saw my grandmother, after she had crossed, in the window of my home. She scared me, and I asked her to please not come back that way.

For the next few years, the children continued to come to me. I would see them very clearly with their parents. They would show me or tell me something significantly personal they wanted to be relayed to their parents. There was always the same theme in their communication. They were okay, and they were not dead. To be honest, I didn't consider this to be mediumship because I was just talking to kids and telling their parents what they said and that they were okay. These weren't 'readings'; they were just factual visits.

As my meditations and communication with my children and my visits with all the others continued, I began to realize how much more there was to reality. The more I was shown, the more I yearned to learn. Ultimately, I was led to my beloved mediumship mentors, Mavis and Jean. Mavis won my heart when she spoke of the Divine God Source, and I knew I was home.

I now look back at my story, and I see it as an illusion in the only reality there truly is, infinite love and everlasting life. There were no coincidences. My twelve years with Michael taught me how to use my senses to communicate, as he couldn't speak. I needed to know his every thought, his every feeling, with a mother's love to ensure he was comforted, safe, and cared for. Thus, my clairsentience. My claircognizance was fine-tuned. Anthony told me when he was four years old that he was going to leave me when he was eighteen. I responded by telling him it was okay because when you are eighteen, you go to college, and you'll be a big boy. After he crossed, I realized no four-year-old knows you go to college at eighteen. His soul was telling me. He said it in the garage that night. My mother appeared to me three days before Anthony crossed.

I continue to be fully dense in my humanity and experience and acknowledge grief. I was told in meditation this was so I could remain compassionate. I willingly and lovingly accept this, as I know I will transcend my physical body soon enough.

I am honored to now work for those in spirit as a medium. I have countless majestic experiences with loved ones in spirit, only with their trust and with the full blessing and grace of God.

My greatest gift has been the mothers and fathers who have walked the fire and risen before, after, and always alongside me. We are the murmur of the Phoenix, and love transcends all.

About the Author

Lisa Wilcoxson is a spiritual evidential medium, psychic, mystic and mentor. Naturally intuitive and having seen spirit since her teenaged years, Lisa dedicated herself to Spiritual work after both her children transcended. As a tested and certified medium, Lisa is renowned for delivering detailed evidence and stunning connection in readings. She compassionately provides undeniable proof the bonds of love are unbreakable, there is no death, and our lives are forever intertwined. Having overcome great trauma, and with an abundance of gratitude for all the miracles along her path, Lisa's mindful and inspirational guidance and connection has helped bereaved people across the globe. With both her children in spirit, Lisa dedicates much of her time to Helping Parents Heal. She is an affiliate leader for two groups, one dedicated to parents whose special needs children have crossed, and one for parents who have lost all or their only child. She and her husband also support the MISS Foundation. Lisa is available for private readings, group readings and public events, and public speaking about the afterlife, grief and her personal chrysalis towards a joy filled life, as well as private mentorship. Lisa travels the country for events and works internationally via Zoom. Lisa resides in Scottsdale and Sedona, Arizona, with her husband Rick and their two dogs. Visit Lisa online at www.PhoenixMedium.com.

"My soul is from elsewhere,
I'm sure of that, and I intend
to end up there."
~Rumi~
Poet, Mystic
1207 – 1273

Channeling Energy and Dialects of Healing with the Ancients, *Lisa Snyder*

By Lisa Snyder

Welcome. This chapter shares my journey as to how I became an evidential psychic medium that channels healing energy and dialects through the use of my voice. I refer to this energy of Divine Source of Love and Light as "Healing with the Ancients."

I was one of those kids who was often told growing up to "quit being so sensitive". Unfortunately, what felt so natural wasn't welcomed by some of the people closest to me. My aunt told me that at the age of five, I had a conversation with my grandpa as he sat in his chair - after he died of a heart attack. I also remember waking up in the middle of the night and seeing "people" in my dark bedroom until one night, around the age of ten, I became so scared that they quit visiting me. Out of fear, I shut down this natural ability to communicate with those from the beyond until I was ready to embrace these capabilities in adulthood.

My degree and early corporate work experience are in engineering and process flow analysis. Despite my career being technical and left-brained, out of personal interest, I was reading a lot of self-help books that were popular at the time. Once I started my family, I became a stay-at-home mom, and this was when my hunger for a deeper spiritual meaning blossomed. I avidly read books by well-known psychics, became a student of A Course In Miracles, and - knowing I wanted to be of service to others' healing - eventually earned certifications in energy work, massage therapy, and craniosacral therapy.

Offering these healing modalities on a professional basis became my new career path. Meanwhile, I was also noticing wonderful signs over the years from loved ones who

343

had crossed over - including flickering lights, the feeling of a cat in spirit laying on the bed with me, and weird static noises over a landline phone call with nobody else on the other end.

An especially impactful experience happened one spring day when I was with a mom's group at a huge park surrounded by woods with my then four-year-old son, Luke, and his two-year-old sister, Laura. Laura started to take off from the group, so I became distracted and lost track of my fearless little boy. Suddenly, I realized he was no longer with the group and was nowhere in sight. Nobody saw him take off, and my heart dropped. I had never known fear like that in my life! I felt blind as to where to start searching for Luke. I was afraid someone may have taken him, as images of horror went through my mind. Overtaken by panic, I started running in one direction after leaving my little girl with one of the other trusted mothers.

This memory still brings tears to my eyes. There wasn't anyone else in the park to ask if they had seen him. I felt so alone and incredibly guilty for losing track of my son. I started running, and my legs quickly began to feel like rubber. It felt like I had a weird out-of-body experience, and I desperately prayed out loud, "God, please help me!", over and over again.

I was frantically sprinting through the park when suddenly, a woman with a baby stroller appeared and said, "He's over there." She pointed me in the opposite direction of where I had been running, and miraculously, he was there! I was so panicked and grateful; I didn't question who she was or where she came from. Once my son was safe, I wanted to thank that woman, but of course, she was nowhere to be found, and no one else saw her. This was my first major experience with what I believe to be an angel, and I will be forever grateful for the Divine help.

In May 2008, my beloved friend and cat of 16 years, Max, was experiencing kidney failure. One of the hardest things I have ever done was to help him cross the rainbow bridge when it was his time to transition. Although I knew he would be free of pain, I asked him for a sign from beyond that I couldn't possibly miss.

Four weeks later, I had still been waiting for my sign from Max, and one afternoon I was standing near a pond, which seemingly had one-hundred ducks and ducklings in and around the water. This was before mobile phones recorded video, so thankfully, my husband was sitting behind me on a bench to witness what happened next. Suddenly, without reason, every single duck and duckling lowered their heads and walked directly towards me very gently and deliberately - as if in a trance - from all directions. Can you imagine such a wild scenario while still feeling a sense of calm and knowing you are completely safe? The closest ones were almost to my feet when a runner came by, oblivious to this amazing event, and broke the trance. They went back to being their normal duck selves. It was completely magical, and I felt that this was such a huge hello and gift from Max's heart to mine. I will treasure that experience always.

Fast forward to September 2016, when something strange and profound began to happen. I started smelling bonfire smoke in the oddest places - a gymnasium, an enclosed office, and in my car in the middle of a snowstorm. I found the aroma to be very comforting and loving, and I have learned that what I experience is called clairalience, a psychic sense of smell. But that was just the beginning of a new journey for me. A couple of months later, I was lying on a massage table with a trusted massage therapist. I was in a deeply relaxed state and felt safe in this environment. Suddenly, I saw in my mind's eye a Native American chief. My right hand seemed to have taken on a mind of its own and involuntarily started to tap my shoulder, then my hip, then made a clockwise motion over my stomach. I quickly realized it was a healing - a new beginning and a huge step in my spiritual and healing journey.

While still lying on the massage table, I unexpectedly had the compulsion to make a noise - a grunt. It sounded silly and even weird, but in the moment, I felt safe and one with the energy. I was relaxed and present. I felt blended with spirit and knew next to nothing about channeling, but I was ready to trust these new sounds I began to make. I didn't know why this was happening, but over time, I would learn what this was all about.

In May 2018, my father-in-law transitioned after I had just arrived on my very first trip to Sedona, Arizona. I was there visiting a friend and to see the beautiful red rocks that just take your breath away. My mother-in-law called to notify me about his passing. I immediately realized he was communicating his feelings and thoughts directly to me. This was a brand-new experience for me, but I recognized his energy and was able to deliver a message to my mother-in-law while we were on the phone. She had no idea at the time that I could channel, and fortunately, she received the messages as a gift. That same weekend, I brought my first brand-new tarot deck with me and was asked to deliver messages to the spiritually inclined friend I was in Sedona to visit. She also gave me two names to "tune" into, and I realized I was seeing images and feeling information I couldn't possibly have known. Sedona was working its beautiful and transformational magic on me. I knew in my heart that it was time for me to get some training to recognize the way Spirit sent me messages, establish healthy boundaries and intentions, and remain grounded and balanced with this work. I began to look for quality programs that would help me with these intentions, as the voice channeling was coming through me on a regular basis.

The following year, I jumped in with both feet. I studied evidential mediumship with a couple of well-known mediums, practiced in development circles, attended a remote viewing retreat at The Monroe Institute in Virginia, and participated in a week-long in-person meditation event in Oregon. All of these experiences, plus a lot of practice, helped me understand how to work with and navigate through the energy and channeled dialects that were coming through in such an organic and natural way over the past couple of years. In addition, I started receiving a lot of undeniable evidence from the practice sessions.

My daughter and best girlfriend, Laura, is a natural athlete. She moves her body with such grace; it's beautiful to watch. In November 2019, she was a very accomplished collegiate volleyball player in the toughest D2 conference in the country. During the conference tournament, she landed from a jump and immediately knew something was wrong with her left knee. She wasn't in too much pain, so she played out the last two games of her season, but the swelling around her knee became alarming. We were expecting it to be a typical knee injury diagnosis, but it was not. A chunk of hard cartilage had broken loose from the end of her femur, and she needed a very specialized surgery involving the grafting of donor tissue. All the other tissues of her knee were perfectly intact. It was a weird injury, and we were very fortunate that a premiere doctor who treated Olympic athletes had just moved back to Minnesota, where we reside now. Thank you, Source! Unfortunately, it ended her volleyball career, but we all know now that it was meant to happen.

In the months prior to Laura's injury, I found myself thinking that I wanted to be at every game I could possibly attend because "all it's going to take is one injury to end her career." This was something I never thought during all of the years that she had played various sports. When Laura got the diagnosis, I felt in some way I had attracted this - because of the law of attraction. I felt guilty that I brought this upon my daughter when the reality was my psychic senses were forewarning and preparing me for what was to come. I learned that receiving intuitive information about someone else is not necessarily the law of attraction at work. Each person is meant to have their own life experiences, and I might not be privy to the reason behind it.

As a former engineer and now a trained evidential psychic medium, I wanted proof of what I already felt to be true. I knew I was working with high vibrational energy, like Jesus, Buddha, and those of the highest possible frequencies of love and light. But how can that be proven? My mantra was, and continues to be, "trust the process". I believe this is why, in April of 2020, I decided to have a reading with a gifted evidential spirit portrait artist. What I really hoped for was a spirit guide portrait, but since it couldn't be validated with evidence, I was curious enough to agree to see who in spirit would like to step forward for me.

The artist mentioned there were "several spirits around me," and it took a bit for him to tune into one specific person. He eventually drew a woman in spirit, but I didn't recognize her. She was wearing a heart-shaped necklace, and this immediately got my attention because I wear the same necklace when I channel. He suggested I share the picture with others, for I could be the messenger. Since he didn't draw one of "my people" in spirit, he offered to meet with me again at no charge. After asking everyone I could think of about the drawing of the woman, which no one claimed to recognize, I was guided to share it with a private online group for mediums. A woman named Lisa Wilcoxson recognized the information. What happened next still blows me away.

I arranged to meet with the original spirit portrait artist a couple of weeks later. He tuned into my energy again and drew two more people in spirit, but I didn't have the heart to tell him I didn't recognize them either. However, I have learned to trust the process, so I reached out to Lisa right after the appointment with the spirit artist, and the drawings were for her once again! Each time, the artist had drawn a close friend to Lisa, whom each had transitioned before I met her. Spirit was doing a great job of bringing her and I together, and we have become dear friends since then. Lisa is a very gifted evidential medium herself, and both of her children are in spirit. As a parent, I can only imagine the pain of having children on the other side. I will be forever grateful to her boys for orchestrating our friendship. What truly blew me away was the date of the first portrait: it was drawn on the Angelversary of Lisa's youngest son, Anthony! Coincidence? No way.

Source knows exactly what to do. I originally wanted a spirit guide portrait when I met with the artist. As a result of that new friendship with Lisa, I received another unexpected gift - a channeled drawing of Jesus with a story I don't have permission to share yet, but it was definite evidence to confirm what I already knew to be true. I am working with the highest source of love and light.

It never ceases to amaze me how much I can feel intuitively. When I worked with clients in person while I was still doing craniosacral therapy, I could look at them and know where we needed to work before they even said a word. When the pandemic started, I had to close my office and work remotely. Because I feel so much in my hands, I am able to use a pillow in my lap to substitute for the client who used to be on my massage table. For example, one moment, the pillow might feel like we're working on the foot. In the next moment, I'm aware we might be working with their neck. In my mind's eye, I see what part of the body, emotion, or energetic field with which we are working. I might feel brief aches and pains in my own body to show me where a client may have an existing or old injury, and my eyes will spontaneously tear to show me grief and sorrow.

As the client's energy is processing, I will often feel heat on my body, or I may burp, so the releasing energy doesn't stick with me but rather goes through me. These are all physical signs to show me that the client is receiving energetic healing. My head will tingle when someone in spirit is trying to get my attention, and a message may be delivered. The energy isn't coming from me but instead comes through me.

As a voice and channel for Divine Source of Love and Light, I always set the intention for the highest possible vibrational frequency to step forward. I know and feel what I'm working with. It's within each and every one of us. Our greatest teacher isn't a guru outside of us, for our greatest teacher is within because we are all a part of the beautiful Source energy.

A few months later, Laura had her knee surgery - during the pandemic. Visitors weren't allowed in the hospital, so my husband and I stayed in our car waiting for a phone call from the surgeon. It was frustrating not being close to our daughter. Laura knew I'd be there with her on an energetic level, and once again, I was surprised at the information I was given by the connection.

During the surgery, I connected with my spirit team, the doctors, and Laura and started sending healing, supportive energy. Right away, there was a strong, metallic flavor on my tongue, which I believe was a sign the anesthesia and drugs were being administered. Next, I spontaneously started to channel dialects through my voice, and they started to sound mechanical. I knew they were using the drill on her knee to create space for the donor tissue. The sounds transitioned to different dialects, and then it started to calm. I had an awareness her surgery was mostly over when we got the call that they were stitching up her knee. I am so thankful my team found a way for me to be with her in that room and provide me with details I could recognize.

What I have learned through this journey is that Source is always there for us. Ongoing signs, evidence, and client testimonials have convinced the logical, scientific, engineer, and Virgo in me of what I have always felt to be true. The channeled healing sounds that naturally exude through my voice are from the Highest Source of Love and Light. These sounds have evolved and continue to expand to include the Lady of the Lake, Mother Earth, Dolphin, Goddesses, Cave, Wind, and so much more.

Source, along with the individual's soul, knows exactly what is in that person's best interest regardless of whether it is a group or solo session. Different energies, ascended teachers, and angels often step forward for the healings. I am fully present; I never know what's going to happen, and that's the beauty of this work. It's not coming from me, but the sounds and many evolving dialects are coming through me. I am a channel and a voice so the person may integrate an energetic healing in another, vibratory way. It is the same as reading a beautiful poem or looking at a magical piece of art. The inspiration and energy behind the masterpiece are the most important things. I feel honored to channel and share this beautiful healing energy. I know, without a doubt, that we have so much love around us.

When I graduated from engineering school, it never occurred to me I would be working with healing energies. Hindsight is 20/20. It is easy to see now how all of my experiences over the years have helped to shape me into the person I am today. I believe love will always win, and this work is meant to be part of the solution to help raise the vibrational frequency of all involved. An example of this work is below - a channeled message from the ancients, done specifically for this book. I'd like to

349

quickly thank Camille Dan for including my journey in this publication, and I'd also like to thank my good friend, Monica, and my daughter, Laura, for helping me edit my story. Thank you for reading.

Channeled Message from The Ancients:

"Welcome to the energy and love of healing with the Ancients. You — we - are all ancients. We are fully supported, fully protected, and fully loved. Regardless of what your mission is on this temporary human experience plane, we all have our parts to do in the game of life. We are so appreciative and grateful to have the opportunity to share with you our message in this beautiful book, this labor of love.

Do you realize how much love and support is available to all? Do you realize that all one needs to do is ask, and it is truly there for you? It may show up as a flower, a poem, or a book that was the result of someone's loved one helping from the other side. Thank you, Aaron, Camille's son and collaborator in the spirit realm.

We have so much we wish to share with you. There are many opportunities and gifts that are available to all. Each of us is of the One, the Divine, the Source, the Creator. How could it be any other way?

Some have signed up for experiences that transcend human comprehension. Why would one sign up for an experience that could be so painful? Why would one begin to share their story during such times of grief and sorrow? We do not minimize the human emotions. Many of us have experienced these emotions. We have a different perspective. We are here for you.

So now we rejoin the story of Healing with the Ancients. Lisa, the channel, agreed to be a voice for this energy of love and light. It is one of many voices and yet the one voice. We all are a part of that one voice. This energy, this voice, is here for all to connect with. All one needs to do is sit in the stillness and listen with the heart.

We help guide the necessary words and voices through images, feelings, and all the senses to show Lisa where we are directing and sharing energy with the one she is working with. This is an agreement between the higher self, the one Source, and Lisa. We wish to share with you that the energy is for all. The energy is for one. We are one."

About the Author

Lisa and her family live near Minneapolis, Minnesota. She earned her Bachelor of Science in Industrial Engineering from Iowa State University. Lisa is nationally certified in massage therapy and bodywork and certified in energy work and craniosacral therapy. In addition to spending time with family, she appreciates the outdoors through hiking and canoeing, enjoys reading, meditating, deepening her spirituality, and traveling to new places.

Lisa works remotely with clients from all around the world through private individual and group sessions. She hosts weekly livestreams channeling energy and dialects of *Healing with the Ancients* in addition to featuring monthly guests. She has also been a guest energy healer and channel at in-person retreats.

To learn more about Lisa and her work with Healing with the Ancients, please visit: www.LisaSnyderHealing.com.

*"The more I study nature,
the more I stand amazed at
the work of the Creator.
Science brings men nearer to God."
~Louis Pasteur~
Nobel Prize Winning
Chemist, Microbiologist
1822 - 1895*

It's Not Always Cardinals, Dragonflies, Butterflies, and Dimes, *Kathy Moreland*

By Kathy Moreland

I gave my son Austin his first hug on June 23, 2003. I gave him his last hug 17 years later to the day on June 23, 2020. He had just turned 18 less than two months prior. Little did I know the night of that last hug that the next morning I would find him with no vital signs and that I would never feel him physically hug me again. He died peacefully in the ICU two days after I found him. He never regained consciousness. He died as a result of fentanyl poisoning after being sober for months and two years of struggling with substance use disorder. This is the story of how I know he is still with us.

Austin was 13 months old when his father and I met him and his older sister through the miracle of adoption. After struggling with infertility, I knew there was another plan for me and my journey to motherhood. Once we started the adoption process, I would share with others that I was "spiritually pregnant" but that I had no idea what the gestation period would be nor when I would "deliver". Ironically, we waited 18 months to adopt both children -- 9 months each! We fell in love with them both immediately. From day one, Austin was a charming, busy, funny, intelligent, mischievous child. Did I say BUSY?!

Throughout his life, he struggled with anxiety, impulse control, and poor judgment as a result of a brain injury from prenatal alcohol exposure. His birth mother had never been told of the dangers of alcohol in pregnancy and had used alcohol to self-medicate her own anxiety. Both children were eventually diagnosed with fetal alcohol spectrum disorder (FASD). FASD shows up in many ways - the most common being struggles with emotional regulation, impulse control, and judgment. Eighty-five percent of those with FASD struggle with anxiety and depression.

I am a registered nurse, a former nurse practitioner in oncology and palliative care, and a professor of nursing. During my career, spanning four decades, I've been privileged to be present at hundreds of deaths. I've seen my fair share of unexplainable phenomena as death approached for my patients and after they died. I learned to accept that there were things beyond my understanding. I always felt "something" as people died, as if they were leaving the space. In fact, there were times when I would "know" that someone was on their way "out" before I even went into their room. It was a gut feeling, a knowing.

Many of my patients would tell stories of their dearly departed family members visiting them in the days before they died. Initially, I attributed this to the strong drugs we were giving them for comfort, but as time passed, I knew it was more than that and thought, "Who was I to question this?"

I was raised an Anglican. I am not overly religious, but I have always believed that there is more to us that we can understand that we call God. I couldn't quite relate to the concept of heaven and hell and the idea of being judged in order to make it to heaven or that there were "chosen" people. How could a loving God do that? I found congruence with my spiritual beliefs in the practices and principles of Unity Church in my adult years. Experiencing so much death and loss in my work led me to study spiritual practices of ancient cultures, metaphysics, meanings of consciousness, Healing Touch, and other forms of energy work in order to help others heal (myself, really!). This work helped me understand the relationship between our biofield health, our physical health and the connection between all of us. Nursing had a lot to learn, I thought. My belief that we are, in the words of Pierre Teilhard de Chardin, "spiritual beings having a human experience" was affirmed. "We are all one" took on a new meaning for me. The left side of my brain came to terms with quantum theories that explained that our physical body is an illusion and is really a collection of energy. It was only a matter of perspective.

Losing so many patients and grounding myself in the belief that we are always present energetically eased the grief associated with the loss of my grandparents, my parents, and three close, dear friends. I believed they were still around even if I couldn't see them. It was comforting. Little did I know that my work in palliative care, those losses, and my studies in quantum theory and energy work were meant to prepare me for the loss of my son…the most painful loss of my life.

The morning Austin arrested; I awoke uncharacteristically early for no apparent reason. I sensed that something wasn't right. I shrugged it off, having had to deal with these feelings throughout his years of drug use. I went downstairs and had my breakfast, not wanting to check on him in his room in the basement as I usually did. It was so early. I think now his spirit was trying to wake me up as he made his initial transition. He had graduated from high school the day before and had been so happy when he went to bed. His last text to me at 1:30 am earlier that day was, "I love you, Mum." Within minutes of eating my breakfast, his girlfriend ran up from his room and said, "Austin's not breathing!" The nurse in me sprung into action. I found him with the tell-tale signs that he had not been breathing for a while but proceeded to start CPR and get Naloxone that I had in the house. Even in that moment, I felt him there but not in his body. I told him to hold on - that help was coming. I was fortunate to have the first responders arrive quickly, and I went upstairs as I couldn't watch what I knew would be happening. I was fully anticipating that the police would come upstairs shortly to tell me that he was dead.

Surprisingly, they got his heart started. "He's trying to come back," I thought to myself. I arrived at the hospital to be told that he arrested six more times since leaving the house but that he was still trying. I stayed in nurse mode - calm on the outside, holding off the shock so that I could stay logical and make decisions. We had our first miracle. He was still alive.

The first hour I sat with him in the ICU, I could sense him hovering over his body. I heard him very clearly say in my mind's ear, "I'm sorry, Mum. I'm really, really sorry." I told him that he didn't need to apologize. I knew he didn't intend for this to happen. I told him that I was open to a miracle and that no one was giving up on him. The nurse in me knew that even if he survived, his life would likely never be the same. Day one passed, and he showed no signs of upper brain activity. Day two seemed like an eternity. We played his favourite music. I kept talking to him and telling him how much he was loved. I knew his kidneys were failing. At 3 am, the morning of the day we were to take him off life support, the nurse called me back to the hospital. "He is going. I can't hold his pressure any longer. You need to get here." He had made his decision before we had. He knew that coming back into his body would not be possible. Perhaps he was shown what the future would hold. His father, who now lived two hours away, was rushing to get to him. As Austin's pressure continued to drop steadily to levels incompatible with life, I asked him to wait for his dad, who was still 20 minutes away. "I need you to tell whoever is calling you to come with them that THEY HAVE TO WAIT. Tell them 'later' like you always tell me when I ask you to do something! Get back in your body and hold your blood pressure. Your Dad needs to see you."

Miraculously, his pressure stopped dropping as soon as I said that. Our second miracle. His father arrived and was able to spend 15 minutes saying goodbye. We all returned to the room and sat in a sacred circle of love around him. I told him we were all there and that he could now do whatever he needed to do. Within seconds, his pressure continued to drop, the area above his bed was surrounded with gold light, and his beautiful heart stopped in the most peaceful death I had ever witnessed.

There are so many ways in which Austin has let us know he is still with us since that day. His birth mother (whom he had a relationship with) called me just after he died and said that at the precise moment he made his final transition, she had awoken from a very vivid dream. He had come to her and told her not to feel guilty and to be happy. He was alright, he told her. She awoke at precisely the moment when his heart stopped. Throughout the week, lights flickered, he continually sabotaged his sister's cell phone by turning the volume up and down (that had never happened before), and he showed up as a dancing blue orb in videos his sister took at a firework display prior to his funeral. There was no denying that things were not normal. His funeral could not take place for a week because of COVID restrictions and the need for a coroner's examination. On the day of his celebration of life, we put a jar of pickles, some spicey potato chips, and some of his metalwork on the altar - his favourite things. After the service, we arrived home, and sitting on the back windowsill of our kitchen was a black squirrel eating...you guessed it...a dill pickle! Now what made this significant is that there were no gardens in the area that were growing pickle cucumbers, and the squirrel didn't move as I approached the window, AND throughout his life, I had called Austin "Squirrel-sh*t" (lovingly, of course) because he reminded me of Hammy, the squirrel on caffeine in the movie *Over the Hedge*. To say Austin was hyper would be an understatement. I had no doubt that this was Austin letting me know that he was alright. I laughed and cried in spite of myself. Squirrels have become important messengers of his presence. They show up ALL the time and in the funniest places, just like him.

Through those first months, there were other messages. Our favourite song was *Bohemian Rhapsody* by Queen, and like any good Mum who was a teenager in the '70s, I had taught Austin every word, including the head banging actions. It was our favourite thing to do in the car whenever we went for a drive. It took me a month or more to play it after he died. When I did, we were on our boat, and I hoped to sing it as loud as I could over Georgian Bay to honour him. I turned it on with the volume cranked up and did my best *Titanic* "king of the world" position on the front of our boat, ready to wail out our favourite song. I was only a few bars in when without warning, the stereo stopped. NO plausible REASON. I knew it was him. I could almost hear him say, "too painful for you, Mum...you're not ready to hear it." I "knew" it was him. The stereo on the boat has not stopped once since.

A few weeks into my grief, I sought out the services of a renowned energy worker. I told her I felt like a "spiritual Humpty Dumpty" and that I needed to be put back together again. The session was via ZOOM. I had never seen her before. As we started the session, she said, "Are you aware that I am a medical intuit and a medium as well?" I was not. "Your son is here and has a message for you." I was intrigued and happy for the opportunity to hear from him. "He wants you to know that he really sure if he wanted to be incarnate in this lifetime...he had a hard time deciding to come in. He is really sorry for what happened. But he wants to assure you that he would have died much sooner had you not been his mother and that because of you, he learned the lesson in this life that he was supposed to learn. HE IS SO HAPPY now. He's telling me that this was the only way he was going to be okay". I was dumbfounded, sad, and peaceful at the same time. I hadn't told her that my son had died or that he was adopted. Months later, the mother of a friend of Austin's who had also lost her son to fentanyl poisoning told me that a medium had shared that she saw a young man with her son on the other side and described Austin to a tee, including the hat he was wearing the week he died. The medium had no previous knowledge of Austin. "They are together along with many of their friends, watching over the others. They are free." She sent me the taped version of her reading. There were many indications that Austin was coming through in the reading.

I've titled this story "It's Not All Cardinals, Dragonflies, Butterflies and Dimes" because I can't count the number of times people have asked me if Austin comes to me in these forms. Cardinals? He would never choose that. Dragonflies? He was afraid of them. Butterflies? Nope! Dimes? Maybe. I have found many around the house that didn't seem to be where I had looked previously. I thank him and keep them in a jar by his picture just in case they are from him. Austin shows up in many forms, and I feel he directs me to know when it is him. It's an inner knowing - a feeling inside. Squirrels, mourning doves sitting outside my window, giant carp coming up to our boat (when they never did before) are amongst the ways in which he has let his presence be known. They don't just show up. They engage with me energetically (if that makes sense) as if to say, "I'm here, Mum. I hope this makes you smile." He directs me (it feels like a little tap on my shoulder) to look for pictures he forms in the clouds for me, many angels, fish, dragons, numbers, and lots of hearts...all things he drew in this lifetime.

The messages Austin has shared have given me comfort. The shared experiences of others who have gotten messages "beyond the veil", the explanations by mediums about the omnipresence of those we love that have passed have helped ease my grief. I have come to terms with the fact that I will never understand what happens on the other side but revel in feeling so significantly insignificant in it all. Don't get me wrong. I still miss Austin's physical presence SO much, as well as the possibilities of what I hoped his life would be. I've realized that I can let him be without having to let him go. I feel there is a distinction.

The loss of my son has truly left its mark on my life - more than any other loss I've experienced. The grief of it all will be a part of the fabric of me until I make my transition. I will be forever connected to Austin in spirit. I have learned that his messages are his way of reassuring me and comforting me, and they do! My grief persists and is like an invisible lead coat that is always with me. I've realized over time that I can take the lead coat off, enjoy aspects of my life without feeling guilty, and know that I continue to honour the memory of him in his physical form while trusting that he is in a place of perfection, peace, and omniscience. This took time. Grief is sneaky, though. It can still blindside me without warning. It truly is the price of being human and loving someone so deeply.

I honour Austin's legacy now through my advocacy work with Moms Stop the Harm (https://www.momsstoptheharm.com/), a group of persons who have family members who have either died or continue to struggle with substance use disorder. Our goal is to change our failed drug policies and prevent drug-related deaths and suffering. I am also doing work through the Registered Nurses Association of Ontario (RNAO) to reduce stigma and educate healthcare workers about FASD and the care of people who use unregulated drugs. The two FASD classrooms that Austin inspired and attended have annual memorial awards named in his honour. Our family sets a place for him at the table for every special occasion, light candles, and hang his ornaments on the Christmas tree annually. I talk with him every day.

For anyone reading this who has experienced great loss, my heart goes out to you. I would suggest that you stay open to possibilities and pay attention to the subtle messages from your loved ones--those spiritual taps on the shoulder to pay attention, whether it be through animal sightings, dreams, music, electrical anomalies, or cloud pictures. Trust your gut feelings. I've found that I can't force those messages but have to be paying attention for those sometimes-subtle signs. If you suspect that you are being reassured that they are present, YOU ARE PROBABLY RIGHT. Don't always look for the objects that others say represent messages from those "departed". I strongly suspect you will know when it is your loved one that is coming through. I wish you peace.

About the Author

Kathy Moreland is a mother, wife, recently retired registered nurse of 40 years and Healing Touch Practitioner. She lives in southern Ontario. Through her decades of work in palliative care and cancer nursing, she witnessed, firsthand, hundreds of deaths and experienced phenomena beyond conventional explanation. Those experiences led her to study metaphysics and energy work. Little did she know that those studies were preparing her to learn to live with personal losses, particularly the loss of her beloved son Austin at eighteen from an inadvertent fentanyl overdose. She shares her story of losing Austin yet finding him again in another dimension--beyond what is normally expected.

Kathy honours Austin's legacy now through advocacy work with Moms Stop the Harm (https://www.momsstoptheharm.com/), a group of persons who have family members who have either died or continue to struggle with substance use disorder. Their goal is to change our failed drug policies and prevent drug-related deaths and suffering. She is also doing work through the Registered Nurses Association of Ontario (RNAO) to reduce stigma and educate healthcare workers about FASD, Fetal Alcohol Spectrum Disorders, and the care of people who use unregulated drugs. The two FASD classrooms that Austin inspired and attended have annual memorial awards named in his honour.

Austin-2 weeks after he was adopted

Austin

*"The present is the only
things that has no end."
~Erwin Schrodinger~
Nobel Prize Winning
Physicist
1887 – 1961*

The Ring, *Brenda Shenher*

By Brenda Shenher

My two Grandmothers, Katie Ortman Schenher and Eva Ruchienski Kesslering, have been my creative inspiration and the source of my personal resiliency for as long as I can remember. Among their many gifts, Grandma Katie gave me my tenacious work ethic, and Grandma Eva gave me her sense of style and grace.

This is the story of Grandma Eva's onyx ring and how it came to be given to me.

Eva Ruchienski was born in Bulgaria in 1906. She immigrated to Canada with her family of two parents and 10 siblings around 1912. The family settled on a piece of government-issued land in the southern part of the Province of Saskatchewan. The practice of opening up Western Canada by the labour of European Immigrants who were to create farms, break up the land, grow communities, and develop the agricultural industry was commonplace at the turn of the 20th Century.

The seven sons in the Ruchienski family were kept at home to break up the land, cut trees, pick stones, and plant and harvest the crops, and the daughters were sent out to work as seasonal domestic servants to other homesteads. My grandmother was one of those "hired girls" beginning at around twelve years old.

When Eva was about 19 years old, she was working at a farmstead where she met a young man and they fell in love. He proposed to her with a square cut black onyx ring with a small diamond in the centre. He was a Dutch Protestant, and she was a German Catholic. He came to my great grandfather to ask for Eva's hand in marriage. My great grandfather, Pius, told him to return in one week with the papers to show that he would settle on a homestead of his own and be able to support and care for

Eva. In one week, he returned, and Pius sent out his wife, Amelia, to meet him. Pius instructed Amelia to tell the young man that he would not be marrying Eva, ever, as he was not of the correct ethnicity or religion and was to go away and never return. Eva was heartbroken and hysterical but powerless against her father's decision.

Within six months, on a cold January day, in 1926, Eva was married to a man of her father's choosing who was ten years her senior but of the right Ethnic and religious background. This was my grandfather, Matthias Kesslering. The years passed, and they grew to love each other. They had five children together and participated in their community while developing and growing their homestead into a viable, productive mixed farm.

When Eva was 50 years old, her daughter Helen died from a brain tumor at the age of 19. Then, at the age of 52, her husband, Max (Matthias), died of prostate cancer. As Eva aged, she suffered the sadness of these losses and developed a disease that eventually took her life, Dementia with Lewy Bodies.

As the eldest granddaughter who lived in close proximity to Eva, and before her memory was lost from dementia, I spent many hours with her talking about her youth, her first love, her family and many other things that she had never even discussed with her own children.

Toward the end, Eva lost the ability to speak as the disease slowly eroded that part of her brain. Once, my mother and I were visiting her in the hospital toward the end of her life, and as I sat by an open door and watched Grandma looking over my left shoulder, staring intently at something/someone, I felt a hand upon my left shoulder. I said to my mother, "Aunt Helen is here, and she is coming for Grandma – can you feel her?" My mother said, "No." As a staunch Catholic, she had never been open to any sort of communication from Spirit unless she was in a Church. By then, I had always felt a closeness to my Aunt Helen, whom I had never met. Still, in many ways, I knew that we were kindred spirits and that she inspired me to emulate her brilliant talents of sewing, crocheting, and knitting, and this was the beginning of my pursuit of Costume Design. I knew that Aunt Helen was one of my Spirit Guides and that she was with us that afternoon.

Shortly afterward, my grandmother passed peacefully in the night. It was early March of 1993 and just before she was to turn 87 years old.

Fast forward to Christmas and New Year of 1993 turning to 1994, and I found myself and my daughter taking the last passenger train trip to Calgary to spend the holidays with my daughter's father. As a single mother who was determined to keep a harmonious relationship with my ex and to have that relationship extend to our child was always a priority for me even though my daughter and I lived in a different Province and money was scarce. We conceived our daughter when I was living in Calgary, where I had pursued Film School and experimented with varying facets of creating alternative arts and entertainment. I was hanging out in a very creative social scene and trying to discover the path which would eventually lead me to become a Costume Designer. While working in a fabric store during this time, I met an amazing woman who is still my lifelong friend to this day, Moira.

Moira was half Dutch and half Irish but had been blessed with the gift of the Irish "second sight" and had been a physic medium her whole life without fully realizing it. She, too, was raised a Roman Catholic, and the strictness of that upbringing did not allow any embrace of another concept of Spirit, or of "the other side" except what was sanctioned by the rules of the Church, meaning that it was not accepted or entertained without judgment and skepticism. However, by the winter of 1993, Moira had abandoned the rules of Catholicism and had embraced her gift of mediumship as she studied and refined it by attending workshops, and conventions, building relationships with other mediums, and developing her gifts as a tarot card reader.

While living in another Province, raising a child, attending University full time, and working as a Fashion Stylist for a modeling agency, I had lost touch with my friend for approximately one to two years. Once arriving in Calgary, I called to let her know that I was in town (surprise!), and we made time for an evening together. We arrived at her house, and while our daughters were playing, she offered to read my tarot cards. I jumped at the chance. I shuffled the cards, and she dealt them and began to study them when she stopped abruptly and said, "Maybe you can tell me who this is...?" I looked at her, confused as she continued, "About two weeks ago this woman came to me and she won't leave me alone...she is middle aged maybe around 50, she has beautiful white hair of which she is very proud and vain, and she has sort of a jowly square face with a downward turn to her mouth, and she sits in her chair all day, rocking, and watching tv." I immediately teared up. "That is my grandmother, Eva." I knew beyond a doubt that it was her. "She passed away last March."

Moira said, "Well, she has been bugging me for over two weeks, and I couldn't figure out who this is or why she is coming to me!" Moira then slowly went into a trance-like state (I witnessed this before and knew she was connecting to the other side), and I sat quietly, waiting. Eventually, Moira began to speak, and she said, "She is with a very tall silver-haired gentleman. He is wearing a white shirt open at the neck and suspenders on dark pants. He is very handsome."

"I think that is my grandfather, Max," I whispered.

Moira continued, "She wants you to find a ring. She wants you to have it. It is in a blonde wooden dresser, but also it might be buried in a box at the base of a tree, so look in two places. It has a black stone."

I was fully crying by now.

Moira continued, "Tell them (the family) that everything is ok and that I am having the time of my life!"

Shortly after this, Moira emerged from her trance-like state and asked me what she had said. I repeated my grandmother's words, and we marveled at how this had occurred. I had no idea that my friend had developed her mediumship gifts to this degree. She had no idea who my grandmother was or that she had passed over. She had never seen a photo of my grandparents, so how would she know that my grandpa always wore a white dress shirt with suspenders or that my grandmother had snow-white hair and jowls? How would she know of the hours that my grandma wiled away, alone in front of the tv, dreaming of her lost loves? And she had no idea that I was coming to Calgary for Christmas or even that I would be coming to visit her.

It was miraculous. It was a significant gift as my grandmother was non-communicative at the end of her life.

I returned to my small town in Southern Saskatchewan, where I was about to do my internship in order to finish my Education Degree, and my daughter and I were staying with my parents. I then told my very Catholic, earth-bound parents about Grandma reaching through the veil to communicate to us all about how she had reunited with her beloved husband and that she was finally happy again. Both of my parents had tears in their eyes as the presence of Spirit moved them during the relaying of the words from my grandma. My mother said, "Yes, my dad always wore a white shirt with suspenders every day." After speaking, my mother went into her bedroom and brought out a small wooden box. Within it was the black onyx ring that Grandma wanted me to have. My mother was sentimental and wasn't big on sharing her stuff, but she was so moved by Grandma's wishes that she gave me, the eldest granddaughter, the ring that meant so much to Eva.

In 2015, while Costume Designing the Netflix Mini-Series, *Tokyo Trial* and shooting in Lithuania, I gave my ring to the Dutch lead Actress to wear in a pivotal piano playing scene. I wished to immortalize the ring in honour of my grandmother's story, and the fact that a Dutch actress wore it bought it home to its origins of purchase by my grandmother's first love, a Dutch man.

I believe that full-circle moments are driven by something greater than what the frail and limited human consciousness can understand. I believe that full-circle moments are where Spirit lives and where we can embrace our connectivity to the past, the present, and for the future.

About the Author

Brenda Shenher is a Costume Designer for Film, Television and Theatre. She has worked in Film since 1994 and has been Costume Designing since the year 2000. She was born and raised on a mixed farm near Viceroy, Saskatchewan where, with her enrollment in the Viceroy 4-H Club at the age of 10, she learned to sew, and that skill set has served her throughout her years working in the Arts and Entertainment Industries. She built her career in Film in Saskatchewan but has enriched her resume by designing throughout Canada as well as The United States, different parts of Europe and Japan. Her work has been seen in Cinemas and at Festivals throughout the World including two Premieres at Cannes, three at TIFF and one at Sundance. Her work is also seen on Netflix, FX, Canal+, BBC, CTV, CBC, and on many more international networks. She has been nominated for a Gemini Award as "Best Costume Designer" for *Corner Gas* in 2004. She has also had multiple nominations for SMPIA Awards, winning for *Falling Angels* in 2005: she was nominated and won the Leo Award for Best Costume Design for *Mr Hockey: the Gordie Howe Story in* 2014 and was recently nominated for a CAFTCAD Award for Best Costume Design for an Independent Feature for *Supergrid.* She is also an Educator and has taught seminars in Canada, Fiji, France, and Lithuania. She lives and works from Toronto, Ontario and Assiniboia, Saskatchewan, Canada.

> *"Hope is being able to see that there is light despite all of the darkness."*
> *~Desmond Tutu~*
> *Bishop, Theologian*
> *Human Rights*
> *Anti-Apartheid Activist*
> *1931-2021*

Soul to Soul: Proof, *Linda Rampling*

By Linda Rampling

Christopher Mark Rampling: 24/4/1979 -? /9/2017: Please, try not to judge. Also, it is imperative to have an open mind. It is extremely difficult to write the facts about when my world grew even darker. I'll try my utmost to be succinct in sharing the essential elements, which are all, sadly, true. Essentially, this is proof of how our consciousness lives on after we leave the body, which I'm wishing to share through the knowledge my son has given to me. It is important because it can allay fears: the type of fear where we'll think we will never see our loved ones ever again – you will. Fears with 'death' – no such thing. I hope what I'm about to share with you, dear reader, will help quash all your fears.

We truly are energy!

I've left a question mark about Christopher's exact day of passing because no one really knows.

Italy September 2017: The holiday destination, which for months, I'd been looking forward to. Here we are, my partner of several years and my five-month-old cocker spaniel, Beau - named after Beau Brummell. (Yep, crazy, but fun!) In case you didn't know Brummell was an important figure in Regency England. We, the three of us, were luxuriating in first-class accommodation, with an extremely comfortable bed, and yet, exhausted and needing a good night's rest, I couldn't fall asleep.

As the world was beginning to wake up, my eyes closed: finally, I fell fast asleep, which is when I saw my late husband, John. He looked so handsome! I always thought he was a good-looking man and oh so charming. Now, here he is, in my dream. It was incredible how healthy he looked. Younger, too. I noticed his clothes; a smart-looking jacket, possibly linen, but not the creased look, which is how most of my linen clothes appear. His jacket looked lighter in colour than the trousers. Yes, it was white but textured, which is why I thought it to be linen.

Of course, at that time, when I saw John, I didn't understand the significance of his visit.

Frankly, it wasn't unusual to see my husband in my dreams. Within days of his passing, John would either show up in a dream or play with the lights in my house. His most amazing efforts were with my computer:

John: A wonderful message from my late husband. It was a Sunday afternoon a few months after John, my husband, had passed, and I'd decided to write a letter to my son. He was in the U.K. (I reside in France), my son, twenty-three going on seventy, but could charm the birds from the trees and...fool everyone. More about that later.

Christopher: AKA Chris. He appreciated his name, but he'd decided to shorten it because Christopher sounded too formal for his liking. Back to the letter: I sat in front of my desktop wondering how to address another of his problems. I tapped the letters: D e a r C h r i s. When I found I could not move forward, I would tap T, and the letter M would appear. Tap H, and I'd get a Z. This continued for some time. Truly extraordinary!

A very dear friend, Tim, happened to be staying with me... thank goodness because I wondered if I was going crazy. So, I asked my friend to witness what was happening. He laughed and told me it was my husband. Really? This was interesting considering Tim was a non-believer in 'Life After.' I've since been told to call anything that is not logical or unappealing, 'interesting.' It's the polite way of saying...well, it's interesting!

My desktop computer appeared to be going crazy, which is why I gave up trying to type my communication to Chris, a letter, which I would have printed off. Now we're talking the bygone era, which required an envelope and stamp to be posted. My screen was just jumbled letters, making no sense whatsoever. I knew the next day I had a French language lesson. As usual, I hadn't done my homework, so I went in search of my books. I looked in all the usual places, but with no luck. Before my husband passed, we'd decided to learn French together. He'd make our French teacher laugh; he'd flummox her with Latin probably because he couldn't, at that stage, concentrate fully on what we were being taught. Not only was he charming, but he was also very clever. Unable to find my French theory book, I decided to look for John's book, which I found almost straight away. Odd! Where was mine? I sat down with John's book to revise. As I opened the book, an envelope fell out. I recognized John's handwriting on the envelope, which was addressed to our son, Chris. Was that his intention when he was playing with my computer?

September 2017: Italy is beautiful. Having previously driven from where I live in Southern France along the magnificent coastline to the Italian French border, I was excited. I'd driven this route several times before, the scenery was truly breath-taking. Italy wasn't exactly on my bucket list because I'd previously visited on several occasions. Travel was different now. I had my Beau, which meant I couldn't do the usual trips to Cape Town, certainly not when I have a young four paws. Of course, in retrospect, I think this was all part of my late husband, or perhaps my guide's plan.

A little bit of my history: When John and I moved to Southern France we arrived with our family dog, the very handsome German Shepherd, a gentle giant we named Jordan. Tragically, within a month of John's passing, our beautiful GSD was diagnosed with lung cancer. He was subsequently buried in my front garden, whereby I vowed no more four-legged friends. By now I had plans, a huge 'bucket list' of countries I wished to visit. I'd witnessed too much sadness. I wanted to escape, whereby travel was the best option.

Beau, 2017: My saviour, gifted from my guides? You decide. I'm in the garden centre looking to buy a pair of hardwearing pruning gloves. I knew this local garden centre sold pets: including birds, fish, rabbits, and dogs. I always felt compelled to take a little look, with no intention whatsoever to purchase. This day was no exception. There he was: A cute blue roan cocker spaniel puppy. Absolutely no way was I going to purchase a puppy, let alone from a store. If I should ever…ever consider a dog, I'd visit a rescue home. The next day, I found myself back in the garden centre, to my amazement the puppy was still there, yep, still "For Sale." Four days later, having not found any decent gardening gloves, I returned to the store. Yep, puppy still for sale.

A couple of days later some friends arrived from the UK. I cannot recall thinking about the puppy. However, on the return journey, back to the airport to bid my friend's a fond farewell, I announced the possibility of purchasing a cocker… if, and it was a big if, he or she was still there, he or she was going to be mine. My friends were astonished. In fact, they were horrified. Never in my wildest dreams did I, at this stage in my life, consider having responsibility for another living soul. Stranger things have happened.

Having dropped my friends off at the airport, there I was, back at the garden centre, nose pressed against the glass, and to my astonishment, the cocker was still there. I was seeing what was to become my saviour in the form of a cocker spaniel. Of course, within minutes, he was mine. Oh, my goodness me! How did that happen, and why?

Holiday: Hmm? I didn't dare look at my bucket list. I had this little bundle of energy; nevertheless, I still had the yearning to travel, I love a change of scenery. Always having itchy feet and a need to discover different cultures, I considered driving over the border. Beau had been chipped, owned a passport; he was fit for travel. Being reasonably close to Spain, I'm there quite a lot, therefore, didn't consider it as a holiday destination. I wished to wander further afield; nevertheless, I couldn't wander too far with a young dog, which is why Italy became the idyllic holiday destination.

The year…being a blur because it feels like yesterday, however, for you, dear reader, I looked it up: 2017.

September 2017: The day came when we were moving from the comfortable contemporary accommodation to the castle. Leaving the stylish and extremely luxurious house was difficult. On this morning, the skies were cloudy, and rain was threatening. However, always the optimist, I hoped everything would be fine and, besides, I was looking forward to enjoying a good lunch! The finest Italian, freshly cooked pasta. I'd previously reserved a table after doing a bit of research to find one of the best restaurants in the area. After arriving at our destination, we dropped our bags off, walked Beau, and headed for the restaurant. Again, I can't recall anything about it, which is unusual for me. I do remember that it was good, and I recall the walk afterwards because the rain had stopped long enough to explore where we were staying. Sadly, the rain didn't hold off long enough for a decent walk, so we made our way back to our apartment in the rather cold and ugly castle. I remember looking through my photographs, on my iPad, before chatting to a girlfriend via Facebook messenger. Along the top of my iPad appeared a message from my daughter. She was asking where I was and was I alone?

I bid farewell to my friend and answered the message from my daughter, Richenda. I was curious to know why she wanted to know if I was alone. What sort of question is that? She phoned and blurted out that Christopher's body had been found. I felt nauseous, and I couldn't catch my breath. I walked up and down trying to gather my thoughts before phoning my daughter back.

My son's body had been found by the plumber. According to what my daughter had been told, Christopher's body had been in a room for two or three days before being discovered. My daughter was frantic about the possibility he'd passed from a heart attack. Richenda has four boys, her eldest, Nathan, had passed several days after open-heart surgery, understandably worried for her sons. She was petrified history was repeating itself.

With no knowledge of what had happened to my son, I attempted to placate her. She was adamant it was heart problems; her father had been diagnosed with cardiomyopathy. Yet again, I attempted to put her straight because his heart problem was caused by alcohol. He'd passed December 20th, 2001, after an operation on a brain tumour. Glioblastoma was nothing to do with my husband's heart. It was odd how, in that moment, after hearing about the loss of my son, I was overwhelmed with trying to reassure Richenda and how she didn't have to worry about heart issues with her sons.

I had to get to the truth! I phoned the local police station, where he lived, but sadly got nowhere. They were not going to tell me, no matter who I said I was. Days later, I was told the police officer was wrong in being unhelpful. After getting nowhere with the police station, I attempted to logically think about whom to contact. I guessed Christopher's body had been found in the room of a house, where I once dropped him off, many moons ago. Whereby I contacted the Landlord. He picked the phone up on the second ring.

Once I told him my name, he said he recognized my voice, conveyed how sorry he was, and how he had been trying to contact me. He went on to explain how Chris owed money for the room he was renting, plus how he wanted access to the room…something about the radiator, which is how Christopher's body was found.

The workman pushed the door open, didn't initially see my son's body. Apparently, he was sitting 'upright with a pizza on his lap.' This is where I heard the first lie surrounding the mystery of my son's passing.

After making the call to my son's Landlord, the Police station, and various people to try and understand what had happened, I fell into bed. Of course, I was wide awake, willing my son to appear. I needed a sign from him. I still had not connected the vision of my husband, Christopher's father, in the dream. Oddly, that very night, my dog, Beau, who's usually very good, showed signs of anxiety. I put it down to him reacting to my sadness. He chewed a wire on a lamp. His persona was different.

We packed to return home. Thankfully the rain had eased up. As we walked back to the car, I looked towards the busy road and contemplated walking in front of a fast, moving vehicle. My mind was in turmoil: the loss of my grandson had been unexplainably horrendous. After my husband passed, my grief plummeted to new lows, but I didn't want to feel a victim. Now, as I walked towards the car, I just wanted to end my life. I looked towards the moving vehicles on the busy road. I was holding Beau's lead. He was my responsibility: I was his world. I could not do it! It was Beau that made me reconsider my demise. I got into the car and put that thought on hold.

When I arrived home, I once again contacted the Police station, on this occasion I was given a name and number of an officer. The lady on the switchboard put me through to that Police Officer. Yes, thankfully, he was the first officer on the scene. No, my son did not have a pizza on his lap. He very kindly told me what he saw. My son's body was on the floor. The officer continued to explain how he thought, while standing, my son had trouble breathing and fell onto the bed before sliding to the floor.

All the while he was talking, I was confused as to why the Landlord would tell me my son had a pizza on his lap. Through the fog in my brain, I heard the words interview, hospital, and machete. What? I asked him to repeat because I didn't understand. The police officer I was listening to had previously met my son, when he visited the hospital where my son was a patient. Christopher had previously been attacked by a rather demented person with a machete. The officer explained that it was a few months prior to the day when he was called to where my son's body lay.

He continued to convey to me how he thought my son was such a lovely, charming young man. 'Eloquent and quietly spoken.'

By now, I was shocked, but also angry! What happened to the person that had attacked my son? Was he in prison? I then listened to how absolutely nothing came of that 'case' because my son refused to make a statement.

I told the officer how I'd been told my son's body was found with a pizza on his lap and how assumptions were made he'd choked. He told me they were all nonsense: false allegations. My head was still reeling from learning my son had been brutally attacked with a machete. My son's body had been taken to a hospital in Reading for the post-mortem examination. I should expect to receive the toxicology and histology results within a few weeks.

Later that day, while sitting in the living room, I noticed Beau was following something. He appeared to be looking into the middle of nowhere. My instincts kicked in. I knew my son was in the room. Beau didn't appear spooked. In fact, he was very calm. It was slightly puzzling to me. Why could my dog see Chris, but I could not?

Christopher Mark Rampling 0-8 years: I couldn't have wished for a better child: Christopher was perfect. Loving, kind, bright, I was so proud of him. I wasn't the only one who thought he looked like an Angel. In hindsight, I think, indeed, I know he got away with far too much, particularly while he attended Primary School. The teachers used to tell me how he always looked so innocent 'with his beautiful big blue eyes...and his charm!' Oh, dear! When Christopher was very young, my husband and I did notice how he was a little different. I cannot recall his age, but it was way before he started school. He would recite passages from the Bible. Neither John nor I were religious, so it was mystifying where he'd learnt the quotes from. I'm now guessing Christopher, when so young, carried the memory from his past life.

Probably more to do with society than the Bible is why I was Christened. My husband was ten years older and previously married. Apparently, to wed in a church, one had to be Christened, which is what he did. I wasn't that hypocritical. John and I were wed in Pietermaritzburg's Town Hall in 1976. I'd previously flown to Johannesburg, on my own. I always had a passion for Africa. As for religion, John would jokingly say how he believed in all: 'Buddhism, Hinduism, Islam,

Confucianism, Taoism, Christianity, and Judaism... one of them could be the "real deal".

Chris M. Rampling. Changes: I remember like it was yesterday. Christopher was age eleven. I was preparing supper when Christopher announced he saw boys 'smoking' from a glass bottle. Sadly, I had no idea what he was referring to. Yes, of course,

I later discovered he was referring to a bong. Was he telling me he'd tried it? Or was he genuinely curious? Was that the very start of his personal path to destruction?

Everything Happens for a Reason: I needed to get to the UK. I'm not sure why, but it was important for me to see my son's body before being released to the funeral directors. Flight to Stansted was booked then cancelled due to Air traffic Control going on strike. On the way back from Italy, my car developed an engine problem. I couldn't go anywhere until a mechanic fixed it. I was on an emotional roller coaster. Eventually, after days of more anguish, I landed in England. The very next day, I drove to the hospital, having previously made an appointment to view the body. I walked into the mortuary on my own, where I was met by a very young man. He led me into a small room, where I saw my son laid out in the middle of the room.

Raw Emotions: I cannot describe my emotions. No words could convey what I was feeling the second I saw the corpse of my once beautiful boy. As I moved slowly to his side, I noticed marks on his forehead. I asked the lad, who had shown me into the room if he knew how they had got there. We both examined the scuff marks on my son's forehead. He had no knowledge as to what they were, which is when I decided to take a photograph. Then this would be proof, should it be needed in the future.

After a few days in the U.K, I returned to my home in France. There was to be an inquiry into the death of my son. The body was not going to be released anytime soon. According to the coroner, it was just in case they needed to take more samples. Within a week or so, I received a call from the coroner, he had received a few of the toxicology and histology results. It would seem my son had overdosed on heroin and alcohol. He told me not all the results were back. Other biopsies were going to take a little longer to analyse. Nevertheless, the very sad verdict my son, Christopher had killed himself with a mix of heroin and alcohol, which was, very sadly, the cause of his demise. Was this suicide? I didn't think so. My son has three daughters; he adored those little girls. However, apart from his daughters, he had very little else going on in his life, which is why many made the incorrect assumption of suicide.

Christopher's voice: A few months earlier, a friend introduced me to play the online game, Words with Friends. I never had time to play until after my son passed. Wide awake in the small hours of the night, Words with Friends was my go-to.

I tried to still my mind with meditation, get into bed, and hope to fall straight to sleep. Most nights, it worked. This night my son, Chris, came to me in a dream. He told me he was sorry, and he loved me. I told Christopher I loved him and how I wished I could talk to him, to hear his voice. He said we could talk to one another. At that moment, I woke up. I lay still for a few minutes, going over and over the dream. I wanted him to come back, so I kept my eyes closed, but my mind was too busy going over everything we said to one another.

That was it. I was wide awake. I sat up in bed and switched my bedside lamp on so I could see to unplug my iPad from its charge cable. I went straight into Words with Friends to see who, at that crazy hour in the morning, would be online for a game. I placed a few letters and waited. Not surprising, there didn't appear to be many people playing. While I waited for someone to take their turn, I came out of the app on my iPad and went straight to my photographs. I looked at the photograph of my son, the one I'd taken of him in the mortuary. While staring at his face, I heard my son's voice: "That's not me anymore, Mum."

Funeral: Thankfully, it wasn't raining. My partner and I sat in the car, parked opposite the crematorium. At my insistence, in case we got caught in traffic, grateful, we'd arrived early. As I sat in the car, I recognised some familiar faces. Christopher's school friends began to arrive. They'd taken the day off work. I hoped he could see who was there.

During the funeral, I focused on being strong for my daughter. I didn't want to break down. No child wants to see their parent crying. A parent must always be seen to be strong. No weaknesses allowed. How did I do it? Easy!

I was born nine years after the end of World War II. My father, from a very young age, was my hero. Sadly, he had a dark side, which now I know to be from what he experienced and saw while serving his King and country. I quickly learnt, from a very young age, if I stupidly burst into tears, unless I was bleeding from every orifice, I was deemed to be a baby. Even though I was a child, I soon learnt to keep control of my emotions. No one likes to be ridiculed. I certainly didn't, particularly by the one person I adored.

Arriving at the crematorium, unsure if Richenda would attend. Previously it was a yes, then a no…and so it went… I got out of the car to greet some of Christopher's school friends. I turned to look at the sky when I saw a vision of loveliness: Richenda had decided to attend. My daughter had warned me not to cuddle her, she didn't want to cry. I knew exactly how she felt. I didn't want to break down, either. Towards the end of the service, I noticed Richenda looking down at her mobile phone. She realised I was curious to know what she was doing. She tilted her mobile, whereby I could see a picture of Chris, my son, her brother with her son, my beautiful grandson, Nathan, he was sitting on Christopher's lap. That's when tears pricked my eyes. I bit deep into my cheek to keep the tears from spilling.

This was a ceremony to say farewell. I felt at peace. Sad, nevertheless, justified in my thinking this was his soul's plan. Strange how he and I became estranged, was it meant to be? Did it lessen my grief? In a way, I think it did.

Chris, early teens: Just after my father passed in May 1994, I noticed a huge difference in my son's behaviour. He was becoming a rebellious fifteen-year-old. Hormones raging, he was discovering who he was and what he thought he wanted. Yes, perhaps I wasn't strict enough. We were not as strict with him in the same way we were with our daughter.

His very first crime: He'd been invited to a party. It was a Saturday evening. He had been good all week, so he was allowed to go out. I was aware of the landline constantly ringing and Chris was either sneaking into the study or darting upstairs to my bedroom where he'd take the calls. I happened to be cleaning my teeth in the ensuite bathroom when he was on one of the calls. I assumed, from what I heard, he was planning to meet up with some lads before the girl's party. Sadly, it was a more sinister plan, which led to him being arrested and subsequently doing time in prison.

While he was in Reading Remand, I visited him every single day – perhaps I should have shown tough love. Once the crime had been heard in Crown Court, he was then moved to a different prison for young men. Christopher being sent to prison was the second of many heartbreaks. The first was the crime he'd committed.

The Latter Years and Estrangement: My son was in self-destruct mode! No amount of money we paid to ensure he'd take a different path, or, indeed, the wonderful opportunity my late husband offered him, with the prospect of a decent career; a good honest future, nothing could deter him. Sadly, I would hear how Chris was charming while sober. When he drank, alcohol it would bolster his ego further. In Christopher's mind, while under the influence, he was the Incredible Hulk, or, because he'd become heavily involved with drugs, he was untouchable. I used to think he mixed with all the wrong people, whereby I'd constantly make excuses when, in truth, he was the wrong element. He met a woman who became the mother of his children while he was, once again in prison. Apparently, they met via a friend. She didn't work in the prison.

Chris suffered with Slap Face Syndrome, also now known as Slap Cheek. I've very recently, within minutes of writing this paragraph, been told it is caused by Parvovirus. Oh, my word! Chris told me he would have walked through fire, do whatever it takes to eradicate the overwhelming embarrassment he experienced when his face flushed like a beacon.

Chris was about seven or eight years old, when he was attacked by a Jack Russell terrier. My husband and I were looking to buy a particular property, unfortunately, there was no warning of a dog.

Chris was trailing behind the rest of us. We'd all wandered through the kitchen, where the dog was under the table. Just like me, he loved animals and, in particular, dogs. Chris being knee-high to a grasshopper, would have seen the dog and possibly went to stroke it. Within minutes we were racing Chris to hospital, where he endured a few stitches to his face, all close to his eye. About three years after the first dog-attack, he was yet again attacked by the neighbour's dog, which they kept as a guard dog.

Honestly? I didn't ever notice his cheeks turning red, but it became a huge problem in his psyche, causing him to walk out of work, subsequently losing the job. He, at one time, had the world at his feet. He was scouted by Chelsea Football Club. John, Chris, and I drove to Battersea, where we watched him play in trial matches, but he threw it all away. He wasn't in the right frame of mind.

As his mother, it was my job to be there for him, but once he reached a certain age, I could not tell him who to be. I disliked his choices. I could see with certain happenings he thought they were the easy option; nevertheless, they were his choices, which he had to take responsibility for.

Years later, after another spell in prison, he phoned telling me that he and the woman he'd met were expecting a baby. He was very apprehensive, telling me he couldn't look after himself, let alone a child. As it happens, they had twins. I prayed his paternal instinct would be a major turning point, and I hoped they'd both be sensible, mature, and be loyal, and kind to one another. It was too much to hope for.

Prior to discovering the girlfriend was pregnant, Chris was out of prison on good behaviour. Any misdemeanour, and he would immediately be sent back. Chris and the girlfriend were sitting in a restaurant deciding what to eat. He felt his face burning up and looking red, so he walked out. They had a blazing row. He kicked her car, sadly, she had him arrested. This time he went on the run. He phoned telling me how his life was dire. I felt so helpless as I heard the anxiety in his voice. He told me, as he always used to, "I love you, Mum." He gave himself up and went back to prison. It was while he was in prison the girlfriend found out she was pregnant. His life became even more complicated.

The girlfriend phoned, telling me she was pregnant, plus how the relationship with my son was toxic. Therefore, because she'd experienced an extremely volatile relationship with someone else prior to my son, she wasn't prepared to have Christopher back. She was emphatic about not wanting contact.

Wind their story forward: Imagine how surprised I was to learn not only did they have another child, but as soon as he came out of prison, they were residing with one another. I'd wondered why the calls from my son had stopped! When I stopped receiving his letters and phone calls, I'd tried contacting him via the prison but was told he'd been released.

Around the time Christopher went back to prison, he seemed to have another female in his life who was very pleasant. He'd previously given me her phone number. It was indeed surreal; however, I was grateful to her because it was another way of knowing my now estranged son and his little family were safe – albeit short term.

The change in my son's persona was soul-destroying. I hoped the fact he was now a dad would give him a sense of responsibility plus be less hostile. I truly do believe he wanted to change. While the girlfriend was away from the house, he'd phone. Generally, we'd have a good catch-up. He'd tell me how he wished I lived down the road, whereby we could meet up. During a couple of his calls, I could hear his concern about the demon drink. How he was troubled that the girlfriend would easily get through a bottle of gin, plus she'd put her name down for Social Housing in Ascot. He later discovered his name was not included.

He'd share the worry with me about her drinking and smoking habits. He desperately needed a different lifestyle. We'd chat for a couple of hours, then he'd lower his tone of voice to a whisper, telling me she's back. The call would abruptly end. I learnt from the Police he was being hauled over the coals because he now had children; his daughters were being used as a weapon against him, and more worryingly, depending on the perspective, Social Services were aware.

Sadly, Christopher and the mother of his children had a co-dependent relationship. When drunk, angry, or high on drugs, he'd phone me. Those phone calls would be at all hours during the night. The girlfriend would be in the background adding fuel to the fire. I'd wake from a deep sleep to hear my son slur his words of anger, usually with Back to Black by Amy Winehouse, playing in the background. I would ask where the girls were but be met with an abusive answer. I usually just listened to the tirade. He was drunk and angry with the world. He also felt very sorry for himself. Of course, he'd re-write history. By this stage, he was an adult, and I felt he should face the music for his bad choices. In my heart, I knew we had a strong bond, but I couldn't haul him out of the quagmire he'd found himself in. There seemed to be no going back, which is why, when hearing my son had passed, I was shocked, but not surprised.

Last hug from my son: A few days before his thirtieth birthday. He passed when he was thirty-eight. At that time, as well as my home in France, I had another house in the UK where he and the girlfriend came to stay. I cooked all his favourite food, and he was happy when he arrived, but I could tell he was craving something. Intuitively I knew he was unhappy. He wanted to drown his sorrows in alcohol. They were to stay for a few days, but after asking me for more money – not for him, but to pay the girlfriend for the petrol - they left within 36 hours. He gave me a huge hug: I'll never forget it. He whispered in my ear, "I love you, Mum, and always will." That was the last day I saw him alive. Eight years later, I saw him again in the mortuary. The bond between a mother and child never really diminishes. Although I'm no longer physically able to cuddle him, he's always letting me know he's close by.

Inquest: My daughter and I arrived separately for the inquest. We were travelling from different parts of the country. I was inexplicably apprehensive. Even though my instinct told me my son had not taken his own life, I still wasn't sure what to expect.

As I climbed the stairs of the very old, fusty building, I was aware of a very pleasant fragrance. It was comforting because I guessed it was the perfume my daughter had chosen to wear that day. As I followed the sign to where the inquest was going to take place, I was happy to see Richenda sitting outside. We didn't have to wait very long before we were called to sit in front of the Judge. It was decided my son did not take his own life.

The local press accosted me outside the Ladies' loo. Do these people have no moral code? They wanted answers, which I was not prepared to give. Thinking of my daughter and grandchildren, who were relatively local, I appealed to their better nature; I asked them not to print this story. To my knowledge, I don't think they did.

More Proof from My Son: Friend's, Nic and Mark, had very kindly invited me to stay over for supper. When I arrived, Nic had something she wanted to share. Collecting her daughter, Hazel, from school was the perfect alone time for a private chat. Mark's father had also recently passed away. Nic explained to me how her sister-in-law knew of a Spiritual Medium and Clairvoyant.

The Medium was booked into the local community centre for a public demonstration. Nic, Mark, and the in-laws excitedly bought tickets in the hope of getting a message from Mark's dad. One hundred and fifty people were gathered in the community centre. Many were already seated by the time Nic, Mark, and family arrived, so they stood at the back of the room. They listened, wishing to hear evidence from Mark's dad, hoping to learn he was okay.

There happened to be an elderly lady in the front row who claimed everyone the Medium brought through. Of course, the crowd was growing slightly irritated. The Medium was pacing the stage when he stopped abruptly, telling the audience, this is nasty. He was appearing to talk to the spirit that was obviously communicating with him.

Dan, the Medium, was asking if it was suicide. Then he exclaimed, "No, it wasn't suicide!" He asked if anyone could relate to this. Dan continued with the spirit's message how his body was not discovered for several days. At this point, Nic thought of my son. Christopher's body had not been discovered for several days. Again, the woman in the front row claimed it was a message for her. A few in the audience sighed.

Dan dramatically tapped his forehead in a chopping motion. Asking what's that…it looks like a wound. At this point, Nic remembered me telling her how shocked I was when the police officer mentioned the machete attack. The woman in the front row was still saying it was a message for her. Without provocation, Dan, looked to the back of the room, directly at Nic, asking if it meant anything to her. The woman in the front row was still insisting it was for her… just as she'd insisted that everyone he brought through was for her.

Unfortunately, Nic and family didn't receive a message from Mark's dad, but we're all positive in thinking it was Christopher ensuring I knew it was not suicide. I knew he wouldn't leave his daughters. I know it was important for Chris to convey the message: my son, Christopher, did not commit suicide.

There had been many times when Chris would tell me how his life was not going anywhere. I recall a particular moment in time when I had to go into hospital for a procedure. I mentioned to Chris because I was going into a U.K. hospital. He told me that if something happened to me, he'd end his own life. That was nine years before he passed. Since that time, although his lifestyle had not improved, he had three daughters. Christopher's three girls gave him every reason to live.

More Evidence: Seven months later: I was about to get into bed when I looked down to see my iPad, which had previously died on me, was now fully charged, with about six messages. The one message which really stood out was from a friend my son attended school with. James and Chris were once partners in crime, unfortunately, quite literally.

I've learnt to forgive. Love is all that matters. Before opening the other five messages, I was drawn to the FB message from James. I think he was a little reticent about how to convey this message; his preamble was about him not really believing...possibly wondering if I would be annoyed, thinking he was totally and utterly crazy. Yes, I understood. In truth, I was overjoyed! James finally got to the point: His girlfriend had visited a psychic medium. The Medium asked if her partner had recently lost a friend by the name of Chris. Attached to the message was a recording of his girlfriend with the Medium. I was left with no doubt. My son wanted to convey he was okay. Chris seized the opportunity through James, his girlfriend, and the psychic.

I loved all the signs I was receiving from my son, but I was concerned I could be keeping him on this Earth; stopping him from moving to whatever was supposed to be next, which is when, out of the blue, as I have discovered these things happen – it's called synchronicity - I discovered Suzanne Giesemann.

Suzanne Giesemann: Medium, Mystic, Spiritual Teacher, Afterlife Connections. Suzanne is a former Navy Commander and Commanding Officer who served as an aide to the Chairman of the Joint Chiefs of Staff on 9/11. From U.S. Commander to Messenger of Hope. I found an email address and wrote asking her opinion about my concerns with seemingly preventing my son from doing what he should be doing, learning, even. Suzanne responded with a positive point of view. She suggested I continue to talk to him and watch for signs. The signs had been there from the very day my son transitioned when my husband, John, appeared in my dream. John was simply telling me he'd be there to meet our son. I truly believe John had somehow manipulated the situation with Beau. Remember? I wanted to travel, no more animals. Within hours of being told about my son's passing, Beau gave me a purpose to carry on.

Afterlife: In my sixty-seven years, come March, it will be sixty-eight; I have experienced so many signs to prove there is something beyond 'death.' My mother used to do Automatic Writing; she'd converse with my grandparents soon after they'd passed. My mother shared various spiritual happenings with me.

One day she made a Ouija board. She literally cut out twenty-eight paper squares, twenty-six with the alphabet, individual A to Z, which she proceeded to place in a circle, onto the kitchen table. For the other two paper squares, she wrote a "Yes" on one and a "No" on the other and placed them in the centre of the circle of paper squares with the alphabet. She then placed an upturned glass with the Yes and No on either side.

I was spellbound as my mother proceeded to ask if anyone was there. The glass slid back and forth, spelling out words in answer to her questions or answering with a simple Yes or No. Even to this day, I recall how my finger was bobbing nervously on the rim of the base of the glass. I was fascinated because I could see my mother was not pushing the glass when it came whizzing in my direction. It was impossible to pull the glass. Amazingly, after my mother asked yet another question, the glass couldn't move as swiftly. There was something tiny, dried on the table, a tiny speck, where the glass could not simply slide over. Now, as an adult, I often think about that moment: if and it's a big 'IF' my mother or I was...let's say assisting the glass, it would have glided over the minuscule dust particle, which was not visible to even my, then, good eyesight, but the glass had several attempts then went round. Incredible!

My father arrived home from work: he was furious with her. That was the one and only time my mother communicated with her 'deceased' parents in my presence. After witnessing my mother communicating with deceased loved ones, plus all my numerous experiences dating back to when I was about eight, I thought it was time to do a little more research. So, I signed up for Suzanne Giesemann's Expand Your Innate Mediumship Skill with Soul-to-Soul Communication course, along with many other people from around the world. The course was perfect, exactly what I required.

Towards the end of the course, although Suzanne had opened a Facebook page specifically for everyone in the course, I branched out with my own Facebook page, aptly calling it Advancing Awareness. We could only have access to Suzanne's FB page for a few more months, so it made perfect sense to try and keep as many people as possible in communication. I also attended weekly gatherings to help hone my soul energy communication further. Someone would read the invocation, and then we'd meditate for about ten minutes, or until someone spoke up with a message.

It was a Monday, possibly a year ago. I'd received the Zoom link, whereby I eagerly clicked on. I offered to be the moderator. Within twenty minutes, one of the ladies in the gathering mentioned a gentleman reading a Newspaper. Many other details, too, whereby it became apparent, this is my father! I was in tears because he mentioned how proud he was, and more important, how sorry he was for the way he'd treated me.

While I attempted to control my emotions, we moved on to another person in the group. She had a young lad with a BMX bike… he has very blonde hair and big blue eyes. Now he was showing her Star Wars characters. She looked directly at me. Telling me this is an English lad. I knew it was my son. Through my tears, I managed to utter a few words of positivity recognising my son. It was an accident, she said. By now, I was sobbing. This was all my grief welling up. You know when you cry, and you cannot catch your breath? That was me. It was a guttural, deep, and unrecognisable emotion that had been obviously dormant for too long. Rather embarrassed, I released my feelings. I simply loved the fact my dear papa had come through, plus it would seem he brought my son, Chris, too.

Soul-to-soul group: The fantabulous Tuesday gathering has been up and running for almost a year. We're an informal group of people from all over the world. I host the Zoom gathering, sending the Zoom link via email every Monday, plus posting onto our FB page. When I haven't invited an eminent guest speaker, we'll read an invocation and meditate for Soul-to-Soul communication. Chloe will often convey a message from Chris, which is so heart-warming to hear.

Leigh: 2019, I was gifted a DNA kit with a year's membership for Ancestry.com, where I discovered cousins. I first met Grant, Leigh's brother. A wonderful, good-looking — as you'd expect — family-orientated man. I discovered Grant's younger sibling, Leigh. I looked Leigh up via social media — so easy to do that nowadays. I noticed we had similar likes and appreciation of All Things Unknown — or so it would seem. I felt compelled to meet her.

We have since met, albeit via social media and via Zoom; nevertheless, we get along like a house on fire. I've often thought about how Chris would get along with Grant and, in particular, Leigh and her son and daughter James and Michaela. It's as if Chris is telling me, "They're our people, Mum, I love them, you'll love them, too."

Leigh and I are so different, but the same. We are a contradiction, but our energy is most definitely on the same page. Without a doubt, we share the same genes, but it is more than biology, which is so important. She and I just appreciate how much more there is to 'life'.

Leigh is in our Tuesday Soul-to-Soul group. During one of our gatherings, Leigh shared: She was on the ladder decorating, in the house on her own, radio music playing when she heard a loud voice almost shout, "Chris." She turned to see who was in the room. The room was empty. I wonder if my son was trying to warn Leigh. A few days later, Leigh's stepmother, Anita, tragically passed. However, within days of Anita's passing, she conveyed, through one of our Mediums, how she was when she was a younger woman while here on Earth. She was a bit of a party girl. Then more accurate details of how she passed. The best part: How is she now? She's fine.

I'm secure in the knowledge that my son, Christopher Mark Rampling, is also fine; he came here to experience and learn. I've learnt to connect with his soul, his energy, and our love, which will never die.

About the Author

Linda Rampling is a photographer, artist, author, enthusiast in conservation, lover of nature, environmentalist. "I just keep on going - riding over those waves, where I learnt very quickly in a world of warriors, to be a warrior, and never to lower my standards. Enjoying every second of my life with my five 4paws; two dogs and three rescue cats. Meditating every day while I walk through the vineyards in Southern France. The earth and nature have become my church; it's where I worship and feel free." Linda is the founder of *Soul-to-Soul* and Facebook Group *Advancing Awareness*

Christopher Mark Rampling

Chris with Rollo, our Golden Retriever

Chris at 19

"One thing you should know, no matter where I go, we'll always be together."
Christopher Robin to Winnie the Pooh.
AA Milne from the book, Winnie the Pooh, October 14, 1926

"Perhaps they are not stars, but rather openings in heaven where the love of our lost ones pours through and shines down upon us to let us know they are happy."
~Eskimo Saying~

Jaden Speaks, *Jessica Baumeister*

By Jessica Baumeister

My name is Jessica, and as far as I can remember, since I was a little girl, I have always wanted to be a mother and have children one day. So, my motherhood journey began at the age of 19 with my first son Ryan in 1995, and I was absolutely in love. I had my second son Brandon at 21 years old in 1998, and at 24 years old in 2001, I had my 3rd son, Jaden. Jaden was unexpectedly born with Down Syndrome, Autism, and had many serious health complications from the start. At 26 years old, I had my last child, a beautiful baby girl, Alyssa, in 2003, and she was a year and a half younger than Jaden.

Jaden continued to struggle with his chronic medical conditions. He stopped breathing in my arms at a month old and needed life supports to aid him. He was given a permanent tracheostomy and feeding tube shortly after. Unfortunately, the trach had silenced his voice and cries from that moment on. Jaden was then diagnosed with a heart condition known as an atrial septal defect that would require open-heart surgery at seven months old. After ten months in the hospital, Jaden was finally stable enough to come home right before his first birthday.

I then started to teach Jaden some simple sign language since his trach compromised his communication and voice. At two and a half years old, Jaden was diagnosed with a second heart condition and needed another open-heart surgery to repair his mitral valve. At four years old, Jaden was officially diagnosed on the autism spectrum PDD type (pervasive developmental disorder).

Despite Jaden's fragile life in and out of the hospital, he had the biggest personality and the best sense of humor. He absolutely loved his big brothers and little sister as we had always been a very tight-knit family and still are. Jaden loved to play in water and rain regardless of his trach, and he also learned to put his thumb over his trach to vocalize. He loved to dance and had a great rhythm to the music. He often enjoyed imitating his favorite cartoons, *SpongeBob*, *Elmo*, and *Spaceballs* the movie. He would at times laugh himself silly while finger painting the wall with poop. He was a little pistol, resilient, funny, stubborn, and full of life.

Jaden often endured more than his share of criticism and neglect to outright physical abuse with cigarette burns from another. The abuse, in turn, caused Jaden to strike out at others aggressively, pull his hair out from the stress of it, bang his head out of sheer frustration or spit at others constantly out of self-defense and sensory overload.

As Jaden grew bigger, he was harder for me to lift, but it was even harder to find in-home nursing and respite care despite my ongoing advocating for it. He was more than most could handle, and most caregivers usually walked out the door after a few days. With the nursing shortage and lack of support, I began to break down and wear thin from the mounting stress load of so much more than I can say. I finally hit what is known as caregiver burnout, and my own mental and physical health was suffering greatly. I was severely sleep-deprived and tired on a soul level.

As Jaden turned nine years old in 2011, the mounting stress and lack of support were more than I could bear. I was then diagnosed with fibromyalgia, adrenal fatigue, and severe depression. I remember one night within that time being woken by sheer panic and genuine fear that I was going to die. I could not shake this feeling for anything that night, and I even thought about writing a Will as the feeling of impending death was so profound. Yet, I was not ready to die.

It is not easy to put into words what followed a few weeks later; however, I found myself in a white room with no corners or edges. I stood in front of three gray-haired older men sitting side by side on a type of platform. The only way I can describe it was like a panel of judges, yet they did not judge me, even once. In fact, they were a presence of pure wisdom and absolute love. They did not speak in words with their mouths but from their soul through their eyes. I was upset, frantically pacing back and forth in front of them. I felt the need to protest for my need to stay on earth. I was not ready to die yet and did not want to leave my children. It's as if I needed to plead my case to continue on with life. I had no idea how long my plea lasted as time did not seem to exist within that space. The three men just calmly listened with so much care and concern. The next thing I knew, I was right back in my kitchen, wondering what the heck just happened, but what I did know was that the feeling of my impending death had lifted.

A few months after that took place, in January of 2012, Jaden was rushed to the hospital with constant diarrhea and vomiting. He was very sick and was admitted to the hospital in the ICU. The doctors ran tests, MRI scans, and x-rays. The results were devastating. Jaden was in total septic shock from a twist in his intestines. He was rushed back to emergency surgery to see if there was any chance of repair or survival. The surgeon returned to me after about 20 minutes and said, "I am so sorry. There is nothing we can do. This is not a survivable situation." Jaden was then brought back to his room in the ICU on full life support so that we could say our goodbyes. I was absolutely devastated and in shock. I crawled in bed next to my son and held him until his last breath that night on January 7th, 2012. We let go with the utmost dignity, love, gratitude, and respect for one another.

Despite my grieving heart, from the moment of my son's death, I felt a massive shift in my entire being. I wasn't quite sure what was happening to me at the time, but it was as if I was broken open in the most magnificent way. I began to see and feel the world so differently around me. The colors were brighter, the sounds were intensely louder, and I could see energy streams from my hands. It was what I now know to be my great awakening; an activation on a spiritual level was unfolding. I began to see and hear spirit, and I was able to heal with my hands or direct healing energy to myself and others.

My grief seemed to come in waves, along with so many questions. I was soul searching, questioning everything I thought I knew or was taught in church growing up. I wondered where my son was and if he was okay. Was anyone looking after him? Was he at peace, and did he know just how much I loved him? So many questions started to surface as I fell asleep that night. Suddenly I found myself at the children's hospital where Jaden and I had spent so much of our time. I was on the General Pediatrics floor visiting some other children that were very sick and getting ready to pass away. I walked into a big patient room with three beds and their pulled curtains dividing them.

I went to the first child lying there in bed, held their hand, prayed for them, and then the second child. After the second, I walked over to the third child and pulled the curtain back. I was startled and screamed for the nurse in disbelief and confusion. My son was sitting there in his bed. I didn't understand why he was here. He had already died and went home to Heaven. I tried to shake off the confusion, walked over, and sat next to my son in tears.

Jaden looked so alive, healthy, and whole. As I sat next to him facing him, he spoke to me so clearly for the first time but not with his mouth, with his heart through his eyes. He said, "Mom, it's okay. I am alive and well! Thank you so much for being the wonderful mom you always were, and I loved you more than you realized, Mom. Thank you for all you have done for me." Of course, I had tears flowing from my eyes. Jaden reached out and wiped my tears away, and said, "I love you, mom." When I woke up from this very vivid dream visit, I sat up in bed and just cried tears of joy that I could see my son and finally hear him say I love you for the first time. Little did I know that this was just the beginning of many more incredible spirit visits, communications, and signs from my son.

I remember one night crying, missing my son, and I felt him sit next to me on the bed. The mattress sunk as he sat there with me, and I could see with my own eyes. He just sat with me in my grief and held my hand with so much love and compassion. After about two to three minutes, I felt Jaden get up off of the bed as the place on the mattress where he sat rose back up.

About a few weeks after that, I was sitting at my kitchen table thinking about my son, and a single house fly kept flying around my head, very persistent. It would not let up, so I got up to move to another room. As I left the kitchen, I stopped and turned around with thought and wonder. The fly was flying around me even more. I asked, "Jaden is that you!?"

I felt so silly asking that to a fly, but in the same breath of wonder, I reached out my hand and asked, "Jaden, if that is you coming to say hi as this little fly, can you come land in my hand?" As soon as I said that the fly landed in my hand and stayed there staring at me!

I was perplexed but so intrigued. I started talking to Jaden out loud and thanking him for showing me that he was still with me. I felt so silly talking to this little fly in my hand and thought, am I losing my mind? I then asked Jaden, "If this really is your spirit coming to say hello can you give me another sign?" As soon as I asked that, the little fly walked from the palm of my hand up to my forearm and did a complete circle around the new SpongeBob tattoo with Jaden's name I got in memory of him! I was so blown away and so amazed at the same time.

I thanked Jaden, and the fly for coming to say hi, and then the little fly flew off. However, it would not be the last time Jaden has used a fly to come and say hello in a tangible way. He has done this repeatedly over the years, and I have even captured it on video many times since then. At first, I was confused, was my son now living as a fly? Soon after, I learned that everything is energy, and spirit energy can manipulate or emerge with anything else to bring us those signs of hope and love in many ways from the afterlife.

Over the months, I would receive so many other amazing signs from Jaden. He has left me pennies at my feet out of nowhere, white feathers would fall in front of me in my house. I received very clear communication with Jaden's voice through the TV or coming through the radio stations. Lights would go off and on.

Jaden would also send individuals with Down syndrome in my direction to give me hugs. For Jaden's first birthday in Heaven, I bought him an Elmo foil balloon. It would follow us around the house, and that balloon stayed in the air for about a month-and-a-half after.

After about eight months, I got another incredible spirit visit from my son. I was lying down one night, and just as I was about to doze off, I felt tugging on my arm pretty strong and heard Jaden calling out, "Mom, Mom, wake up." I opened my eyes, and my son was very clearly standing right next to my bed. I looked at him, and he said, "Mom, come on, get up, let's go!"

As I wiped my eyes and sat up in bed, Jaden said again, "Mom, come play!" He took off and ran from my room across the hall to his bedroom and flipped the light on. I was calmly amazed to see my son looking so alive and so happy again. So, I jumped out of bed and followed him into his bedroom. He was jumping up and down on his bed, laughing. I walked over to him smiling, and he jumped from the bed into my arms. We just hugged a moment as he slid down on his feet and darted out of his bedroom into the kitchen, and said, "Come on, Mom, let's play!" So, I followed Jaden around the house playing, flipping the lights off and on as he always did in life. I remember noticing that my son's Down Syndrome features were more subtle, and his scars were gone from all of his many surgeries. He looked so well and more alive than ever. After a while, I told my son, "I love you. Mommy's going to go back to bed now." He looked up and said, "Okay, Mom, I am not going anywhere. We have so much more to do, learn, and teach others together."

I nodded my head with a soft smile in complete agreeance and went back to bed. The next morning, I woke up with this very strong and clear understanding that my son and I would work together to share his story and perspectives from the heavens. To have an opportunity with a voice and a chance to speak about his life and help teach others from his experience.

So, in 2014 that is just what we did. We formed a Facebook group called *Jaden's Way Speaks From Heaven* and collaborated with some beautifully gifted mediums to channel Jaden and share his story with all.

Now in 2022, I would like to give Jaden a chance to provide us with some of his feedback on the afterlife. (As channeled by psychic medium Michelle Grey)

Mom: Well, hello, my beautiful son!

Jaden: Hi Momma!

(Jaden comes in wearing a t-shirt, jeans, black and white sneakers, a baseball cap, and a red superhero cape).

Mom: So, since we are writing this wonderful chapter together, I wanted to ask you some questions about the afterlife, signs from your loved ones, and so forth from your experience…

Jaden: Of course, Mom, let's do it!

Mom: Wonderful, Sweetie! So, I want our first question to be about you so our readers can get a little better understanding of you. So briefly, many people want to understand why you chose to come into the flesh with Down Syndrome, Autism, and to be so medically fragile?

Jaden: Hm, that's a big one. First of all, I just want to say, when some "neurotypical" people look at me and my life with disabilities, which I call super abilities, and say or think, oh that is really unfortunate, or that is a really sad life, or I can't imagine being in that position, etc. From my point of view, coming into my life and body

392

was not sad to me. My life was all I knew. In fact, my life was full of feeling, love, and color. Sure, there were times that I couldn't say or express how I felt in ways I wished I could or times I felt captive in my own body or felt frustration, absolutely as all of us do in life. But that was my human condition and what I planned for before I was born. Why? So, I can experience the world in a more tactical way, communicate with my body in different ways, and see life through my eyes and from this perspective. It was like a kaleidoscope, and I could see, hear, and feel in layers. What I mean by that is when your other senses are taken away, it's like the volume gets turned up in other areas. I also came in for you, Mom, my family, and so many more. It was like soul family planning. I also feel life experience is not about longevity, it is about richness, and I got that!

Mom: Yes, you did, Son, and I agree, it's not about quantity but quality.

Jaden: Exactly, exactly!

Mom: My next question for you is what was your transition like to the afterlife or which word do you prefer?

Jaden: I call it Home because it is our real home. What is it like to transition? Well, it feels like a butterfly. It is like a caterpillar that is in a cocoon, and when it is time to break out of that cocoon, a beautiful, brilliant, bright yellow butterfly bursts free. It is so light and free, like gliding on the wind with zero heaviness or anything weighing it down. It is like being carried in the loving arms of your mother, father, and everything you love all at once. It feels like being hooked in through the heart space with liquid gold.

Mom: Wow, Son, how amazing! Okay, honey, my other question is, how are signs from our loved ones achieved? What does the process of that look like? One of your most notorious ways of coming to me was with a fly so let's start with that.

Jaden: (big smile) So for the fly, as with birds, butterflies, or anything else, everything is consciousness. You can think of it as a network, and everything living is connected and interwoven within that network. This network almost looks like a grid with all these little wires running through it. In spirit, we are still connected to the network. The only difference is that we have the ability to see the whole network, not just an aspect of it. Human beings, for the most part, tend to walk around with a sort of shield or blinders on, so they are not as easily influenced. But things like birds, butterflies, babies, animals, and the like are very open and easier to influence to give signs from spirit because they are pure form and it's very natural to them. It's like a little door in their brains that is wide open, and there is a wire running along through that door, and spirit can send a signal down through that wire to the brain that says move over that way or go that way. Oh, just like when you would get hugs from me through individuals with Down Syndrome mom.

Me: Oh my gosh, Son, yes!

Jaden: So, in those cases, Mom, you would be out at the grocery store or coffee shop, and a person with Down Syndrome would be walking in your direction, so I would send a signal through that wire that says, see that woman walking towards you, could you please give her a hug for me, thank you. Then the person with Down Syndrome would give you a hug from me.

Mom: (my eyes tear up) I loved those hugs so much, son. There were just days I missed that beautiful DS face and energy. I had received so many hugs over the years from the time you died from random individuals with DS, I always knew those hugs were sent from you, Son, and I was always so thankful for them.

Jaden: You're always so welcome, Mom! Another thing while we are on the topic, almost all individuals with Down Syndrome and Autism are very open to spirit, again pure form. They can usually feel, sense, or even see spirit.

Mom: That makes a lot of sense. I can see that, Son. Can it also be difficult for our loved ones to send us signs?

Jaden: Sometimes, it can depend on the atmosphere, conditions, or frequency. Meaning it is harder to send those signals through if there is a lot of heaviness, dense or busy thoughts, closed off, lack of faith, etc. There needs to be light, easy, open, free-flowing energy coursing through the network. Think of it like the internet. It can get backed up and run slow when more people are online, making it a bit more difficult to send a signal successfully along the network.

Mom: So fascinating.

Jaden: It also depends on the soul of your loved one because each soul can do things differently from the next. Some humans will often feel or think, well, why doesn't my loved one in spirit send me signs like that or appear in front of me? Maybe I am

394

not loved as much or worthy enough? Some readers may even be thinking this right now, but that is not it at all. It takes a lot of energy to get our signs and messages across, so please know your loved ones are trying to reach out.

Mom: So, to kinda sum it up, the messages or signs from our loved ones in spirit are achieved through consciousness, influence, and intent, right?

Jaden: You got it, Mom!

Mom: Okay, Sweetie, my next question is, what do you do in Heaven?

Jaden: Oh boy, there are tons and tons of things to do in the heavens. For me, I like to run and play, ride my go-cart, hang out with my friends and families here and on earth. I am also a guide not only to you and my family but also to many around the world, as well. I help guide a lot of individuals and their families with specific needs. Heaven/Home is pretty much tailored uniquely to each soul experience.

Mom: Okay, Honey, my last question is, what would be your most important advice for those going through loss and the grieving process?

Jaden: For all that are reading this, it's to know that we never really "lose" our loved ones. One of the biggest reasons my mom and I are doing this work together is to help give others some bit of peace and faith that this life on earth is all part of the human experience, but just a small part of who we truly are. We simply shed our physical bodies, but that's about it. We also need to acknowledge that the grieving process is also very real for humans, just as it is valuable. Mom, you know firsthand that there are a lot of golden nuggets in the process of grieving.

Mom: So many.

Jaden: We need to remember to be compassionate and gentle with ourselves. To begin to understand that we ARE with you every step of the way. So, when you feel ready, reach out to your loved ones in spirit, talk to them, and feel that unbreakable love in your heart space that never dies.

Mom: Beautiful. Thank you so much, Son!

Our passion and work together are to share Jaden's story with others about the afterlife, Jaden's transition Home, and to give others a soft reminder of peace, faith, and healing. To be able to channel other amazing spirits from the heavens who also lived life with disabilities or who were unable to speak in life, to share their own stories, heal, and to learn together.

What my son has taught me throughout his life on earth and now from the heavens has changed my entire outlook on life and death. In life, he taught me such compassion not only for others but for myself as well. He taught me the value of surrender. Jaden taught me how to truly live. He taught me grace, mercy, the value of vulnerability, patience, and love on a grand scale. He taught me how to laugh at a good poop joke and not take everything so seriously.

In death, Jaden has taught me that there truly is no death. We shed our physical bodies but continue on in spirit form.

We are all energy, and that energy can not be destroyed; it simply changes from one form to another. I also no longer fear death or see death as the end. Jaden helped me understand that the grey-haired men I was talking to were actually my heavenly council and that I was about to die of a broken heart, but with so much love and grace, Jaden took my place instead.

Jaden has taught me, our family, and so many friends around the world, about his story, his love, faith, his healing hugs, spiritual guidance, and we would love to share it with you too.

About the Authors

Come check out Jaden and Jessica on Facebook and say hi. They can be found under Jessica Marie Tatro, and *Jaden's Way Speaks From Heaven* Facebook group.

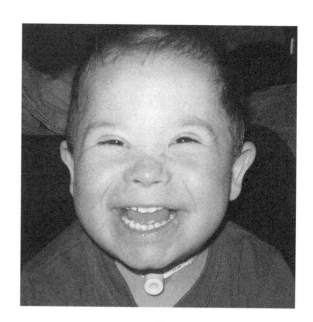

Jaden

Jaden and Jessica

> *"What happens after death is so unspeakably glorious that our imagination and our feelings do not suffice to form even an approximate conception of it. The dissolution of our time-bound form in eternity brings no loss of meaning."*
> *~Carl Jung~*
> *Psychiatrist, Psychoanalyst*
> *1875 – 1961*

Mirrors, *Sharon Kotchetovsky*

By Sharon Kotchetovsky

I live in Bucks County, PA, with my husband of 43 years. Together, we raised three children. Our son Scottie was/is our youngest. We have two daughters, and through a lot of joy, laughter, emotional upheaval, and struggle, we have always put family first. My husband and I come from families of long marriages and several siblings. Having children was something we discussed just a few months into our relationship. We were confident that we would be good parents. But, like a lot of parents, we were woefully unprepared for most of the challenges we would face in raising our children. That is not to say we had nothing but challenges. We have beautiful, wonderful, funny memories of dance recitals, art shows, Christmases, birthdays, vacations, hockey, gymnastics. The list goes on and on. The years of raising our three children were the happiest times of our lives, and neither of us has a lot of regrets about those years. With that said, since the death of our youngest and even before that when he was struggling with alcoholism and drug addiction, we (me especially) have lamented over things we should have done or could have done to be better parents.

We are not and have never been particularly religious, although we both have our beliefs and personal understandings of spiritual values and a shared interest in the mystery of consciousness. It was not a subject or a philosophy we brought up in everyday conversations with our children as they grew up. Still, it was/is something that we don't avoid talking about when mysterious phenomena and life challenges present themselves in our lives.

We were in our early twenties when we got married and had all three of our children before I reached the age of twenty-nine. I, much more than my husband, often wonder if the fact that we were young, immature parents contributed to the alcohol and drug abuse that two of our children went through in their late teens and twenties. With everything that I have read and listened to, before and since the death of our son, about trauma and addiction, I have often been racked with guilt for things I did or said, or didn't do or say in their younger years, which may have contributed to their choices and the struggles that ensued because of those choices. I know by being a member of the wonderful organization Helping Parents Heal that many parents have had similar dilemmas. But knowing that and reading the posts of other parents on the HPH Facebook page did not always work to relieve my guilt. That was something I had to work through and walk through daily for many months after our son passed. The desperation of those feelings at times was overwhelming, along with the grief.

I have slowly begun to sort out some of this guilt and come to terms with the imperfect way I parented. I have worked diligently through meditation, prayer, journaling, and reading to forgive my shortcomings and remind myself not to forget the things I did that helped my kids. I worked to keep an open mind to learn all I could about addiction and how it can present itself in some very tricky ways. We, as a family, have learned to overcome the stigma of addiction and alcoholism and accept it as a condition that needs to be handled with respect and love rather than shunning and shame.

When I was pregnant with my first child, my imagination would always see a little boy with dark curly hair. That is probably just a typical fantasy of a pregnant woman dreaming of what her child might look like. By the time I was pregnant with my third child (Scottie), I was pretty sure I would be having another little girl based on my first to two pregnancies. How little we know of what is to come. In those days, ultrasounds were done, but they didn't always reveal the sex of the child, so we were prepared for anything.

When the day came, and I went into labor, I was calm, the day was warm for March, and I felt ready. When his head emerged, my first thought was, "She looks just like her sisters." Then that little body (well, not that little – 8.6lbs) slid out, and Wow!!! I was thrilled, amazed, ecstatic! We had a boy! I was a proud mother. In fact, this feeling of pride for my children never faded for me. No matter what trouble they got into or what struggles they had, I always had a sense of pride that they were mine. I knew their gifts and talents. I had faith in their strong personalities. I know children are never really ours. As Kahlil Gibrand says in The Prophet, "Your children are not your children. They are the sons and daughters of Life's longing for itself." (Gibrand, Kahlil, 1927, The Prophet, Alfred A. Knopf) But most parents tend to take ownership of and responsibility for their children from the second they are born, and it is a confusing lesson to learn that you can't always, and sometimes actually shouldn't, take care of your child for too long.

This little boy stole my heart. Not because he was a big smiler, he didn't giggle very often, and he took longer to speak words than either of his sisters. There was something thoughtful about him, something serious about him. People would say that he takes after my husband, who is also a man of few words like his son. I just sensed something introspective about him, and I was a little too protective of him at times. My daughters, in their teen years, would often tell me, "He's your favorite." I would joke with them about it, saying things like, "He is just easy." In many ways, raising a boy was a little easier than raising girls. Don't get me wrong, I love my daughters like crazy, and they each know it. I can't explain my fascination with Scottie... He still fascinates me in many ways. I miss him with such a longing that I find it hard to think straight.

After ten-plus years of struggling to overcome alcoholism and drug addiction, our son took matters into his own hands and intentionally overdosed on fentanyl and heroin. In his true, kind, considerate way, he sent our family a group text to let us know he was "leaving". The sheer panic that ensued in the hours that followed that text can't be described. Our hearts and souls will never be what they were when he was in our company. He knew we loved him more than anyone in his life loved him, but, in his mind, he seemed to think this would be the best thing he could do to keep us from worrying about him or continuing to try to help him get "better."

The place in my heart that still has a hole in it can never be filled by anyone but him. However, the dreams, signs, and synchronicities that have occurred since he left this world have been so incredible that it is impossible to believe that he is "really" gone.

In fact, for me, he has never been gone. I often talk to him out loud and sometimes laugh at the responses I get in my mind. I made the decision to contribute my chapter about him to this anthology, and two days later, I had a dream of him telling me he was writing a book about something that would explain something. I feel he is with me as I write this.

My communication with my son has come to me in dreams and signs, both physical and mental, and in what the famous and often quoted founder of psychoanalysis, Carl Jung, described as synchronicities. One of these synchronicities transpired as I was in the middle of reading *Memories, Dreams, Reflections* by C.G. Jung (1989, Random House). I had a dream where I was holding a small mirror, and I saw Scottie standing behind me. The next day, I went back to reading the book, and in chapter XI, On Life after Death, I came to a page where he is exploring the concept that the dead know only what they knew at the time of their death, Carl Jung states "Hence their endeavor to penetrate into life in order to share in the knowledge of men. I frequently have a feeling that they are standing directly behind us, waiting to hear what answer we will give them and what answer to destiny." When I read this, I froze. I thought of that dream the night before, where Scottie was standing behind me in the mirror. It gave me the feeling that he was so near and so interested in what I was doing.

In the first months that we, as parents, were becoming aware of Scottie's battle with alcoholism, before any drug use, we were in denial. Afterall, he was a teenager and, like many teenagers, had tried drinking at parties, and he would grow out of it. It took us a couple of years to come to the realization that he was not like most teenagers, he could not control his urge to drink, and it had become something he was doing on a daily basis. By this time, we were on high alert and in complete rescue mode. However, we were still convinced that we could talk him out of it with suggestions of sticking with his woodworking hobby, pursuing his music, continuing to play ice hockey. We thought we knew a lot about alcoholism because both my husband and I had siblings, parents, and grandparents who had their lives ruined by this addiction. My own brother had died in 2006 as he daringly crossed a highway while under the influence. This was an uncle that my son adored as a child, and when he started facing his own struggles with alcohol, he asked me if I thought he was like my brother. At that time, I could not fathom it, and I said, "No."

As the months turned into years, there were rehabs, meetings, counseling, and even two months in county prison. After those two months, Scottie stuck to a program and stayed clean and sober for three years. All was going well. He had a young woman he loved. He was working in an apprenticeship program with the Ironworkers Union several nights a week, attending AA meetings, even speaking at large meetings as a guest. He was engaged when he and his fiancée decided that having a drink on weekends was probably safe. As we waited and watched, his world began to fall apart.

By the end of that third year of sobriety, he was once again struggling with drinking and now heroin. For the next four years, there were several stays in rehabs, most for no more than thirty days which is what insurance would cover. The longest stay was ninety days. We all thought, this is it, he's on his way! He had made such a commitment! He made good friends even though most of them were from other states. He was back to work. He was going to meetings, or so we thought. Somewhere in the months between December of 2015 and March of 2016, I began to realize that he was once again struggling to maintain sobriety. He turned 30 in March, and when I called to wish him a happy birthday, I knew.

By April of 2016, he returned to a familiar rehab, but I didn't feel the relief I had felt in the past when he had checked into rehab. I also didn't get a feeling from him that he was enthusiastic about recovery or anything else. I was getting scared. For the next two months after he checked out of rehab, it was touch and go. We (me, my daughters, my husband) knew he was struggling with the addictions and with his mental health. He had been diagnosed with anxiety and depression at the rehabs he had been in but refused to continue with the medications that had been prescribed. I think once he left rehab, he was determined to get healthy without medication. He must have wanted so badly to be strong or "normal" and really just wanted to leave this perceived weakness behind him.

In June of 2016, he picked up a girlfriend from rehab and set out across the country without letting us know he was leaving. At that time, he had been staying with us because his house was for sale. He had wanted to move a little closer to us or possibly go back to Florida, where he had success with rehab and made close friends. None of these things were ever to happen. Once he returned from his trip across the country, things were going downhill fast. He was facing jail time for an earlier DUI he had gotten while sitting in his parked car. He did not want to return to rehab, believing it was just a waste of money. He was sad and aimless and addicted to heroin. We pleaded with him. We asked him whether he was afraid of dying with these drugs, which we knew now were often laced with fentanyl. His response was, "I don't want to die, but I'm not afraid." He said this because he was convinced that he could control his doses, and if he could do that, he could control the disease.

This timeline is painful to recount, and it doesn't paint the whole portrait of Scottie. It only describes his downfall, his only downfall, albeit a deadly one. What I wanted to shout from the rooftop in the days and months after Scottie left this world was this: I learned from this beautiful human being how to be a better person. His sensitivity toward others was apparent even as a small child.

Once, after a family gathering, while coming home in the car, we were all pointing out the difficult personalities and character flaws of some of the people we had just spent time with. My son, who was about eight years old at the time, said things like, "I think he's funny, or I like her, or she was nice to me." We stopped immediately, ashamed of ourselves for only pointing out the others' flaws. I never forgot that. Scottie was like that, always seeing the good qualities of another person and giving them credit for their gifts or talents. He was patient. He could wait for hours while I tried to learn a song he liked on the piano, repeating the sequence of notes over and over again until I got it. He would sit with his nephew, watching him build something out of Legos with his tiny fingers and never interfere or take over to get the project done faster. He wasn't the loudest one in the room, but he had impeccable timing and was often the funniest one. He did a perfect imitation of his dad that would have the rest of us holding our sides in laughter. He mastered any skill he set his mind to, whether it was building a crane tower out of Kinex at age nine or playing a difficult riff on the guitar that he mostly learned to play on his own. He would practice for hours and take his guitar everywhere.

He was charming in a quiet way. When he walked into a gathering in his cool, quiet way, people gravitated to him, feeling his warmth and acceptance. Animals gravitated to him too. On one occasion, at a lake with a group of friends, a duck swam up to him as he floated on a raft. His friends were dumbfounded because this duck would not leave his side. That duck stayed with him in and out of the water for over an hour! His friends still mention it in Facebook posts. I told this story at his funeral because the duck is a symbol of connection to family and friends, according to the renowned intuitive Colette Baron-Reid.

He was kind to the point that I feel it could have been a weakness because his sensitivity toward another person's insecurity could be too allowing at times. He did have a temper, and it could be quick and strike with force but only when pushed to the brink. That unpredictable, hidden temper got him in trouble a few times when he was drinking and left him with guilt that he could not resolve. He had a very hard time forgiving himself even long after others had forgiven him.

My first dream communication came two months after losing Scottie. In that dream, we were standing in a pool. I hugged him, and he hugged me. We were both crying. He said, "You can't understand." He dove away, and I couldn't find him. Then, one of my grandsons pointed him out to me. As he stood up in the pool, I said, "I just want to talk to you. I won't take up too much of your time." He dove away again. That dream was so real. I felt him hugging me. I felt him crying. I have spent the last five-plus years on a mission to understand. I still don't completely understand, and I have come to terms with the fact that I never will, but since that time, I have explored more about consciousness and our eternal spirits than I ever would have had I not had the life-altering experience of losing my precious son.

With his guitar playing and singing skills, Scottie often entertained small crowds at parties and open-mike nights. He loved to play and sing Johnny Cash songs, and his deep voice was so much like Cash's that it was uncanny. A crowd favorite was *I Walk the Line*. About three months after his death, my daughters and I were out to lunch at a very nice restaurant in Phila, the type of restaurant where you might hear some trendy jazz playing or maybe some cool Latin playlist. As we sat down at the beautifully set table, I said, "Listen." We froze. The song playing was *I Walk the Line* by Johnny Cash. We knew somehow Scottie had joined us for lunch.

Another dream I had in the first year that was so visceral I was sure I had been with him was of him sitting in the back seat of my car, and his dad was asleep in the passenger's seat. Scottie's arm was resting on the center console, and I was holding his arm and leaning on his shoulder. Meanwhile, his other hand was on his dad's shoulder as he slept. I turned and said, "I wish you could stay and hang out." He nodded, but he had a duffle bag with him, and he got out of the car. This dream reminded me of the times of departure we had when he would leave to go to rehab.

Then, there was the morning I was sure that I woke up and he was standing at the bedside. I said, "You're here!" He looked wonderful with his plaid flannel shirt on and baseball cap. Then, I actually did wake up, and to this day, I can't tell if I dreamed it, or he actually appeared there.

The physical signs I have received have been many. About four months after his passing, while on the phone talking about him to his girlfriend, a heart shape formed on the griddle I was drying. I had cleaned the griddle and turned the flame on to dry it. This heart shape was an exact replica of the heart rock he had given me one day when he was a small boy. I have kept that rock on my windowsill in the kitchen ever since that day. I took it as a vivid sign that Scottie was in on this conversation that I was having with his girlfriend. I have tried since then to dry that griddle over the flame and have never seen that heart shape appear again.

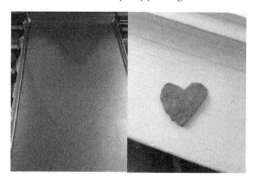

Another astonishing physical sign I got and then questioned for hours was a day after I sat with the first medium I had ever seen. Before losing my son, I will admit, I thought mediums were in the category of fortune-tellers. They were for people's entertainment at parties or events or TV shows. Several months into my grief, a friend who lost her son to suicide just five months before my son took his own life, questioned me about whether I had seen a medium. I said, "No, I don't think I'm ready for that." She had been to see this young woman whom she was extremely impressed with and recommended that I see her. I was so nervous about seeing this medium I didn't even tell my family or close friends, thinking that they would either not approve or just feel sorry for me that I would go to such lengths to try to see my son. Anyway, that sitting was literally head expanding. I felt like my head had grown in size when I got in the car to leave. During that sitting, the medium mentioned hair several times (along with other incredible evidence), but she wasn't sure why and I couldn't help her. I was just so overwhelmed with the other facts about my son she was telling me. How could she possibly know this stuff??

So, a little back story. I have my children's graduation portraits sitting on a chest of drawers in a room upstairs. Before my son went to have his portrait taken in his junior year of high school, he had grown his hair out. His hair was very thick and curly, just like I imagined during my first pregnancy. I begged him to get his hair cut before having his photo for the yearbook taken, telling him he would regret it later if he didn't. Nope. He wasn't going to do it. But, the day after the photo was taken, he went and got his hair cut short. Just to get me, I swear. We laughed about that a lot as the years went by.

Anyway, back to the incident. The day after that first reading, in the early evening, I stood next to this chest of drawers with the senior portraits on it. I was just standing there staring out the window because the sun was going down, and it was pretty. Then, boom! This framed photo of him falls forward. I froze in my tracks, wondering how in the hell it fell over because it was one of those that lean back on a stand, but it had fallen forward, face down. I checked for any water from the plants around it. I checked the window — it was closed. There were no fans in the room. I couldn't figure it out, but my adrenaline was pumping. The next day, I knelt in front of this photo staring at it, and it hit me - the hair! That's what all the talk of hair was about in that reading that I couldn't relate to at the time. I am convinced that my son's energy was in that room as I stood by that window that evening, and he used it to push that framed photo over. As if to say, "Mom! My Hair, My Hair! Now, do you get it?!?" I could feel him laughing at me.

I have to say something about numbers here. Scottie passed on 6/22/2016. Since that time, as haunting as it may seem, I have seen the number 622 so many times on clocks, license plates, road signs, etc. My daughter has also seen it repeatedly, and we often notify each other when it starts popping up for us. His birthday is 3/08/1986, and that number appears in some very synchronistic ways, too. On his first birthday without him, my daughter and I went to breakfast to talk about him. We were both still very sad, but we were talking about seeing 622 showing up all the time. We finished eating our breakfast which wasn't much, and the waitress put the bill on the table. We turned it over and gasped. It was $6.22 - he definitely likes to hang out with us.

I have five or six thick journals now, mostly about dreams, signs, meditations, synchronicities, and a lot of soul-searching questions. I keep track of the signs. I take photos when I can.

My son had to write a song in one of the rehabs as a therapy practice. My husband and I happened to be visiting him as he was writing it, and I helped him write some verses. The song was titled "I'm Amazing". After he died, I turned it into "You're Amazing" in my own head and decided to get a license plate that reads URMAZNG. One day, I was driving in the rain, in a very down mood and feeling very frustrated. I said, "Please! I need a sign." Not long after I said that I was sitting at the light, and the car next to me honked. My first thought was, "What the hell?" I looked over to see two young guys trying to tell me something. Reluctantly, I rolled down the window to hear them say, "You're Amazing! Your license plate!" I was so taken off guard that I just smiled and said thank you. Then, it occurred to me — my sign! Thank you, Scottie! You're Amazing!

As I write this, it has been over five and a half years since I saw Scottie, yet I feel like my relationship with him has developed into a more open communication. I noticed this began becoming more evident to me as I slowly let go of my guilt and many of my fears that he might not be happy. I realize that those are very human worries and concerns, so I forgive myself for not understanding that sooner. These days, my interactions and conversations with my son are a little easier, and as that began to happen, I've noticed that my dreams of him have become more casual and less full of my worries and concerns. I wonder if he were still here with us, would our relationship have progressed like this. Of course, I will never know that, but for some reason, it gives me comfort to think that it would have been similar. I love you, Scottie. You're my favorite boy in the whole wide world. I can see you rolling your eyes and laughing at me.

One more thing. I took a break from writing this chapter to go on a planned camping trip that lasted eighteen days. While traveling, I was also working on poems for a class I was taking. The teacher of the class would send us "seed" ideas each week. So, a few days ago, I wrote down several ideas for a poem. One was about a visit from a cardinal that had taken place about three or four years ago, just one to two years after Scottie had transitioned. I took an early morning walk to decide about which idea I wanted to write. When I returned to our site, I sat in the chair, and my attention was drawn to my left because of a familiar bird call. There sat a cardinal in a branch in the only tree at our campsite. The incident that I wrote the poem about was this: One morning (that three to four years ago), getting ready to take a walk, I stood in front of a mirror and saw a cardinal in the pine tree behind me, outside the window. I thought about my friend who said cardinals were always her sign for her mother. I sort of froze and thought, "Could that be a sign from Scottie?" Well, for the next two weeks, that cardinal returned several times. Not only did he return, but he tapped on that window many times, drawing me from other rooms to see what the noise was and every time it was him. I had an overwhelming knowing that my son was doing his best to let me know, "I'm still here!"

About the Author

Sharon Kotchetovsky lives in Bucks County, PA with her husband of forty-three years and their three children, two daughters and a son (in spirit). All Sharon's occupations since becoming a parent offered her the time to be around her growing children and to satisfy some of her interests. Sharon was a mortgage loan officer for twelve years and a realtor for nine years. She is now retired and spends her time taking poetry and writing classes. She enjoys yoga which she has practiced for the past fifteen years and walking near her home. She also loves to golf with her husband. Sharon and her husband recently purchased a travel trailer in which they have taken several trips and plan to take more in the near future. She always has her journal with her to record a dream or a sign that she knows will occur.

"Life and death are one thread,
the same line viewed
from different sides."
~Lao-Tzu~
Chinese Philosopher
6th Century BC

Remember the Love, *Pearl & Maxie Richman*

By Pearl and Maxie Richman

Pearl

I was born on August 25th, 1958. My father was a Holocaust survivor who married my Canadian-born mother. I was the youngest of three girls, my sister Annabelle being the eldest and my sister Arlene being the middle child. We were each four years apart, but despite our age gap, we were bonded by the trauma and chaos of our family dynamic. My father was extremely abusive on many levels, and although I did not bear the brunt of it, I was a witness to its ramifications and existed in a climate of pain, volatility, and unpredictability. My mother was a constant source of comfort and guidance through these years despite her own suffering. She did her best to keep our family together, but unfortunately, the weight of the damage was too heavy to carry. When I was twelve years old, she made the difficult decision to leave my father in order to protect my sisters and me. Even though divorce was frowned upon at this time, she knew she needed to get us away from him to ensure our safety and, frankly, our survival.

Arlene was an incredibly intelligent, beautiful, and talented woman, but unfortunately, the years of abuse she suffered manifested in severe addiction and mental illness. She fought this battle for the majority of her adult life until "the pain became too excruciating" to live, which were the words she left in her suicide note. She ended her life on December 28th, 1999, at the age of 47.

Annabelle was my protector and loved me fiercely. There was no one I laughed harder with. She was brilliant, creative, artistically gifted, passionate about social justice issues, and had an inner strength and magnetic energy that was undeniable. She was

410

an incredibly talented counsellor and turned her traumatic history into her mission: to help and advocate for abused women and children. She founded a charity called Court Support and Counselling Services, which supported women through the process of bringing their abusers to justice. She was inspired by her own experience of being the first woman in Canada to pursue charges of incest in federal court after the statute of limitations was lifted. That being said, after years of failed relationships and poor physical health, her mental health began to decline. As she continued to lose her independence, her will to live was also lost. She ended her life on her own terms on October 23rd, 2016.

My life took a more promising direction. After my mother left the marriage, we were left with nothing and had to rebuild our lives. My mother and I were each other's lifelines, and we were inextricably bound together. I went on to university to become a teacher, while my mother began York University as a mature student with a grade 8 education. She went on to become a master's in social work. I got married and had a family. My husband Steven and I wanted to create an atmosphere of safety, unconditional love, and transparency for our family. We have two beautiful children, Maxie and Cole, who became the centre of our world. Even though my shared history with Anabelle and Arlene was traumatic, somehow, I was able to create a beautiful life for myself and my family. I felt that it was my responsibility to end the cycle of abuse…and I did. Annabelle and Arlene were an incredibly important part of Maxie and Cole's childhood and upbringing. Time spent with my kids was the happiest and most fulfilled I've ever seen my sisters. Annabelle and Arlene both left an indelible imprint on both of them.

Maxie

I was born on July 12th, 1990. Some of my earliest and most joyful memories revolve around time spent with both Anabelle and Arlene, or 'Abelle' and 'Aunty Ar' as I called them. Because neither had their own children, my brother Cole and I were treated as their own. I remember playing 'Boom Chugga Chugga' with Arlene, where she would bounce me on her knees and let me fall through her legs as she caught me, both of us squealing with joyous laughter. Because I was so young when she passed, my memories of her have faded, but the love I hold in my heart for her will never die. Annabelle and I had an extraordinary connection. We are alike in so many ways, and she often told me she thought I came from the wrong womb! She would take my brother and I on so many adventures; to the exhibition, on long drives to see the Christmas lights, to Chinatown to try exotic fruits, and she would create story worlds that were infused with moral lessons, like 'Jimmy the Litterbug' who warned us of the dangers of smoking and littering and 'Peter the Polar Bear' who advocated for climate change reform. Over the years, as I grew up, our relationship developed into more of a friendship. We would spend hours at her apartment talking, laughing, cooking, and listening to soul music on her record player. She would always have special treats at her house that I wasn't allowed at home, like bacon and cinnamon buns. We were so close that I came out to her about my sexuality two years before I told the rest of my family and friends, including my parents. I loved both of my aunts fiercely, and although they are not here physically, I feel their spirit and their love guiding and protecting me every single day.

The experiences enclosed in this chapter are reflective of our individual and collective experiences with the afterlife. Our journey towards spirit started after Arlene passed away, but our awareness of signs was awakened in 2016 after the passing of Annabelle. As such, the experiences outlined in this chapter are more closely associated with her. Although we feel the presence of Arlene, we've had more profound moments of spiritual connection with Annabelle.

Pearl

Since Arlene passed away, I was continually visited by a red cardinal in my backyard. I wasn't aware at the time that cardinals are said to represent our loved ones lost. I was always so comforted by their presence that I knew they had to mean something profound. Once, I was driving up north and when I looked to my right, travelling alongside my car window was a cardinal...I just knew it was Arlene, and I smiled. Another time, many years later, after both Arlene and Annabelle died, I was walking along Alcorn Ave. on a bright, sunny day and to my delight, right on the sidewalk directly in front of me there were two bickering cardinals, pecking at each other. I stopped and smiled because I knew it was them. I greeted them by saying, "Hi Annie and Ar!" and then they flew off. It was so comforting to know they were together. My belief that the cardinals were visits from heaven was confirmed the first time I met with a medium 22 years ago, just after Arlene passed away. Just as she began the session, she asked me if I had an affinity toward cardinals. I was so anxious about the session and the notion of cardinals representing my sisters that I burst into tears and said a resounding, "Yes!". She told me to turn around and look out the window. And there, to my astonishment, was a cardinal perched on a birdbath. It stayed there for a good 15 minutes. I cannot tell you how comforting that was because I knew Arlene was with me during that profound reading.

412

Arlene

Annabelle

A couple of weeks after Annabelle passed away, I woke from a fitful sleep with a very strong vision. My sister appeared to me, screaming with urgency, "Sell the condo, sell the condo!!" I could recall the vision with such clarity. It was as if she were right there. Her white hair and beautiful blue eyes implored me to act. You see, all Annabelle wanted to do was leave a financial legacy for Maxie and Cole. That's why she bought the condo in the first place... so that she had something of substance to leave them when she died. Little did she know that her impact, on so many levels, was far greater and more enduring than she could ever have imagined.

Maxie

I was in New York in February of 2016, 4 months after Annabelle passed away, with one of my close friends as a weekend getaway. At the time, I was in a lot of emotional pain for many reasons, one of which was the loss of my aunt which left a huge void in my heart. One day we were walking through the streets of New York aimlessly, and I saw a man on the street right in front of me selling Mangosteens. Importantly, Mangosteens are native to Indonesia and Malaysia and are hard to come by in North America, let alone on the streets of New York. However, during one of our fruit tours of the markets in Chinatown, Annabelle and I discovered this delicious fruit, and it quickly became our favourite. She would often bring them over as a treat, and we would search for them on our subsequent visits to the markets.

I would have bumped right into him if I hadn't seen the man selling the mangosteens! Something from deep within me told me to buy a bag, so I listened. When I had the bag in my hands, I opened it to pick one out, but I heard a soft, gentle voice that said, "Wait," and again, I listened. We must have walked at least two more hours, stopping at different art vendors on the street and retail stores selling clothing and souvenirs, all as I was carrying the precious bag of fruit with me. We walked and walked until finally, we ended up on the High Line overlooking the Hudson River. We were exhausted from our walk and took a moment to sit and rest on two lounge chairs we found. My friend was lying down on one and me on another. She had her headphones in listening to some music, yet again, I heard that same gentle, quiet voice. This time it whispered, "Now." And again, I listened. I slowly began to reach into the bag, pick out one of the fruits, and peel it. I removed one of the segments and put it in my mouth, savouring every bite of the sweet, juicy flesh. At that very moment, I felt an overwhelming sense of euphoria. It is difficult to describe, but it was a sense of peace and tranquillity that I hadn't felt in years, or ever! It honestly felt as if Anabelle was wrapping her arms around me and her spirit entered my body, calming me and soothing my emotional unrest. The feeling lasted the entire time I was eating the Mangosteens, and just as quickly as it came on, it ceased. I knew it was her. I felt her entire presence surrounding me and holding my pain for me. Even if just briefly, I knew that she was trying to comfort me and that the peace I felt was an extension of what she was feeling, wherever she was. It took me a few minutes to get my bearings after this profound experience. My friend and I got up from our chairs and started to walk down the Highline towards the exit. As we were leaving, I came across a mural that must have been at least 25 feet tall, with a poem written by the artist Zoe Leonard on it that read:

"I want a dyke for president I want a person with aids for president and a want a fag for vice president and I want someone with no health insurance, and I want someone who grew up in a place where the earth is so saturated with toxic waste that they didn't have a choice about getting leukemia. I want a president that had an abortion at sixteen and I want a candidate who isn't the lesser of two evils and I want a president who lost their last lover to AIDS, who still sees that in their eyes every time they lay down to rest, who held their lover in their arms and knew they were dying. I want a president with no airconditioning, a president who has stood on line at the clinic, at the DMV, at the welfare office and has been unemployed and layed off and sexually harassed and gaybashed and deported. I want someone who has spent the night in the tombs and had a cross burned on their lawn and survived rape. I want someone who has been in love and been hurt, who respects sex, who has made mistakes and learned from them. I want a Black woman for president. I want someone with bad teeth and an attitude, someone who has eaten that nasty hospital food, someone who crossdresses and has done drugs and been in therapy. I want someone who has committed civil disobedience. And I want to know why this isn't possible. I want to know why we started learning somewhere down the line that a president is always a clown; always a john and never a hooker. Always a boss and never a worker, always a liar, always a thief never caught."

415

And that was my aunt...always fighting for the underdog, always questioning power structures, and always thinking bigger and beyond the realities of our current state of being. I felt like that poem was her way of saying, "If you didn't think that was me, here I am." I had always wondered about the afterlife, but this was my first experience of being embodied by it.

Pearl and Maxie's Shared Experiences

To give the following section some context, throughout her life, Anabelle struggled with many physical limitations. She never felt at home in her body. As such, she did not want to carry this burden with her into her death and decided to be cremated rather than have a traditional Jewish burial. She always loved being in the water because that is where she felt weightless, which allowed her to be free of the constraints of her body. Her other wish was to have her ashes spread in the sea of her favourite place on earth, Barbados. She always spoke of feeling completely accepted and not judged when she was there. She had close friends that lived there that she felt very connected to and who she frequently visited until she could no longer travel due to her poor physical health. Six months after her death, we honoured her wish and took a trip to Barbados alongside two of her closest friends. The moment we landed and stepped off the plane, the four of us felt her presence and energy VERY strongly, and it stayed with us for the entirety of the trip. Once we settled in, we all gathered on the beach, took a collective deep breath, and took in the breathtaking beauty surrounding us. We knew in that moment why she loved this island so dearly.

The next morning, we met the captain at his boat. He was taking us out into the Caribbean Sea to honour her wishes. The boat was surprisingly beautiful.... how fitting for our Annabelle. The sun was sparkling, warm, and luminous. Annabelle would have described the day as a "sparkler"! After a 30-minute ride out, we decided on the spot that felt right. We brought fresh-cut flowers with us and started the ceremony, each speaking words of love about Annabelle. After each of us was done, we threw our flowers into the sea. We tenderly removed the box from the velvet bag containing her ashes. Then, gently, we each took some of her ashes and let the wind carry her to sea. While our music was playing, the song *Lost Boy* by Ruth B, came on. As we held her in our hands and began to sprinkle her ashes into the beautiful blue water, the lyrics gripped us:

"He sprinkled me in pixie dust and told me to believe

416

Believe in him and believe in me
Together, we will fly away in a cloud of green
To your beautiful destiny
As we soared above the town that never loved me
I realized I finally had a family
Soon enough, we reached Neverland
Peacefully, my feet hit the sand."

It was most certainly her message to us that she was finally home and at peace.

On our way back to shore, we quietly reflected on the experience we just had. Maxie looked up into the sky and saw the sun framing a cloud in the shape of a heart with an arrow going through it. We were all astonished at this sign and quickly grabbed our phones to capture the moment. Another reaffirmation that Annabelle was with us.

Pearl kept behind a small amount of Annabelle's ashes so that she could place them on Arlene's grave in Toronto so that she could have them both close when she visited the cemetery. When calling her mom to discuss this choice, her mom encouraged her to follow Annabelle's final wishes and allow all of her remains to rest where she wanted them to be. Pearl agreed. Later that afternoon, at dusk, the four of us met on the beach to release the rest of her ashes. The weight of this final act was not lost on us. We found a quiet, calm part of the beach where no one was around us, and the water was very calm. The notion that we were carrying her ashes came with a strong sense of duty and responsibility, especially for Pearl, as she held Annabelle's ashes high above her head as a final act of sisterly protection. We waded into the calm water waist deep and spread the rest of her ashes around us. Unspoken, there was a collective sense of needing some space from each other to process the multitude of emotions we were experiencing during this final act of love. Meray walked deeper into the water, and Maxie, Pearl, and April were spread out about 20 feet from each other behind her. Maxie remembers being able to hear Meray's cries and feeling how much pain she was in at that moment, but she was not sure if Meray still needed space or was in need of comfort, so she stayed back and began to float in the water looking up at the sky. After about 10 seconds, Maxie began to feel the water starting to move her toward Meray, which was odd as the water was completely calm with no current. Gaining speed by the second, Maxie was shocked by what was going on. She was moving unnaturally fast, in a straight line, directly towards where Meray was standing up ahead. When she was about 5 feet away, the water stopped moving her, and she gently floated up behind Meray and wrapped her arms around her, embracing her and holding her tightly. Both broke down sobbing, but it felt more like a release than pure sadness. It was as if Annabelle knew Meray needed support at that moment and chose Maxie to be the conduit of her comfort, as she knew Maxie would be able to hold that space for her. We were all in complete awe of what we had just seen and felt, but that was not our last sign.

On our final day of the trip, we went down to the beach to take one last dip in the beautiful water and savour our final moments in Barbados. Maxie was the last one to come out of the water, and on her way back, she noticed there was a small piece of paper folded under the foot of her pool chair. At first, she thought it might just be garbage, but something was telling her to pick it up. As she unfolded the paper and read what was inside, she was in complete and utter shock. It was an acknowledgment page that had somehow been perfectly ripped out of a book. The message read:

"This book has many midwives. So many people have played a part in bringing it into the world that to name them individually would take a separate volume. I have, I hope, thanked them in person along the way, but would like to acknowledge their importance again here. Each has contributed something unique and invaluable: some at a specific moment; some over a longer period; some over a lifetime. Thank you, each and every one of you, for helping me tell this story. I am blessed by your kindness."

ACKNOWLEDGMENTS

This book has many midwives. So many people have played a part in bringing it into the world that to name them individually would take a separate volume. I have, I hope, thanked them in person along the way, but would like to acknowledge their importance again here. Each has contributed something unique and invaluable: some at a specific moment; some over a longer period; some over a lifetime.

Thank you—each and every one of you—for helping me tell this story. I am blessed by your kindness.

We had always known that Annabelle's final wish was not to be buried but rather, cremated, with her ashes spread in the Caribbean Sea. She intuitively knew that this final act of love would give her the freedom she always wished she had. We had all supported her in different ways and at different times in her life, so finding this 'acknowledgment' (literally) felt like her final thank you. Although the message was about helping her throughout her life, it was almost as if she was thanking us for helping her complete her journey to the other side.

We left the beach completely overwhelmed by the many incredible signs and connections we experienced over the week. It was time to pack up and head to the airport. The moment we got into the taxi and closed the doors, a Stevie Wonder song, Overjoyed, started playing, and we all looked at each other immediately in astonishment. You see, not only was Stevie Wonder one of her favourite artists but so was this song. It was almost as if she was communicating how 'overjoyed' she was that we were able to deepen our connections with each other through this experience and that we were able to honour her in a way that brought both her and us peace.

These profound spiritual experiences reaffirmed our belief that our loved ones who have passed are really not gone but exist in a different form. If we keep our hearts and our minds open, we can nourish this connection with them whenever and wherever we are. Each and every time we do, whether it is through messages, signs in

419

nature, songs, or even pages from a book, it brings us an immense amount of comfort knowing they are right beside us in every moment of our lives. This knowing is deeply healing.

Annabelle left this poem in her will to bring us comfort. We hope it does the same for you.

> *When I come to end of the road*
> *And the sun has set for me,*
> *I want no rites in a gloom-filled room.*
> *Why cry for a soul set free?*
> *Miss me a little but not too long,*
> *And not with your head bowed low.*
> *Remember the love that we once shared*
> *Miss me but let me go.*

About the Authors

Mother and daughter, Pearl and Maxie Richman are passionate and dedicated students of kindness, love, and inclusivity. Pearl has been a teacher for almost 35 years and has nurtured a love of children and creativity in Maxie, who has her master's in Child Study and Education from The University of Toronto. With a plethora of mutual interests that include styling, design, writing, and advocacy, Pearl and Maxie set out to modernize the Passover Haggadah by curating *The Haggadah* and *Hug-It-Out*, a companion Haggadah for kids. Both are interlaced with important themes of resilience, acceptance, and self-love, framed within the context of spirituality and intersecting gender, sexual, cultural, and racial identities.

Pearl's mother, Maxie's grandmother, Lil and Pearl's sisters, Maxie's aunts, Annabelle and Arlene, are the inspiration behind their books and their deep and evolving relationship to Spirit.

www.thehaggadahcollecive.com

Dedication
♡

If you look carefully, you can see a blue string connecting every page of your Haggadah. The colour blue is symbolic of the colour of the sea, and the sea resembles the sky, and the sky resembles spirituality! The blue thread is said to promote the highest spiritual connection.

What does that mean? What is spirituality?

Well, the meaning of spirituality is pretty personal, but in general it can be described as a feeling of connection to something greater than ourselves. It can be a connection to nature, the universe, the energy that flows through all of us, and even God. It is about trying to turn off your thoughts and turn on the feelings of your heart and listening to your wise inner voice. It is about believing that there is a special place inside each and every one of us that we can go to for answers, guidance and truth.

The blue thread represents this connection. Even though we cannot see it with our eyes, we can feel it with our hearts. People who love each other are always connected by a very special string made of love. Even when we are not with the people we love, that feeling still exists.

There are two very special people we would like to dedicate this book to, Annabelle and Arlene, Maxie's aunts and Pearl's sisters. Even though they are not with us anymore, the blue string of love still connects us to them. In fact, the characters Annie and Arnie are named after them. Annabelle always said, "trust what you feel" which means to trust your inner voice when it whispers your truth. Both Annabelle and Arlene LOVED kids and they loved to make them laugh and share stories with them.

We love and miss them very much, but know the blue string will always keep our hearts connected.

With Love,

Pearl and Maxie

Dedication to Annabelle and Arlene in the book, Hug-It-Out, Co-written by Maxie and Pearl

"You are not a drop in the ocean.
You are the ocean in a drop."
~Rumi~
Poet, Mystic
1207 - 1273

Oceans of Love, *Lisa Arnold*

By Lisa Arnold

I always knew I would be a mom. There was never a question in my mind. I met the love of my life, my eternal mate, Jim, in my last year of college, at just twenty years old. Honestly, if it didn't seem out of the perfect order of things, I would have had children with him right away. We immediately recognized each other as soul mates. To him, this meant he knew me long before this human journey. I believed him, although I never delved into the true testament of this declaration. At least not until recently.

After we married, I quickly learned that being a mom was natural. The greatest choice I've ever made in my life. Well, besides spending eternity with my incredible husband. These were simple choices. I just followed my heart. My boys are four years apart, and we named them all D names, so they are our 3Ds. Forever. Devin is 25, easy-going, thoughtful, and sweet as can be. He recently learned what it's like to feel the love of being a parent to his fur baby, Bentley. He is such an awesome Daddy to that sweet pup. My youngest, Dylan, is a junior in high school and is 17 years old. He loves the performing arts and is such an advocate for others' rights, from humans to animals to this beautiful planet Earth. He adores his puppy, Bella, just like his big bro. Then there is Derek (Derry), my free-spirited child. He quite literally is a free spirit now.

In September 2020, at the age of 20, Derry "passed away". I put that term in quotations because I know with all my heart that he hasn't actually passed anywhere. He is not lost or gone. In my family, we try not to use those words. We rarely say died because we believe that only refers to the physical body. Our favorite term is "transitioned". I hesitate to share how he transitioned because I believe that the "how" is just a means to the next stage of a soul's evolution. I believe that before a soul chooses to re-emerge into its full non-physical expression, the soul is already so much closer to perceiving the bigger picture of life. THERE IS NO SEPARATION! So, although it may appear from the human view that they are not ready for the next stage of being, I believe a soul will never transition unless it chooses. Derry used a drug overdose as his means of transition.

As for Derry's present existence, he is now 21. We all celebrated his 21st birthday with him right by our sides. Derek cherishes his family, or "Familia" as he'd sometimes call us. When in physical form, Derry spent most of his time with his "tribe", his friends, as I'm positive he continues to do now. He loves to surf, fish, and skateboard. He barely wears shoes or a shirt. He uses a shoelace as a belt and most often wears clothes that don't even belong to him, lol. Just ask his friends what they are missing from their wardrobe, and I'm pretty certain you'll find it in his closet.

As you may have noticed, I am talking about him in the present tense. That is how we talk about him in our family and with his friends; to him and about him in the here and now just like we do for anyone we can see with our human eyes.

When Derry first transitioned, I'm not going to lie and say it didn't bring me to my knees screaming and crying. It did, and there are moments, sometimes days, it still does. I wanted to rewind time, yet simultaneously accepted this as my place in this time and space reality. My first question to my husband was, "Will we ever be happy again?" He is so reassuring. He answered with a comforting positive, "YES!" So, from this moment, I continued on my spiritual journey.

Since I was a young child, I have questioned life. At least, life from the perspective of "Live, Die, Heaven". I could not find my comfort in this sequence. I wanted to know more. I now know my exploration was my soul talking to me, my soul guiding me. My greater being wants my human me to live the best physical life possible. It is my belief that in order to do this, I must listen to my intuition and my feelings, spending less time on electronics like my phone and instead more time in nature. I've realized living this human life is an experience for my soul! I've awakened to the knowing that I'm an eternal being playing a role in this play called "Life".

The first months after Derry's transition to life after life, I intently explored the internet in search of those who believed like me that our children live on. I found

Suzanne Giesemann, the renowned medium, and teacher, who still inspires me today. Channeling from her spirit guides, *Sanaya*, are so insightful and resonate with my greater being. Her teachings just fit! I went on to find Dr. Mark Pitstick, the well-known author who, like Suzanne, shares so much that I just know is my truth.

My next discovery was Elizabeth Boisson, co-founder of *Helping Parents Heal*. How comforting to share this journey with so many others in this group that understand how I feel. I refer to them as family, who selflessly offer someone to listen, group meetings, endless resources, and many endearing friendships from near and far. In the first couple of months before returning to work, I spent many an afternoon or evening on their online calls. I soon realized how many other people shared similar beliefs. My already open-minded spirituality just continued to evolve as it does to this day.

I quickly found my solace, intuitiveness, and heart to hearts with my boy, walking or meditating in nature. Nature just is, without question. Animals, the ocean, the sky, the trees, it has all the answers. I had to learn to listen and allow the knowing we already have within us. I began walking with my sweet pup, Bella, for what seemed like hours a day. During these walks, I find some of the most synchronous physical signs and engage in insightful chats with my baby boy. Sometimes I ask a question and, without hesitation, get an answer. I spin it and add his voice to the answer through my human filter, but the content is clearly his guidance.

The knowing is felt, not thought. Of course, I like hearing his voice, and Derry inspires me to hear it in his comforting tone. My boy is amazing at providing me with visuals of this grand picture of life in a way my human brain can process. These visuals have helped me grow outside of these human limits I have placed upon myself. One of the first visions from him that I remember was only a couple of months after his transition. He showed me that we, he and our physical family, participated in a kind of mud run. I was watching myself on a television screen participating in these games of exhilaration, challenge, joy, and satisfaction. While I was watching, Derry kind of just showed up to watch, too, only he had finished the run. We all congratulated him and were so excited for him. His perspective, which I've come to learn I can share with him when I focus, is so broad. The whole big picture is crystal clear.

Another time he shared with me that life is a whole pizza pie. He has the perspective from the middle observing all our slices of life. In this vision, I'm living, where I am his Momma, and he is my boy. He said that I can always find him anywhere. There is no sequential timeline, like there is in human form. Things that haven't yet happened from my point of view already exist in this slice of life. So incredible!

Derek told me that we all drive a different vehicle, meaning our bodies. Some like luxury, some like simplicity, some care about transportation, while others think it's not important. Some really tend to their vehicles. Others don't. You get the idea. All the while, though, we all know we are not our means of transportation but are the drivers of these vehicles. Our bodies are simply our transportation or experience for this go-around.

Probably my most relatable analogy he gave me is this play called "Life". We are all actors who agreed excitedly to play specific roles in this soft-scripted play. By soft script, I mean the story line was mostly set but with plenty of room for improv, which represents our human choices. The actors are from our soul family, and I believe we agree to different roles in each incarnation. In this particular drama, Derry and all of his family agreed he would transition before us. We knew it would be a human struggle, yet from our souls' points of view, we would always know who we really are, the beautiful, loving pure actors that only know peace, love, and joy. We are sitting in the audience with Derek cheering ourselves on. We incarnate for the experience. Every time we incarnate with a new experience, our souls expand universally.

Through all of his analogies, Derry has taught me the most valuable piece of knowledge that has awakened me to my core. I am always the awareness, the soul, having this human experience. I am never not me. He is never not him. I live side by side with my boy eternally from both his perspective and mine, depending upon where I focus at the time. I wholeheartedly believe that when we sleep, we fully re-emerge into our non-physical selves. The body rests, and the soul adventures with our children. Sometimes we are even fortunate enough to remember. Other times we just wake with a feeling of familiarity, like we were just with them before the brain gets involved and tries to convince us otherwise. Ignite that flame of intuition. Know you were just with them and agree to leave doubt behind. These beliefs are where happiness lives. Remember, the only real separation is through our human senses. We are eternal souls simply having a human experience.

Let's talk signs!! This is just so much fun! Almost immediately after Derry's transition, my family began playing Theme of the Day (TOD) with our boy. I would meditate and quiet my mind, and the first word that came to mind was the TOD. We write it on a chalkboard for our family to see. Then we look for the signs. They always come through. Derry is so creative in how he lets these signs come across. Sometimes we realize the signs already came days before we chose or continue on for days after, which is no time from Derry's perspective. I suggest you give it a try. Be playful and open-minded. Our loved ones in spirit are quite creative.

One day that stands out, in particular, was Owl Day. I meditated that morning during a hypnagogic state and had three visions. One was an owl, which I immediately knew was TOD. The second was Derry and me sitting on a park bench near a pond with ducks and geese. The third vision was Derry on the open deck of a beach house on the top floor with his shirt off. He was waving his shirt in his hand like a flag. The beach house framed the walkway entrance to a beach. When I awoke, all the visions were crystal clear, and I knew exactly where the bench was located. On Saturdays after Derry transitioned, my husband, my youngest, and I coined Saturdays as "Adventure Saturday" and began doing just that...adventuring. Well, Owl Day fell on a Saturday; hence the adventure began. When I woke up, I yelled, "I know where we are going today!" So, off to The Market Common we went. It was a beautiful day. Before even arriving there, my husband, while scrolling through Facebook, saw a post about the Christmas tree brought to The Rockefeller Center for the tree lighting ceremony in New York City. Let me preface that our last physical vacation with Derek and my boys was the winter before at the same time of year in NYC. We just missed the tree lighting ceremony but still saw the magnificent tree and had all the holiday feels of Christmas in the city. It was a first time for all of us and is a treasured memory. This made the sign for the owl even more synchronous. In that social media post, Jim saw an owl in that Rockefeller tree!! An owl!! Because it was such an unusual circumstance, it started showing up all over social media. In fact, at one point, my phone did something I had never seen before. It started scrolling Facebook really fast, like the pages of a book. My husband witnessed this. It went on for a few seconds only to randomly stop on a stranger's Facebook profile. I opened his feed to his first post, having no idea who this man was or what had just happened. It was a collage of pictures all about the famous Rockefeller owl. We could just feel our boy aligning this day like a scavenger hunt for us.

Next, we went on to visit The Market Common. We walked around the pond where the benches are located just like I saw in my vision, only to notice there was a market that day with lots of vendors. We decided to check it out. One of Derek's buddies is named Muddy Mike. He crafts incredible pottery. He had a booth that day at the festival unbeknownst to us. After our hellos, I proceeded to tell Mike about the game we play, and today's TOD is an owl. He seemed a bit surprised, and I wasn't sure why. A few days prior to this day, TOD was an octopus, so I felt a nudge to buy the beautiful Octopus mug, which remains a favorite of mine today. When I inspected the craftsmanship carefully, I noticed Mike's signature emblem. It's an owl!! He puts it on every piece. This certainly explained the surprised look on his face. Just wow!!

After leaving The Common, we decided to get sandwiches and head to Garden City, where Derry spent most of his last physical summer with his friends and his girlfriend surfing and chilling. We drove to so many different lots until we found a spot where we could see the ocean from in the car. The perfect spot opened up. After eating my sandwich, I told Jim and Dylan I was going to sit on the beach and talk to Derek. I was Zen gardening the sand with a stick and, without thinking, had drawn the perfect jellyfish. I called my husband to come to take a picture as I felt it was TOD for the next day. When Jim and I were leaving the beach, I commented how the railings of this beach house near the entrance were all weathered. My husband said he liked the look, though, which brought us to further inspect the whole house. When we looked up, I noticed the deck was just like the one I saw Derry standing on, waving his shirt. The only difference is Derry wasn't standing there, but on the railing was a life-sized ceramic owl!! No other decoration but that. AN OWL! It was a day more special than I can possibly convey to you in words.

There have been journal entries full of signs and synchronicities that have cast away the shadow of doubt in my experience. More often than not, the TOD clearly shows itself on the shows we regularly find ourselves watching. One day it was waffles. How will that ever show up? How about on the show, *The Office*?! An episode I hadn't yet seen featuring quite a bit of dialogue about waffles on that very day!!

Another stand-out TOD was milk. I guess my kid likes food, in the physical perspective, and still now! So, we were watching a new *Schitt's Creek* episode since we love comedies to bring some lightness into our lives. It was all about milk!! Illegal, unpasteurized milk!! Another TOD was softball. When I heard softball in my head, I doubted it and changed it to baseball because Derry loved baseball when he was younger. When my dad came home from work, I told him TOD was baseball. He said, "Are you sure it's not softball because I found a bright colored one outside at work." Well, I switched back to my first instinctive thought Derry gave me, a softball. Later watching *Schitt's Creek* again, the episode was all about softball!! I can't make this up!! One day, I will spend time re-reading my journals and writing memoirs of my signs and synchronicities just to provide hope and instill belief in others.

This is the perfect segue to share everyday signs and synchronicities from my child through license plates, bumper stickers, signs, numbers, birds, flowers, feathers, nature in general, songs, and so much more. On the day of Derry's transition, we saw a beautiful white egret, which in itself isn't unusual where we live, but it was as if this angelic creature knew right where we would be before we even knew. I quickly learned that the egret isn't the only special messenger from my boy. Seagulls, eagles, cardinals, and of course, the owl have all made multiple special appearances in unexpected places with the most perfect timing. As if these free-spirited flying souls aren't enough, their magical feathers fall off and leave a trail that reminds us that our children are always close. All ways. It's incredible when you open yourself to the possibility, better yet, the probability that our children are communicating with us quite easily.

I've learned to read license plates. Their meaning to me is instantaneous, like reading words from a book. I'm not saying that the translation would necessarily resonate with anyone else, yet to me, the message is always so clear. It's so much fun!! Songs are similar. The messages in the songs are so often relevant to my thoughts, recent conversations with someone, or maybe circumstances I'm physically living. Then, there are the repeated angel numbers or the numbers that might represent a significant date. The quantity of times and variety of places these numbers appear is undeniable. To negate them as "coincidence" would be more challenging than simply accepting that we are all part of a much grander design. A picture that only the soul's eyes can fully understand. Have fun with it!

Our children and our transitioned loved ones are always present. We just need to raise our vibration to a frequency that aligns with theirs, our greater beings, and the universe. This high vibration is where the magic lives. Only it's not a place but a state of being. One we can all have at least glimpses of during this physical lifetime. I say, "at least", because I propose to live one foot in Utopia while trying to mirror image that beautiful existence right here in the physical world. Together, we can help awaken each other and achieve peace, compassion, joy, and experiences in this earthly realm. We can experience heaven on Earth. No matter our experience in the physical form, we will all transition to the grandest reality. We can't get it wrong, but we can decide on our physical reality regarding the quality. "Live Ya Life and Love Ya Life", says the legend Derek Scott Arnold. I hear ya, baby. I plan to live by these words right by your side. Oceans and same same.

About the Author

Lisa is the grateful mother of 3 boys, her 3Ds, and has been married to her soulmate for more than 25 years. Although originally from Massachusetts, Lisa and her husband have resided in peaceful coastal South Carolina for just over 17 years. Home truly is where the heart is. They have family both near and up north and spend time visiting their distant relatives. Recently, they purchased a vintage camper and have begun experiencing adventure outdoors. Their sweet fur baby, Bella, loves accompanying them on trips. At least weekly, they love to babysit their precious grandpup. Lisa loves to write poetry to accompany her husband's beautiful photography. Their family goal is to become more mobile to continue to explore magnificent countryside. Their boys, both physical and spirit, are always along for the ride. All ways.

"True self is non-self, the awareness that
the self is made only of non-self elements.
There's no separation between self
and other, and everything is interconnected.
Once you are aware of that
you are no longer caught in the idea
that you are a separate entity."
~Thich Nhat Hanh~
Monk, Poet, Teacher
1926-2022

Everyday Spirituality; Living and Loving Life in Full Expression, *Chloe and Ellen*

By Chloe Whilding & Ellen McKendry

Have you ever felt like events in your life were 'meant to happen'? Like you were just a tiny cog in a great big machine, one singular drop in an ocean of consciousness? Have you ever met someone who transforms your entire existence? Raises your vibration beyond comprehension? Have you wondered if it was all purely by chance or if things were being orchestrated by someone or something bigger?

Adverse life events led to awakenings for us both individually and we found ourselves living an existence that didn't hold space for contemplation or self-evolution or provide support for open and loving connections to be nurtured. We both found ourselves in unfulfilling careers, unfulfilling relationships, and a generalised feeling that there was a different path to take out there for us. We both found ourselves seeking out knowledge from as many spiritual sources that could be found via videos, books, forums, online meetings, and groups and trying to gain clarity on how to shake off and break free from the inner discontentment and feeling of being trapped in the current human experience that felt so dense and heavy. We have come to realise that everything seems to have happened in its divine timing for a purpose and meaning, and to know our meeting each other was most definitely something that had been pre-planned, pre-destined, and masterminded from across the veil.

Chloe's Story

I grew up in Coventry, UK, with two siblings and regularly attended a Church of England Charismatic Church. Introduction to Source was fraught with contradictions, but ultimately, I remember feeling inner peace and a loving connection as an intuitive empath from a very young age. Having what could be described as psychic abilities, such as intuitively sensing danger, death, and reading people's energy, produced fear and anxiety due to my Christian upbringing who deemed these abilities as either of the occult or would only be valid if they had been given as a gift from God and only to be used on Sundays, not to experiment with, and definitely not something that was already innate to me. It felt like a contradiction of being told to be spiritual but forced to stay within the constricted provided narrative and within the accepted parameters of their understanding and beliefs rather than my own experience. The God I was introduced to was a harsh and judgmental God who was jealous and would punish us for making "mistakes". This was not the inner experience I was having, and I felt very confused for most of my childhood.

Spirituality was a changing and constantly evolving part of my life. The biggest catalyst for change came in the form of the breakdown of my marriage and, within two months, the physical death of my dad in the Summer of 2020. These two huge life events catapulted me inwards, navigating the journey of grief and allowing myself to feel the emotions that came up and proactively reading books, meditating, and taking part in spiritual events and workshops that could help me make sense of everything I was experiencing. I wanted to make sure everything I felt was positively expressed and processed and believed that this would ensure I came out as best a version of myself as possible, for my own sake and the sake of my two daughters, who were nine and six at the time. A big spiritual jump forward came from an eight-week course that was designed to expand innate mediumship skills with soul-to-soul communication. The main goal for me at this time was that I would be able to understand the skills I had always felt I had and establish an open channel to communicate with Dad. Not only did I connect with him, I connected with many souls and spirits, spirit guides, and spirit animals.

My dad came through to me in his own distinctive style! He was always very quirky, light, and humorous. He encouraged me from the outset to lighten the vibrations, laugh, and spread joy through all my interactions with others. He "pops" into my mind's eye nearly every day. If he feels I am getting bogged down in my human story, he'll do a funny dance or sing a song to me. Equally, if he misses his granddaughters, he will use me to hug them, so he can feel their embrace. On many occasions, he has given the girls messages of hope and encouragement through me, either by speaking through me as a channel or by giving me images to convey to them. The main symbol he uses to reassure me that he is still with me is a heart. I find them in places I would not expect them! These have included coffee cups, cloud shapes, bath bubbles, petals on my path. Once, I was out for a walk with my Mum, talking about my upcoming divorce and how stressful it all was. I was feeling particularly downtrodden and found myself getting increasingly anxious about the future when I turned to look down at the pavement, and there was a heart-shaped earring on the ground! Some might say that it was wishful thinking and that I was just noticing heart shapes more than usual, but I believe that Dad and my spirit guides/helpers encourage me to spot these signs and synchronicities. It has been wonderful in particular to be able to provide comfort to Ellen with her son, who transitioned this dimension, via messages and channelled writing with reassurances that he's ok, that he left when he was supposed to, and to remind her not to blame herself; it was as it was 'meant to be'. Being able to support my partner with such tenderness is an incredible way to share our love.

I have felt nothing but love and light from the other side, no fear, or darkness. Regularly meditating or spending time in the peace and quiet helps me connect with my higher self and those in spirit, fundamentally leaving me with a sense of peace and reassurance that all is ultimately well.

I don't know where my spiritual journey will take me, but I am eager to learn and cultivate a relationship with Ellen, our children, and the wider community that stands on the foundations of love and respect for each other. Developing spiritually has clarified my own innate abilities to reach people from all walks of life, in my day-to-day interactions or at work as a Registered nurse, educating and developing people while being in a conscious flow of divine energy.

Ellen's Story

My childhood was firmly placed and grounded in the world of structure and academic achievements, with religion and spirituality playing no prominent part in the day-to-day busy family life as one of four children. I remember feeling there was most definitely a set path laid out ahead for me by my parents; an expected route to be taken with education, career choices, and even relationships with no deviations. Decisions and choices were based on ration, logic, and science, which for me didn't make any sense; I experienced the world in a whole range of emotions (my own and others! The way of an empath, I guess!) colours and gut feelings. I just always felt like so many things couldn't just be explained away as 'nonsense' knowing I had predictive dreams, anxiety far greater than my years should've felt, out-of-body experiences, and visions of colours around people and animals. Yet the magic I could feel and see was never allowed to be mentioned, and the unseen was to be unspoken of; a general ethos of if it couldn't be easily explained, then it didn't happen. As a teenager, I was drawn to a very different experience than most; I wasn't down the park with friends, I wasn't at the local village pub drinking and hanging out, I was saving my part-time wages to attend weekly meditation meetings and clearing circles, completing healing courses and soaking up as much spiritual knowledge and practice as possible, a strange dichotomy between the day-to-day life I was living and the inner world of my higher self I was learning. I then spent several years travelling solo through over 40 countries, absorbing the stories and experiences of the land and people I came across, feeling more alive and in tune with the patterns and flow of the universe than ever, freely living and free flowing.

Life in my early twenties, however, seemed to throw me off the path I was on, and I became tied into the human story of fitting in, finding jobs, struggling to make soul connections, and found myself very unhappy in a life that didn't feel quite like the one I thought I should be having; there was no magic. After years of suffering with mental health problems, having multiple miscarriages, and a marriage breakdown, I gave birth to my son in 2019, and something in me suddenly became aware that I had to be better, get better, feel better and knew that there had been more than this and that it might be possible to feel that feeling of being alive and connected again.

I reached out to old friends lost along the way, completed a spiritual development course, and found my entire life brightening up and shifting all around me, and in all aspects too; new house, new job, new friends, and meeting an amazing new partner in Chloe. I had honestly never felt such a spiritual connection like ours to another human before. We started doing weekly meditations in a zoom group together, reading books and passages of writings to each other that had resonated before but now seemed to be more real than ever, and the signs and messages of loved ones over the veil came flooding through as if now I was living wholly and able to express myself fully. I was now an open channel to receiving them freely now. I have yet to figure out exactly where my spiritual journey will take me. At the moment, I'm enjoying learning to trust the messages and visions I receive and getting validation from others I have had messages for. Whether I am able to use these gifts as a career and escape the mundane rat race of 'normal' jobs, I don't know, but it's exciting to think that there's so many possibilities out there, and with the team of helpers behind me I will be fully supported and guided along the way.

As well as receiving messages and images of loved ones for fellow members of the zoom group we belong to, I found most days Chloe's dad would pop a funny song or message into my head, would let me know when Chloe or her daughters needed a hug and now even write channelled letters through me to her. He shows me him playing and looking after my lost babies that didn't get to spend time on this earth plane with me, and he very proudly tells me that he is the conductor of the life orchestra we are playing in, taking full credit for the coordination of events that led to the meeting of Chloe and I when we were both ready to accept and experience the deep love we have and progress together spiritually, modest isn't he!

Our Journey

We often talk about how we felt prior to meeting each other and how much our lives have shifted just before and during our relationship. Prior to knowing each other, we both separated from our partners in the same week a year before we met. We both took stock of our lives and chose to take a leap into a new unknown territory of navigating it as single parents. We had both spent several nights contemplating our right to be here, seeking answers to our purpose and questioning whether the life experiences we were suffering were all part of the story or if we had just got it horrifically wrong. We then followed the synchronistic hints and guidance that led to us ultimately finding each other when we were spontaneously thrust onto the platform of online dating! Ellen was about to delete her account after a few transient message exchanges that felt shallow and contrived. Chloe, encouraged by her friend and a few glasses of gin, tentatively dipping her toes in for the first time when the 'like' came through from Ellen within a few minutes of her account being live! Our first conversations flowed as easily as the ocean, and it felt like the soul connection we didn't know was actually possible, a familiarity of past lives lived in unison, and a coming together of like-mindedness. Having always jokingly said that time is merely a social construct, we found time would fly by, hours lost in conversations and sharing of stories.

Our lives have continued to intertwine with such a free-flowing pace, a unique harmonious resonance that is always feeling divinely led and supported, our children blending wonderfully as if they were always meant to be part of a tribe together, our continued hours and hours lost in each other's worlds and pasts, coming across uncanny similarities and twists that must seem so strange and coincidental to others. We both know; however, our journeys have been as they have for a higher purpose and learning. As our connection has deepened, we have found ourselves joining each other in meditative states, talking soul language in our sleep to each other, and channelling joint messages for practice sitters in spiritual circles. We have been able to channel writing for each other from across the veil, people often comment on our unique combined energy, our interwoven feeling of light, and we have repeatedly been told via spirit messages from others that we have come together for a great purpose this lifetime; no pressure!

Being able to live and love so fully and freely feels like such an honour and gift to us both and being able to have the chance to reunite our spiritual beings is the greatest gift of all. There is no doubt we have had many incarnations together, but with the world, in its shifting current state, we feel there is a real sense of commitment and drive to assist the common universal stream of consciousness forward; wish us luck as we continue living this life in its fullest expression of light and love!

About the Authors

Chloe and Ellen live in Norfolk, UK where they are raising their 3 children. Chloe is a specialist nurse and Ellen is an artist and advisor and between them have studied and trained in many different fields of health and spirituality including Emotional Freedom Therapy and Reiki. They are currently working on their own channeled and self illustrated Oracle card deck, continue to provide joint spiritual readings and hope to use their innate spiritual gifts and training to work more in the field in the future.

Chloe's Dad, Keith Greaves

The hearts Chloe and her daughters
have received from Keith

Acknowlededgments

My deepest gratitude and appreciation to every author who contributed a chapter, foreword, and endorsement to this anthology, especially those authors in spirit who assembled their book club across the veil, gathered us all together, and guided us to share our beautiful stories and memories in their honour for this labour of love.

Special acknowledgement and thanks go to Suzanne Giesemann creator of Messages of Hope, Sandra Champlain creator of We Don't Die, Dr. Sonia Rinaldi co-founder and research director of IPATI, The Psychic Lawyer Mark Anthony JD, Dr. Mark Pitstick of creator of Soul Proof and director of the Soul Phone Foundation, Elizabeth Boisson co-founder of Helping Parents Heal, Robert Ginsberg co-founder of Forever Family Foundation, Jane Asher Reaney creator of The Next Room, Linda Rampling creator of Advancing Awareness, Sherry Gallant the Wellness Medium, Lisa Snyder creator of Healing With the Ancients, and Jonathan Dan creator of the mystical and magical cover art for this book for the extra attention they generously gave to the creation and promotion of this wonderful anthology project.

Extra special acknowledgement, thanks, love, and hugs go to Antonio Di Cintio for his patience, attention, support, and love through hard times and good times on my journey of grief and spiritual awakening.

Made in the USA
Columbia, SC
23 July 2022

63889498R00251